SQL THE ONE

SQL THE ONE

MICROSOFT SQL SERVER INTERVIEW GUIDE

UDAY ARUMILLI

Notion Press

Old No. 38, New No. 6
McNichols Road, Chetpet
Chennai - 600 031

First Published by Notion Press 2016

ISBN 978-1-946390-97-4

"This book is dedicated to the

Most Inspiring & Successful Person I know

Sri. Nandamuri Taraka Rama Rao (Sr.NTR)"

CONTENTS

About the Book

The book discusses about Microsoft SQL Server interview experiences, questions and answers for a range of SQL DBA's and SQL Server professionals. These questions have been collected from the people who attended interviews at various multinational companies across the world.

Initially from 2009 whenever I attended an interview I started capturing interview questions, experiences and framed into a self-reference guide. Post that I started gathering interview experiences from my friends and colleagues. In 2013 we have got an idea of authoring a book which can be a big reference guide for any typical SQL DBA. After that we concentrated on latest interview experiences and started approaching our blog followers and requested them to share their interview experiences. We used to help them in finding the answers and added those questions and answers into our guide. Once we find a list of questions asked in an interview we put efforts to cover the best answer for the given question. You may find the lengthy answers for almost all of the questions. From our experiences we can mostly see thread questions in technical interviews which means you are not just asked "WHAT" and also you will be tested on "HOW," "WHEN" and "WHY." We recommend our readers to understand the concept and drive the interview process.

All interview questions are categorized which makes easier for reviewing while preparing for an interview. The book presented these questions and answers from both interviewer and interviewee prospective. Staring form basics it takes you to in depth internals which are useful for the range of DBA's from fresher to lead roles. This book primarily focusing on interview preparation, apart from that it can also be useful for a quick review for SQL Server topics.

These questions and answers were asked in interviews conducted for different level of positions at various organizations. Positions include that SQL DBA, Senior SQL DBA, SQL Server SME, SQL Server Database Architect, SQL Server Performance Tuning Specialist, SQL Database Engineer, SQL Database analyst, Database Consultant, Lead DBA consultant, Application SQL DBA, Core SQL DBA, Development SQL DBA etc. on both service oriented and product oriented organizations that ranges from start-ups to the IT industry Big Techies.

For any SQL Server DBA there are three plus points with this book. 1. This book has been prepared from the interview prospective; 2. It covers wide range of SQL Server versions from 2005 to 2016; 3. All interview questions have been categorized. These points will make the book as unique and helpful for any SQL DBA for a quick review and interview preparation.

As the reader of this book, you are our most important critic and commentator. We value your opinion and want to know what we're doing right, what we could do better and any other words of wisdom you're willing to pass our way. You can email or write me directly to let me know your valuable feedback.

About the Author

Uday Arumilli: Was born and brought up in a small village called "VENTURU" located in Andhra Pradesh, India. He is a post graduate in Computer Science from Andhra University College of Engineering. He is having a decade experience with Microsoft SQL Server in designing, developing, administrating, maintaining and optimizing enterprise database systems for the world class organizations. He is having a rich experience in building database applications using one of the finest platforms "SQL Server" with the lowest possible cost. He is also experienced in freelancing, blogging and consulting database solutions. Currently, he is associated with a database architect role and architecting Microsoft SQL Server database systems with specific focus on cloud. You can find more about the author and material related to these topics on his blog. He can be reached through his personal email, blog, Facebook, Twitter or LinkedIn.

Blog: www.udayarumilli.com

Email: udayarumilli@gmail.com

LinkedIn: http://in.linkedin.com/in/udayarumilli

Facebook: https://www.facebook.com/udayarumilli

Twitter: https://twitter.com/udayarumilli

ACKNOWLEDGMENTS

First and foremost I should thank my parents, grandparents and my entire family (C.D.Raju, C.S.N.Murthy, Prakash Chava and Satheesh Duggina) for giving me the best. I would like to thank my guru "Rama Rao Gampala" for his professionalism, technical knowledge, and commitment to this project. I'd also like to thank my close friends "Raj Chowdary Rayudu" and "Bhanu Prasad Kota" for their everlasting support during the tough times. Special big thanks to "Sudha Duggina" & "Harika Vundavilli" for their support and frequent words of encouragement, they kept me going and this book would not have been possible without them. I would like to thank my colleagues, blog followers for sharing their interview experiences. I would also like to thank Notion Press for giving me the opportunity to write this book.

Finally I would like to express my gratitude to the many people who saw me through this book; to all those who provided support, talked things over, read, wrote, offered comments, allowed me to quote their remarks and assisted in the editing, proofreading and design.

Special Thanks

Paul S. Randal

Brent Ozar

Robert Sheldon

Klaus Aschenbrenner

Thomas LaRock

Pankaj Mittal

Glenn Berry

Jonathan Kehayias

John Sansom

Harsh Deep Singh

Brian Knight

Pinal Dave

Vinod Kumar M

Rama Rao G

&

All Microsoft SQL Server MVP's & FTE's

CHAPTER 1

SQL SERVER ARCHITECTURE

Interview Questions and Answers

Introduction: This chapter takes you through the SQL Server Architecture related interview questions and answers. This is one of the most common areas where any SQL DBA, SQL Developer and MSBI engineers can expect questions in technical interviews. Answers are explained in detail, while you are preparing for an interview one should understand the concept and make a note on key points. These questions and answers are deals with the below topics:

- SQL Server High & Low Level Architecture
- Transaction Log Architecture
- Query processing Architecture
- Memory Architecture
- New Features added in 2008, 2008 R2, 2012, 2014, 2016

SQL Server High & Low Level Architecture

1. Can you explain SQL Server Architecture?

Ans:

You might be asked this question to know how you strong in SQL internals. You need not draw the diagram but you should be able to explain the components available and how they work. I have seen this question on interviews at Microsoft (IT and GTSC), Amazon, Barclays, Pythian, CA and E&Y. So let's understand how components work and you just need to know how communication happens from end client to the database page.

There are total 4 major components in SQL Server Architecture:

- Protocol Layer
- Query Processor/Relational Engine
- Storage Engine
- SQLOS

Each and every instruction must be interact with these 4 components. High level SQL Server Architecture can be explained in 4 steps as below:

- The Protocol Layer receives the request from the end client and translates it into the form where SQL Server Relational Engine can understand and work on it.

- The Query Processor accepts the T-SQL batches processes and executes the T-SQL batch. If data is required the request is passed to Storage Engine
- The Storage Engine manages the data access and service the requested data.
- The SQLOS takes responsibility of operating system and manages locks, synchronization, buffer pool, memory, thread scheduling, I/O etc.

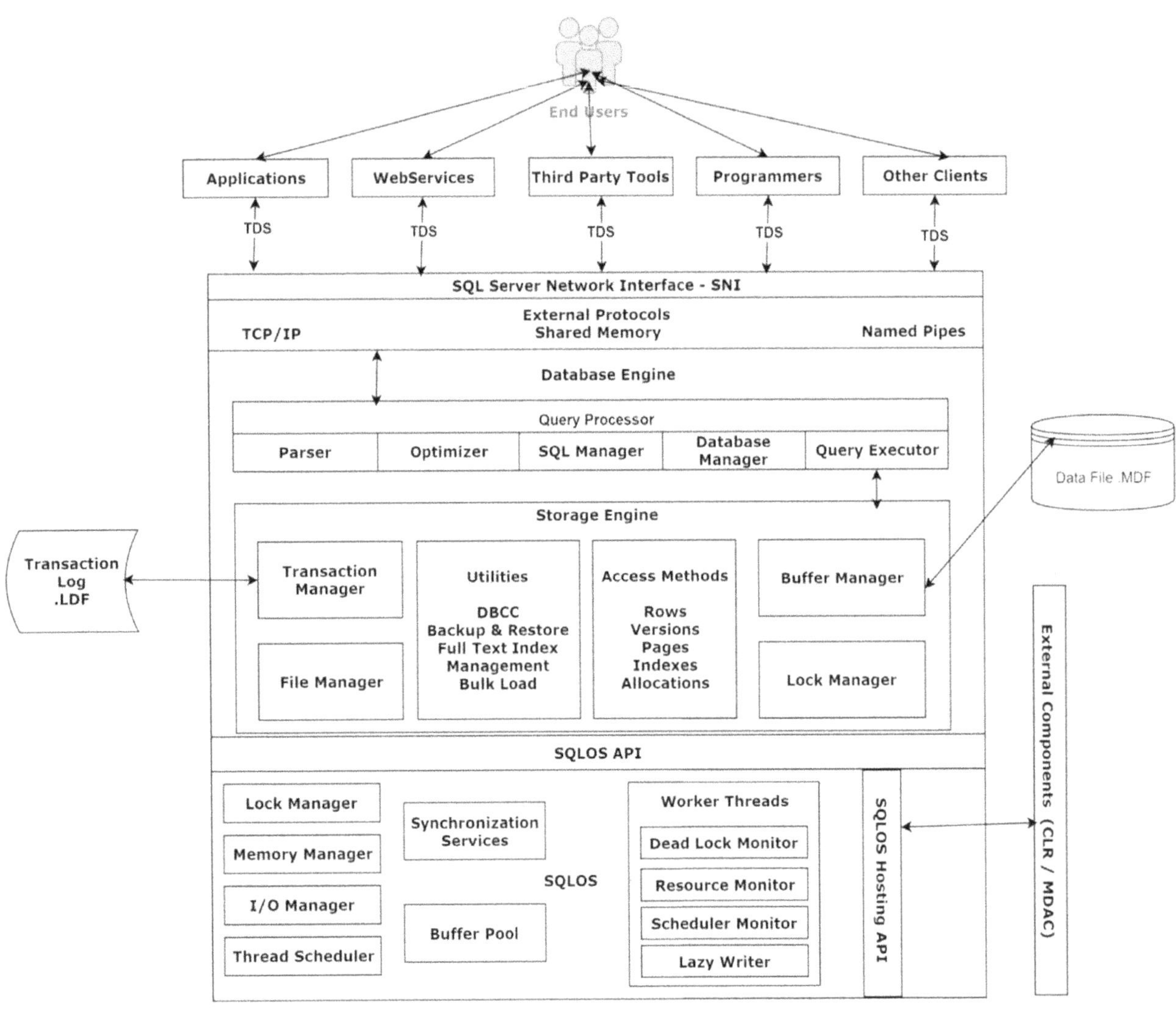

Fig 1.1

2. Can you explain the SQL Server Protocol Layer?

Ans:

End clients/Applications should use a protocol to communicate with SQL Server Database Engine. Data is transferred in the form of TDE (Tabular Data Stream) packets over the network. SNI (SQL Server Network Interface) takes the responsibility of encapsulating TDE packets on a standard communication protocol. SQL Server supports 4 types of network protocols:

Shared Memory:

Clients using the shared memory protocol can only connect to a SQL Server instance running on the same computer; it is not useful for most database activity. Use the shared memory protocol for troubleshooting when you suspect the other protocols are configured incorrectly.

- Server – Machine 1
- Clients – Machine 1

TCP/IP:

TCP/IP is a common protocol widely used over the Internet. It communicates across interconnected networks of computers that have diverse hardware architectures and various operating systems. TCP/IP includes standards for routing network traffic and offers advanced security features. It is the most popular protocol that is used in business today.

- Server – Machine 1
- Clients – WAN (Any machine from any network)

Named Pipes:

Named Pipes is a protocol developed for local area networks. A part of memory is used by one process to pass information to another process, so that the output of one is the input of the other. The second process can be local (on the same computer as the first) or remote (on a networked computer).

- Server – Machine 1
- Clients – LAN (Any machine from LAN)

VIA:

Virtual Interface Adapter (VIA) protocol works with VIA hardware. This feature is deprecated from SQL Server 2012.

3. Can you explain phases and components in SQL Server Relational Engine?

Ans:

We are giving a detailed description for each component and phase. This is only for your understanding. When you are preparing for an interview you just need to quickly review these phases and components.

Query Processor/Relational Engine process a T-SQL batch in 5 phases:

- Parsing
  - ✓ Parsing
  - ✓ Binding
- Compiling
- Optimizing
  - ✓ Cache Lookup
  - ✓ Normalizing
  - ✓ Optimizing

- Caching
- Executing

There are various components involved on above 5 phases. They are:

- Parser
- ALGEBRIZER
- T-SQL Compiler
- Optimizer
- SQL Manager
- Database Manager
- Query Executer

4. Can you explain each phase in detail? To simplify the question how SQL Server relational Engine works in processing SQL queries?

Ans:

Here we'll see how SQL Server Relational engine process a SQL Server query in all phases.

Parsing:

It converts high level language to machine understandable language.

- **Parser:** Parser checks for correct syntax, including the correct spelling and use of keywords and builds a parse/sequence tree.
- **Binding/ALGEBRIZER:**
    - ✓ It Loads Meta data for tables and columns
    - ✓ Checks whether tables and columns exist,
    - ✓ Add information about required conversions to the sequence tree.
    - ✓ Replaces references to a view with the definition of that view and performs a few syntax based optimizations.
    - ✓ These syntax optimizations include converting right outer joins to equivalent left outer joins, flattening sub-queries to equivalent join syntax, and simplifying some negative expressions etc.

Compiling:

- The query processor looks for statements for which optimization is not required.
- These statements Ex. variable declarations and assignments, conditional processing with IF, iteration with WHILE etc.
- These statements don't require optimization but needs to be compiled through the T-SQL language compiler.
- Compilation is only for special T-SQL statements which are not required any optimization.

Optimizing:

The primary goal of this phase is to produce a best cost based execution plan. Not all queries are sent for optimization. Queries like DDL are compiled into an internal form and queries like DML sent to the optimizer.

- **Cache Lookup:** First it verifies if matching plan is already exists in procedure cache. If exists then it skips the next process and go to execution phase.
- **Normalizing:** Query is first broken down into simple fine grained form.
- **Optimizing:**
  - ✓ Designs the best cost based plan based on various parameters.
  - ✓ Here the cost factor is not based on time but on resource (I/O, CPU, Memory etc.) consumption.
  - ✓ Parameters include data volume, type of operations, cardinality, indexes, statistics, configurations, access methods etc.

Caching:

Now optimizer stores the prepared plan to procedure cache.

- When a user process inserts an execution plan into the cache it sets the current cost equal to the original query compile cost
- Thereafter, each time a user process references an execution plan, it resets the current cost to the original compile cost
- When memory pressure exists, the Database Engine responds by removing execution plans with zero cost from the procedure cache.
- The Database Engine uses the resource monitor and user threads to free memory from the procedure cache

SQL Manager:

This component takes care of the execution of stored procedures. It is responsible for deciding as to when a stored procedure needs recompilation and for storing the plan cache for reuse by other stored procedures. It also manages auto parameterization.

Database Manager:

The database manager handles access to the metadata needed for query compilation and optimization, making it clear that none of these separate modules can be run completely separately from the others. The metadata is stored as data and is managed by the storage engine, but metadata elements such as the data types of columns and the available indexes on a table must be available during the query compilation and optimization phase, before actual query execution starts.

Executing:

Query executer component of Relational Engine takes care of this execution. It acts as the despatcher of the commands mentioned in the execution plan. The query executer works in association of the Storage engine as each command needs to access the database.

5. Can you be able to explain the Storage Engine role?

Ans:

Actual data processing happens in Storage Engine. Initially SQL Server Storage Engine consist components that requires to manage entire data processing but later on some of the components has been divided into a separate module called SQLOLS. Now SQL Server Storage Engine contains below components:

- Access Methods
- Locking Operations
- Transaction Services
- Utility Commands

Access Methods:

- The access methods are nothing but programming unit codes and these are called when server requested for data.
- It requests the data/index pages, creates the OLE DB row-set which can be returned to the relational engine.
- The access methods contain code to open table, retrieve qualified data, and update data.
- The pages are not retrieved rather the request to the buffer manager is made.
- The manager serves the page in the cache or reads from the disk.
- The access methods include Rows, Pages, Indexes, Versions, and Allocations.

Locking Operations:

- Locking is a crucial function of a multi-user database system such as SQL Server.
- Locking operations make sure that SQ: Server transactions following the configured ISOLATION level.
- It manages compatibility between the lock types, resolves deadlocks, and escalates locks if needed. The locking code controls partition, schema, table, page, and row locks as well as system data locks.

Transaction Services:

- This component makes sure that all transactions are atomic which means they are following ACID properties.
- In SQL Server, if there is a system failure before the transaction is committed, all the work is rolled back. Write ahead logging has the ability to roll back work in progress or roll forward committed work.
- This component coordinates with the current locking code and manages the transactions accordingly.

Utility Commands:

This is the other component of SQL Server Storage Engine for controlling utilities such as:

- DBCC Commands
- Full-text Index Population and Management

- Backup and Restore Operations
- Bulk Load Operations

6. Can you briefly explain about the component SQLOS?

Ans:

SQLOS is an operating system inside SQL Server. This is a module and controls the end to end data access, processing and management. Below are the roles of SQLOS:

- Memory management
- Scheduling
- IO management
- Synchronization Services
- Thread Management
- Worker Management
- Framework for Locking management
- Framework for Transaction management
- Deadlock detection
- Utilities for Dumping
- Utilities for Exception handling

7. When I say compile and execute a SQL Batch does it means compiler compiles each line of code?

Ans:

Compilation is only for special T-SQL statements which are not required any optimization. Ex: Variable declaration and assignment etc. We usually say compile a stored procedure. This means compile and optimize the procedure. Compilation is required for non DML commands and optimization is required for DML commands.

8. What is a record and what are the different types available?

Ans:

A record is the physical storage associated with a table or index row. There are different types of records available in SQL Server:

Data Record: Stores table rows in a heap or in the leaf level of clustered index. Data records are stored on data pages.

Index Record: We can differentiate index records into two types, those that store non-clustered index rows and those that comprise the b-tree that make up clustered and non-clustered indexes. Index records are stored on index pages

Text Record: Stores LOB values

Ghost Record: These are records that have been logically deleted but not physically deleted from the leaf level of an index.

Other Record: There are also records that are used to store various allocation bitmaps, intermediate results of sort operations, and file and database metadata

9. What is a Page?

Ans:

The fundamental unit of data storage in SQL Server is the page.

Page size is 8kb and 128 pages = 1 MB.

Page starts with the header of 96 bytes that is used to store page number, page type, the amount of free space on the page, and the object id that owns the page. The maximum size of a single row on a page is 8060KB. But this restriction is relaxed for tables which are having VARCHAR, NVARCHAR, VARBINARY, TEXT and IMAGE columns.

10. What is ROW_OVERFLOW_DATA allocation unit?

Ans:

When the total row size of all fixed and variable columns in a table exceeds the 8,060 byte limitation, SQL Server dynamically moves one or more variable length columns to pages in the ROW_OVERFLOW_DATA allocation unit.

This is done whenever an insert or update operation increases the total size of the row beyond the 8060 byte limit. When a column is moved to a page in the ROW_OVERFLOW_DATA allocation unit, a 24-byte pointer on the original page in the IN_ROW_DATA allocation unit is maintained. If a subsequent operation reduces the row size, SQL Server dynamically moves the columns back to the original data page.

11. What is an EXTENT?

Ans:

An extent is eight physically contiguous pages or 64 KB.

That means 16 Extents = 1 MB.

There are two types of Extents. Uniform Extents and Mixed Extents.

Uniform extents are owned by a single object;

Mixed extents are shared by up to eight objects

12. What are the different types of Pages?

Ans:

PFS (Page Free Space): Percentage of free space available in each page in an extent. The first page on any database data file is always a PFS page.

GAM and SGAM (Global Allocation Map & Shared GAM):

- GAM: Extents have been allocated: 1 – Free space 0 – No space
- SGAM: Mixed Extents have been allocated: 1 – Free Space + Mixed Extent and 0 – No space
- Each GAM/SGAM covers 64000 extents - 4 GB.

- ➢ The second page on any database data file is always a GAM page
- ➢ *The third page on any database data file is always a SGAM page.*

DCM (Differential Changed Map): This tracks the extents that have changed since the last BACKUP DATABASE statement. 1 – Modified, 0 – Not modified

BCM (Bulk Changed Map): This tracks the extents that have been modified by bulk logged operations since the last BACKUP LOG statement. 1 – Modified, 0 – Not modified (Used only in bulk logged Recovery model)

In each data file pages are arranged like below

File Header → PFS → GAM → SGAM → BCM → DCM → Data and Index Pages

Along with that we have three different data pages

- ➢ Data
- ➢ Index
- ➢ Text/Image (LOB, ROW_OVERFLOE, XML)

13. What are the "Files" and "File Groups"?

Ans:

Files: There are three types: Primary- .MDF, Secondary - .NDF and Log files - .LDF

File Groups: There are two, Primary File Group – All system tables and User Defined - Depends

All secondary files and user defined file groups are created to optimize the data access and for partitioning the tables.

14. What are the Pros and Cons of File Groups?

Ans:

Advantages:

- ➢ Using FILEGROUPS, you can explicitly place database objects into a particular set of database files. For example, you can separate tables and their non-clustered indexes into separate FILEGROUPS. This can improve performance, because modifications to the table can be written to both the table and the index at the same time. This can be especially useful if you are not using striping with parity (RAID-5).
- ➢ Another advantage of FILEGROUPS is the ability to back up only a single FILEGROUP at a time. This can be extremely useful for a VLDB, because the sheer size of the database could make backing up an extremely time-consuming process.
- ➢ Yet another advantage is the ability to mark the FILEGROUP and all data in the files that are part of it as either read-only or read-write.

Disadvantages

- ➢ The first is the administration that is involved in keeping track of the files in the FILEGROUP and the database objects that are placed in them.
- ➢ The other is that if you are working with a smaller database and have RAID-5 implemented, you may not be improving performance.

15. What is Instant File Initialization and how it works?

Ans:

On Windows systems when SQL Server needs to write something on disk, first it verify that the hard disk space is trustworthy means the space is readable. The verification process is:

- SQL Server writes zeros to the file
- This process is known as zeroing process
- SQL Server uses single thread for zeroing process
- The actual operation that triggers this verification should wait until this verification process completed.

If Instant File Initialization is enabled for SQL Server, it skips the zeroing process for data files and reduces the wait time.

16. What are the database activities that get benefit from Instant File Initialization?

Ans:

- Creating a new Database
- Restoring a database from backup file
- Increasing database data file size manually
- Increasing database data file size due to Auto Growth option
- TEMPDB creation at the time of SQL Server restart

Note: Remember growing log file still uses the zeroing process

17. How to check if Instant File Initialization is enabled for a SQL Server

Ans:

Enabling trace flags (3004, 3605) enable writing zeroing process information into SQL Server error log. If Instant File Initialization is enabled for SQL Server we can't see zeroing process messages for data file where we can still can see zeroing process messages related to log files something like "Zeroing Completed On ...._log.LDF."

18. How to enable Instant File Initialization?

Ans:

In order for SQL Server to be able to perform instant file initialization the SQL Server service account must be granted the Perform Volume Maintenance Task security permission. This can be done by using the Local Security Policy Editor.

- Run lusrmgr.msc on the server to find the appropriate group name for each instance of SQL Server.
- Run secpol.msc on the server.
- Under Security Settings on the left, go to Local Policies and under that to User Rights Assignment.
- Under Policy on the right side, go to "Perform volume maintenance tasks" and double click on it

- Add SQL Server group created by SQL setup (standalone) or cluster domain group (for clusters)
- Restart SQL Server

Note: If your SQL Server service account is already in part of Windows Local Administrators Group then we need not add it to the Volume Maintenance Task. Also IFI doesn't works if Transparent Data Encryption (TDE) is enabled.

19. Have you ever implemented Instant file Initialization in any environment? If yes did you observe any performance gain?

Ans:

Yes! I have enabled this option in most of the environments I worked and I strongly suggest enabling it.

I have clearly seen the performance gain by enabling Instant File Initialization. An example:

- Restoring a database from the backup (160 GB) – 3Hr 47Min
- After Enabling Instant File Initialization the same operation took – 2Hr 8 Min

20. Does Instant File Initialization is enabled for SQL Server by default?

Ans:

No! By default IFI is not enabled for SQL Server as there is a slight security risk.

As you may know, when data is deleted from disk by the operating system, it really is not physically deleted; the space holding the data is just marked as being (space) available. At some point, the older data will be overwritten with new data.

- When Instant File Initialization is not enabled: Data is zeroed out before writing anything on that page.
- When Instant File Initialization is enabled: There is a slight security risk here. When a new database is created those new pages are not zeroed out and there is a chance that newly allocated pages might contain previously deleted data and one can read that data using a recovery tool.

Transaction Log Architecture

21. Can you explain the Transaction Log logical architecture?

Ans:

Each log record is identified by a unique number called LSN (Log Sequence Number). A log record contains the LSN, Transaction ID to which it belongs and data modification record.

Data modification record: It's either operation performed or before and after data image

- When recorded "Operation Performed"
  - ✓ Transaction committed - Logical Operation is permanently applied to the data
  - ✓ Transaction rollback – Reverse Logical Operation is applied to the data.

- When Recorded "Before and After Data Image"
  - ✓ Transaction committed – Applied the after transaction image
  - ✓ Transaction rollback – Applied the before transaction image

22. Can you explain the Transaction Log physical architecture?

Ans:

The transaction log is used to guarantee the data integrity of the database and for data recovery.

The SQL Server Database Engine divides each physical log file internally into a number of virtual log files. Virtual log files have no fixed size, and there is no fixed number of virtual log files for a physical log file.

The only time virtual log files affect system performance is if the log files are defined by small size and growth increment values. If these log files grow to a large size because of many small increments, they have lots of virtual log files. This can slow down database STARTUP and also log backup and restore operations.

23. There is a big change happened in SQL Server Log architecture on SQL Server 2014. Do you have any idea on that?

Ans:

Yes! VLF creation algorithm got changed from SQL Server 2014 which results into a smaller number of VLF when compared to the earlier (Before 2014) algorithms.

Before SQL Server 2014:

- Up to 64 MB: 4 new VLFs, each roughly 1/4 the size of the growth
- 64 MB to 1 GB: 8 new VLFs, each roughly 1/8 the size of the growth
- More than 1 GB: 16 new VLFs, each roughly 1/16 the size of the growth

From SQL Server 2014:

- Is the growth size less than 1/8 the size of the current log size?
- Yes: create 1 new VLF equal to the growth size
- No: Use the Formula (8 VLF if Auto Growth > 1/8 of total log file)

Note: You can find examples and other VLF related questions in the chapter SQL DBA – General

24. What do you know about Checkpoints?

Ans:

Checkpoints flush dirty data pages from the buffer cache of the current database to disk. This minimizes the active portion of the log that must be processed during a full recovery of a database. During a full recovery, the following types of actions are performed:

- The log records of modifications not flushed to disk before the system stopped are rolled forward.
- All modifications associated with incomplete transactions, such as transactions for which there is no COMMIT or ROLLBACK log record, are rolled back.

Before a database backup, the Database Engine automatically performs a checkpoint so that all changes to the database pages are contained in the backup. Also, stopping a server issues a checkpoint in each database on the server.

25. What is the Active Log?

Ans:

The section of the log file from the Min-LSN to the last-written log record is called the active portion of the log, or the active log. This is the section of the log required to do a full recovery of the database. No part of the active log can ever be truncated. All log records must be truncated from the parts of the log before the Min-LSN.

26. What is Write Ahead Transaction Log?

Ans:

SQL Server uses a write-ahead log (WAL), which guarantees that no data modifications are written to disk before the associated log record is written to disk.

Data modifications are not made directly to disk, but are made to the copy of the page in the buffer cache. The modification is not written to disk until a checkpoint occurs in the database. A page modified in the cache, but not yet written to disk, is called a dirty page. The internal process that actually goes on:

- Copy of the data pages are pulled and placed in buffer cache
- Applied the operation on the pages that are on buffer cache
- Write the log record details (Pages modified) to Disk
- Write/flush/apply the page to the disk

If step 4 happens before the step 3 then rollback is impossible. SQL Server takes the responsibility of writing the log details to disk before flushing the dirty pages.

Query Processing Architecture

27. Do you have any idea on SQL Server Batch/Task Scheduling?

Ans:

Each instance must handle potentially thousands of concurrent requests from users. Instances of SQL Server use Microsoft Windows threads, or if configured, they use fibers, to manage these concurrent tasks efficiently. This includes one or more threads for each server Net-Library, a network thread to handle network I/O, and a signal thread for communicating with the Service Control Manager.

Each instance of SQL Server has an internal layer (SQL OS/Kernel) that implements an environment similar to an operating system. This internal layer is used for scheduling and synchronizing concurrent tasks without having to call the Windows kernel.

Connection: A connection is established when the user is successfully logged in. The user can then submit one or more Transact-SQL statements for execution. A connection is closed when the user explicitly logs out, or the connection is terminated.

Batch: An SQL batch is a set of one or more Transact-SQL statements sent from a client to an instance of SQL Server for execution.

Task: A task represents a unit of work that is scheduled by SQL Server. A batch can map to one or more tasks.

Windows thread: Each Windows thread represents an independent execution mechanism.

Fiber: A fiber is a lightweight thread that requires fewer resources than a Windows thread. One Windows thread can be mapped to many fibers.

Worker thread: The worker thread represents a logical thread (Task) in SQL Server that is internally mapped (1:1) to either a Windows thread or, if lightweight pooling is turned ON, to a fiber. The mapping can be done till the free worker threads available. (Parameter: Max worker Threads)

28. Any idea how Thread and Fibber Execution happens?

Ans:

Microsoft Windows uses a numeric priority system that ranges from 1 through 31 to schedule threads for execution. Zero is reserved for operating system use. When several threads are waiting to execute, Windows dispatches the thread with the highest priority.

By default, each instance of SQL Server is a priority of 7, which is referred to as the normal priority. The priority boost configuration option can be used to increase the priority of the threads from an instance of SQL Server to 13. This is referred to as high priority.

The performance of any instances running at normal priority can be adversely affected. Also, the performance of other applications and components on the server can decline if **priority boost** is turned on.

29. I have a web application and the backend is SQL Server. A user logged into the application, updated his details and submitted the request. The request includes a set of select statements and update statements. Now I wanted to know the step by step procedure for how the request reaches the database and work done. Can you be able to demonstrate?

Ans:

At Client:

1. User enter data and click on submit
2. The client database library transforms the original request into a sequence of one or more Transact-SQL statements to be sent to SQL Server. These statements are encapsulated in one or more Tabular Data Stream (TDS) packets and passed to the database network library. SNI (SQL Server Network Interface) takes this responsibility.
3. The database network library uses the network library available in the client computer to repackage the TDS packets as network protocol packets.
4. The network protocol packets are sent to the server computer network library using the server chosen network protocol (Ex TCP, Named Pipes etc.)

At Server:

5. The extracted TDS packets are sent to Open Data Services (ODS), where the original query is extracted.
6. ODS sends the query to the relational engine
7. A connection established to the relational engine and assigns a SID to the connection

At Relational Engine:

8. Check permissions and determines if the query can be executed by the user associated with the request
9. Query sends to Query Parser
   - It checks that the T-SQL is written correctly
   - Build a Parse Tree\Sequence Tree
10. Parse Tree sends to "ALGEBRIZER"
    - Verifies all the columns, objects and data types
    - Aggregate Binding (determines the location of aggregates such as **GROUP BY**, and **MAX**)
    - Builds a Query Processor Tree in Binary Format
11. Query Processor Tree sends to Optimizer
    - Based on the query processor tree and Histogram (Statistics) builds an optimized execution plan
    - Stores the execution plan into cache and send it to the database engine

At Database Engine:

12. Database engine map a batch into different tasks
13. Each task associated with a process
14. Each process assigned with a Windows Thread or a Windows Fiber. The worker thread takes care of this.
15. The Thread/Fiber send to the execution queue and wait for the CPU time.
16. The Thread/Fiber identifies the table location where the data need to be stored
17. Go to the file header, checks the PFS, GAM and SGAM and go to the correct page
18. Verifies the page is not corrupted using Torn page Detection/Check SUM
19. If new pages are required then it allocates a new page and it updates the below locations
    - PFS
    - Page Header – Checksum/Torn Page Detection (Sector info)
    - BCM
    - DCM
20. It issues the appropriate lock/latch on that page; pick that page from disk (MDF) to memory (RAM).
21. It applies the required modification on the page in Memory

22. All operations are logged into Transaction log file (LDF)
23. These pages are known as dirty pages as the same page differs in between memory and disk.
24. Once all required modification done on that page and transaction committed, the transaction in LDF are marked as committed and pages in memory wait for the checkpoint to be happened.
25. Once checkpoint happens all dirty pages are written to disk (MDF) and in LDF filled VLF files will be cleared if DB is in simple recovery mode or if it is in full recovery mode then it will wait for log backup to be happened.
26. In this entire process the
    - **Memory manager:** Take care of allocating buffers, new pages etc.,
    - **Lock manager:** Take care of allocating appropriate locks on the objects/pages and releasing them when task completed. It also take care Latches at physical level.
    - **Thread Scheduler**: Schedules the threads for CPU time
    - **I/O manager**: Establish memory bus for read/write operations from memory to disk and vice versa
    - **Deadlock\Resource\Scheduler Monitor:** Monitors the processes
    - **Lazy Writer:** Will be issued by SQL Engine to flush pages from memory to disk, when there is no sufficient memory available
27. Once the process is completed the result set is submitted to the relational engine and follow the same process for sending back the result set to client application.
28. The connection will be closed and the SID is removed

Memory Architecture

30. How Min and Max server memory options impact memory usage from SQL Server?

Ans:

The **min server memory** and **max server memory** configuration options establish upper and lower limits to the amount of memory used by the buffer pool of the Microsoft SQL Server Database Engine. The buffer pool starts with only the memory required to initialize. As the Database Engine workload increases, it keeps acquiring the memory required to support the workload. The buffer pool does not free any of the acquired memory until it reaches the amount specified in **min server memory**. Once **min server memory** is reached, the buffer pool then uses the standard algorithm to acquire and free memory as needed. The only difference is that the buffer pool never drops its memory allocation below the level specified in **min server memory**, and never acquires more memory than the level specified in **max server memory**.

31. What are the different types of memory?

Ans:

Physical Memory: The actual memory installed on mother board.

Virtual Memory: Total Physical Memory + Page File

Page File: When available memory can't serve the coming requests it starts swapping pages to disk to the page file. The current page file size we can get from "sysdm.cpl" à Advanced à Performance Settings --> Advanced

Cached memory: It holds data or program code that has been fetched into memory during the current session but is no longer in use now.

Free memory: It represents RAM that does not contain any data or program code and is free for use immediately.

Working Set: Amount of memory currently in use for a process. Peak Working Set is the highest value recorded for the current instance of this process. Consistently Working Set < Min Server Memory and Max Server Memory means SQL Server is configured to use too much of memory.

Private Working Set: Amount of memory that is dedicated to that process and will not be given up for other programs to use.

Sharable Working Set: Shareable Working Set can be surrendered if physical RAM begins to run scarce

Commit Size: The total amount of virtual memory that a program has touched (committed) in the current session. Limit is Maximum Virtual Memory that means Physical RAM + Page File + Kernel Cache.

Hard faults/Page Faults: Pages fetching from the page file on the hard disk instead of from physical memory. Consistently high number of hard faults per second represents Memory pressure.

32. How SQL Server acquires and releases Memory to/from OS?

Ans:

When SQL Server is using memory dynamically, it queries the system periodically to determine the amount of free memory. Maintaining this free memory prevents the operating system (OS) from paging. If less memory is free, SQL Server releases memory to the OS. If more memory is free, SQL Server may allocate more memory. SQL Server adds memory only when its workload requires more memory; a server at rest does not increase the size of its virtual address space.

33. What is Virtual Address Space (VAS)?

Ans:

- A virtual address is a binary number in virtual memory that enables a process to use a location in primary storage (main memory) independently of other processes.
- This provides a layer of abstraction between an application and physical memory so that the operating system can choose the most efficient way to use physical memory across all the processes.
- For example, two different processes can both use the memory address 0xFFF because it's a virtual address and each process has its own VAS with the same address range.
- The size of the virtual address space is determined largely by the CPU architecture.
- 32 bit can have Max 2 ^ 32 = 4 GB VAS and 64 bit will have 2 ^ 64 = Almost 16 Trillion GB VAS – 8TB is CAP

34. I have restarted my windows server. Can you be able to explain how memory allocation happens for SQL Server?

Ans:

Memory allocation is always depends on CPU architecture.

32 Bit:

- Initially allocates memory for "Memory To Leave" (MTL) also known as VAS Reservation (384 MB). This MTL value can be modified using the start parameter "–g"
- Then Allocates memory for Buffer Pool = User VAS – MTL (Reserved VAS) = Available VAS
- Maximum BPool Size = 2048 MB – 384 MB = 1664 MB.

64 Bit:

- Allocates Memory for Buffer Pool based on Maximum Server Memory configuration
- Non-Buffer Pool Memory region (MTL/VAS Reservation) = Total Physical Memory - (Max Server Memory + Physical Memory Used by OS and Other Apps)
  - ✓ Ex: Windows Server is having 64 GB physical memory; SQL Server Max Server Memory = 54 GB and OS and other apps are using 6 GB than the memory available for
  - ✓ Non-BPool (MTL/VAS Reservation) = 64 – (54+6) = 4 GB
  - ✓ Max Buffer Pool Size = Max Server Memory = 54 GB

35. What are all the objects that use MTL/Non-BPool memory allocated for SQL Server?

Ans:

- Connections with Network Packet Size higher than 8KB (8192 bytes)
- Memory allocated by Linked Server OLEDB Providers and third party DLL's loaded in SQL Server process
- Extended Stored Procedures or sp_OAcreate calls
- XML Documents
- Query Plans with the size > 8 KB
- SQL Server CLR
- Backups using larger MAXTRANSFERSIZE parameter
- Memory consumed by memory managers when memory requested for more than 8 KB contiguous allocation
- Memory for threads (stack size is 2 MB in 64-BIT SQL)

36. What is "Lock Pages in Memory"?

Ans:

- As you may know how memory allocation on windows operating system SQL Server occupies memory as much as it can based on the configurations and available memory.
- When windows operating system encounter a memory pressure it starts asking SQL Server to release memory and that released memory will be paged to page file.
- When Lock Pages In Memory is enabled for SQL Server Service Account then SQL Server can lock the pages and need not release memory when OS forcing to release.

37. Can you technically explain how memory allocated and lock pages works?

Ans:

Windows OS runs all processes on its own Virtual Memory known as Virtual Address Space and this VAS is divided into Kernel (System) and User (Application) mode.

Default: No Lock Pages in Memory is enabled

- SQL Server memory allocations made under User Mode VAS using VirtualAlloc() WPI function.
- Any memory that allocates via VirtualAlloc () can be paged to disk.
- SQLOS resource monitor checks QueryMemoryResourceNotification windows API and when windows sets Memory Low notification, SQLOS responds to that request by releasing the memory back to windows.

Lock Pages in Memory is Enabled for SQL Server:

- SQL Server memory allocations are made using calls to the function AllocateUserPhysicalPages () in AWE API.
- Memory that allocates using AllocateUserPhysicalPages () is considered to be locked. That means these pages should be on Physical Memory and need not be released when a Memory Low Notification on Windows.

38. Does "Lock Pages In Memory (LPIM)" enabled by default in SQL Server 2008 R2/2012?

Ans:

No! As per Microsoft documentation it's not. We need to enable it.

39. When to choose Lock Pages in Memory option for SQL Server?

Ans:

- When using Old windows servers – SQL Server 2005 on Windows Server 2003
- When working with 32 Bit servers and AWE is enabled
- When using Windows 2008 R2/2012 R2 and above still seeing hard trims happening SQL Server process memory.

Note: If you are using the latest windows systems and configured SQL Server memory settings as per the business requirement we need not worry about Lock Pages in Memory.

40. How to enable Lock Pages in Memory for SQL Server?

Ans:

We can enable by adding SQL Server service account to "Lock Pages in Memory" in group policy editor.

- Open Group Policy Editor using the shortcut "GPEDIT.MSC"
- Computer Configuration
- Windows Settings
- Security Settings

- Local Policies
- User Rights Assignment
- Right Side "Lock Pages In Memory"
- Right Click Properties
- Add SQL Server DB Engine service account
- Restart SQL Server

41. Can you tell me the difference between Logical Reads and Physical Reads?

Ans:

Logical Reads:

- Logical read indicates total number of data pages needed to be accessed from data cache to process query.
- It is very possible that logical read will access same data pages many times, so count of logical read value may be higher than actual number of pages in a table.
- Usually the best way to reduce logical read is to apply correct index or to rewrite the query.

Physical Reads:

- Physical read indicates total number of data pages that are read from disk.
- For a query when required pages are not found on cache memory it picks the required pages from Hard Disk and keep those pages on cache memory for further usage. This is known as physical read.

42. What is In-Memory OLTP?

Ans:

In-Memory OLTP is Microsoft's latest in-memory processing technology. In-Memory OLTP is optimized for Online Transaction Processing (OLTP) and integrated into SQL Server's Database Engine. In-Memory OLTP originally introduced in SQL Server 2014 and it mainly features two new data structures:

- Memory-Optimized Tables
- Natively-Compiled Stored Procedures

43. What are Memory-Optimized Tables?

Ans:

Memory-optimized tables store their data into memory using multiple versions of each row's data. This technique is characterized as 'non-blocking multi-version optimistic concurrency control' and eliminates both locks and latches thereof allowing the best concurrency control which leads to the significant performance improvement. The main features of Memory-Optimized Tables are:

- The entire table resides in memory
- Rows in the table are read from, and written to, memory
- Multiple versions of rows can be managed In-Memory

- Eliminates locks and latches
- The option of durable & non-durable data
- Data in memory-optimized tables is only read from disk during database recovery

44. What are Natively-Compiled stored procedures?

Ans:

A natively-compiled stored procedure is a SQL Server object that can access only memory-optimized data structures such as memory-optimized tables, table variables, etc. Features of a natively-compiled stored procedure:

- It is compiled to native code (DLL) upon its creation
- It can only interact with memory-optimized tables
- Aggressive optimizations take time at compile time
- The call to a natively-compiled stored procedure is actually a call to its DLL entry point

45. What is the architecture for In-Memory OLTP? Does it's a separate component or how SQL Server handles a request when they need both disk based and memory optimized objects?

Ans:

SQL Server 2014 and 2016 are having hybrid architecture by combining the both traditional database and In-Memory OLTP engine. There are 4 components created in In-Memory architecture

In-Memory OLTP Compiler:

This is for compiling "stored procedures" which are created as "Natively Compiled Stored Procedures" and also it compiles the incoming request to extract the natively compiled stored procedure dll entry point.

Natively Compiled SP's and Schema:

It holds the compiled code for natively compiled stored procedures.

In-Memory OLTP Storage Engine:

It manages user data and indexes of the memory optimized tables. It provides transactional operations on tables of records, hash and range indexes on the tables, and base mechanisms for storage, check pointing, recovery and high-availability. For a durable table, it writes data to FILESTREAM based FILEGROUP on disk so that it can recover in case a server crashes. It also logs its updates to the SQL Server database transaction log along with the log records for disk based tables. It uses SQL Server file streams for storing checkpoint files.

Memory Optimized Table FILEGROUP:

The most important difference between memory-optimized tables and disk-based tables is that pages do not need to be read into cache from disk when the memory-optimized tables are accessed. All the data is stored in memory, all the time. A set of checkpoint files (data and delta file pairs), which are only used for recovery purposes, is created on files residing in memory-optimized FILEGROUP that keep track of the changes to the data, and the checkpoint files are append-only. Operations on memory-optimized tables use the same transaction log that is used for operations on disk-based tables, and as always, the transaction log is stored on disk.

New Features added in 2008, 2008 R2, 2012, 2014, 2016

46. What is the new Features Added in SQL Server 2008/2008 R2/2012/2014/2016?

Ans:

Here we'll list of news features added in SQL Server versions. Most of the times in interviews you are asked a question "What are the new features added in SQL Server XXXX?" To simplify the answer we are just giving the single line abbreviations. While preparing for an interview just have a quick look and try to remember 4 to 5 features on current working and last version. Let's say you are currently working on 2012 then you need to look for 2012 and 2008 R2.

Features are categorised for DBA, Developer and Security. That doesn't mean that SQL Developer need not look into DBA section or vice versa. This is just to make it more readable, when a feature is more related to Developer we added in Developer section when a feature is more relevant administration part it will be in DBA section. Also we are not covering insights for MSBI.

SQL Server 2008

SQL DBA:

Activity Monitor: Great tool to showcase resource utilization and performance using GUI.

Policy Based Management: The ability to manage standards on multiple servers

Enhanced Database Mirroring: Automatic data page repair and compressing outgoing log stream

Resource Governor: We can configure it to control SQL Server resource utilization and workload.

External Key Management: Provides a comprehensive solution for encryption and key management.

Hot Add CPU: Adding resources online without downtime.

PowerShell: SQL Server 2008 ships with PowerShell snap-in built on .Net framework 2.0.

Table Compression: Compress data and index pages to save memory and I/O.

Backup Compression: Native backup compression.

Performance data collection: Centralized data repository for storing and reporting performance data

Extended Events: Event collection is easier now compares to running a trace

Security:

TDE - Transparent Database Encryption: Encrypt database without code changes

Change Data Capture: Track data changes.

SQL Auditing: the ability to audit at the server, database and table levels.

SQL Developer:

File-stream Data: To store binary large objects out on the file system.

Multi-Server Queries: being able to submit a batch of queries against multiple servers simultaneously.

Object Explorer Details: 36 possible columns of information about a database

Object Search: Searches for all objects within the selected scope: server, database, tables

SSMS Debug: the ability to debug any Transact-SQL within SSMS using breakpoints etc.

Intellisense in SQL Server Management Studio: interactive help support similar to Visual Studio.

Plan Freezing: Now we can lock down query plans

Spatial Data Types: Geometry and Geography

DATE/TIME Data Types: DATE, TIME, DATETIMEOFFSET

CLR Enhancements: User-defined aggregates and User-defined types now enhanced up to 2GB.

Table-Valued Parameters: It allows stored procedures to accept and return lists of parameters.

MERGE command: For incremental load using INSERT, UPDATE and DELETE operations.

HIERARCHYID Datatype: Provides tree like functionality among the data elements in a table

Grouping Sets: An extension to the GROUP BY

Filtered Indexes and Statistics: We can create non clustered index on a subset of a table

Object Dependencies: New DMV's provided for reliable information on depending objects

Sparse Columns: Columns that are optimized for the storage of NULL values.

SQL Server 2008 R2

SQL DBA:

SQL Server 2008 R2 Datacenter: Supports 256 logical processors

SQL Server Utility: Central repository control for multiple SQL Servers

Multi Server Dashboards: Dashboards showing combined server data can be created.

SQL Developer:

Master Data Services: To manage enterprise central database

Data-Tier Application: To map Database and Visual Studio builds

Stream Insight: Can analyse streaming data on the fly

Unicode Compression: New algorithm for Unicode storage

PowerPivot for SharePoint and Excel: Process datasets and reports.

Report Builder 3.0: Improved visualizations for SSRS

Parallel Data Warehouse: Data warehouses to be scaled over several physical SQL Servers.

SSMS enhancements for SQL Azure: SSMS support for cloud

SQL Server 2012

SQL DBA:

Licensing Model: It's not based on sockets introduced new core based licensing model

Edition changes: Introduced new BI edition and retired Datacenter, Workgroup and standard for small business.

ALWAYSON availability: Provides both Disaster Recovery and High Availability

Enhanced PowerShell Support: More CMDLETS introduced

Windows Server Core: Core is the GUI less version of Windows that uses DOS and PowerShell for user interaction SQL Server 2012 supports Windows Core

SQL Azure Enhancements: DB size limit increased to 150 GB, Azure data sync allows hybrid model etc.

SQL Developer:

Indirect checkpoints: Now we can configure checkpoint intervals database wise

Column Store-Index: Stores columns on page instead of rows

SSDT: BIDS is now SSDT SQL Server Data Tools.

File Table: Builds upon FILESTREAM and SQL Server can access windows files on non-transactional

Sequence objects: an alternative for IDENTITY property

THROW: Improved error handling

New Conversion Functions: PARSE, TRY_PARSE, TRY_CONVERT

New Logical functions: CHOOSE, IIF

New String functions: CONCAT, FORMAT

New Date & Time functions: DATEFROMPARTS, DATETIME2FROMPARTS, DATETIMEFROMPARTS, DATETIMEOFFSETFROMPARTS, SMALLDATETIMEFROMPARTS, TIMEFROMPARTS.

ROWS and RANGE: Support for Window framing on result sets

LAG and LEAD: To get the previous and next rows data

New Rank distribution functions: PERCENT_RANK, PERCENTILE_CONT, PERCENTILE_DISC and CUME_DIST

OFFSET/FETCH: Supports paging for ad hoc queries

FORCESCAN: New table hint

WITH RESULT SETS: More control on stored procedure returned result set metadata

sp_describe_first_result_set: Advanced version for SET FMTONLY option. Also DMV's added for this

Statistical Semantic Search: Advanced feature builds upon the existing full-text search

Data Quality Services- DQS: A service added to MDS for advanced data profiling and cleansing

Power View: Light weight tool for BI reports

BI Semantic Model: Hybrid model that allows one data model will support all BI experiences

Big Data Support: ODBC driver for SQL Server that will run on a Linux platform etc.

Security:

User-Defined Server Roles: Customization for Server Roles

Database Audit: Like SQL Server Audit and it performs audits database level

Contained Databases: Users can be added on a database without login can easier migration

SQL Server 2014

SQL DBA:

Standard Edition Memory Capacity: Increased to 128 GB whereas 2012 standard editions it is 64 GB.

SQL Server Developer Edition is free: Microsoft made SQL Server 2014 Developer Edition license free.

ALWAYSON AG more secondary's: 2012 supports 4 whereas 2014 supports up to 8 secondaries

ALWAYSON AG readable secondaries: Readable secondaries remain online even though primary replica is down.

Add Azure Replica Wizard: Helps us to create asynchronous secondary replicas in Windows Azure

Buffer Pool Extension: SQL Server 2014 enable users to use Solid State Disk (SSD) to expand the SQL Server 2014 Buffer Pool as non-volatile RAM (NvRAM).

RG I/O control: In 2014 Resource Governor can also be configured to control the physical I/O.

Backup Encryption: SQL Server 2014 introduced native backup encryption. It supports several encryption algorithms AES 128, AES 192, AES 256, and Triple DES.

Managed Backup to Azure: SQL Server 2014 native backup supports Windows Azure with auto scheduling

SQL Developer:

In-Memory OLTP Engine: We can enable memory optimization for selected tables and stored procedures.

Updateable Column-store Indexes: On SQL Server 2012 to utilize the column-store index, the underlying table had to be read-only. SQL Server 2014 eliminates this restriction. In 2014 Column-Store Index must use all the columns in the table and can't be combined with other indexes.

Cardinality Estimator Improvements: Cardinality Estimator redesigned in SQL Server 2014.

Delayed Durability: Introduced delayed durable transactions. A delayed durable transaction returns control to the client before the transaction log record is written to disk. Durability can be controlled at the database level, COMMIT level, or ATOMIC block level.

Partition Switching and Indexing: The individual partitions of partitioned tables can now be rebuilt.

Lock priority for Online Operations: The ONLINE = ON option now contains a WAIT_AT_LOW_PRIORITY option which permits you to specify how long the rebuild process should wait for the necessary locks. We can also be able to configure terminating the blocking process related to rebuild.

Incremental Statistics: Now we can create partition level statistics by using the option INCREMENTAL

Inline Specification for Indexes: Inline specification of CLUSTERED and NONCLUSTERED indexes is now allowed for disk-based tables. Creating a table with inline indexes is equivalent to issuing a create table followed by corresponding CREATE INDEX statements. Included columns and filter conditions are not supported with inline indexes.

SELECT ... INTO Enhancement: This statement now can be operated in parallel

Power View and Power BI: Power View now in 2014 supports OLAP cubes along with the tabular data. Power BI for office 365 is a cloud based BI solution.

Security:

SELECT ALL USER SECURABLES: A new server level permission. When granted, a login such as an auditor can view data in all databases that the user can connect to.

CONNECT ANY DATABASE: A new server level permission when granted, a login can connect to any existing/future database in that instance. Combine with SELECT ALL USER SECURABLES or VIEW SERVER STATE to allow an auditing process.

IMPERSONATE ANY LOGIN: A new server level permission when granted, allows a middle-tier process to impersonate the account of clients connecting to it, as it connects to databases.

SQL Server 2016

SQL DBA:

SQL Server Developer Edition is free: Microsoft made SQL Server 2014 Developer Edition license free and same continued with SQL Server 2016 Developer Edition.

ALWAYSON Enhancements: Standard Edition will come with AGs support with one database per group synchronous or asynchronous, not readable (HA/DR only). 3 sync replicas supported whereas it was 2 in SQL 2014. Listener will be able to do round-robin load balancing of read-only requests on multiple SECONDARIES. Now supports Microsoft DTC. SQL Server ALWAYSON to Azure Virtual Machine

Database Scoped Configurations: The new ALTER DATABASE SCOPED CONFIGURATION allows us to control database level configurations. Ex: Parameter sniffing at database level.

Striped Backups to Microsoft Azure Blob Storage: In SQL Server 2016, SQL Server backup to URL using the Microsoft Azure Blob storage service now supports striped backups sets using block blobs with the maximum backup size of 12.8 TB.

File-Snapshot Backups to Microsoft Azure Blob Storage: In SQL Server 2016, SQL Server backup to URL now supports using Azure snapshots to backup databases in which all database files are stored using the Microsoft Azure Blob storage service.

Managed Backup: In SQL Server 2016 SQL Server Managed Backup to Microsoft Azure uses the new block blob storage for backup files. It supports automatic and custom scheduling, backups for system databases and backups for databases with simple recovery model.

No need to enable Trace flag 4199: Most of the query optimizer behaviours controlled by this trace flag are enabled unconditionally under the latest compatibility level (130)

TEMPDB enhancements: Trace Flags 1117 and 1118 are not required for TEMPDB anymore. When TEMPDB is having database files all files will grow at the same time based on growth settings. All allocations in TEMPDB will use uniform extents. By default, setup adds as many

TEMPDB files as the CPU count or 8, whichever is lower. We can have the control on TEMPDB configuration while installing SQL Server 2016.

New Default Database Size and AUTOGROW Values: For model database these default values are changed in 2016. Default data and log file size is 8 MB and auto-growth is 64 MB.

MAXDOP option for DBCC: Now we can specify MAXDOP option for DBCC CHECKTABLE, DBCC CHECKDB and DBCC CHECKFILEGROUP.

Replication Enhancements: Replication supports memory-optimized tables and replication support enabled for Azure SQL Database.

SQL Developer:

Column-Store Index Enhancements: A read-only non-clustered COLUMNSTORE index is updateable after upgrade without rebuilding the index. Also COLUMNSTORE indexes can be created for In-Memory tables

Live Query Statistics: Management Studio provides the ability to view the live execution plan of an active query.

Query Store: It can quickly find the performance differences caused by changes in query plans. The feature automatically captures a history of queries, plans, and runtime statistics, and retains these for your review. It separates data by time windows, allowing you to see database usage patterns and understand when query plan changes happened on the server.

Temporal Tables: SQL Server 2016 now supports system-versioned temporal tables. A temporal table is a new type of table that provides correct information about stored facts at any point in time.

Built-in JSON support: Java Script Object Notation (JSON) SQL Server 2016 enables ability to move JSON data to SQL Server tables using various clauses and functions. Ex: FOR JSON, OPENJSON, ISJSON, JSON_VALUE, JSON_QUERY, JSON_MODIFY

PolyBase: PolyBase allows you to use T-SQL statements to access data stored in Hadoop or Azure Blob Storage and query it in an ad-hoc fashion. It also lets you query semi-structured data and join the results with relational data sets stored in SQL Server. PolyBase is optimized for data warehousing workloads and intended for analytical query scenarios.

Stretch Database: SQL Server migrate historical data transparently and securely to the Microsoft Azure cloud. SQL Server handles the data movement in the background based on the policy we can configure. The entire table is always online and queryable. Stretch Database doesn't require any changes to existing queries or applications the location of the data is completely transparent to the application.

In-Memory OLTP Enhancements: To be frank it's not just enhancements. In-Memory OLTP on 2014 is just a trail version and in 2016 this is the first version where we have seen lot of things has been fixed and supported.

In-Memory – ALTER TABLE is log-optimized, and runs in parallel: Only the metadata changes are written to the log also now it can run in parallel.

In-Memory Statistics: Now statistics are updated automatically

In-Memory Parallel Scan: Memory-optimized tables, and hash indexes, are now scannable in parallel.

In-Memory – LOBs with large row size: Now memory optimized tables can have LOB type columns

In-Memory – TDE and MARS: MARS and TDE support enabled for In-Memory optimized tables

In-Memory T-SQL support: SQL Server 2016 overcomes the maximum limitations on 2014 In-Memory OLTP T-SQL Support. Now In-Memory OLTP supports OUTPUT clause, UNIQUE index, FOREIGN KEY, Alter, Schema changes, Triggers, Check constraint, UNIION, UNION ALL, DISTINCT, OUTER JOIN, Sub queries and lot many native features supports in 2016 In-Memory optimized tables and natively compile stored procedures.

Foreign Key Relationship Limits: SQL Server 2016 increases the limit for the number of other table and columns that can reference columns in a single table from 253 to 10,000.

Support for UTF-8: BULK INSERT, BCP Utility and OPENROWSET now support the UTF-8 code page.

TRUNCATE TABLE – Partition: The TRUNCATE TABLE statement now permits the truncation of specified partitions.

ALTER TABLE Enhanced: Now allows actions to be performed while the table remains available.

NO_PERFORMANCE_SPOOL: New query hint can prevent a spool operator from being added to query plans.

DROP IF: Really useful feature. It drops the object if it exists in database.

sp_execute_external_script: Advanced Analytics Extensions allow users to execute scripts written in a supported language such as R.

COMPRESS – DECOMPRESS: Functions to convert values into and out of the GZIP algorithm.

New DATETIME: DATEDIFF_BIG, AT TIME ZONE functions and sys.time_zone_info view are added to support date and time interactions.

STRING_SPLIT and STRING_ESCAPE: New string functions added

Security:

Row-Level Security: This is a predicate based access control.

Always Encrypted: Encrypt entire data (Data file, Log file, Backup, Communication Channel) and only application can see the data.

Dynamic Data Masking: Dynamic data masking limits sensitive data exposure by masking it to non-privileged users.

Transparent Data Encryption Enhanced: TDE supports Intel AES-NI hardware acceleration of encryption. This will reduce the CPU overhead of turning on Transparent Data.

AES Encryption for Endpoints: The default encryption for endpoints is changed from RC4 to AES.

New Credential Type: A credential can now be created at the database level in addition to the server level credential that was previously available.

CHAPTER 2

SQL SERVER INSTALLATIONS AND UPGRADES

Interview Questions and Answers

Introduction: This chapter takes you through the SQL Server Installation and Upgrades related interview questions and answers. This is one of the most common areas where any SQL DBA can expect questions in technical interviews. These questions and answers are deals with the below topics:

- SQL Server Licensing
- Service Accounts and Network Protocols
- Installation
- Upgrade
- Troubleshooting Scenarios
- SQL Server Components and Capacity Specifications

SQL Server Licensing

1. Do you know how licensing happening in SQL Server?

Ans:

Prior to SQL Server 2012:

Microsoft SQL Server could be purchased as either a Server/CAL (Client Access License) licensing model or a (physical) Processor licensing model.

Server/CAL model: The server was licensed and each user (person or device) needed a CAL.

Processor licensing model: When number of users is large we can go for Processor License which is licensed based on number of physical processors.

From SQL Server 2012:

Microsoft SQL Server 2012: Introduced Core Licensing Model which is licensing number of cores for each processor.

Let's say I have 6 Processors and each processor is having 8 cores.

SQL Server 2008 R2 Enterprise: 6 Processor License required

SQL Server 2012 R2 Enterprise: 6X8 = 48 Core License required

Note: Each Core License price is ¼ of one Processor License. So when we are running ratio of 4 cores per processor end cost doesn't change and it's almost same for both 4 Processor License and 16 Core License. This is a very basic difference and it needs a lot of patience to understand SQL Server Licensing models.

2. How licensing differs from Physical and Virtual machines in SQL Server 2012?

Ans:

Physical:

- All cores in the server must be licensed
- A minimum of 4 core licenses required for each physical processor

Virtual:

- Individual virtual machines may be licensed (as opposed to all cores in the physical server)
- A minimum of 4 core licenses per virtual machine

3. Did you get a chance to know the price of SQL Server any version/edition?

Ans:

- SQL Server 2012 Enterprise – Per Core $6874
- SQL Server 2012 Standard – Per Core $1793/Per Server $898
- SQL Server 2012 Client Access License (CAL) – $209

4. Apart from processor and cores what are all the other things that we need to consider while licensing?

Ans:

There is lot of things need to be considered while planning for SQL Server license:

- Number of processors
- Cores for each processor
- Physical/Virtual
- Processor Type
- Core Factor (Based on Processor Type)
  - ✓ AMD – Core Factor – 0.75
  - ✓ Single Core Processor – Core Factor – 4
  - ✓ Dual Core Processor – Core Factor – 2
  - ✓ All other processors – Core Factor – 1
- Number of Packs
- Mirroring and High Availability
- Software Assurance Rights
- License Mobility

5. How Mirroring and High Availability impact SQL Server license?

Ans:

ACTIVE – PASSIVE: Mirrored configurations or active-passive cluster/failover configurations do not require licenses on the mirror. This doesn't apply if you are using a combination of mirrored and active databases on mirrored/passive node.

ACTIVE – ACTIVE: Clusters or ALWAYSON High Availability Groups do need licensing for every active node within the group.

6. What is Software Assurance Rights?

Ans:

When you upgrade from SQL Server 2008 R2 (or below) to SQL Server 2012 using your Software Assurance rights you can continue to use your existing license model until the end of your Software Assurance cycle. This means that if you have CPU licenses under SQL Server 2008 R2 you can continue to use those CPU licenses under SQL Server 2012 until your Software Assurance expires. Once it expires you will need to true up on the number of CPU Cores.

7. What is License Mobility?

Ans:

License Mobility flexi benefit available under Software Assurance, customers can reassign licenses between servers as often as necessary within a server farm

8. How types of processor impact the SQL Server license?

Ans:

Here is the basic formula for calculating total licenses required:

Total Licenses Required = Two Processors X Cores per Processor X Core Factor

- Two processors, four cores per processor, Dual Core, Intel = 2 x 4 x 2 = 16 licenses
- One processor, four cores, Intel = 1 x 4 x 1 = 4 licenses
- Two processors, AMD 61XX model, eight cores 2 x 8 x 0.75 = 12 licenses

Note: when ordering the licenses, you must divide the number of licenses by two to determine how many 'packs' to order.

9. Starting from SQL Server 7 to 2016, from which edition the licensing model has been changed?

Ans:

Processor core licensing model introduced in SQL Server 2012. Microsoft has moved away from counting sockets to a new core-based licensing model. The Enterprise edition can be licensed only per core. The list price is $6,874 per core. The Business Intelligence edition is licensed only per server; it goes for $8,592 per server. You must also purchase Client Access Licenses (CALs) per user. The CAL price has increased to $209 per CAL. The Standard edition has the option of being licensed either per core or per server; it costs $1,793 per core or $898 per server.

Also from SQL Server 2014 Microsoft made SQL Server Developer Edition free which can be used for enterprise development and testing environments.

Service Accounts and Network Protocols

10. What is a service account?

Ans:

Based on the selected components while doing the installation we will find respective service to each component in the Windows Services. E.g. SQL Server, SQL Server Agent, SQL Analysis Services, SQL Server integration Services etc. There will be a user for each and every service through which each service will run. That use is called Service Account of that service.

11. Your customer sent you a request to suggest a service account for production SQL Server installation. How do you suggest the correct service account for SQL Server?

Ans:

I would suggest based on the business requirement. In most of the cases we would use Domain User accounts:

When to use Domain User Account:

- ➢ SQL Server interacts with other servers, services or resources on the network ex: Files Shares
- ➢ SQL Server services uses linked servers to connect to other SQL Servers on the network
- ➢ Use a low privileged domain user account for running SQL Server services.
- ➢ Domain user account is the most recommended account for setting up SQL Server services that interact with other servers on the network.
- ➢ Domain User Account is controlled by Windows active directory thereof domain level policy on accounts applies to SQL Server service account as well.

When to use Network Service Account:

- ➢ Never recommend to use Network Service Account for running SQL Server services
- ➢ These accounts are shared with other services running on the local computer
- ➢ Network Service Account is a built-in account that has more access to server resources and objects than user accounts of local user groups
- ➢ Any SQL Server services that runs on Network Service Account, can access network resources by using the credentials of the computer account.
- ➢ This account shows up as "NET AUTHORITY\NETWORK SERVICE" when configuring SQL Server Services.

When to use Local User Account:

- ➢ SQL Server doesn't interact with other servers, services or resources on the network (ex: Files, Shares, Linked Servers, Etc.)
- ➢ Use a low privileged local user account for running SQL Server Services.

When to use Local System Account:

- ➢ We don't recommend local system account for running SQL Server services.

- Local System Account has more permission
- It is a very high-privileged built-in account created by Windows OS
- Local System Account has extensive privileges on the entire local system and acts as a computer on your company's network.
- This account shows up as "NT AUTHORITY\SYSTEM" when configuring SQL Server services.

When to Use Local Service Account:

- This is a built-in windows account that is available for configuring services in windows.
- This account has permissions as same as accounts that are in the users group, thus it has limited access to the resources in the server

12. What are the network protocols that SQL Server supports?

Ans:

Stand-alone named and default instances support the following network protocols:

- Shared memory
- Named pipes
- TCP/IP
- VIA

Shared Memory:

Clients using the shared memory protocol can only connect to a SQL Server instance running on the same computer; it is not useful for most database activity. Use the shared memory protocol for troubleshooting when you suspect the other protocols are configured incorrectly.

Server – Machine 1

Clients – Machine 1

TCP/IP:

TCP/IP is a common protocol widely used over the Internet. It communicates across interconnected networks of computers that have diverse hardware architectures and various operating systems. TCP/IP includes standards for routing network traffic and offers advanced security features. It is the most popular protocol that is used in business today.

Server – Machine 1

Clients – WAN (Any machine from any network)

Named Pipes:

Named Pipes is a protocol developed for local area networks. A part of memory is used by one process to pass information to another process, so that the output of one is the input of the other. The second process can be local (on the same computer as the first) or remote (on a networked computer).

Server – Machine 1

Clients – LAN (Any machine from LAN)

VIA:

Virtual Interface Adapter (VIA) protocol works with VIA hardware. This feature is deprecated.

Note Shared memory is not supported on failover clusters.

13. Do we need to grant Administrator permissions on the Windows server to SQL Service account to run the services?

Ans:

No, it is not required. It's not mandatory to grant Administrator permissions to the service account.

14. What permissions are required for a user to install SQL Server on a server?

Ans:

User through which we are installing SQL Server must have administrator permissions on the Windows server.

Installation & Upgrade

15. What are the different releases of SQL Server? We usually talk about RTM, RC, SP, CU etc. right, what are the different releases of a SQL Server product and what do you know about them?

Ans:

- *CTP (Community Technology Preview):* It's Beta release of SQL Server product.
- *RC (Release Candidate):* A release candidate (RC) is a beta version with potential to be a final product, which is ready to release unless significant bugs emerge.
- *RTM (Released to Manufacturing):* It is the original, released build version of the product. This is the actual product software that we get on DVD or ISO file from MSDN.
- *CU (Cumulative Update):* Cumulative updates contain the bug fixes and enhancements up to that point in time that have been added since the previous Service Pack release and will be contained in the next service pack release.
- *SP (Service Pack):* Larger collection of hotfixes that have been fully regression tested. In some cases delivers product enhancements.
- *GDR (General Distribution Release):* GDR packages contain only security and critical stability issue fixes. GDR fixes should not contain any of the CU updates.
- *LDR/QFE/Hot Fix (Limited Distribution Release/Quick Fix Engineering):* LDR packages contain "other" fixes that have not undergone as extensive testing, and resolve issues that only a fraction of the millions of users might ever encounter. QFE updates include CU fixes.

16. What are Shared Features Directory and its usages?

Ans:

This directory contains the common files used by all instances on a single computer e.g. SSMS, SQLCMD, BCP, DTExec etc. These are installed in the folder "<drive>:\Program Files\Microsoft SQL Server\(100\110\120)" where <drive> is the drive letter where components are installed. The default is usually C drive.

17. What is a SQL Server Instance?

Ans:

An instance of the Database Engine is a copy of the sqlservr.exe executable that runs as an operating system service. Each instance manages its own system databases and one or more user databases. An instance is a complete copy of an SQL Server installation.

18. Type of Instance and maximum no. of instances which can be installed on a server.

Ans:

There are two types of Instances.

- Default instance
- Named Instance
- Each computer can run maximum of 50 standalone instances of the Database Engine. One instance can be the default instance.
- The default instance has no name. If a connection request specifies only the name of the computer, the connection is made to the default instance or with IP address and the port number.
- A named instance is one where you specify an instance name when installing the instance. A connection request must specify computer name/IP Address and instance name/Port number in order to connect to the instance.

19. Can we install multiple instances on the same disk drive?

Ans:

Yes, we can install multiple instances on the same disk drive because each installation creates its own folder with the below format MSSQL11.INSTANCENAME.

20. What is a collation and what is the default collation?

Ans:

Collation refers to a set of rules that determine how data is sorted and compared. Character data is sorted using rules that define the correct character sequence, with options for specifying case-sensitivity, accent marks, kana character types and character width.

Default collation: *SQL_Latin1_General_CP1_CI_AS*

21. What is the default port of a SQL Server instance?

Ans:

SQL Server default instance by default listen on 1433 port.

22. Can we change the default port of SQL Server, How?

Ans:

Yes, it is possible to change the Default port on which SQL Server is listening.

- Click Start > All Programs > Microsoft SQL Server 2012 > Configuration Tools >SQL Server Configuration Manager
- Go to SQL Server Configuration Manager > SQL Server Network Configuration > Protocols for <Instance Name>
- Right Click on TCP/IP and select Properties
- In TCP/IP Properties dialog box, go to IP Addresses tab and scroll down to IPAll group. Now change the value to static value which you want to set for SQL Server port.
- Make sure Dynamic Port ls empty (Remove 0).

23. How to get the port number where the SQL Server instance is listening?

Ans:

Below are the methods which we can use to get the port information:

- SQL Server Configuration Manager
- Windows Event Viewer
- SQL Server Error Logs
- sys.dm_exec_connections DMV
- Reading registry using xp_instance_regread

24. What is a FILESTREAM?

Ans:

FILESTREAM was introduced in SQL Server 2008 for the storage and management of unstructured data. The FILESTREAM feature allows storing BLOB data (example: word documents, image files, music and videos etc.) in the NT file system and ensures transactional consistency between the unstructured data stored in the NT file system and the structured data stored in the table.

25. What are the file locations for Server components?

Ans:

Server components are installed in directories with the format <instanceID>\<component name>. For example, a default or named instance with the Database Engine, Analysis Services, and Reporting Services would have the following default directories:

- ✓ <Program Files>\Microsoft SQL Server\MSSQL.1\MSSQL\Database Engine
- ✓ <Program Files>\Microsoft SQL Server\MSSQL.2\OLAP\for Analysis Services
- ✓ <Program Files>\Microsoft SQL Server\MSSQL.3\RS\for Reporting Services

26. What about SSIS, Notification services and client components?

Ans:

SQL Server Integration Services, Notification Services, and client components are not instance aware and, therefore, are not assigned an instance ID. Non-instance-aware components are installed to the same directory by default: <system drive>:\Program Files\Microsoft SQL Server\(90\110\120)\. Changing the installation path for one shared component also changes it for the other shared components. Subsequent installations install non-instance-aware components to the same directory as the original installation.

27. List out the default path for the SQL Server components.

Ans:

Example Folder Name 2008 R2: MSSQL10_50.SQL2008R2

Example Folder Name 2014: MSSQL12.SQL2014

- Database Engine server components

  \Program Files\Microsoft SQL Server\MSSQL.*n*\MSSQL\Binn\
- Database Engine data files

  \Program Files\Microsoft SQL Server\MSSQL.*n*\MSSQL\Data\
- Analysis Services server

  \Program Files\Microsoft SQL Server\MSSQL.*n*\OLAP\Bin\
- Analysis Services data files

  \Program Files\Microsoft SQL Server\MSSQL.*n*\OLAP\Data\
- Reporting Services report server

  \Program Files\Microsoft SQL Server\MSSQL.*n*\Reporting Services\ReportServer\Bin\
- Reporting Services report manager

  \Program Files\Microsoft SQL Server\MSSQL.*n*\Reporting Services\ReportManager\Bin\
- SQL Server Integration Services

  <Install Directory>\[90/100/110/120/130]\DTS\
- Notification Services

  <Install Directory>\[90/100/110/120/130]\Notification Services\
- Client Components

  <Install Directory>\[90/100/110]\Tools\
- Components that are shared between all instances of SQL Server

  \Program Files\Microsoft SQL Server\[90/100/110/120/130]\Shared\

28. Can we change the directory while adding new features?

Ans:

Can't! You must either install additional features to the directories already established by Setup, or uninstall and reinstall the product.

29. What are the log files generated while Installing\Upgrading\Applying (packages) SQL Server on Windows machine?

Ans:

Summary.txt

This file shows the SQL Server components that were detected during Setup, the operating system environment, command-line parameter values if they are specified, and the overall status of each MSI/MSP that was executed.

Location:

%program files%\Microsoft SQL Server\(100\110\120\130)\Setup Bootstrap\Log\

Note:

To find errors in the summary text file, search the file by using the "error" or "failed" keywords.

Summary_engine-base_YYYYMMDD_HHMMss.txt

Generated during the main workflow

Location:

%Program files%\Microsoft SQL Server\(100\110\120)\Setup Bootstrap\Log\<YYYYMMDD_HHMM>\

Summary_engine-base_YYYYMMDD_HHMMss_ComponentUpdate.txt

Generates during the component update workflow

Location:

%programfiles%\Microsoft SQL Server\100\Setup Bootstrap\Log\<YYYYMMDD_HHMM>\

Summary_engine-base_20080503_040551_GlobalRules.txt

Generates during the global rules workflow

Location:

%programfiles%\Microsoft SQL Server\100\Setup Bootstrap\Log\<YYYYMMDD_HHMM>\

Detail.txt

Detail.txt is generated for the main workflow such as install or upgrade, and provides the details of the execution. The logs in the file are generated based on the time when each action for the installation was invoked, and show the order in which the actions were executed, and their dependencies.

Location

%\Microsoft SQL Server\100\Setup Bootstrap\Log\<YYYYMMDD_HHMM>\Detail.txt.

Note:

If an error occurs during the Setup process, the exception or error are logged at the end of this file. To find the errors in this file, first examine the end of the file followed by a search of the file for the "error" or "exception" keywords.

Detail_ComponentUpdate.txt

Detail_GlobalRules.txt

MSI log files

The MSI log files provide details of the installation package process. They are generated by the MSIEXEC during the installation of the specified package.

Location

%programfiles%\Microsoft SQL Server\100\Setup Bootstrap\Log\<YYYYMMDD_HHMM>\<Name>.log.

Note:

At the end of the file is a summary of the execution which includes the success or failure status and properties. To find the error in the MSI file, search for "value 3" and usually the errors can be found close to the string.

ConfigurationFile.ini

The configuration file contains the input settings that are provided during installation. It can be used to restart the installation without having to enter the settings manually. However, passwords for the accounts, PID, and some parameters are not saved in the configuration file.

Location:

%programfiles%\Microsoft SQL Server\100\Setup Bootstrap\Log\<YYYYMMDD_HHMM>\

SystemConfigurationCheck_Report.htm

Contains a short description for each executed rule, and the execution status

Location:

%programfiles%\Microsoft SQL Server\100\Setup Bootstrap\Log

\<YYYYMMDD_HHMM>\

30. How many SQL Server log files can be retained in the SQL Server error logs be default?

Ans:

By default, there are seven SQL Server error logs; Error log and ERRORLOG.1 through ERRORLOG.6. The name of the current, most recent log is ERRORLOG with no extension. The log is re-created every time that you restart SQL Server. When the ERRORLOG file is re-created, the previous log is renamed to ERRORLOG.1, and the next previous log (ERRORLOG.1) is renamed to ERRORLOG.2, and so on. ERRORLOG.6 is deleted.

31. Is it possible to increase the retention of Error log files and How?

Ans:

Yes it is possible to change the number of Error logs retention. We can follow the below steps to change the Error log file retention.

- Open SQL Server Management Studio and then connect to SQL Server Instance
- In Object Explorer, Expand Management Node and then right click SQL Server Logs and click Configure as shown in the snippet below.
- In Configure SQL Server Error Logs window you can enter the value between 6 and 99 for the number of error logs and click OK to save the changes

32. What is the installation log file location for SQL Server?

Ans:

Summary.txt:

C:\Program Files\Microsoft SQL Server\(90\100\110\120\130)\Setup Bootstrap\LOG

All other files:

C:\Program Files\Microsoft SQL Server\(90\100\110\120\130)\Setup Bootstrap

\LOG\<Date_Time>\

Here you find logs for each individual component as well as the actions performed at the time of installation.

33. What information stored in Summary.txt?

Ans:

This file has information on the installation start and stop time, installed components, machine name, product, version and detailed log files. Although this file differs slightly based on selected installation components, this file does not have any user names, passwords, service accounts, ports, etc. This file does have a high level log and references to the detailed files which will be reviewed next.

34. Is there any possibility to find out the "SA" password from log files?

Ans:

No! Clear Passwords not stored at anywhere.

While installing SQL Server, SA password validation and confirmation is logged on few setup related log files. But the actual password is never stored in clear text during the database services installation. There are other places where we may see SA and service account password logged (Not in Clear Format) is the temporary file location "C:\DOCUME~1\ProfileName\LOCALS~1\Temp*.tmp" but these files are removed at the end of SQL Server installation.

35. I have applied a SP/CU on 2012 instances. Where we can find the log files?

Ans:

Check the folder with the latest data and time

C:\Program Files\Microsoft SQL Server\(90\100\110\120\130)\SetupBootstrap\LOG\

<YYYYMMDD_HHMM>\<Summary_ServerName_Date_Time>

Other files like component wise files are also located in the same folder.

36. Which component performs the configuration check while installing the SQL Server?

Ans:

- As part of SQL Server 2005/2008 R2/2012/2014 Setup, the System Configuration Checker (SCC) scans the computer where Microsoft SQL Server will be installed.
- The SCC checks for conditions that prevent a successful SQL Server installation.
- Before Setup starts the SQL Server Installation Wizard, the SCC retrieves the status of each check item, compares the result with required conditions, and provides guidance for removal of blocking issues.
- All of the SCC checks items are network enabled; checks can run on a local computer, as well as in remote and cluster situations.
- The system configuration check generates a report which contains a short description for each executed rule, and the execution status. The system configuration check report is located at %programfiles%\MicrosoftSQL Server\120\Setup Bootstrap\Log\<YYYYMMDD_HHMM>\.

37. What are the things involved in installing SQL Server 2008 R2/2012/2014/2016?

Ans:

- Determine capacity requirements for SQL Server. Ex: Memory, CPU, Space etc.
- Determine the required features based on your business requirement
- Determine the required Network protocol
- Determine the backup plan
- Determine the High Availability and Disaster Recovery plan
- Determine the folder paths for SQL binaries, Backups, User Database, TEMPDB & Other System Database MDF, LDF
- Determine the list of logins required for SQL Server and Service Accounts
- Determine the configuration values Ex: Instant File Initialization, Lock Pages, Max Server Memory, DAC etc.
- Make sure we are also including the latest Service Pack/Cumulative Update
- Review Microsoft suggested Prerequisites
- Be sure the computer meets the system requirements for SQL Server
- Make sure Software and Hardware are matching
- Review Security Considerations for a SQL Server Installation
- Run SCC to identify the blocking issues and resolve before go ahead.
- Make sure you have administrator permissions on the computer where SQL Server will be installed. If you install SQL Server from a remote share, you must use a domain account that has read and execute permissions on the remote share.

- Verify that the disk where SQL Server will be installed is uncompressed. If you attempt to install SQL Server to a compressed drive, Setup will fail
- Pause antivirus software while installing SQL Server
- Stop all services that depend on SQL Server
- Most importantly document all requirements properly

38. List out the Instance-Aware and Instance-Unaware Services

Ans:

Instance-aware services in Microsoft SQL Server include:

- SQL Server Database Engine
- SQL Server Agent
- Analysis Services
- Reporting Services
- Full-Text Search

Instance-unaware services in SQL Server include:

- Notification Services
- Integration Services
- SQL Server Browser
- SQL Server Active Directory Helper
- SQL Writer

39. What is a silent installation and how can we use this feature?

Ans:

The procedure to install SQL Server instance through command line using ConfigurationFile.ini file in "Quite" mode is known as Silent installation.

40. What is "ConfigurationFile.ini" file?

Ans:

SQL Server Setup generates a configuration file named ConfigurationFile.ini, based upon the system default and run-time inputs. The ConfigurationFile.ini file is a text file which contains the set of parameters in name/value pairs along with descriptive comments. Many of the parameter names correspond to the screens and options which you see while installing SQL Server through the wizard. We can then use the configuration file to install SQL Server with the same configuration instead of going through each of the installation screens.

41. What is the location of ConfigurationFile.ini file?

Ans:

We can find the configuration file in the C:\Program Files\Microsoft SQL Server\110\Setup Bootstrap\Log folder. There will a subfolder based on a timestamp when the SQL Server 2012 installation was done.

42. Can we install SQL Server using a configure file?

Ans:

Yes! We can prepare a configuration file. While installing SQL Server the path to the configuration file is specified in the **"Ready to Install"** page in the configuration file path section. Cancel the setup without actually completing the installation, to generate the INI file.

File Location and Name:

%programfiles%\Microsoft SQL Server\110\Setup Bootstrap\Log

\<YYYYMMDD_HHMM>\ConfigurationFile.ini.

43. How to install a SQL Server using configuration file?

Ans:

From Command prompt locate the setup.exe file location and can install using config file.

Setup.exe/ConfigurationFile=MyConfigurationFile.INI

Instead of specifying passwords inside the config file specify them explicitly as below.

Setup.exe/SQLSVCPASSWORD="***********"/
AGTSVCPASSWORD="*************"/ASSVCPASSWORD="*************"/
ISSVCPASSWORD="*************"/RSSVCPASSWORD="*************"/
ConfigurationFile=MyConfigurationFile.INI**

44. What are the security considerations for a SQL Server installation?

Ans:

- Enhance physical security for file locations: Data/Log file, Backup, ERRORLOGs etc.
- Use firewalls
- Isolate services
- Run SQL Server services with the lowest possible privileges
- Do not use default port 1433
- Disable XP_CMDSHELL
- Remove access to Public role for extended stored procedures
- Disable NetBIOS and server message block
- Use Windows Authentication if possible
- Use strong passwords for SQL logins
- Always enable password policy checking
- Disable SQL Server browser service if not required
- Disable SA account or rename it
- Revoke guest user access
- Disable unused features of SQL Server
- Enable Audit for SQL Server logins
- Limit the number of SYSADMIN roles
- Limit the Windows Server access

45. What are the minimum Software requirements to install SQL Server 2012?

Ans:

- Internet Explorer 7 or a later version is required for Microsoft Management Console (MMC), SQL Server Data Tools (SSDT), the Report Designer component of Reporting Services, and HTML Help
- SQL Server 2012 does not install or enable Windows PowerShell 2.0; however Windows PowerShell 2.0 is an installation prerequisite for Database Engine components and SQL Server Management Studio.
- NET 3.5 SP1 is a requirement for SQL Server 2012 when you select Database Engine, Reporting Services, Replication, Master Data Services, Data Quality Services, or SQL Server Management Studio, and it is no longer installed by SQL Server Setup.
- Dot NET 4.0 is a requirement for SQL Server 2012. SQL Server installs .NET 4.0 during the feature installation step. SQL Server Express does not install .NET 4.0 when installing on the Windows 2008 R2 SP1 Server core operating system. You must install .NET4.0 before you install SQL Server Express on a Windows 2008 R2 SP1 Server core operating system.

SQL Server Setup installs the following software components required by the product:

- Dot NET Framework 4 1
- SQL Server Native Client
- SQL Server Setup support files

46. What are ways of migrating SQL Server from lower version to higher version?

Ans:

If you want to upgrade a SQL Server instance from SQL Server 2008 R2 to SQL Server 2012/2014, below are the different ways you can do this migration.

In-Place Upgrade: In this method, existing instance of SQL Server will be upgraded to higher version, thus we end up with one instance of SQL Server with higher version i.e., SQL Server 2012. Here the instance name remains same, so application connection string remains the same, only change that may be required is to have latest connectivity drivers installed.

Side-By-Side Upgrade: In this method a new instance of SQL Server 2012/2014 is installed on same server or a different server and them all User databases, Logins, Jobs, configuration settings need to be configured or created on the new SQL Server instance.

47. What are the differences between In-Place Upgrade and Side-By-Side Upgrade?

Ans:

- In In-Place Upgrade, instance name does not change, so no need to change the connection string, but in side-by-side upgrade, instance name will be different if new instance is installed on same server, if installed on other server, and then the server name will change and will result in requirement to change to the connection string.
- In-Place upgrade has risk or additional down time in case the upgrade fails which ends up with clean up and reinstalling everything clean and during this entire process, there will

be huge amount of downtime required. In side-by-side upgrade, we are installing a new instance or even on a new server, so any failures will not affect the existing SQL instance, which will continue to serve the clients.

- Side-by-side migration has lot of addition tasks like backup and restore of user databases on new instance, create logins, fix orphan users, configure SQL Server settings appropriately, Create all the required jobs, etc. In-Place upgrade does not require much changes as everything will be migrated and readily available to use.
- Rollback of SQL Server instance in in-place method is not possible, but is fully possible in side-by-side upgrade.
- Amount of downtime is more with in-place upgrade compared to properly planned side-by-side upgrade.

48. What are the advantages and disadvantages of Side-by-side and In-Place upgrade?

Ans:

Pros & Cons: In-Place:

Pros

- Easier, mostly automated
- Generally fast overall process
- Requires no additional hardware
- Applications remain pointing to same server/database name

Cons

- Less granular control over upgrade process
- Instance remains offline during part of upgrade
- Not best practice for all components
- Complex rollback strategy
- Not recommended for SSAS

Pros & Cons: Side-by-side:

Pros

- More granular control over the upgrade process
- Original database left unchanged; allows for testing of new database
- Single occurrence of database downtime
- Relatively straightforward rollback strategy

Cons:

- Usually require additional hardware
- Server/database name changes
- Not practical for VLDB unless utilizing SAN(Beware of "loss of quick roll-back")

49. What's the practical approach of installing Service Pack?

Ans:

Steps to install Service pack in Production environments:

- First of all raise a change order and get the necessary approvals for the downtime window. Normally it takes around 45–60 minutes to install Service pack if there are no issues.
- Once the downtime window is started, take a full backup of the user databases and system databases including the Resource database.
- List down all the Start-up parameters, Memory Usage, CPU Usage etc. and save it in a separate file.
- Install the service pack on SQL Servers.
- Verify all the SQL Services are up and running as expected.
- Validate the application functionality.

Note: There is a different approach to install Service pack on SQL Server cluster instances. That will be covered in SQL Server cluster.

50. What is Slipstreaming? And when it is introduced?

Ans:

It is a term used to describe merging original source media with updates in memory and then installing the updated files. Slipstreaming has been supported by Windows Operating systems for a while but has been added to SQL Server 2008 service pack 1. Slipstream allows you to go to the latest and greatest, initially it was introduced with SQL Server 2008 service pack 1 and a CU for service pack 1.

When we got a request to install SQL Server 2012 with SP1 we can do it in a one go by using slipstreaming procedure that means we can include both SQL Server 2012 and SP1 media files on one folder and can be installed in a single go. Before SQL Server 2008 SP1 we had to install service packs or cumulative updates separately.

51. I have installed SQL 2008 Database Engine component to an instance and now I want to add features to this instance using slipstream. How do I add features to an existing instance?

Ans:

In theory you just run the slipstream build again to add features. However, setup will fail since setup does not correct detect that it is installed and needs to be patched versus installed. In this case, you need to add features using original media and then patch using the service pack installer. We don't support features within an instance at different levels, so ensure features within an instance are at the same patch level.

52. What if I did not copy the ia64 and x64 folders to my original media which is necessary for slipstreaming. Can I still install x86?

Ans:

Technically, it will work. But we do not recommend skipping merging all architectures since at some point a user might install one of these architectures. If you merges x86 but not x64, you media is inconsistent. If at a later point in time, you run x64, the result will be unpredictable.

53. I already have SQL Server 2008 instance and now I want to update to service pack 1. Do I need to use slipstream?

Ans:

No, slipstream will not work when the product is already installed.

54. Can I slipstream in any CU?

Ans:

In general, yes. However, you need to ensure the CU will work the original release (RTM) or SP. For example, if you are slipstreaming Service Package 1 (SP1), then only CUs based on SP1 can be slipstreamed into the installation. If you are not slipstreaming a service pack, then you need to ensure the CU is for the original release.

55. I slipstream original media SQL Server 2008 R2/2012 with SP1 and installed. After installation if we rollback SP1 does all features Rollback and the installed SQL Server is same as SQL Server 2008 R2/2012 fresh installation?

Ans:

Essentially, it is the same. However some of the components (e.g. SNAC, MSXML 6, and Setup support files) can't be rolled back. The core features: Database Engine, Reporting Services, Analysis Services, and the other shred components will be rolled back.

56. Can I use slipstream to upgrade from SQL Server 2000/2005 to SQL Server 2008 R2?

Ans:

Yes!

57. Is there a way to find out when a patch/SP was last applied to an instance?

Ans:

- Start SSMS, open help menu and go to "about"
- Run Select @@version
- Run SELECT SERVERPROPERTY('productversion'), SERVERPROPERTY ('productlevel'), SERVERPROPERTY ('edition')
- Run XP_READERRORLOG and from the result set we can find the version details
- By checking through the SQL Server log file from bootstrap folder
- If nothing worked as far as I know only option there would be to look at the add/remove programs list (or dump this data from the registry to make it easier to deal with) and get that info from there. SQL Server doesn't track that within the system databases.

58. Which is the environment you suggest to apply first when a new service pack/cumulative update released?

Ans:

I always suggest applying first on staging environment which is a Pre-PROD. PROD we can't directly apply but also remember development environment also lot of dependencies and if something goes wrong it holds/delays the deliverables.

59. Is it mandatory to restart the Windows server after installing SQL Server service pack?

Ans:

No, it's not mandatory to restart Windows server after installing SQL Server service pack but it is always a good practice to do so.

60. How to check the SQL Server version and Service pack installed on the server?

Ans:

```
SELECT
convert(VARCHAR(50),SERVERPROPERTY('productversion')) AS 'Product_Version',
convert(VARCHAR(50),SERVERPROPERTY ('productlevel')) AS 'Product_Level',
convert(VARCHAR(50),SERVERPROPERTY ('edition')) AS 'Edition',
@@VERSION AS 'Full_Details';
```

61. How to slipstream a Service Pack or Cumulative Update with the SQL Server installation?

Ans:

- Download all required SP and CU to local folder ex: U:\SQLUpdate
- Extract zip.exe files into the same folder. Ex: U:\SQLUpdate
- Open command prompt as administrator
- Change the path to SQLSetup file folder. Ex: E:\.\X64\.\SQLSetup
- Run below command

  setup.exe/action=install/UpdateEnabled=TRUE/updatesource= "U:\SQLUpdate"

62. Did you observe any change in slipstream between SQL Server 2008/R2 and 2012 versions?

Ans:

On SQL Server 2012 the old slipstream feature is in "Deprecated Features." Before 2012 we need to give as a separate paths for each CU and service pack but from 2012 we can extract all required updates to one single folder and we can input that folder to installation command.

On SQL Server 2008 R2/2008:

D:\setup.exe/Action=Install/PCUSource=D:\SP1Folder/CUSource=D:\CU1Folder

On SQL Server 2012:

Keep all required slipstream files on a single folder. In this case SP1 and CU1 on a folder "D:\SQLUpdate"

D:\setup.exe/Action=install/UpdateEnabled=TRUE/updatesource= "D:\SQLUpdate"

63. Can you quickly tell me few things which should not be missed after migrating SQL Server to newer version?

Ans:

- Change Compatibility to the current version
- Run DBCC UPDATEUSAGE - DBCC UPDATEUSAGE(<database_name>) WITH COUNT_ROWS
- Update statistics on all tables with full scan
- Check fragmentation and based on results do index reorganize or rebuild
- Recompile all stored procedures "sp_recompile"
- Refresh all views using "sp_refreshview"
- Fix orphan user/login problems
- Check SQL Server and windows error logs
- Make sure all server objects moved properly
  - ✓ Linked Servers
  - ✓ DDL Triggers
  - ✓ Jobs/Maintenance Plans
  - ✓ Operators
  - ✓ Alerts
  - ✓ DBMail
  - ✓ Proxy Settings/Credentials
  - ✓ Other Objects
- Take a full backup for all databases

64. Have you ever applied Cumulative Update on SQL Server? If yes there is a known problem with CU updates do you know that?

Ans:

Yes! Installation of the Cumulative Update is similar to the installation of a Service Pack. Cumulative Updates are not fully regression tested thereof we should be very careful in applying the CU, do a proper testing on Non-Prod environment before applying to Production environment.

But there is good news from Microsoft. It recommends ongoing, proactive installation of SQL Server CUs as they become available. SQL Server CUs are certified to the same levels as Service Packs, and should be installed with the same level of confidence. Applicable for All CU released after January 2016.

65. How do you determine whether to apply latest Service Packs or Cumulative Updates?

Ans:

Below are the common reasons for installing Service Packs or Cumulative Updates:

- If SQL Server is experiencing any known issue and it is found that the issue was fixed on a particular Service Pack or CU

- When security updates released
- Service Packs we can apply with the confidence as these are well tested before public release.

66. What are the pre-requisites before installing a service pack or Cumulative Updates?

Ans:

On critical servers, it is important to make sure to follow all the pre-requisites before installing service pack or Cumulative Updates, so that there are no issues after patching the critical production servers.

- Install the service pack or CU on test server with similar setup
- Check for any errors in SQL ERRORLOGs or Eventlogs
- Test the application thoroughly to make sure it works without any issues.
- Document and Test the Rollback plan on test server to make sure that we can rollback successfully in case of any issues after applying the patches.
- Backup all System and User databases and verify that they can be restored.

67. Can you upgrade SQL Server 2008 SP2 Standard Edition to 2008 R2 Developer Edition?

Ans:

You can't change the edition of the installed instance as far as I know, but you could install a second instance with the Developer edition, or uninstall the Standard edition, install Developer edition and attach the user databases.

68. Does upgrade advisor analyse the remote instances?

Ans:

Upgrade Advisor can analyze remote instances of SQL Server, except for SQL Server Reporting Services. To analyze Reporting Services, Upgrade Advisor must be installed and executed on the report server.

69. How to upgrade a SQL Server 2000 to SQL Server 2008?

Ans:

First we should get answers for what kind of upgrade are you doing an in-place or side-by-side upgrade? The different approaches will result in different checklists. The safest approach is the side-by-side upgrade. You can do this either by using a backup and restore or detach/attach of the database files. I'd suggest using the backup & restore as the safer approach. Here are the things I'd do:

- Run Upgrade Analysis tool from Microsoft. Address any issues raised there, first.
- Identify DTS packages. These must be migrated by hand, unless you buy PragmaticWorks excellent software. Rebuild the DTS packages as SSIS.
- Script out all SQL Agent jobs.
- Script out all security
- Backup the systems and validate the backups (preferably by restoring them to another system)

- Run the security script on the new system
- Run the restore on the new system.
- Validate the databases by running DBCC
- Manually update all statistics
- Run the SQL Agent script

70. Can you detach a SQL Server 2008 R2 database and attach it to a SQL Server 2012 server?

Ans:

Yes. SQL Server 2008 R2 databases are compatible with SQL Server 2008. However, that attaching a SQL Server 2008 R2 database to SQL Server 2012 automatically upgrades to a SQL Server 2012 database and the database is then no longer usable by the SQL Server 2008 R2.

71. Can you detach a SQL Server 2012 database and attach it to a SQL Server 2008 R2 server?

Ans:

No. The only way to move a SQL Server 2012 database to a SQL Server 2008 R2 server is by transferring the data using a method such as Data Transformation Services (Import/Export),SSIS, BCP, or use of a query between linked servers.

72. How long will it take to upgrade SQL Server databases?

Ans:

Many factors affect the amount of time needed to upgrade SQL Server Databases. Depending on the complexity of each database, Size of databases, the hardware platform, number of processors, disk subsystem, and amount of RAM plays a significant part in the amount of time required for the upgrade. Selecting "data validation" during the setup increases the amount of time needed to perform the upgrade by a factor of two.

73. When you upgrade a SQL Server, the upgrade wizard seems to stop responding and fails sometimes. Why?

Ans:

If applications or services have open ODBC connections to the SQL Server during the conversion process, they may not allow the SQL Server to shut down completely. The conversion process will not proceed on to the next step if it does not receive verification that the SQL Server has been completely stopped.

74. I have upgraded SQL Server 2008 Instance to SQL Server 2014. How to roll back the upgrade?

Ans:

- *In-place upgrade:* IT's very time consuming as everything has to be uninstalled and need to install a fresh copy of SQL Server 2008 instance.

- *Side-by-Side Upgrade:* We just need to redirect applications to use SQL Server 2008 instance instead of SQL Server 2014 as the old/legacy instance is still available in side-by-side upgrade.

75. What are the parameters should be considered while choosing the upgrade process?

Ans:

Components: A certain upgrade strategy might not be possible because the component does not support it. For example, there is no in-place upgrade for SSIS from SQL Server 2000; Microsoft recommends that you upgrade most SQL Server 2000 SSAS components.

Versions and Editions: The in-place upgrade strategy does not support all paths between versions and editions. For example, to upgrade a SQL Server 2000 Enterprise Edition instance to SQL Server 2012 Standard Edition, you must perform a side-by-side upgrade because SQL Server Setup does not support an in-place upgrade path.

Partial upgrading: To transition only a few databases on a server to SQL Server 2012/2014 and leave the rest on the legacy version, you must use a side-by-side upgrade.

Upgrading over time: To transition databases gradually, a few databases at a time, from a legacy instance to SQL Server 2012/2014, you can only use a side-by-side upgrade.

Effect on applications: If your organization requires minimal disturbance to the existing applications and users, you may want to choose an in-place upgrade if possible.

Availability: Both an in-place upgrade and a side-by-side upgrade require that the databases be unavailable for a certain amount of time. The amount of downtime required depends primarily on the size of the data sets. At first, it might seem that an in-place upgrade would be faster than a side-by-side upgrade because the data is not transferred from one server to another. However, an in-place upgrade also requires time for the installation of SQL Server 2012/2014. In a side-by-side upgrade, SQL Server 2012/2014 is already installed on another instance. If the data transfer proceeds quickly and few changes are needed on the new instance, a side-by-side upgrade might be faster than an in-place upgrade.

76. While planning for SQL Server to a new version what do you suggest your development team?

Ans:

Ask your development team to have a look at:

Discontinued features: Features that doesn't support

- Use of *= and =* is no longer supported from SQL Server 2012 and above
- Use COMPUTE/COMPUTE BY doesn't supports from SQL Server 2012

Deprecated features: Features do supposed to use as these will be discontinued in future version

- Do not use sp_addtype instead use "CREATE TYPE"
- Avoid using datatypes text, ntext, image instead use VARCHAR(MAX), NVAARCHAR(MAX) and VARBINARY(MAX).
- Make sure all T-SQL statements end with semi colon ;

Breaking changes: Features for which functionality changed

- For example on SQL Server 2012 and above the ALTER TABLE statement allows only two-part (schema.object) table names. If you mention dbname.schema.object this results in failure.

Note: Not just development team DBA should also review all these changes to make sure all existing features are compatible with the newer version or find out the alternatives.

77. What are the different tools available while upgrading SQL Server?

Ans:

- SQL Server Upgrade Advisor
- DTS xChange
- Microsoft® Assessment and Planning Toolkit 3.2
- SQL Server Upgrade Assistant
- SQL Server Best Practices Analyser
- System Configuration Checker
- SQL Server: Deprecated Features Object Counter
- Custom tools

78. What is the sequence to install service packs or hotfixes on an instance of SQL Server that is part of Log Shipping/Database Mirroring/Replication/Failover Clustering environment?

Ans:

When an instance of SQL Server is configured as part of Log Shipping, Database Mirroring, Replication, or Failover Clustering environment, it is important to install service packs or hotfixes in a correct sequence otherwise we may get unexpected issues.

Log Shipping:

There is no required sequence to apply a service pack or hotfix for Primary, Secondary and Monitor servers in a Log Shipping environment. The following is my preferable to apply service pack or hotfix:

- Apply the service pack or hotfix on the Monitor server.
- Apply the service pack or hotfix on the all Secondary servers.
- Apply the service pack or hotfix on the Primary server.

Database Mirroring:

If you install service packs or hotfixes on servers in a database mirroring environment, you need to determine the role of the servers. If there are many mirroring sessions configured on the server, you need to determine all possible roles that could be. For instance, if the server is acting as a mirror server for any database mirroring session, update the server as the mirror role for all mirroring sessions. To do this, follow these steps:

- If a witness server is configured in the database mirroring session, disable the automatic failover during the update process. To do this, remove the witness server from the mirroring session.
- If the safety level of the database mirroring session is OFF (asynchronous mode), change the safety level to FULL (this is required in step 3).
- Make sure all database mirroring sessions to be in Synchronous mode and synchronized.
- Pause the database mirroring sessions that are present on the server.
- Install the service pack or hotfix on the mirror server.
- Resume the database mirroring sessions.
- Perform manual failover (all the mirroring sessions on this principal server) to the mirror server so that mirroring server assumes the principal role.
- Pause the database mirroring sessions as step 4.
- Install the service pack or hotfix on the new mirror server (previous principal server).
- Resume the database mirroring sessions.
- If you changed the safety level in step 2, change the safety level back to OFF.
- If the database mirroring session has a witness server undo the changes made in step 1

Replication:

In a replication environment, there is no preferable sequence to apply service pack or hotfix for non-bidirectional replication typology. However, for bi-directional replication typology such as merge typology or transactional replication with updateable subscriptions, you must upgrade Distributor, Publisher, and Subscribers in the following order:

- Apply the service pack or hotfix on the Distributor server.
- Apply the service pack or hotfix on the Publisher server.
- Apply the service pack or hotfix on the Subscriber server

Failover Clustering:

Before SQL Server 2008, if you want to install a service pack or hotfix, you must install the setup on the Active node (node that currently runs SQL Server services). When running the setup it will launch simultaneously "remote silence" on all passive nodes.

However from SQL Server 2008 onwards the service pack or hotfix deployment is changed to reduce the downtime. Now, you must install the service pack or hotfix on the passive node first. To do this, following these steps:

- Apply the service pack or hotfix on the passive node (or all passive nodes if you have more than one).
- Reboot the passive node.
- Failover the SQL Server failover cluster to the passive node (and the passive node becomes active now).
- Apply the service pack or hotfix on the new passive node (previous active node).
- Reboot the passive node.

79. How to apply service pack to SQL Server in cluster environment in SQL Server 2008 R2?

Ans:

- First need to test applying the service pack on a test server to make sure that the application does not break after applying the service pack or cumulative update.
- On a two node cluster, make sure SQL Server instance and MSDTC and Cluster groups are all on one node of the cluster, which will become the active node.
- Perform backups of System and user databases.
- Remove the passive node from the SQL Server resource possible owners list.
- Install the service pack on the passive node.
- Add the passive node back to the SQL Server resource possible owners list.
- Failover SQL Server instance to node where we applied the Service Pack.
- Check error logs to make sure upgrade scripts completed successfully and latest version is reflected in SSMS and SQL error log.
- Remove the new passive node from the SQL Server resource possible owners list.
- Install the service pack on the new passive node.
- Add the passive node back to the SQL Server resource possible owners list.
- Failover SQL Server instance to the newly upgraded node.
- Check Error logs to make sure upgrade scripts completed successfully and latest version is reflected in SSMS and SQL error log.
- Test the application.

Note: We can also skip removing and adding node names from possible owners but this is the recommended approach.

80. How do you install Service Packs or CU on SQL Server 2012 instances with ALWAYSON Availability Group databases?

Ans:

With ALWAYSON Availability Group databases, we can install service packs or CUs with minimal downtime to the end users, but there can be impact if secondary replicas are used for reporting purposes. Below are the steps to install Service Packs or CU on SQL Server 2012 instances with ALWAYSON Availability Group databases.

- Make sure that the ALWAYSON Availability Group is running on one node, which will be the active node.
- Backup all the System and User databases.
- Install the service pack or CU on the secondary replica.
- Test the secondary replica, by checking ERRORLOGs and eventlogs to make sure there are no failures or errors.
- Failover ALWAYSON Availability Group to secondary replica which will now become new primary replica.

- Backup all system databases.
- Install the service pack or CU on the new secondary replica.
- Test the new secondary replica, by checking ERRORLOGs and eventlogs to make sure there are no failures or errors.
- Failover ALWAYSON Availability Group to the secondary server which will now become the primary server.
- Verify and Test the application.

Troubleshooting Scenarios

81. Can a Service Pack or Cumulative Update be uninstalled to roll back in case of failures?

Ans:

- We cannot uninstall a service pack or Cumulative Update on SQL Server 2005 or lower.
- Starting with SQL Server 2008, we can uninstall a service pack or Cumulative Update from control panel à Add or remove programs à view installed updates window.

82. Since you are an experienced DBA you might have seen the issue "SQL Server service is not starting" right? Can you describe the top 3 common reasons that cause SQL Server service failure?

Ans:

- Service account password changed but not updated at SQL Server Services
- System databases not available or not accessible. Ex: Files might be deleted or corrupted
- STARTUP parameters having incorrect path locations ex: Master database file location is wrongly specified in SQL Server start-up parameters.

83. From your experience can you describe the top reasons that cause SQL Server installation failures?

Ans:

- Missing supporting software. Ex: DOTNET Framework
- Missing Supporting Files
- Corrupted Binaries/Files
- Access dined
- PowerShell not installed
- Partial Uninstallation of previous instance
- Unsupported versions
- Registry corruption
- Using Wrong Services Accounts
- Anti-virus blocking the installation

84. What are the common issues you faced in upgrading SQL Server?

Ans:

Common causes

- SQL Server or the machine running the upgrade loses its network connection.
- The database in which you were working has run out of log or data space.
- You are not allowed to perform an update to a table.
- The database is corrupted.
- The database is not available (still in recovery) It may be unavailable if the upgrade program begins to work before SQL Server finishes performing recovery after start-up.
- Unable to restart the server

Can identify the issue from the upgrade log files and resolve the issues and rerun the upgrade advisor

85. Have you ever come across with the problem ".MSP or .MSI files are missing" while installing or patching a SQL Server? What are these files?

Ans:

Yes! Starting from SQL Server 2005 till the recent installation of SQL Server 2014 I have seen this issue lot many times while installing SQL Server and applying service packs.

.MSI and .MSP:

When a product is installed by using Windows Installer, a stripped version of the original .msi file is stored in the Windows Installer cache. Every update to the product such as a hotfix, a cumulative update, or a service pack setup, also stores the relevant .msp or .msi file in the Windows Installer cache. Any future update to the product such as a hotfix, a cumulative update, or a service pack setup, relies on the information in the files that are stored in the Windows Installer cache. Without this information, the new update cannot perform the required transformations.

Default Folder for the Windows Installer Cache:

%windir%\installer

86. What are the most common reasons that causes ".MSP/.MSI file missing" issues and how to resolve these issues?

Ans:

These are the ***most common reasons*** that cause Windows Installer cache files missing:

- Windows Installer Cache files are deleted/removed accidentally
- User don't have proper access to the Windows Installer Cache folder
- Firewall or Antivirus is blocking the access
- Downloaded SQL Server ISO is corrupted
- Installing SQL Server from CD/DVD

If it is a permissions issue the problem can be resolved very easily but if the files are deleted in any case then the resolution will be bit difficult.

Repair: Try to run SQL Server installation with REPAIR from command prompt

Copy Missing Files using VB Script: As Microsoft suggested there is a VB script "FindSQLInstalls. vbs script" this we can find out from Microsoft support forums. This can identify the missing files and copy them from the original media.

Copy Missing Files Manually: Manual copy is easy for missing .MSI files. But for .MSP there is a different procedure.

- **Copying .MSP:**
  - ✓ Collect the complete details about missing file from the error message, from the setup log file.
  - ✓ Copy the same file from the original media to the Windows Installer cache folder.
- **Copying .MSI:**
  - ✓ Collect the complete details about the missing file from the error message, from the setup log file.
  - ✓ We should be able to find out details about Original MSP and Cached MSP details.
  - ✓ For .MSP files file name will be changed when copied from original media to Cache folder.
  - ✓ We need to do the same thing identify the original file name from original media and copy the file into Windows Installer Cache folder and rename the file as you see in setup logs.
- Windows Cache Folder is: %windir%\installer
- Original Media file location:
  <Drive>:\SQL2014_ENU--x64\x64\setup\sql_engine_core_inst_msi\

87. What is the most critical issue you faced while installing SQL Server 2012? You can tell me the recent one.

Ans:

We had a bad experience with SQL Server 2012 SP1.

Problem:

- When SP1 released our team has applied on 5 staging machines.
- There was no problem with the installation, it went on well but soon we come to know that there were performance issues.

RCA:

- When I did a RCA found it was due to high CPU utilization and we have seen there were a lot of warnings in event log on "SQL_Tools_Ans."
- Further investigated and found 90% CPU utilization is from msiexec.exe and it was running continuously thereof problems started.
- We quickly gone through MSDN sites and found there were lot of other people facing the similar kind of issues.

Solution:

- Immediately we have uninstalled SQL Server 2012 SP1 from all staging machines.
- Next minute CPU utilization came down and we didn't see msiexec.exe on running processes list.
- This issue got fixed in SQL Server 2012 SP1 CU2

88. Can you describe any strange issue that you faced while installing SQL Server?

Ans:

Problem:

When we were installing SQL Server 2008 R2, setup continues to install setup support files, the windows suddenly disappeared and next the next window never shows up. Same issue repeated when we tried to install it again.

RCA:

Found an error message from temp folder log file "SQLSetup_1.log" and the error message is "Failed to Launch Process" and "Failed to launch local setup100.exe.

Resolution:

- We followed a difficult process to resolve this issue but it worked out. Make sure you have taken the backup for Windows Registry.
- Save this file as .reg

  [HKEY_LOCAL_MACHINE\SOFTWARE\Microsoft\Microsoft SQL Server\100
  \Bootstrap]
  "BootstrapDir"="C:\\Program Files\\Microsoft SQL Server\\100\\Setup Bootstrap\\"
  [HKEY_LOCAL_MACHINE\SOFTWARE\Microsoft\Microsoft SQL Server\100
  \Bootstrap\Setup]
  "PatchLevel" = "10.50.1600.00"
- Run the saved file
- Copy files from source to destination:

Source – SQL Server Setup File/Media	Destination – Server Local Disk
X64/X86 file	C:\Program Files\Microsoft SQL Server\100\ Setup Bootstrap\SQLServer2008R2
Setup.exe	C:\Program Files\Microsoft SQL Server\100\ Setup Bootstrap\SQLServer2008R2
Resources folder	C:\Program Files\Microsoft SQL Server\100\ Setup Bootstrap\SQLServer2008R2

Note: One of my colleagues had the same issue on other instance while installing SQL Server 2008 R2 and the problem got resolved after installing PowerShell 2.0. As per MSDN blogs the same problem exists in 2008, 2008 R2, 2012, 2014.

89. Since we are looking for a person who is good in understanding and expertise in SQL Server installations and upgrades. Can you tell me one last issue you faced while installing SQL Server 2012 or 2014?

Ans:

Problem:

SQL Server 2012 installation failed with an error message "The identities of the manifests are identical but their contents are different."

RCA:

- This was a known issue with Visual C++ 2005 runtime library setup.
- A security update was missing for Visual C++ 2005.
- On SQL Server Setup there is an .MSI file which merged with merge modules of Visual C++ 2005 runtime library.

Resolution:

- Download and install Microsoft Visual C++ 2005 Service Pack 1.

  Or
- Slipstream SQL Server 2012 with CU1 as the issue got fixed in CU1

90. Have you ever participated in SQL Server Upgrades? If yes can you quickly describe an issue that you faced in SQL Server upgrades?

Ans:

Problem:

We faced an issue while we were upgrading from SQL Server 2005 to SQL Server 2008 R2. SQL Server 2008 R2 upgrade setup wizard has been failing at upgrade rules page due to "Security Group SID (Security Identifier)" rule failure.

RCA:

- I have verified upgrade log files from setup bootstrap folder.
- When checked it's clearly showing that it is reading the account details from windows registry and the SID's which are in registry are not matching/mapping with the account names.
- These accounts are used for SQL Services.

Resolution:

- From the log file we got the SID and the registry key details.
- We have verified the registry and found the same values as in error log file
- We have verified the actual/correct SID for these failed accounts from command prompt just type WHOAMI/GROUPS.
- When compare values are not matching with the registry.

- ➢ Performed a backup for windows registry and updated SID with the original values for the failed accounts.
- ➢ Then restarted the windows machine and re-run the migration wizard and this time it executed without any issue.

91. While installing SQL Server 2008 I am hitting the error: "The setting 'PCUSOURCE' specified is not recognized." How do you resolve it?

Ans:

If you have followed the slipstream instructions, ensure the path to PCUSOURCE does not contain spaces. The setup does not handle the spaces as expected. The quick workaround is to rename the PCUSource path so it does not contain any spaces. You can confirm this is the problem by viewing the Detail_ComponentUpdate.log located at %programfiles%\Microsoft SQL Server\100\Setup Bootstrap\Log\<last session>. Search for "PCUSource." If you see commas in the PCUSource path, this is the issue.

92. You are trying to install a service pack on your SQL Server 2008 R2/2012; service pack is ended with a failure. When you try to check the log file there is no log file/folder generated with that date on location: C:\Program Files\Microsoft SQL Server\110\Setup Bootstrap\log\. But all existing log files are there in that location. Have you ever faced it earlier?

Ans:

Yes! We faced it while applying SP1 for SQL Server 2012 instance. The installation got failed but we couldn't be able to find any log file/folder generated on that date.

RCA:

- ➢ When we verified there are two files created Summary.txt and Details.txt on D drive.
  D:\Program Files\Microsoft SQL Server\110\Setup Bootstrap\log\
- ➢ Summary.txt: Didn't give much information on failure
- ➢ Detail.txt: Found there are error messages "Could not find a part of the path 'C:\Program Files\Microsoft SQL Server\110\Setup Bootstrap\Log\20150519_003216\MSSQLSERVER'.
- ➢ The path is clearly exists but it's not able to locate it.
- ➢ Windows setup environment variable for "Program Files" location. This we can know by using run button and type %programfiles%. When we tried it it's locating D drive program files.

Resolution:

- ➢ Change the environment variable location for Program Files to C drive.
  HKEY_LOCAL_MACHINE\SOFTWARE\Microsoft\Windows\CurrentVersion
- ➢ Updated below values in registry
  ProgramFilesDir –> C:\Program Files
  ProgramFilesDir (x86) –> C:\Program Files (x86)

- After the change I just logged out and logged in.
- I was able to install SQL Server 2012 SP1 without any issue

93. We have upgraded databases from SQL Server 2005 to SQL Server 2014 and now the upgrade hits the production. Unfortunately a part of application is not supporting SQL Server 2014. Do we need to Rollback entire process to SQL 2005? Is that the only solution? If it is the only way! Since the databases at production transactions are being running and the data has been updated. How do you handle this?

Ans:

Since you said a Part of Application is not working properly with SQL Server 2014. This means it should be caught in test environment which should be done before the production environment.

However, after the upgraded SQL Server 2014 instance goes into production and starts capturing new data, there will come a point in time when enough new data has been captured that a rollback is no longer realistic.

- *In-place upgrade*, if you encounter problems after the system is in production, making adjustments or "patches" to the new application would be a better option than attempting a rollback.
- *Side-by-Side upgrade*, you could employ SSIS to transfer new data from the SQL Server 2014 instance to the legacy SQL Server 2005 to bring it current. Depending on the complexity of the data, this could be a difficult process.

SQL Server Components and Capacity Specifications

94. What are the various Editions available in SQL Server 2012 version?

Ans:

Below are the various editions available in Microsoft SQL Server 2012

- SQL Server 2012 Standard Edition
- SQL Server 2012 Enterprise Edition
- SQL Server 2012 Business Edition
- SQL Server 2012 Express Edition
- SQL Server 2012 Web Edition
- SQL Server 2012 Developer Edition

95. What is the change you most liked in SQL Server 2016 installation procedure?

Ans:

Till SQL Server 2014 we did not have the capability to create multiple TEMPDB files based on the number of cores during installation, it used to be taken care by DBA after installating SQL Server. In SQL Server 2016 the install wizard includes TEMPDB configuration feature on the Database Engine Configuration page. As per best practices, TEMPDB data files can be 8 or the number of cores whichever is less and this configuration can be doen during the installation itself.

Most Common Questions:

Below is the list of questions that will be asked in interviews for a range of positions starting form junior DBA to senior level.

96. What is the minimum recommended memory for SQL Server 2008 R2/2012/2014/2016?
97. What is the minimum recommended CPU for SQL Server 2008 R2/2012/2014/2016?
98. What are the pre-requisites for SQL Server 2008 R2/2012/2014/2016?
99. What are the components got installed with SQL Server 2008 R2/2012/2014/2016?
100. What are the maximum capacity specifications for SQL Server 2008 R2/2012/2014/2016?
101. Can you be able to identify the SQL Server version based on version number?
102. Do you have any idea bout SQL Server Version code name?

Below tables will answer all of these questions. Remember that we have collected these details for the highest edition for each version. Ex: Enterprise for 2016/2014/2012 and Datacenter for 2008 R2. We believe this will give you a quick reference for interview preparation.

SQL Server Requirement Specifications:

Version	Hard Disk	Memory	Processor Speed	Processor Type	OS Support	Software
SQL Server 2016	6GB	4GB	2.0 GHz	X64 Processor: AMD Opteron AMD Athlon 64 Intel Xeon with Intel EM64T support Intel Pentium IV with EM64T support	Windows Server 2012 Foundation To Windows Server 2012 R2 Datacenter	.NET Framework 4.6 Windows PowerShell
SQL Server 2014	6GB	4GB	2.0 GHz	x64 Processor: AMD Opteron, AMD Athlon 64, Intel Xeon with Intel EM64T support, Intel Pentium IV with EM64T support x86 Processor: Pentium III- or faster	Windows Server 2008 SP2 To Windows Server 2012 R2 Datacenter	.NET Framework 3.5 SP1 & 4.0 Windows PowerShell
SQL Server 2012	6GB	4GB	2.0 GHz	x64 Processor: AMD Opteron, AMD Athlon 64, Intel Xeon with Intel EM64T support, Intel Pentium IV with EM64T support x86 Processor: Pentium III- or faster	Windows Server 2008 SP2 To Windows Server 2012 R2 Datacenter	.NET Framework 3.5 SP1 Windows PowerShell
SQL Server 2008 R2	4 GB	4GB	2.0 GHz	AMD Opteron, AMD Athlon 64, Intel Xeon with Intel EM64T support, Intel Pentium IV with EM64T support	Windows Server 2003 SP2 To Windows Server 2012 R2 Datacenter	Windows Installer 4.5 or Later .NET Framework 2.0 SP2 & 3.5 SP1

Fig 2.1

SQL Server Editions and Components Report:

Newly introduced – Marked with Green

Version	Editions	Component Type	Component
SQL Server 2016	Enterprise Standard Web Developer Express	Server Components	Database Engine
			Analysis Services
			Reporting Services
			Integration Services
			Master Data Services
			SQL Server R Services
		Management Tools	Management Studio
			Configuration Manager
			Profiler
			Database Engine Tuning Advisor
			Data Quality Client
			Data Tools
			Connectivity Components
		Documentation	SQL Server Books Online
SQL Server 2014	Enterprise Business Intelligence Standard Web Developer Express	Server Components	Database Engine
			Analysis Services
			Reporting Services
			Integration Services
			Master Data Services
		Management Tools	Management Studio
			Configuration Manager
			Profiler
			Database Engine Tuning Advisor
			Data Quality Client
			Data Tools
			Connectivity Components
		Documentation	SQL Server Books Online
SQL Server 2012	Enterprise Business Intelligence Standard Web Developer Express	Server Components	Database Engine
			Analysis Services
			Reporting Services
			Integration Services
			Master Data Services
		Management Tools	Management Studio
			Configuration Manager
			Profiler
			Database Engine Tuning Advisor
			Data Quality Client
			Data Tools
			Connectivity Components
		Documentation	SQL Server Books Online
SQL Server 2008 R2	Datacenter Enterprise Standard Developer Workgroup Web Express Compact	Server Components	Database Engine
			Analysis Services
			Reporting Services
			Integration Services
		Management Tools	Management Studio
			Configuration Manager
			Profiler
			Database Engine Tuning Advisor
			Business Intelligence Development Studio
			Connectivity Components
		Documentation	SQL Server Books Online

Fig 2.2

Capacity Specifications:

When specification changed comparing to previous version – Marked as green

Parameter	SQL Server 2016	SQL Server 2014	SQL Server 2012	SQL Server 2008 R2
Maximum Memory - Standard	128 GB	128 GB	64 GB	64 GB
Maximum Memory - Enterprise / DC	Operating System Maximum	Operating System Maximum	Operating System Maximum	Operating System Maximum
Maximum CPU - Standard	4 Sockets or 24 Cores	4 Sockets or 16 Cores	4 Sockets or 16 Cores	4 CPU
Maximum CPU - Enterprise / DC	Operating System Maximum	Operating System Maximum	Operating System Maximum	Operating System Maximum
Bytes per index key	Clustered index - 900 Nonclustered index - 1700	900	900	900
Bytes per foreign key	900	900	900	900
Bytes per primary key	900	900	900	900
Bytes per row	8060	8060	8060	8060
Clustered indexes per table	1	1	1	1
Columns per index key	16	16	16	16
Columns per foreign key	16	16	16	16
Columns per primary key	16	16	16	16
Columns per SELECT statement	4096	4096	4096	4096
Columns per INSERT statement	4096	4096	4096	4096
Columns per UPDATE statement	4096	4096	4096	4096
Connections per client	Maximum value of configured	Maximum value of configured	Maximum value of configured	Maximum value of configured
Database size	524,272 terabytes	524,272 terabytes	524,272 terabytes	524,272 terabytes
Databases per instance of SQL Server	32767	32767	32767	32767
Filegroups per database	32767	32767	32767	32767
Files per database	32767	32767	32767	32767
File size (data)	16 terabytes	16 terabytes	16 terabytes	16 terabytes
File size (log)	2 terabytes	2 terabytes	2 terabytes	2 terabytes
Instances per computer	Stand-alone - 50 Failover Cluster With Shared Disk - 25 Failover Cluster With SMB - 50	Stand-alone - 50 Failover Cluster With Shared Disk - 25 Failover Cluster With SMB - 50	Stand-alone - 50 Failover Cluster With Shared Disk - 25 Failover Cluster With SMB - 50	Stand-alone - 50 Failover Cluster - 25
Nested stored procedure levels	32	32	32	32
Nested subqueries	32	32	32	32
Nested trigger levels	32	32	32	32
Nonclustered indexes per table	999	999	999	999
Parameters per stored procedure	2,100	2,100	2,100	2,100
Parameters per user-defined function	2,100	2,100	2,100	2,100
REFERENCES per table	253	253	253	253
User connections	32,767	32,767	32,767	32,767
XML indexes	249	249	249	249

Fig 2.3

Version, Service Pack and Build Report:

Version	Code Name	RTM	SP1	SP2	SP3	SP4
SQL Server 2016		RC3				
SQL Server 2014	Hekaton	12.0.2000.8	12.0.4100.1			
SQL Server 2012	Denali	11.0.2100.60	11.0.3000.0 / 11.1.3000.0	11.0.5058.0 / 11.2.5058.0	11.0.6020.0 / 11.3.6020.0	
SQL Server 2008 R2	Kilimanjaro	10.50.1600.1	10.50.2500.0 / 10.51.2500.0	10.50.4000.0 / 10.52.4000.0	10.50.6000.34 / 10.53.6000.34	
SQL Server 2008	Katmai	10.0.1600.22	10.0.2531.0 / 10.1.2531.0	10.0.4000.0 / 10.2.4000.0	10.0.5500.0 / 10.3.5500.0	10.0.6000.29 / 10.4.6000.29
SQL Server 2005	Yukon	9.0.1399.06	9.0.2047	9.0.3042	9.0.4035	9.0.5000
SQL Server 2000	Shiloh	8.0.194	8.0.384	8.0.532	8.0.760	8.0.2039
SQL Server 7.0	Sphinx	7.0.623	7.0.699	7.0.842	7.0.961	7.0.1063

Fig 2.4

CHAPTER 3

SQL SERVER SECURITY

Interview Questions and Answers

Introduction: This chapter takes you through the SQL Server security related interview questions and answers. This is one of the most common areas where any SQL DBA or SQL Developer can expect questions in technical interviews. These questions and answers are deals with the below topics:

- Password Policy
- Server, Database and Application Roles
- Contained Database
- New Security Features
- SQL Injection
- SQL Server Audit
- Impersonation
- Proxy Accounts
- Transparent Data Encryption
- Policy Based Management
- Security General
- Security Strategies

Password Policy

1. Do you know about password policy in SQL Server? Have you ever implemented this?

Ans:

Yes! While creating a new login we do make sure 3 options enabled. We never miss this especially in enterprise environments.

- Enforce Password Policy
- Enforce Password Expiration
- User Must change password at next login

2. If password policy is enforced; can you tell me the new password rules and policies to make sure the password is strong?

Ans:

Password Complexity: When password complexity policy is enforced, new passwords must meet the following guidelines.

- ➢ Password should not contain the login name or computer name
- ➢ Password should not be "password," "admin," "administrator," "SA," "SYSADMIN"
- ➢ Password minimum length 8 and maximum 128
- ➢ Password contains characters from three of the following four categories:
  - ✓ Latin uppercase letters (A through Z)
  - ✓ Latin lowercase letters (a through z)
  - ✓ Base 10 digits (0 through 9)
  - ✓ Non-alphanumeric characters such as "!," "$," "#,""%"

3. I am creating a SQL login with the password = "password" also enabled "Enforce Password Policy." Surprisingly the login got created without any warning or error. Why it accepted the simple password even when password policy was enabled?

Ans:

As I said earlier SQL Server password policy follows the hosted windows server password policy. There might be chance that windows may not enable the complex password policy.

4. How to check current or existing password policy on a windows server?

Ans:

From the Run window open security policy wizard using "secpol.msc"

Server, Database and Application Roles

5. What are the SQL Server access control components?

Ans:

SQL Server access control components are the entry level points for SQL Server Security and takes responsibility for protecting data.

Principals: Entities that can be authenticated to access the SQL Server resources. For example, your Windows login can be configured as a principal that allows you to connect to a SQL Server database. SQL Server supports three types of principals: logins, users, and roles. Logins exist at the server level, users exist at the database level, and roles can exist at either level.

Securable: SQL Server resources that can be accessed by a principal. Securables are the actual resources you're trying to protect, whether at the server level (e.g., availability groups), database level (e.g., full-text CATALOG), or the schema level (e.g., table or function).

Permissions: Types of access granted on a securable to a specific principal. For example, you can grant a Windows login (the principal) the ability to view data (the permission) in a specific database schema (the securable).

6. What are the fixed server level roles?

Ans:

- SYSADMIN: Can perform any activity
- ServerAdmin: Can change server configuration, restart, shutdown server
- SecurityAdmin: Can manage server level logins, also can manage db level if they have permission on DB
  - ✓ Granted: ALTER ANY LOGIN
- ProcessAdmin: Can kill a process on an instance
  - ✓ Granted: ALTER ANY CONNECTION, ALTER SERVER STATE
- DiskAdmin: Can manage the disk files
  - ✓ Granted: ALTER RESOURCES
- BulkAdmin: Can perform BULK INSERT
  - ✓ Granted: ADMINISTER BULK OPERATIONS
- SetupAdmin: Can add and remove linked servers
  - ✓ Granted: ALTER ANY LINKED SERVER
- Dbcreator: Can create, alter, drop and restore any database on the instance
  - ✓ Granted: CREATE ANY DATABASE
- Public: Default role for newly created login

sp_helpsrvrolemember: List out the members mapped with the server roles

7. What are the Database roles available?

Ans:

- db_accessadmin: Granted: ALTER ANY USER, CREATE SCHEMA, Granted with Grant option - Connect
- db_backupoperator: Granted: BACKUP DATABASE, BACKUP LOG, CHECKPOINT
- db_datareader: Granted - SELECT
- db_datawriter: Granted – INSERT, UPDATE and DELETE
- db_ddladmin: Granted – Any DDL operation
- db_denydatareader: Denied - SELECT
- db_denydatawriter: Denied - INSERT, UPDATE and DELETE
- db_owner: Granted with GRANT option: CONTROL
- db_securityadmin: Granted ALTER ANY APPLICATION ROLE, ALTER ANY ROLE, CREATE SCHEMA, VIEW DEFINITION
- dbm_monitor: Granted: VIEW most recent status in Database Mirroring Monitor

sp_helprolemember: List out the members mapped with the server roles

Note:

Fixed database roles are not equivalent to their database-level permission. For example, the **db_owner** fixed database role has the CONTROL DATABASE permission. But granting the CONTROL DATABASE permission does not make a user a member of the **db_owner** fixed database role.

8. What are the security related CATALOG views? Where the security related information stored on?

Ans:

Server Level:

- Sys.server_permissions
- Sys.server_principals
- Sys.server_role_members
- Sys.sql_logins

Database Level:

- Sys.database_permissions
- Sys.database_principals
- Sys.database_role_members

9. What are the extra roles available in MSDB?

Ans:

- db_ssisadmin: Equals to SYSADMIN
- db_ssisoperator: Import/Delete/Change Role of own packages
- db_ssisltduser: Only can view and execute the packages
- dc_admin: Can administrate and use the data collector
- dc_operator: Can administrate and use the data collector
- dc_proxy: Can administrate and use the data collector
- **PolicyAdministratorRole:** can perform all configuration and maintenance activities on Policy-Based Management policies and conditions.
- ServerGroupAdministratorRole: Can administrate the registered server group
- ServerGroupReaderRole: Can view and the registered server group
- dbm_monitor: Created in the MSDB database when the first database is registered in Database Mirroring Monitor

10. What are the SQL Server Agent fixed database roles available?

Ans:

SQLAgentUserRole:

- Ability to manage Jobs that they own

SQLAgentReaderRole:

- All of the SQLAgentUserRole rights
- The ability to review multi-server jobs, their configurations and history

SQLAgentOperatorRole:

- All of the SQLAgentReaderRole rights
- The ability to review operators, proxies and alerts
- Execute, stop or start all local jobs
- Delete the job history for any local job
- Enable or disable all local jobs and schedules

11. What is application role in SQL Server database security?

Ans:

Application roles are database level roles like database roles. We can create them and assign permissions to them just like regular database roles but we can't map users with them. Instead, we provide a password to unlock access to the database. Here it is how it works:

- Create a login on SQL Server for application user
- Create an application role on the corresponding database.
- Give the application role password to the user
- User will have access to login to SQL Server but doesn't have any access to the database including public role.
- He/she just need to provide the password to unlock the access to the database
- EXEC sp_addapprole 'App_Role_Name', 'Password'
- Once it is executed successfully the user will get all rights that your app role have on that database.

12. Have you ever implemented App Roles on your environment?

Ans:

We tried to implement on 2008 R2 for one of the client. But we observed few problems with application roles. Application roles are not working properly when connection pooling is set to ON at application side.

Contained Database

13. What is a contained database in SQL Server?

Ans:

Before 2012 all databases are Noon-Contained databases. A user defined database can be created as a contained database by specifying the option "Containment Type" in database properties. But before that the contained database property has to be set at instance level. Contain database contains all database metadata in that database only instead of storing it in master database.

- Most of the metadata that describes a database is maintained in the same database.

- All metadata are defined using the same collation.
- User authentication can be performed by the database, reducing the databases dependency on the logins of the instance of SQL Server.
- The SQL Server environment (DMV's, XEvents, etc.) reports and can act upon containment information.
- The containment setting of a database can be NONE, PARTIAL or FULL. But only NONE and PARTIAL are supported on SQL Server 2012.

14. What are the advantages and disadvantages of a contained database feature?

Ans:

Advantages:

- User authentication can be done at database level.
- Contained databases have less dependency on instance then conventional databases. Objects & features of each database can be managed by themselves, reduce workload of system database & SQL instance.
- Easier & faster to migrate databases from one server to another. Errors related to missing users and orphan users are no longer an issue with contained databases.
- Contained database users can be Windows and SQL Server authentication users.
- Contained database user can access only contained database objects. They cannot access system databases and cannot access server objects.
- Contained databases can be used with HADR (Always On).
- Maintaining database settings in the database, instead of in the master database increase security & flexibility. Each database owner has more control over their database, without giving the database owner SYSADMIN permission.

Disadvantages:

- A database owner has more control on contained database, User can create contained database users without the permission of a DBA that can lead to security issues & data theft threat
- Contained databases cannot use replication, change data capture, change tracking, numbered procedures, schema-bound objects that depend on built-in functions with collation changes
- Before changing containment settings at database level from NONE to PARTIAL, contained databases feature needs to be enabled at instance level
- To connect to contained database, you need to specify database name in default database option
- Contained database user can access other databases on the Database Engine, if the other databases have enabled the guest account

New Security Features

15. What is the new security features added in SQL Server 2012?

Ans:

Default Schema for Windows Group Logins: Let's say we have a Windows account [MyDomain\WinAdmin]. If someone from this group logged in [MyDomain\User1] and tried to create an object then there will be a new schema created like [MyDomain\User1].Table. This issue got fixed in 2012. In 2012 we can assign a default schema for the Windows Group accounts.

User Defined Server Roles: Till 2008 R2 we have user defined roles at database level, 2012 allows us to create a Server level user defined roles which gives us more control in handling security.

Contained Database: Easier database migrations as it contains user and login information on same database instead of in Master.

Data Protection: Supporting Hash Algorithm-256 (SHA-256) and SHA-512.

Auditing: Native support/feature for auditing the database environment by creating the Audit specifications. We can also create user defined audits. Ex: We can create an Audit specification to trace all events for a specific login and write all these event details into Audit Log. We can also filter the events.

16. What is the new security features added in SQL Server 2014?

Ans:

Functionality Enhancement for TDE: In 2014 Transparent Data Encryption takes the normal backup and then applies the Encryption before writing it to the disk. It allows backup compression is useful when TDE enabled. TDE applies on compressed backup.

CONNECT ANY DATABASE: This is a new server level permission which can allow a login to connect all existing and future databases in the instance. This can be helpful when we need to give permissions for audit purpose.

IMPERSONATE ANY LOGIN: This is a new server level permission which gives us more control in giving/denying impersonate access to logins.

SELECT ALL USER SECURABLES: A new server level permission. When granted, a login such as an auditor can view data in all databases that the user can connect to.

17. What is the new Security features added in SQL Server 2016?

Ans:

Always Encrypted:

- This is a new feature which is useful for managing highly sensitive data
- Unlike TDE it encrypts data at rest means physical files (Data, Log and Backup), data in memory and data in communication channels.
- TEMPDB is uninvolved from encryption
- Encryption can be applied to column level.
- A driver that encrypts and decrypts the data as it is sent to the database server is installed on the client.
- Application connection string must be changed.

Row Level Security:

- This is first introduced in Azure SQL Database. Now it's part of on-premises feature from SQL Server 2016.
- Data need not be encrypted but we can restrict the users to see the sensitive data. No master keys or certificates required as there is no encryption
- Row-level security is based on a table-valued function which evaluates user access to the table based on a security policy that is applied to the table.
- The access levels only applies to SELECT, UPDATE, DELETE operations but anyone who is having INSERT permissions can insert rows.
- Only problem with this is using user defined functions to control user access which is a huge disadvantage from performance prospect.

Dynamic Data Masking:

- Masks data at select time based on user or database roles (Mainly for Read-only Users).
- It actually doesn't change the data but mask data based on the user who access that data.
- For example I have a columns called "CredNo" to store customer creditcard number. If I mask this column then it will be viewed as 22XXXXXXXXXX56.
- But as I said data is not modified only this logic applied and data is masked based on the user/role.
- A SYSADMIN or db_owner can view the actual data.
- We can use 4 different types of functions to mask data; Email, Partial, Default, Random

SQL Injection

18. What is SQL Injection and why is it a problem?

Ans:

SQL Injection is an exploit where unhandled\unexpected SQL commands are passed to SQL Server in a malicious manner. It is a problem because unknowingly data can be stolen, deleted, updated, inserted or corrupted.

19. How can SQL Injection be stopped?

Ans:

Development\DBA:

- Validate the SQL commands that are being passed by the front end
- Validate the length and data type per parameter
- Convert dynamic SQL to stored procedures with parameters
- Prevent any commands from executing with the combination of or all of the following commands: semi-colon, EXEC, CAST, SET, two dashes, apostrophe, etc.
- Based on your front end programming language determine what special characters should be removed before any commands are passed to SQL Server

- Research products or services to scan your code and web site on a regular basis to prevent the issue

Network Administration:

- Prevent traffic from particular IP addresses or domains based on network statistics
- Review the firewall settings to determine if SQL Injection attacks can be prevented
- Remove old web pages and directories that are no longer in use because these can be crawled and exploited

20. How to recover from SQL Injection?

Ans:

If for some reason the resolution implemented does not resolve the problem and the SQL Injection attack occurs again, the quickest path may be to do the following:

- Shut down the web sites
- Review the IIS logs to determine the commands issued and which web page\command has the vulnerability
- Convert the code to determine which tables were affected and the command issued
- Find and replace the string in your tables
- Correct the web page\command that has the vulnerability
- Test to validate the issue no longer occurs
- Deploy the web page\command
- Re-enable the web sites

21. Do you know the different types of SQL Injections?

Ans:

Inband: Data is extracted using the same channel that is used to inject the SQL code. The retrieved data is presented directly in the application web page.

Out-of-band: Data is retrieved using a different channel (ex: An email with the results of the query is generated and sent to the tester).

Inferential or Blind: there is no actual transfer of data, but the tester is able to reconstruct the information by sending particular requests and observing the resulting behaviour of the DB Server.

22. What are the different techniques used in SQL Injection?

Ans:

Union Operator: In a SELECT statement, making it possible to combine two queries into a single result or result set.

Boolean: use Boolean condition(s) to verify whether certain conditions are true or false.

Error based: This technique forces the database to generate an error, giving the attacker information upon which to refine their SQL Injection.

Out-of-band: technique used to retrieve data using a different channel (e.g., make a HTTP connection to send the results to a web server).

Time delay: use database commands (e.g. sleep/delay) to delay answers in conditional queries. It is useful when attacker doesn't have some kind of answer (result, output, or error) from the application. If time delay statement works means the web page is vulnerable.

23. What are the most common symbols/operators used for SQL Injection?

Ans:

- Symbol - Quotes (')
- Symbol - Semicolon (;)
- Symbol – SQL Comments (-- or/****/)
- Keyword - OR
- Keyword - UNION
- Concatenate - +
- Dynamic SQL - EXEC
- XP_SMDSHELL

Note: It's for SQL Server, this list might change based on RDBMS

24. Can you take an example and explain how SQL Injection actually happens?

Ans:

Let's say a financial firm built an online application for their customers. Customers can login using their email ID and password. Let's imagine that the parameter sanitization is not properly doing in application layer. Now a hacker wants to try SQL Injection at this website:

Hacker Checks the Vulnerability:

- First try using email and password as below: Observe single quote at the end

  EmailID: test@testmail.com'

  Pwd: test@123
- Result Observation:
  - ✓ If this parameter is properly sanitized in application layer then the code should ignore this single quote and search for the email test@testmail in database, since this email is not available it should return message something like "Wrong User Name or Pwd"
  - ✓ If this parameter is not properly sanitized in application layer then the SQL Statement may looks like:
  - ✓ SELECT Column1, Column2 From Table Where EmailID = "test@testmail.com";
  - ✓ Obviously this statement fails and application might return an error message like "Database Error" or "Internal Error."
- Application returns the error message: "Database Error" or "Internal Error." Hacker found the key information "Parameters are not sanitized properly."

- ➢ Application Handles Errors properly: Parameters are not properly sanitized but errors are handled in a proper way and returned the message "No user with this Email"
- ➢ If application handles error messages properly then hacker will try to apply other techniques:
  - ✓ Try to get user names: Email ID: test@testmail.com' OR full_name like '%joy%'
  - ✓ Guess column name: Email ID: test@testmail.com' OR email is null
  - ✓ Making condition true: Email ID: test@testmail.com' OR 1 = 1
  - ✓ Test Vulnerability: Email ID: test@testmail.com'; DELAY 10
  - ✓ Test Vulnerability: Email ID: test@testmail.com' UNION SELECT 1

Now Hacker will try actual Injection Attack:

- ➢ Hacker is already tried and he/she knows that the website/application is vulnerable. Can you imagine the impact if hacker tries below statements?
- ➢ Get the table name

  Email ID: test@testmail.com'; SELECT Top 1 Name From sys.objects WHERE TYPE = 'U'
- ➢ Drop the table name

  Email ID: test@testmail.com'; Drop Table Customer

  Email ID: test@testmail.com'; Drop Table Users
- ➢ Hacker knew one of the member EmailID joel@gmail.com and can you imagine if he/she can be able to update this account with his email ID:

  Email ID: test@testmail.com'; UPDATE Customers SET Email = 'test@testmail.com' WHERE email = 'joel@gmail.com'
- ➢ Once he confirmed that the email ID is updated successfully he can easily log into the website using the option "Forgot Password." When forgot password the password will be sent to hacker account and he can reset it. Then he could be able to log into JOEL account and stole his information.

25. What are the different ways to prevent SQL Injection?

Ans:

Sanitize Parameters: Define acceptable symbols for the input parameters and scrutinize at application before passing them to database.

Error Reporting: Make sure errors are handled properly and error information is not returning to the end user.

Hide Schema: Create views and hide the actual table structure and give access on views.

Querying Database: Use stored procedures for all database processing; avoid using queries in front end instead initiate a call to stored procedure by passing the sanitized input parameters.

Privilege: Use least privileged user account for web applications and make sure no admin rights issued for application users.

Dynamic SQL: Always use SP_EXECUTESQL instead of EXEC

XP_CMDSHELL: Make sure application user doesn't have access to XP_CMDSHELL.

Isolate the Web Server: Make sure SQL Server/database server is not sharing with web server.

Remove Unused: Remove all unused users and logins and stored procedures

Audit: Perform a detailed Audit on database systems

SQL Server Audit

26. What are the ways to perform audit in SQL Server?

Ans:

In SQL Server There are various solutions available for auditing:

- SQL Trace
- SQL Profiler
- C2 Auditing
- Common Criteria Compliance
- DML Triggers
- DDL Triggers
- Logon Triggers
- Change Data Capture
- Extended Events
- SQL Server Audit

SQL Trace: It was introduced on SQL Server 2000. By using this we should be ready to handle the performance impact on a busy server but it provides the very fine grained auditing solution. SQL Trace use stored procedures sp_trace_create, sp_trace_setevent and sp_trace_setstatus.

SQL Profiler: SQL Profiler is an API/front-end for SQL Trace. Using profiler might heavily increase load on your database server. We can choose events, columns, filters from API.

C2 Auditing: Introduced in SQL Server 2000. It audits stored procedure execution, creation and deletion of objects and login audit. We can't choose the events rather audit everything or nothing. The main problem with this feature is server get shutdown when an event is not able to log.

Common Criteria Compliance: It is an alternative for C2 audit. It was introduced in SQL Server 2005 SP1 but is only available in Enterprise, Development and Evaluation Editions of SQL Server. It takes care of 3 things. A) Overwrite memory with known bits before handover it to new resource. B) Audit both failed and successful logins. C) Give more precedence to Table level DENY over Column Level GRANT.

DML Triggers: Can audit database level DML operations Ex: INSERT, DELETE, UPDATE

DDL Triggers: Can audit server level DDL operations Ex: CREATE, DROP ALTER

Logon Triggers: Can audit user logins but it fires only when use is able to successfully login to the server. It can't be able to audit failed logins.

Change Data Capture: Introduced in SQL Server 2008 and can audit DML changes. This feature harvests the SQL Server transaction log as part of the sp_replcmds process, for changes to data on the tables for which it was enabled.

Extended Events: Introduced in SQL Server 2008 as a replace for SQL Trace, events were limited on 2008 but this feature is enhanced on 2012 by supporting all events that supports on SQL Trace. It's a light weighted feature thereof less performance impact.

SQL Server Audit: Introduced in SQL Server 2008 but limited to Enterprise edition. In SQL Server 2012 Server Level auditing is also available for standard edition users. This is the best way to perform secure audits with the less performance impact. There components needs to be configured "Server Audit," "Server Audit Specification" and "Database Audit Specification."

27. I have a premium SQL Server 2012 database where data is highly sensitive. My requirement is to audit all "Delete" operations against the table "CCTran" on database "OrgStore." Can you describe the steps required to configure SQL Audit to fulfil this requirement.

Ans:

Create Audit:

- On SSMS Connect to SQL Server 2012 instance
- Go to Security and expand à Audits
- Create "New Audit"
  - ✓ Audit Name: Give a Name – "Audit_OrgStore"
  - ✓ Audit Destination: "File"
  - ✓ File Path: "M:\Audit"
  - ✓ Note: Leave defaults for remaining parameters as we have enough space available.
  - ✓ Click Ok à New Audit will be created

Enable Audit:

- Go to Audits and enable the Audit "Audit_OrgStore"

Create Audit Specification:

- Now we need to choose "Database Audit Specification" or "Server Audit Specification"
- Our requirement is for auditing an operation Delete at database level we need to create a "database Audit Specification"
- Go to database OrgStore à Expand Security à Database Audit Specification
- Create a new Database Audit Specification:
  - ✓ Name: "DBSpec_audit_Delete"
  - ✓ Audit: Select the Audit we have created "Audit_OrgStore"
  - ✓ Audit Action Type: From the list select "Delete"
  - ✓ Object Name: CCTran
  - ✓ Principal Name: estore_user (user account that should be audited)
  - ✓ Click on OK and the Database Audit Specification will be created

Enable Audit Specification:

- Enable the Database audit Specification "DBSpec_audit_Delete"
- Now Audit is configured for the given requirement.

Test SQL Audit:

- Execute Delete statements against the table "CCTran" from database "OrgStore"
- These statements will be logged in audit file located on "M:\Audit" folder.
- This file can't be open using text editor, we need reporting services or we can use T-SQL statement:

  "SELECT event_time, action_id, statement, database_name, server_principal_name FROM fn_get_audit_file ('M:\Audit\Audit-*.sqlaudit', DEFAULT, DEFAULT); "

Impersonation

28. I logged into SQL Server using an account called "DBA" and now can we be able to impersonate temporarily to execute few statements?

Ans:

Yes! We can use "EXECUTE AS."

SELECT SUSER_SNAME ();

EXECUTE AS LOGIN = 'SA';

SELECT SUSER_SNAME ();

After the statement "EXECUTE AS LOGIN" if you execute any query that will be executed as user SA.

29. What is "WITH EXECUTE AS OWNER"?

Ans:

- This is known as impersonation and it is available from SQL Server 2005 to SQL Server 2016.
- When we create a stored procedure WITH EXECUTE AS OWNER means that the stored procedure will run as DBO (database owner) and it can perform anything in that database.
- Any user who is having permission to execute that stored procedure can run that stored procedure as the "db owner."
- User A - Don't have a permission to INSERT/DELETE/UPDATE on table T
- Stored Procedure USP is created WITH EXECUTE AS OWNER
- Inside the procedure there are INSERT and UPDATE issuing on Table T
- If you give execute permission on stored procedure "usp" to user "A" then user can be able to execute the procedures which indirectly INSERT/UPDATE data on table T.
- This is very useful when we need to restrict access for users on sensitive data.
- Make sure user doesn't have access to stored procedure code.

30. What are the impersonation options available?

Ans:

There are basically five types of impersonation available:

- SELF: The specified user is the person creating or altering the module
- CALLER: This will take on the permissions of the current user
- OWNER: This will take on the permissions of the owner of the module being called
- "user_name": A specific user
- "login_name": A specific login

31. Does this user impersonation is possible only with stored procedures?

Ans:

No! Impersonation can be used with below:

- Stored Procedures
- Functions
- DML triggers
- DDL triggers
- Queues
- T-SQL Batch

32. As you suggested we have started using WITH EXECUTE AS OWNER. But still my client is not ready to use WITH EXECUTE AS OWNER as the code executes under DBO user. Any other way we can implement this?

Ans:

Yes! Instead of impersonating owner use a proxy userID.

- Create a user at database without login. That means no user can be logged in and connect to database under this user.
  CREATE USER [Truncate_Tab] WITHOUT LOGIN;
- This is a proxy user ID that we are creating for internal security purpose.
- Now grant ALTER permission to this proxy user ID Truncate_Tab
  GRANT ALTER TO [truncate_Tab];
- Then in that stored procedure replace the "Owner" with this proxy user ID
  WITH EXECUTE AS 'Truncate_Tab'
- Now the stored procedure executes under this proxy user ID.

Proxy Accounts

33. What is the proxy account in SQL Server?

Ans:

When a SQL Job is created the job executed under SQL Server Agent service account. There are certain scenarios where the service account requires highest privileges. Giving highest privileges to SQL Server Agent service account is allowed in enterprise environments, in those cases we do create a proxy account we'll give all required permissions to this proxy account. This proxy account can be mapped to SQL Agent Job/job step thereof the particular job/step runs under the highest privilege account through proxy.

34. How to create and use Proxy account?

Ans:

- Create Credential
- Create Proxy
- Associate Proxy with Subsystem
- Grant Permissions to Use Proxy
- Specify Proxy to Use for Job Step

35. What are the various scenarios where we may need to use PROXY account with SQL Server agent?

Ans:

- Executing SSIS package
- Need to work with OS commands – Ex: NET STOP/START commands
- Communicating with other machines on network
- PowerShell Scripts
- Replication Agents
- Analysis Services Commands

Transparent Data encryption

36. What is Transparent Data Encryption?

Ans:

TDE is designed to protect data by encrypting the physical files of the database, rather than the data itself. Its main purpose is to prevent unauthorized access to the data by restoring the files to another server. With Transparent Data Encryption in place, this requires the original encryption certificate and master key.

- TDE is introduced with SQL Server 2008 Enterprise edition
- TDE purpose is secure by encrypting database physical files
  - ✓ Data File (.MDF/.NDF)
  - ✓ Log File (.LDF)
  - ✓ Backup File (.bak)
- Data is not encrypted while transferring between databases or when communicating with application. Connection encryption has to be done using Secure Socket Layer (SSL) or Internet Protocol Security (IPSec). There are new features (always encrypted) added in SQL Server 2016 to encrypt data during the network transfer.

- TEMPDB physical file is also encrypted when TDE is initially enabled for the first time in that instance.

37. What are the advantages and disadvantages of TDE?

Ans:

Advantages:

- Implementation of TDE does not require any schema modifications or code changes.
- The decryption process is invisible to the end user
- TDE enabled databases can be participated in Logshipping, Mirroring, Replication and from 2012 we can add these databases to ALWAYSON Availability Groups.
- The performance impact due to TDE is minimal. As per Microsoft it's 3 to 5 % and it may vary based on data and infrastructure.
- The encryption is applied at physical file level thereby no much impact on indexes.

Disadvantages:

- Before SQL Server 2016 TDE protects data at rest (Data Files, Log Files, Backups) but data in communication channels or in memory is vulnerable.
- Do not enable both TDE and compression which may impact your database performance very badly.
- Data still available to SYSADMINs with proper rights
- In-Memory OLTP log records are encrypted if TDE is enabled but data in a MEMORY_OPTIMIZED_DATA FILEGROUP is not encrypted if TDE is enabled.
- If you miss to backup of your server certificates or master key there is no way that you can recover data from encrypted database backup.
- TDE is expensive feature as it is available with Data Center/Enterprise Edition only.

38. How to implement Transparent Data Encryption?

Ans:

- Create a Database master key for master database
- Create a certificate that's protected by the master key.
- Create a special key that's used to protect the database. This key is called the database encryption key (DEK) and we secure it using the certificate.
- Backup Keys and Certificate
- Enable encryption for the user database

39. How to know the list of all databases for which TDE enabled in a given instance?

Ans:

Use the DMV sys.dm_database_encryption_keys with sys.databases will give you TDE enabled database details.

40. How to disable/decrypt the TDE for a database?

Ans:

- Alter the database and set the option ENCRYPTION to OFF
- It will take time based on the size of the database. Wait until the database decryption is done.
- Drop the database encryption key for this database.
- Restart the SQL Server Instance

Note: It's recommended to take a backup of Master Key and Certificate before reversing TDE.

41. Does TDE supports in all SQL Server High Availability and Disaster Recovery features?

Ans:

Yes! TDE supports in all HA and DR options provided by SQL Server

Replication: It supports but there are lots of problems we need to deal with. Certificate must be installed on all subscribers and data is not encrypted as it is distributed

Log Shipping: Data encrypted on Primary and Secondary databases

Database Mirroring: Data encrypted on principal and mirror databases

Failover Clustering: There is one copy of shared data.

ALWAYSON Availability Groups: We have to configure using T-SQL

42. What is the SQL Server Edition support for TDE?

Ans:

- TDE is introduced in SQL Server 2008 Enterprise Edition.
- TDE supports only in enterprise edition of SQL Server 2008, 2008 R2, 2012, 2014 and 2016.
- TDE also supports in Developer Edition as well but it is only supposed to use with Development and Testing environments.

43. Does TDE prevent the security administrator or database administrator from seeing the data in the database?

Ans:

No! TDE protects the data at rest, but an authorized user such as a database administrator or security administrator can access the data in a TDE-encrypted database. To prevent an SA or DBA from accessing selected parts of the data, you need to use application-level encryption.

44. Is there any performance impact for using TDE?

Ans:

- Yes! Performance overhead is involved in using TDE.
- The encryption and decryption process do require additional CPU cycles.
- As per Microsoft documentation the overhead for using TDE ranges from 3 to 30 based on the type of workload

- Also TEMPDB needs to be encrypted which is also causes some performance degradation
- If compression and TDE is enabled on same database then we might see some serious performance issues.

Policy Based Management

45. What is Policy Based Management?

Ans:

As the name implies this feature is to define and implement policies/standards for SQL Server across the enterprise. This feature is introduced with SQL Server 2008. It easier the policy/standard implementation across all SQL Server instances from a centralized server.

Advantages:

- Define database standards based on your corporate/client requirement
- Selective implementation which means if you want to give exception for one of the instance we can do that.
- The entire policy management is automated
- After running the policy/standard check if you find any issues those issues can be fixed by clicking a button.

46. Usually what kind of database standards will be implemented in enterprise environments?

Ans:

Standards can be implemented for 3 levels, Instance, Database and Object Level.

Naming Standards: Acceptable strings for a database name or a stored procedure name

Security Policies: Security Policy must be checked to true for all logins

Configurations: Auto Shrink must be turned off on all instances.

47. How to implement Policy Based Management?

Ans:

In order to understand Policy Based Management we should know below terms:

- Target: An entity that is managed by Policy-Based management; e.g. a database, a procedure etc.
- Facet: A predefined set of properties that can be managed
- Condition: A property expression that evaluates to True or False; i.e. the state of a Facet
- Policy: A condition to be checked and/or enforced

Implementing a Policy:

- Create a Condition
  - ✓ Facet "Database"
  - ✓ Field "@AutoShrink"
  - ✓ Operator "="
  - ✓ Value as "False"

- Create the Policy
  - ✓ Create a new policy: Give a name
  - ✓ Map the condition: Map the condition that we have created in first step
  - ✓ Execution Mode: Select the correct execution mode based on the requirement
- Evaluate a Policy
  - ✓ Simply execute/evaluate the policy which checks the given condition and reports it.

48. What is the option execution mode in creating a new policy in policy based management?

Ans:

The option execution mode plays a vital role in policy execution. There are total 4 modes available:

On Demand: This is the default mode. Policy is evaluated only when you manually execute it

***On Schedule*:** We can create a schedule to evaluate the policy. It creates a SQL Agent job and executes it and logs the failed conditions in Windows Event Log

On Change - Log Only: Evaluates policy when any facet changed and log the events into Windows Event Log when there is any violation

On Change – Prevent: Evaluates policy when there is a facet changes happens and It prevent the change if it violates the policy condition.

Security General

49. You are assigned as a database architect for one of the premium project. Client asked you the question "What are the areas where we should configure proper security principles and need to follow best practices?" How do you answer the question?

Ans:

Physical Security: File location and Server access

Network Security: Connection encryption and data transfers, firewalls

Service Accounts: Use the lease privileged service accounts

Authentication: Windows or SQL, Enable password policy, use strong passwords

Authorization: Least privileged logins, restrict SYS Admin

Sensitive Data: Data Encryption, Backup Encryption, Obfuscate data when restored to non-prod, use views/stored procedures and other object to restrict direct access on tables.

SQL Injection: Follow the best coding practices

Disaster Recovery: Proper planning for login movement/migration to secondary/replica/standby/passive server. Create backup for server security certificates and attach with backup files.

Patching: Never miss applying security patches and service packs

Auditing: Last but the most important step do configure the best audit mechanism and check the reports and take the appropriate action if you see anything suspicious.

50. **Since we are looking for a SQL Server SME, we would expect you to define and implement security best practices in our enterprise database environment. From your experience can you list out few points to enforce security for SQL Server?**

Ans:

Providing security for SQL Server is nothing but making sure that the right people have access to the right data. When we start working with a client we do provide and implement a security best practices guide. I may not list out entire points in detail but here are the bullet points:

- Use strong passwords for all accounts and make sure the password policy is enabled for all logins.
- Minimize the number of SYSADMINs allowed to access SQL Server.
- Give users the least amount of permissions they need to perform their job.
- Use stored procedures or views to allow users to access data instead of letting them directly access tables.
- When possible, use Windows Authentication logins instead of SQL Server logins.
- Don't grant permissions to the public database role.
- Remove user login IDs who no longer need access to SQL Server.
- Avoid creating network shares on any SQL Server.
- Turn on login auditing so you can see who has succeeded, and failed, to login.
- Ensure that your SQL Servers are behind a firewall and are not exposed directly to the Internet.
- Using server, database and application roles to control access to the data
- Securing the physical database files using NTFS permissions
- Disable SA account if not possible use an un guessable password
- Create customized database roles and server roles
- For critical databases make sure TDE (Transparent Data Encryption) is enabled
- Define and implement the best practices and coding standards to prevent SQL Injection
- Periodically perform the database security audits
- For end user restrict direct access to tables instead use views, stored procedures
- Restrict physical access to the SQL Server
- Disable the Guest account
- Isolate SQL Server from the web server
- Choose either of the service to run SQL Server (Local User – Not an Admin, Domain User – Not an Admin)
- Restrict the remote administration (TC)
- If SQL Server authentication is used, the credentials are secured over the network by using IPSec or SSL, or by installing a database server certificate.
- Do not use DBO users as application logins

- Firewall restrictions ensure that only the SQL Server listening port is available on the database server.
- Remove the SQL guest user account.
- Remove the BUILTIN\Administrators server login.
- Apply the latest security updates/patches
- Enable only the required network protocols
- Disable NETBIOS and SMB protocol unless specifically needed.
- Do not expose a server that is running SQL Server to the public Internet.
- Configure named instances of SQL Server to use specific port assignments for TCP/IP rather than dynamic ports.
- Use extended protection in SQL Server 2012 if the client and operating system support it.
- Grant CONNECT permission only on endpoints to logins that need to use them. Explicitly deny CONNECT permission to endpoints that are not needed by users or groups.

51. When we need to talk about "SECURITY" in SQL Server what are the features that helps us implementing the security policies?

Ans:

We have plenty of features in SQL SERVER to enforce the security. The major features include:

- Password policies
- Policy Based Management
- Transparent Data Encryption
- Backup Encryption
- Always Encrypted
- Dynamic Data Masking
- Limited metadata visibility (system Tables to CATALOG Views)
- DDL triggers
- User-schema separation
- Impersonation
- Granular permission sets
- Security CATALOG views
- SQL Audit

52. In SQL Server what is a securable?

Ans:

A securable is any database entity or object that can be secured or managed with permissions. At the very highest level, this would be the server itself. Securable include databases and all associated objects.

- Server Level Securable:
  - ✓ Endpoint
  - ✓ Login
  - ✓ Database
- Database Level Securable:
  - ✓ User
  - ✓ Role
  - ✓ Application Role
  - ✓ Assembly
  - ✓ Message Type
  - ✓ Route
  - ✓ Service
  - ✓ Remote Service Binding
  - ✓ Fulltext CATALOG
  - ✓ Certificate
  - ✓ Asymmetric Key
  - ✓ Symmetric Key
  - ✓ Contract
  - ✓ Schema
- Schema Level Securable:
  - ✓ Type
  - ✓ XML Schema Collection
  - ✓ Object
- Object Level Securable:
  - ✓ Aggregate
  - ✓ Constraint
  - ✓ Function
  - ✓ Procedure
  - ✓ Queue
  - ✓ Statistic
  - ✓ Synonym
  - ✓ Table
  - ✓ View

53. What is the Guest user account in SQL Server? What login is it mapped to it?

Ans:

The Guest user account is created by default in all databases and is used when explicit permissions are not granted to access an object. It is not mapped directly to any login, but can be used by any login. Depending on your security needs, it may make sense to drop the Guest user account, in all databases except Master and TEMPDB.

54. What are the permissions required to TRUNCATE a table?

Ans:

In order to execute TRUNCATE command on a table the user should have "ALTER TABLE" permission on that table. TRUNCATE TABLE permissions are default to:

- Owner of the Table
- Member of the fixed database roles
  - ✓ DB_owner
  - ✓ DB_ddladmin
- Member of the fixed Server role SYSADMIN

55. What is the use of BUILTIN\Administrators Group in SQL Server?

Ans:

Any Windows login in BUILTIN\Administrators group is by default a SQL Server system administrator. This single group can be used to manage administrators from a Windows and SQL Server perspective

56. What objects does fn_my_permissions function reports on?

Ans:

- SERVER
- DATABASE
- SCHEMA
- OBJECT
- USER
- LOGIN
- ROLE
- APPLICATION ROLE
- TYPE
- MESSAGE TYPE
- ASYMMETRIC KEY
- SYMMETRIC KEY
- CERTIFICATE
- SERVICE

- REMOTE SERVICE BINDING
- FULLTEXT CATALOG
- ASSEMBLY
- CONTRACT
- ENDPOINT
- ROUTE
- XML SCHEMA COLLECTION

  SELECT * FROM fn_my_permissions (NULL, 'SERVER');

  SELECT * FROM fn_my_permissions ('AdventureWorks', 'DATABASE');

  SELECT * FROM fn_my_permissions ('Employee', 'OBJECT')

57. How to perform backup for Certificates in SQL Server?

Ans:

- Using Native Backup
- Using Backup Certificate Command

58. Name 3 of the features that the SQL Server built-in function LOGINPROPERTY performs on standard logins.

Ans:

- Date when the password was set
- Locked out standard login
- Expired password
- Must change password at next login
- Count of consecutive failed login attempts
- Time of the last failed login attempt
- Amount of time since the password policy has been applied to the login
- Date when the login was locked out
- Password hash

59. What are the page verification options available in SQL Server?

Ans:

Page verification checks help to discover damaged database pages caused by disk I/O path errors. Disk I/O path errors can be the cause of database corruption problems and are generally caused by power failures or disk hardware failures that occur at the time the page is being written to disk. There are two page verification options available "Torn Page Detection" and "Checksum."

TORN PAGE DETECTION:

Works by saving a specific bit for each 512-byte sector in the 8-kilobyte (KB) database page and is stored in the database page header when the page is written to disk. When the page is read from disk, the torn bits stored in the page header are compared to the actual page sector information. Unmatched values indicate that only part of the page was written to disk. In this situation, error message 824 (indicating a torn page error) is reported to both the SQL Server error log and the Windows event log. Torn pages are typically detected by database recovery if it is truly an incomplete write of a page. However, other I/O path failures can cause a torn page at any time.

CHECKSUM:

Works by calculating a checksum over the contents of the whole page and stores the value in the page header when a page is written to disk. When the page is read from disk, the checksum is recomputed and compared to the checksum value stored in the page header. If the values do not match, error message 824 (indicating a checksum failure) is reported to both the SQL Server error log and the Windows event log. A checksum failure indicates an I/O path problem. To determine the root cause requires investigation of the hardware, firmware drivers, BIOS, filter drivers (such as virus software), and other I/O path components.

60. What are database end points?

Ans:

- A SQL Server endpoint is the point of entry into SQL Server.
- Endpoint is the term for the point of connection between a client or server and the network.
- SQL Server routes all interactions with the network via endpoints and each endpoint supports a specific type of communication.
- DBA mostly look into endpoints part when installing SQL Server and working with high availability options like Database Mirroring or allowing HTTP connections to SQL Server
- There are two types: system end Points and User Defined End points
- System End Points: End points are created for network protocols (TCP, VIA, Shared_ Memory, Named_Pipes) and DAC (Dedicated Admin Connection)
- To check all endpoint details "SELECT * FROM sys.endpoints"

61. What is an assembly in SQL Server?

Ans:

Managed database objects, such as stored procedures or triggers, are compiled and then deployed in units called an assembly. Managed DLL assemblies must be registered in Microsoft SQL Server before the functionality the assembly provides can be used. To register an assembly in a SQL Server database, use the CREATE ASSEMBLY statement.

62. What is a principal in SQL Server security?

Ans:

A principal is any entity or object that has access to SQL Server resources. These are:

- Windows domain logins
- Windows local logins
- SQL Server logins

- Windows groups
- Database roles
- Server roles
- Application roles

63. What are some of the pros and cons of not dropping the SQL Server BUILTIN\ Administrators Group?

Ans:

Pros:

- Any Windows login is by default a SQL Server system administrator
- This single group can be used to manage SQL Server from a system administrator's perspective

Cons:

- Any Windows login is by default a SQL Server system administrator, which may leads to a security threat and it is strictly restricted as per any enterprise environment security policy.

64. What is delegation?

Ans:

Kerberos Delegation is lies at Active Directory. There are scenarios where this Delegation required:

- End client is accessing a web service and web service redirecting to SQL Server which is installed on another server. Here webservice delegates the user credentials on behalf of end client.
- End client is accessing a SQL Server and the data retrieval required to connect to another SQL Server instance using linked server. In this case the first SQL Server delegates the user credentials on behalf of end client.

Security Strategies

65. When we connected to a network in enterprise environment we can see the database server installed on that network. Our application security policy strictly says that our backend server should not be visible in network. Can you be able to hide the SQL Server instance?

Ans:

Yes! We can do that. To hide a SQL Server instance, we need to make a change in SQL Server Configuration Manager. To do this launch SQL Server Configuration Manager and do the following: select the instance of SQL Server, right click and select Properties. After selecting properties you will just set Hide Instance to "Yes" and click OK or Apply. After the change is made, you need to restart the instance of SQL Server to not expose the name of the instance.

66. We have a list of 3 SQL Server logins which are dedicated to a critical application. We have given all required rights to those logins. Now my question is we have to restrict the access only to these three logins. Means there are two conditions:

a) No other user should be able to access the database except those three logins

b) Even for those three logins they should be able to run their queries only through the application. If someone login through SSMS and trying to run a query should result into a failure.

Finally there should be only way to running a query is from their application using one of those three logins, there should be no other way to run queries on that database. How do you restrict?

Ans:

- Do not give access to any other login on that database except for those 3 app logins.
- Create a trigger that test each and every query like below

```
IF app_name () in ('SQL Query Analyzer','Microsoft SQL Server Management Studio')
Begin
        Raiserror (.....)
End
Return
```

67. How to resolve the orphan user problem?

Ans:

A database user can become orphaned if the corresponding SQL Server login is dropped. Also, a database user can become orphaned after a database is restored or attached to a different instance of SQL Server. Orphaning can happen if the database user is mapped to a SID that is not present in the new server instance.

- To find out the orphan users

```
USE <database_name>;
GO;
sp_change_users_login @Action='Report';
GO;
```

- To resolve the orphan user problem

```
USE <database_name>;
GO
sp_change_users_login @Action='update_one',
@UserNamePattern='<database_user>',
@LoginName='<login_name>';
GO
```

68. Here is the requirement: We need to give access to a team member on one of the premium database.

a. The user should be able to execute 15 selected stored procedures

b. The user shouldn't be able to check the stored procedure code

c. The user shouldn't have SELECT/INSERT/DELETE/UPDATE/TRUNCATE rights on any database table or view.

d. Except the execute permission that to restricted for the given 15 stored procedures, other than that user shouldn't have any other access on that database.

What is your solution?

Ans:

- First create all 15 procedures WITH EXECUTE AS OWNER. That means the procedure execute as database owner:

  ```
  CREATE PROCEDURE [dbo].[procedure_1]
  WITH EXECUTE AS OWNER
  AS
  BEGIN
  Declaration
  --
  SELECT * FROM Table_1;
  --
  INSERT DATA INTO TABLE_2;
  --
  UPDATE DATA ON TABLE_3;
  END
  ```

- Create a login 'test_login' and map the login to the corresponding database with only Public role no other permission required.

- Now grant execute permission to the newly created user <test_login> on 15 procedures

  ```
  GRANT EXECUTE ON [procedure_1] TO <test_login>
  ----------------------------------------------------------------
  GRANT EXECUTE ON [procedure_15] TO <test_login>
  ```

- Now login with test_login and connect to the database
  - ✓ You can connect to only to the required database in that instance.
  - ✓ You can execute those 15 stored procedures successfully
  - ✓ You can't perform SELECT, INSERT, UPDATE and DELETE on any table or view in that database.

- ✓ You can't even check the stored procedure code
- ✓ You can't do anything except executing those 15 stored procedures.

69. You are delegating permissions on a SQL Server instance to other administrators. You have local, single server jobs on one server that you would like to allow another administer to start, stop, and view the history, but not delete history. This administrator will own the jobs. Which role should you assign?

Ans:

SQLAgentUserRole

SQL Server provides 3 fixed roles for the agent service that limit privileges for administrators. The SQLAgentUserRole is designed for local jobs (not multiserver) that allow the member to work with their owned jobs (edit, start, stop, view history) without deleting the history of any job.

70. We are going to build a database for a premium application where data is highly sensitive. Now we need to design the best security strategy for the below requirement.

There are total 3 different group of people access the database for reporting purpose and data loads.

Ex: Grp1: 30 Tables, 15 Views, 8 PROCs, 2 functions. Grp2: 26 Tables, 18 PROCs etc.

Each group is having a set of database objects on which the other groups shouldn't have any permission.

Ex: Table 1 is belongs to group 1. Means Group 2 and Group 3 shouldn't have any rights on Table1

There are few master tables and these set of tables should be accessible for all 3 groups.

Ex: Common Tables: Currency, TimeZone, Country, Conversion etc should be accessible to all 3 groups.

All 3 group users can have SELECT, INSERT and Execute rights on all their respective objects.

Ans:

- ➢ Create 4 schemas:
  - ✓ Schema1 for holding Group1 related objects: Tables, Views, Procs etc.
  - ✓ Schema2 for holding Group2 related objects: Tables, Views, Procs etc.
  - ✓ Schema3 for holding Group3 related objects: Tables, Views, Procs etc.
  - ✓ Schema4 for holding common objects: Tables, Views, Procs etc.
- ➢ Create all related objects on each schema. Tables, Views, Procs, functions etc.
- ➢ Create synonyms to represent schema level objects. Ex: Create a synonym ORGS to represent a table "schema1.Organization_Sales." It helps in abstracting the internal object name also easier the developer/programmer job.

- Create 3 database Roles: Role1, Role2 and Role3 and Map schemas to Roles
  - ✓ Role1: Schema1 and Schema4
  - ✓ Role2: Schema2 and Schema4
  - ✓ Role3: Schema3 and Schema4
- Grant required permissions on schemas to Roles:
  - ✓ GRANT SELECT, INSERT, EXECUTE on Schema1 and Schema4 TO Role1
  - ✓ GRANT SELECT, INSERT, EXECUTE on Schema2 and Schema4 TO Role2
  - ✓ GRANT SELECT, INSERT, EXECUTE on Schema3 and Schema4 TO Role3
- **This means:**
  - ✓ Members belong to Role1 have SELECT, INSERT and EXECUTE permissions on all objects belongs to Schema1 and Schema4
  - ✓ Members belong to Role2 have SELECT, INSERT and EXECUTE permissions on all objects belongs to Schema1 and Schema4
  - ✓ Members belong to Role3 have SELECT, INSERT and EXECUTE permissions on all objects belongs to Schema1 and Schema4
- Now Map all required users to roles
  - ✓ Role1: Users belongs to GROUP 1
  - ✓ Role2: Users belongs to GROUP 2
  - ✓ Role3: Users belongs to GROUP 3
- That's it the above strategy fulfills the given requirement. It easier the administrator job as below:
  - ✓ New object created on a schema: No action required from DBA
  - ✓ New user added to the group1: Simply add the new user to the corresponding role i.e Role1
  - ✓ Now "Delete" permission required for all users from Group 2: GRANT DELETE ON Schema02 TO Role2
  - ✓ New user required access on Group1 and Group2: Add new user to Role1 and Role2

71. Can we be able to find out who changed the password for a SQL Login? If yes explain.

Ans:

Yes! There are 2 places we can find this information:

- Custom Trace with the event class "Audit Login Change Password" (System default trace doesn't include this event class)
- "masterdb" transactional log file. (Information will be arises if a checkpoint happens), we can read the log file using the undocumented system function fn_dblog

72. How to give permission to view stored procedure code?

Ans:

We have to give "View Definition" (sp_help/sp_helptext) access to user in order to allow a user to access the object metadata/code. This permission can be granted on 4 levels:

- SERVER
- DATABASE
- SCHEMA
- INDIVIDUAL OBJECT

Server Level: User can view any definition on all databases in that instance

GRANT VIEW ANY DEFINITION TO <User Name>

Database Level: User can view all object definitions on that database

GRANT VIEW DEFINITION TO <User Name>

SCHEMA Level: User can view all object definitions on that schema

GRANT VIEW DEFINITION ON SCHEMA :: <Schema Name> TO <User Name>

Object Level: User can view definition of the particular object

GRANT VIEW DEFINITION ON <Object Name> TO <User Name>

73. What are the permissions required to use DMV?

Ans:

To query a dynamic management view or function requires SELECT permission on object and VIEW SERVER STATE or VIEW DATABASE STATE permission.

GRANT VIEW SERVER STATE to <Login Name>

GRANT VIEW DATABASE STATE to <User Name>

74. What is the quickest way to list out all database objects and their permissions to user details?

Ans:

System stored procedure will give us the list of permissions for the objects in that current database.

EXECUTE sp_helprotect

75. We have a role R1 created. This role is granted to INSERT and UPDATE on all tables. I have mapped 20 users to this role R1. Now these 20 users have got the INSERT and UPDATE permission as the role is granted. But now I wanted to DENY INSERT permission for one of those 20 users. Is it possible without detaching that user from the role R1?

Ans:

Yes! It is possible. We need not change anything at role level. Just DENY the insert permission for the single user. That's it. The basic rule is DENY takes the precedence over other permissions.

76. I have opened a session by impersonating another user using EXECUTE AS LOGIN = 'Admin_User'. I have completed executing a batch or T-SQL statements. How can I switch back to my own session without closing the session?

Ans:

Using the keyword REVERT

```
EXECUTE AS LOGIN = 'Admin_User';
-- Admin_User
SELECT SUSER_SNAME ();
-- Switch back to your session
REVERT
--Actual user name which you are currently logged in with
SELECT SUSER_SNAME ();
```

77. We have created a SQL Agent job to execute a SSIS package and the job started failing with the message "Non-SYSADMINS have been denied permission to run DTS Execution job steps without a proxy account." Any idea how to resolve this issue?

Ans:

This error occurs if the account under which SQL Server Agent Service is running and the job owner is not a SYSADMIN on the box or the job step is not set to run under a proxy account associated with the SSIS subsystem. We need to use a proxy, SQL Server Agent impersonates the credentials (Windows User accounts) associated with the proxy when the job step is executed.

78. We recently had a requirement to disable a database user for temporary purpose. After certain period we would request back to enable the user access. Can you explain how to disable a user in a database?

Ans:

There is no direct option for disabling a database user. Removing the user mapping for the corresponding login can restrict the user access to that database. But here the requirement is it should be only for temporary purpose when they required it back we should be able to enable the user with all required roles and permissions. This can be done using T-SQL command:

To disable a user in a database:

```
USE <Database Name>
GO
REVOKE CONNECT FROM "<User Name>"
```

To enable the user back:

```
USE <Database Name>
GO
GRANT CONNECT TO "<User Name>"
```

Note: Please note double quotes, it's mandatory to use double quotes.

79. Our client required to give TRUNCATE permission for one of the programmer and below is the requirement:

The user "PRG01" should be able to truncate 2 tables

Except those 2 tables he/she shouldn't be able to TRUNCATE any other tables

We shouldn't give "ALTER TABLE" permission.

Also for your information these 2 tables are not having/referencing foreign keys

Now tell me what is your solution?

Ans:

There is not a straight forward method to give only TRUNCATE TABLE permission.

- Create a stored procedure by giving the table name as input parameter
- Create stored procedure WITH EXECUTE AS OWNER
- Validate the table name
- TRUNCATE the table when table name matches one of required 2 tables
- If not matches echo a message that user doesn't have rights to truncate
- The procedure looks something like below:

```
CREATE PROCEDURE [dbo].[usp_Truncate] @Tab VARCHAR(60)
WITH EXECUTE AS OWNER
AS
BEGIN
        SET NOCOUNT ON;
        IF (@Tab = 'Mem1' OR @Tab = 'Mem2')
        BEGIN
                DECLARE @QUERY NVARCHAR(100);
        SET @QUERY = N'TRUNCATE TABLE ' + @Tab + ';'
        EXECUTE sp_executesql @QUERY;
        PRINT 'Truncate completed successfully:'+@Tab;
        END
        ELSE
        BEGIN
        PRINT 'You do not have permission to Truncate Table:'+@Tab;
        END
END
```

- Give execute permission for the user "PRG01"

```
GRANT EXECUTE ON [usp_Truncate] TO PRG01
```

- That's it. Now the user PRG01 can truncate only two tables Mem1 or Mem2 and the user can't TRUNCATE any other tables.

CHAPTER 4

SQL Server Backup & Restore

Interview Questions and Answers

Introduction: This chapter takes you through the SQL Server Backup and Restore related interview questions and answers. These questions are helpful for range of database administrators staring from a junior to an expert level DBA while preparing for a technical interview. These questions and answers are deals with the below topics:

- Backup & Restore
- Backup and Restore features in 2014/2016
- Scenarios

Backup and Restore

1. How does the database recovery model impact database backups?

Ans:

The database recovery model is responsible for the retention of the transaction log entries. So based on the setting determines if transaction log backups need to be issued on a regular basis. As we know each and every transaction occurs on database will be logged into transaction log file irrespective of the database recovery model. But the recovery model determines when these logged transactions can be released/removed from log file.

- *Simple:* Committed transactions are automatically removed from the log when the check point process occurs.
- *Bulk Logged:* Committed transactions are only removed when the transaction log backup process occurs.
- *Full:* Committed transactions are only removed when the transaction log backup process occurs.

2. How can I verify that backups are occurring on a daily basis?

Ans:

- Check all backup jobs history
- Review the SQL Server error log for backup related entries.
- Query the MSDB.dbo.backupset table for the backup related entries.
- Review the file system where the backups are issued to validate they exist.
- Write a script to take care of this validation and to send a notification to DBA team when found backup errors/issues.

3. **How do you know if your database backups are restorable?**

Ans:

- Issue the RESTORE VERIFYONLY command to validate the backup. For validating LiteSpeed backups use XP_restore_verifyonly
- Randomly retrieve tapes from off site and work through the restore process with your team to validate the database is restored in a successful manner.

4. **What are some common reasons why database restores fail?**

Ans:

- Sufficient space not available on drive
- User may not have sufficient permissions to perform the restore
- Unable to gain exclusive use of the database.
- LSN's are out of sequence so the backups cannot be restored.
- Syntax error such as with the WITH MOVE command.
- Version problem
- Might be wrong backup location specified
- Service account may not have permissions on backup folder

5. **What are the permissions required to perform backup and Restore?**

Ans:

The user must be a member of either of the below roles

Backup: To perform backup the login must be assigned to any of the below roles

- SYSADMIN – fixed server role
- db_owner - fixed database role
- db_backupoperator – fixed database role

Restore: To perform restore the login must be assigned to any of the below roles

- SYSADMIN - fixed server role
- Dbcreator - fixed server role
- db_owner - fixed database role

6. **What are some common post restore processes?**

Ans:

- Sync the logins and users
- Validate the data is accurate by running DBCC commands
- Notify the team\user community
- If the restore is from PROD to Pre-PROD, cleanse the data to remove sensitive data i.e. SSN's, credit card information, customer names, personal information, etc.
- Change database properties i.e. recovery model, read-only, etc.

7. Explain how you could automate the backup and restore process?

Ans:

- Backups can be automated by using a cursor to loop through each of the databases and backup each one
- Restores can also be automated by looping over the files, reading from the system tables (backup or log shipping) or reading from a table as a portion of a custom solution

8. Can we be able to take the backup for "RESOURCEDB"?

Ans:

No! We can't perform backup for resource DB. But we can take the physical file backup for "RESOURCEDB" MDF and LDF files.

9. How to rebuild the system databases?

Ans:

- To rebuild the master database we have to use setup.exe from command prompt. There is no much difference between 2005 and 2008 except few command line switches.
- Find the setup.exe file (C:\............................\100\Setup BootStrap\Release\setup.exe)
- Run the below command from dos prompt

  c:\Program Files\Microsoft SQL Server\100\Setup Bootstrap\Release>setup.exe

  /QUIET

  /ACTION=REBUILDDATABASE

  /INSTANCENAME=<*Default/Named*>

  /SQLSYSADMINACCOUNTS= <Service Account>

  [/SAPWD=<*Mandatory when using Mixedmode*>]

  [/SQLCOLLATION=<*Give new collation if you want to change default*>]

- When setup has completed rebuilding the system databases, it will return to the command prompt with no messages (It always first prints out the version). Examine the "Summary" log file ([100\110\120]\setup bootstrap\logs) to verify the completion status.

10. What are the things should be considered when we are planning for rebuilding system databases?

Ans:

We usually rebuild the system databases when they are corrupted. Rebuild deletes the databases and recreates it hence all the existing information is vanished.

Before rebuild:

- Locate all recent backup of system databases
- Make a note on MDF and LDF file locations, server configuration, Build/hotfix/sp applied

Post Rebuild:

- Review the summary.txt once the rebuild completes to make sure rebuild completed without any issue.

- Move system databases to the correct location as before rebuild
- Restore all the system databases from existing backups to get our environment back with the all changes.

11. How can we rebuild Resource system database?

Ans:

Run SQL Server installation Setup.exe file and from installation wizard from left navigation pane select "Maintenance" and Click on Repair. It rebuilds the resource database.

12. How to restore MASTER or MSDB database from a valid backup?

Ans:

- Stop and Start the SQL Server Database Engine in Singe User Mode (Using parameter –m)
- Restore the Master Database from SQLCMD prompt
    - ✓ From dos prompt using SQLCMD connect to the SQL Server and run the restore script
    - ✓ RESTORE DATABASE MASTER FROM DISK='D:\MASTER_FULL.BAK' WITH REPLACE
- Stop and start the SQL Server Database Engine in normal mode
- Restore MSDB Database
    - ✓ Connect to management studio and run the restore script for MSDB
    - ✓ RESTORE DATABASE MSDB FROM DISK='D:\MSDB_FULL.BAK' WITH REPLACE

13. What are the new features added for Backup and Restore on SQL Server 2014?

Ans:

Backup Encryption:

- On SQL Server 2014 we can enable encryption while creating native backup either using T-SQL or SSMS.
- Backup encryption supported in SQL Server 2014 Standard, Business Intelligence and Enterprise editions.
- Encryption supports algorithms: AES 128, AES 192, AES 256 and Triple DES.

Backup to URL – Azure Storage:

As expected SQL Server 2014 backup is cloud enabled. Now we can directly perform a backup to Microsoft Azure Storage using the destination as URL. It supports both T-SQL and SSMS UI. To use SQL backup to URL we need:

- An Azure subscription
- Access to Azure using the Azure Portal or PowerShell
- An Azure Storage Account
- A container in the Azure Storage account

Managed Backups:

- This is primarily designed for Small to Medium Business (SMB). This feature "Managed Backups" automates the backup process and directs the backup to Windows Azure storage.
- It works for both when the SQL Server is in our internal premises or in Windows Azure VM.
- Managed Backups can be setup at database level or at instance level.
- Since it directs backup to windows azure, it requires an Azure Subscription and storage account.

14. If we enable managed backup to Windows Azure on which conditions the backup is generated automatically on 2014?

Ans:

A full backup is automatically scheduled to Windows Azure when:

- SQL Server Managed Backup to Windows Azure is enabled with default settings at the instance level
- SQL Server Managed Backup to Windows Azure enabled for the first time for a database
- The log growth since the last full database backup is equal to or larger than 1 GB
- One week has passed since the last full database backup
- The log chain is broken

A log backup is automatically scheduled to Windows Azure when:

- There is no log backup history
- The transaction log space used is 5 MB or larger
- 2 hours have passed since the last log backup
- When the transaction log backup is lagging behind a full database backup

15. Can we control the backup schedules in managed backups on 2014?

Ans:

No! It depends on log usage and other conditions

16. Can we include databases with "simple recovery" on managed backups on 2014?

Ans:

No! Not possible for system databases and for databases which are in simple recovery mode.

17. Can you quickly tell me the process for creating an encrypted backup on SQL Server 2014?

Ans:

- Create a database master key on master database
- Create a Certificate on master database

- Create a Backup and mention all required parameters for encryption
    - ✓ Keyword ENCRYPTION
    - ✓ Algorithm ex: AES_256
    - ✓ Certificate to be used; the one that we created on master.

18. We get an encrypted backup from Server A and the requirement is this backup has to be restored at Server B. Can you quickly demonstrate the steps?

Ans:

Server A:

- Backup the Master Key to a file (.key) using the same password that we used while creating the Master Key
- Backup the certificate to a file (.cer) with a private key. The private key is created using the same password that we used in above step.
- Backup the database using encryption

Server B:

- Restore the Master Key:
    - ✓ First decrypt using the password used on Server A
    - ✓ Then create a new master key
- Open master key: Important step
- Create certificate from the certificate backup created on Server A
- Now we can restore database without specifying any special options as we are restoring from an encrypted backup.

19. Is there any impact if we enable the backup encryption?

Ans:

- Yes! Mainly strain on CPU
- AES-128 is the best algorithm still it uses 20% to 25% extra CPU for encryption
- TRIPLE_DES_3KEY algorithm takes 40% to 45% extra CPU
- We should be very careful on backup timings if backup compression is also enabled along with backup encryption. Because in one of the environment we have seen CPU takes 55% extra while running backup with compression and encryption with TRIPLE_DES_3KEY

20. We are storing backup files on Windows Azure. Can we restore the backup from Windows Azure to our local machine?

Ans:

Yes! We can do that we just need to mention RESTORE <DB NAME> FROM URL = <> WITH CREDENTIALS = <>;

21. What are the new backup related enhancements in SQL Server 2016?

Ans:

Managed Backup Enhancements:

- This feature is introduced in SQL Server 2014
- System databases can be backed up.
- Backup for databases in simple recovery model is possible.
- A backup schedule can be customized based on business requirement rather than log usage.

Backup to Azure – Storage Enhancement:

- SQL Server 2014 supports backup on Page blobs whereas SQL Server 2016 supports backup on block blobs on Windows Azure.
- When we check monthly storage price block blobs are cheaper than page blobs
- Page Blog has limit to 1 TB and block blob limit is 200 GB.
- But we can take a stripe backup maximum up to 64 block blobs which is equal to 12.8 TB.

File – Snapshot Backups on Azure:

- SQL Server 2016 is having a feature File-Snapshot backup for the database files stored on Azure Blob store.
- This will be helpful for SQL Server running on Azure Virtual Machine.
- It throws an error message if we try to perform a File Snapshot backup for the databases which are stored on local drives.

22. Can we perform a tail log backup if .MDF file is corrupted?

Ans:

Yes! We can perform a tail log as long as the LDF if not corrupted and no bulk logged changes.

A typical tail log backup is having two options, 1. WITH NORECOVERY 2.Continue After Error.

WITH NORECOVERY: To make sure no transactions happens after the tail log backup

CONTINUE AFTER ERROR: Just to make sure log backup happens even though some meta data pages corrupted.

23. What are the phases of SQL Server database restore process?

Ans:

- *Copy Data:* Copies all data, log and index pages from backup file to database MDF, NDF and LDF files
- *REDO:* Roll forward all committed transactions to database and if it finds any uncommitted transactions it goes to the final phase UNDO.
- *UNDO:* Rollback any uncommitted transactions and make database available to users.

24. What is the database where we can find the backup and restore information for all databases in that instance?

Ans:

MSDB is the database with the backup and restores system tables. Here are the backup and restore system tables and their purpose:

- backupfile - contains one row for each data file or log file backed up
- backupmediafamily - contains one row for each media family
- backupmediaset - contains one row for each backup media set
- backupset - contains one row for each backup set
- restorefile - contains one row for each restored file
- restorefilegroup - contains one row for each restored FILEGROUP
- restorehistory - contains one row for each restore operation

25. How can full backups be issued without interrupting the LSN's?

Ans:

Issue the BACKUP command with the COPY_ONLY option

26. What is Point in Time recovery?

Ans:

Point in Time Recovery option gives us the ability to restore a database prior to an event that occurred that was detrimental to your database. In order for this option to work, the database needs to be either in the FULL or Bulk-Logged recovery model and you need to be doing transaction log backups.

27. How is a point in time recovery performed?

Ans:

Point-In-Time recovery means we need to recover data till the specific given time. It depends on which backup types are issued. We have a database and we are performing full, differential and transaction log backups. Due to data corruption we need to recover/restore our database till 2:18 PM. We have the latest transaction log file available at 2:30 PM.

- Restore the most recent full backup with the NORECOVERY clause
- Restore the most recent differential backup with the NORECOVERY clause
- Restore all of the subsequent transaction log backups with the NORECOVERY clause except the last transaction log backup
- Restore the last transaction log backup (2:30 PM) with the RECOVERY clause and a STOPAT (2:18 PM) statement.

28. Why don't we just backup SQL Server Database Files (MDF, LDF and NDF) using Windows backup tool instead of SQL Server native backup?

Ans:

- Copying DATA and LOG files may ignore locks and transactions that may be currently in progress, it means that when you attempt to attach that database later you will have a database file that is in an inconsistent state. It will generate errors.

- Also transactional backups may not be easy with windows backup
- Point in time recovery is also a challenge

29. While upgrading SQL Server which one you choose Detach/Attach or Backup/Restore? Why?

Ans:

I would always recommend Backup and Restore

Time Consuming: MDF/LDF files are huge when compared to backup files as these data files contains space for unallocated pages as well.

Database should be in offline: For a premium databases it's not possible to take database offline for a longer time. But for moving MDF/LDF files the source database should be in offline during the copy progress.

Inconsistency: We may not be 100% sure that MDF and LDF files are consistent all the time

Failures: Instead of Copy if Move happens and attach failed then we may lose database

Absolutely No for VLDB: It never been an option for large databases

30. What are the restore options available?

Ans:

When you restore a backup, you can choose from 3 restore option,

- *With Recovery:* Database is ready to use, and user can connect to database, user can change data inside database.
- *No Recovery:* Database is not ready; there are few more backups that have to be applied to this database instance. User cannot connect to database because it is in Restoring Status. (Exception: Not considering Database Snapshots)
- *Standby/Read Only:* Database is ready to use but database is in Read-Only mode, user can connect to database but they cannot change data inside database. A running database con not be changed to standby mode. Only a data in no-recovery state can be moved to standby mode. This is an option that is specified while restoring a database or transaction log.

31. What are Marked Transactions?

Ans:

SQL Server supports inserting named marks into the transaction log to allow recovery to that specific mark. Log marks are transaction specific and are inserted only if their associated transaction commits. As a result, marks can be tied to specific work, and you can recover to a point that includes or excludes this work.

32. What is RESTORE FILELISTONLY option?

Ans:

This SQL returns a result set containing a list of the database and log files contained in the backup set in SQL Server.

```
RESTORE FILELISTONLY FROM AdventureWorksBackups WITH FILE=1;
GO
```

33. What is RESTORE LABELONLY option?

Ans:

It returns a result set containing information about the backup media identified by the given backup device.

```
RESTORE LABELONLY FROM DISK='C:\Backup\Adv_Full.bak'
MediaName   NULL
MediaSetId   23979995-927B-4FEB-9B5E-8CF18356AB39
FamilyCount 1
FamilySequenceNumber    1
MediaFamilyId       86C7DF2E-0000-0000-0000-000000000000
MediaSequenceNumber     1
MediaLabelPresent   0
MediaDescription    NULL
SoftwareName        Microsoft SQL Server
SoftwareVendorId    4608
MediaDate   1/3/16 8:15 PM
MirrorCount 1
```

34. What is piecemeal Restore?

Ans:

A piecemeal restore sequence restores and recovers a database in stages at the file group level, beginning with the primary and all read-write, secondary file groups. Piecemeal restore process allows us to restore the primary file group first and the database can be online and the remaining file groups can be restored while the recovery the transactions are running on primary. Mostly suitable for data warehousing databases.

Consider we have a database of 3 TB whereas on primary file group is a read write FILEGROUP of size 500 GB and we have other files groups which are read-only of size 2.5 TB. We actually need not perform backup for read-only file groups, here we can perform partial backups.

Piecemeal restore process allows us to restore the primary FILEGROUP first and the database can be online and the remaining FILEGROUPS can be restored while the recovery the transactions are running on primary File group. Mostly suitable for data warehousing databases.

35. What are your recommendations to design a backup and recovery solution? Simply what is Backup Check list?

Ans:

Before designing the database backup strategy first we need to analyze the business requirements, Service Level Agreement.

- Determine What is Needed
- Recovery Model
- Select Backup Types
- Backup Schedule
- Backup Process
- Document
- Backup to Disk
- Archive to Tape
- Backup to Different Drives
- Secure Backup Files
- Encrypt or Password Protect Backup Files
- Compress Backup Files
- How Much to Keep on Disk
- Online Backups
- Run Restore Verify only
- Offsite Storage

36. What are all of the backup\Restore options and their associated value?

Ans:

Backup Options:

- Full – Online operation to backup all objects and data in a single database
- Differential – Backup all extents with data changes since the last full backup
- Transaction log – Backup all transaction in the database transaction log since the last transaction log backup
- File – Backup of a single file to be included with the backup when a full backup is not possible due to the overall database size
- File group – Backup of a single file group to be included with the backup when a full backup is not possible due to the overall database size
- Cold backup – Offline file system backup of the databases
- Partial Backup – When we want to perform read-write FILEGROUPS and want to exclude read-only FILEGROUPS from backup. It will be useful for huge databases (Data warehousing)
- Third party tools – A variety of third party tools are available to perform the operations above in addition to enterprise management, advanced features, etc.

Restore Options:

- ➢ Restore an entire database from a full database backup (a complete restore).
- ➢ Restore part of a database (a partial restore).
- ➢ Restore specific files or FILEGROUPS to a database (file restore).
- ➢ Restore specific pages to a database (page restore).
- ➢ Restore a transaction log onto a database (transaction log restore).
- ➢ Revert a database to the point in time

37. Have you ever performed the backup using T-SQL? Can you explain about different backup options?

Ans:

BACKUP [DATABASE/LOG] <File/FILEGROUP>

TO <Backup Device>

MIRROR TO <Backup performed to different locations>

MIRROR TO <>

MIRROR TO < Only 3 mirrors can be specified >

WITH <Options>

Below are the General WITH options

- ➢ Backup Set Options
  - ✓ COPY_ONLY – Full backup on full recovery mode DB with no chain breaking
  - ✓ COMPRESSION | NO_COMPRESSION – DB compression
  - ✓ DESCRIPTION
  - ✓ NAME
  - ✓ PASSWORD – Can assign a pwd, same password required to restore it
  - ✓ EXPIREDATE – Expires after the given date
  - ✓ RETAINDAYS – number of days that must elapse before this backup media set can be overwritten
- ➢ Media Set Options
  - ✓ NOINIT | INIT – Overwrite | Append
  - ✓ NOSKIP | SKIP – Check Backupset expiration before overwritten | No checks
  - ✓ NOFORMAT | FORMAT -
  - ✓ MEDIADESCRIPTION
  - ✓ MEDIANAME
  - ✓ MEDIAPASSWORD
  - ✓ BLOCKSIZE

- Data Transfer Options
    - ✓ BUFFERCOUNT
    - ✓ MAXTRANSFERSIZE
- Error Management Options
    - ✓ NO_CHECKSUM | CHECKSUM
    - ✓ STOP_ON_ERROR | CONTINUE_AFTER_ERROR - Instructs BACKUP to fail if a page checksum does not verify | Continue after error
- Compatibility Options
    - ✓ RESTART
- Monitoring Options
    - ✓ STATS - Shows Percentage completed
- Tape Options
    - ✓ REWIND | NOREWIND
    - ✓ UNLOAD | NOUNLOAD
- Log-specific Options
    - ✓ NORECOVERY – Performs tail log and leave DB in restoring mode
    - ✓ STANDBY – Performs a backup and leave DB in read only mode
    - ✓ NO_TRUNCATE – Specifies that the log not be truncated and causes the Database Engine to attempt the backup regardless of the state of the database

Scenario Based

38. Is it possible to restore a Database backup of SQL Server 2012 to SQL Server 2008/2008 R2?

Ans:

No it's not possible to restore the upper version database backup to lower version.

39. You are leading a DBA team and one of your team members came to you and reported that he has executed an UPDATE command without WHERE CLAUSE on production database. Now that entire table has got updated with the wrong data. How do you handle the situation?

Ans:

That's really an embarrassing situation. I actually faced it earlier in my previous role. The command has been provided by release team and one of our DBA has executed but he immediately identified the problem and reported us. The solution that worked out:

- Made database to single user mode
- Identified the "Transaction ID" and "Begin Time" by reading log file using sys.fn_dblog()
- Performed a log backup

- Created a dummy database on the same instance and restored it with this database latest full backup
- Restored the latest differential backup followed by all transaction log backups except the last one that we have taken.
- Restored the latest transactional backup that we performed in step 3 with point in time recovery. Time we have given as just before the transaction begin time that we identified in step 2
- i.e.: Transaction Begin Time: "2016-07-26 15:26:39" then recover data till "2016-07-26 15:26:38"
- We got our original table in dummy database
- Applied an update statement by joining the same table between original database and the dummy database where we have the correct data and do the required changes.
- Made the original database to multi user mode
- Dropped the dummy database

40. For the accidental situations like "DELETE WITHOUT WHERE," "UPDATE WITHOUT WHERE" or "DROPPING A TABLE" can't we have any other options except restoring full/diff/log file?

Ans:

I don't think we have a native support tool/method to roll back the committed operations. But there are few third party tools which can be really helpful in these situations.

- ApexSQL: ApexSQL Log
- Redgate: SQL Log Rescue

41. What are the issues you faced in backup and restore process?

Ans:

Error 3201 - when performing a backup to a network share:

Where SQL Server disk access is concerned, everything depends on the rights of the SQL Server service STARTUP account. If you are unable to back up to a network share, check that the service STARTUP account has write rights to that share.

Operation System Error/Can't open the backup device:

Either the specified location is missing or the service account under which the SQL Agent is running does not have the permissions on that folder.

Too many backup devices specified for backup or restore:

The most common cause for this error is because you are trying to restore higher version backup on previous version. Ex: 2014 backup on 2012.

An earlier transaction log backup is required:

There are one or more transaction log backups that need to be restored before the current transaction log backup. Using LSN number we can identify the prior log backups.

42. I have my PROD SQL Server all system databases are located on E drive and I need my resource database on H drive how can you move it?

Ans:

No! Only RESOURCEDB cannot be moved, Resource DB location is always depends on Master database location; if u want to move resource DB you should also move master db.

43. I'm trying to restore 85 GB database backup taken from SQL Server 2008 R2 machine to a SQL Server 2012 machine in the Amazon EC2 cloud, using a .bak file and the SQL Management Studio. SQL Management Studio reports the restore reaches 100% complete, and then just hangs indefinitely (8+ hours) using a lot of CPU, until I restart the SQL Server service. Upon restart, SQL again uses a lot of CPU activity for what seems to be an indefinite amount of time, but the DB never comes online?

Ans:

The database is in the process of being upgraded from SQL 2008 R2 to SQL 2012 when you kill it. Check the ERRORLOG in SQL Server and you should see that the database restore is complete and that the database is being upgraded.

This process is normally very quick, but it can take a while to perform depending on the database, especially if you have a lot of pending transactions in the database which must be rolled forward or backward before the database can be upgraded.

44. Let's say we have a situation. We are restoring a database from a full backup. The restore operation ran for 2 hours and failed with an error 9002 (Insufficient LOGSPACE). And the database went to suspect mode. How do you troubleshoot this issue?

Ans:

In that case we can actually add a new log file on other drive and rerun the restore operation using the system stored procedure "**sp_add_log_file_recover_suspect_db.**" Parameters are the same as while creating a new log file.

45. Let's say we have a situation. We are restoring a database from a full backup. The restores operation runs for 2 hours and failed with an error 1105 (Insufficient space on the file group). And the database went to suspect mode. How do you troubleshoot this issue?

Ans:

In that case we can actually add a new data file on another drive and rerun the restore operation using the system stored procedure "**sp_add_data_file_recover_suspect_db.**" Parameters are the same as while creating a new data file.

46. Have you ever encounter the issue "media family on device is incorrectly formed"? If yes what is the reason and how you resolved it?

Ans:

Yes! I have seen this error "The media family on device is incorrectly formed. SQL Server cannot process this media family" lot many times. There are few common cases that raise this error:

- Trying to restore backup from higher version to lower version; Ex: Backup taken from 2014 and trying to restore to 2008 R2.
- Trying to restore a backup using SSMS or T-SQL in a native method when the backup is taken using a third party tool Ex: Litespeed
- Trying to restore a backup file where the backup copy is still in progress.
- Backup file might be corrupted.

Note: When backup is corrupted the error looks like "The file on device '' is not a valid Microsoft Tape Format backup set."

47. See I have an environment, Sunday night full backup, everyday night diff backup and every 45 min a transactional backup. Disaster happened at 2:30 PM on Saturday. You suddenly found that the last Sunday backup has been corrupted. What's your recovery plan?

Ans:

When you find that the last full backup is corrupted or otherwise un-restorable, making all differentials after that point useless. You then need to go back a further week to the previous full backup (taken 13 days ago), and restore that, plus the differential from 8 days ago, and the subsequent 8 days of transaction logs (assuming none of those ended up corrupted!).

If you're taking daily full backups, a corrupted full backup only introduce an additional 24 hours of logs to restore.

Alternatively, a log shipped copy of the database could save your bacon (you have a warm standby, and you know the log backups are definitely good).

48. One of our database full backup size 300 GB, usually my differential backup size varies between 300 MB and 5 GB, one day we were surprised to see the differential backup size was increased to 250 GB? What might be the reason any idea?

Ans:

Your differential backups can easily be nearly as large as your full backup. That means you're taking up nearly twice the space just to store the backups, and even worse, you're talking about twice the time to restore the database.

To avoid these issues with diff backups, ideally schedule the index maintenance to happen right before the full backup.

49. Consider a situation where publisher database log file has been increasing and there is just few MB available on disk. As an experienced professional how do you react to this situation? Remember no disk space available and also we can't create a new log file on other drive

Ans:

Essentially we have to identify the bottleneck which is filling the log file.

As a quick resolution check all possible solutions as below:

- Resolve if there are any errors in log reader agent/distribution agent
- Fix if there are any connectivity issues either between publisher - distributor or distributor
- Fix if there are any issues with I/O at any level
- Check if there is any huge number of transactions pending from publisher
- Check if there are any large number of VLF's (USE DBCC Loginfo) which slows the logreader agent work.
- Check all database statistics are up-to-date at distributer. Usually we do switch off this "Auto Update Stats" by default.
- To find and resolve these issues we can use "Replication Monitor," "DBCC Commands," "SQL Profiler," "System Tables/SP/Function."

If in-case we can't resolve just by providing a simple solution we have to shrink the transaction log file. Below are two methods.

To shrink the transaction log file:

- Backup the log – So transactions in VLF's are marked as inactive
- Shrink the logfile using DBCC SHRINKFILE – Inactive VLF's would be removed
- If you find no difference in size repeat the above steps 1 and 2

To truncate the transaction log file:

In any case we are not able to provide the solution against the increasing logfile the final solution is disable the replication, truncate the log and reinitialize the subscribers.

- Disable replication jobs
- Execute SP_ReplDone procedure. It disable the replication and mark as "Replicate done" for all pending transactions at publisher.
- Backup the transaction log
- Shrink the log file using "DBCC SHRINKFILE"
- Flush the article cache using "sp_replflush."
- Go to distributor database and truncate the table MSRepl_Commands
- Connect to replication monitor and reinitialize all subscriptions by generating a new snapshot.
- Enable all replication related jobs.

50. We have a table which is 1.2 GB in size, we need to write a SP which should work with a particular point of time data?

Ans:

You may need to add insert timestamps and update timestamps for each record. Every time a new record is inserted, stamp it with the DATETIME, and also stamp it with the date time when updated. Also possibly use partitioning to reduce index rebuilds.

51. Consider a scenario where you issue a full backup. Then issue some transaction log backups, next a differential backup, followed by more transaction log backups, then another differential and finally some transaction log backups. If the SQL Server crashes and if all the differential backups are bad, when is the latest point in time you can successfully restore the database? Can you recover the database to the current point in time without using any of the differential backups?

Ans:

You can recover to the current point in time, as long as you have all the transaction log backups available and they are all valid. Differential backups do not affect the transaction log backup chain.

52. How much time taken to take full backup of 500 GB database by using third party tool LITESPEED and without using third-party tool and also how much time taken to restore same full backup using LITESPEED and without third-party tool

Ans:

There is no specific time we can say for BACKUP & RESTORE operation.

It depends on lot of factors like Disk I/O, Network, processors etc.

SQL Server 2012:

- Database Size: **1.2 TB**
  - ✓ Time taken to Backup with Litespeed: **3:20 Hrs (80 % of compression)**
  - ✓ Time Taken to Restore: **6Hrs**
- Database Size: **800 GB**
  - ✓ Time Taken to Backup using Native Method: 11 Hrs
  - ✓ I never tried restoring huge DB in native method mean native backups. But we can do it after 2008 R2 as compression working absolutely fine and when Instant File Initialization is enabled.

SQL Server 2008:

- A Database of 20 GB will take 14 Min to Backup and 22 Min to Restore the Backup

53. Consider a situation where I have to take a backup of one database of 60 GB. My hard drive lacked sufficient space at that moment. I don't find 64GB free on any drive. Fortunately, I have 3 different drives where I can hold 20 GB on each drive. How can you perform the backup to three different drives? How can you restore those files? Is this really possible?

Ans:

Yes it is possible. We can split the backup files into different places and the same can be restored.

- BACKUP DATABASE AdventureWorks
  TO DISK = 'D:\Backup\MultiFile\AdventureWorks1.bak',
  DISK = 'E:\Backup\MultiFile\AdventureWorks2.bak',
  DISK = 'F:\Backup\MultiFile\AdventureWorks3.bak'

- RESTORE DATABASE [AdventureWorks]
  FROM DISK = N'D:\Backup\MultiFile\AdventureWorks1.bak',
  DISK = N'E:\Backup\MultiFile\AdventureWorks2.bak',
  DISK = N'F:\Backup\MultiFile\AdventureWorks3.bak'

54. We have been using SQL Server 2014 and we need to rebuild the system databases due to a corruption in master database. Do we need to get the installation DVD or Media to rebuild system databases?

Ans:

No! Not required. SQL Server can get these original files from a cache location called "Template" folder. These (System Databases) are cached into this folder at the time of installation.

55. Have you ever worked with the Template folder in SQL Server? If yes, can you explain about it?

Ans:

- In earlier version of SQL Server (2000 and 2005) if there is a need to rebuild system databases we need to get the installation media DVD or network share.
- From SQL Server 2008 onwards, we don't need get the installation file DVD or media to rebuild system databases.
- During installation of SQL, setup does the caching of setup.exe (and other files needed for setup) and also the MDF and LDF file in Template folder.
- In this directory you will find master, model, and MSDB database and log files that were copied from your installation source as part of setup.
- SQL Server 2014 Setup.exe location: C:\Program Files\Microsoft SQL Server\120\Setup Bootstrap\SQLServer2014
- SQL Server 2014 Template Folder location: C:\Program Files\Microsoft SQL Server\MSSQL12.SQL2014\MSSQL\Binn\Templates
- Path may be different for SQL Server 2012/2008 R2/2008.

56. Ok, so my instance system databases MDF and LDF files are initially cached to Template folder. My question is when we see any corruption in master database and we need to rebuild the system databases, can we directly copy and use these MDF and LDF files from Template location instead of running REBUILD?

Ans:

- No! We are not supposed to directly copy files from Template location to DATA and LOG folders.
- If we manually copy these files and tries to restart SQL Server it might fail with the errors as it cannot identify the location for MDF and LDF files for other system databases. Reason is simple Master database is a copy of initial DB when it got installed. It contains the default path for MSDB and MODEL database file locations. But in reality we usually don't keep system databases on C drive.

- If we rebuild the system databases, setup would move the files from Template location to the proper location and it modifies the path of other databases which is stored in master database.

57. We have a database with size 800 GB. We are taking full backup on daily basis which was taking 3 to 4 hours of time. You are asked to suggest a proposal for speeding the backup process. What are the various ways you suggest to speed up the backup process?

Ans:

Full and Differential: Why we are taking full backup on daily basis? We can plan for a weekly full backup and daily differential backup and also transactional backup based on SLA for data loss acceptance. Differential backup doesn't take much time when compare to full backup. Make sure the latest differential backup is in safe place as it requires to restore database with the least data loss.

File/File Group backup: Categorize the tables into "Master," "Lookup" and "Transactional" and keep these files into different file groups. Perform backup only on tables where data changes on daily basis. This is one way but we should need to do a lot of research before applying this method. This is really useful when databases are very huge.

Backup database to Multiple Files: If your business is demanding a full backup on daily basis then you can choose this method. Split backup into 3 or 4 files on different drives. Let's say I have a database with 1 TB in size and it is taking 4 hours to perform a full backup, if we split this backup into 4 files on 4 different disks then the full backup time comes to 1 hr. Logic is we have 4 files writing on 4 different physical drives, each drive have a separate thread and all these threads executes in parallel. Remember when we do split backup make sure all these files are available for a successful restore.

Backup during off hours/less traffic: This is one of the best practices in scheduling backup.

Backup to local disk and then archive: Avoid using a network path in backup and make it as three tire architecture. 1. Perform backup to local disk 2. Schedule a job to copy/move from local to network 3. Then you can continue moving to tape.

Backup Compression: This is one technique mostly used when there is a space issue. But sometimes compression can reduce backup time when we have lot of CPU cycles are free and having enough IO bandwidth.

CHAPTER 5

SQL SERVER LOG SHIPPING

Interview Questions and Answers

Introduction: This chapter takes you through the SQL Server Log Shipping related interview questions and answers. These questions are helpful for range of database administrators staring from a junior to an expert level DBA while preparing for a technical interview. These questions and answers are deals with the below topics:

- SQL Server Log shipping
- Log shipping Scenarios

SQL Server Log Shipping

1. What is log shipping?

Ans:

Log shipping provides a way of keeping in step databases that reside on different servers, or on different instances on the same server. It achieves this by automating the process of backing up data from a primary database on one server or instance and restoring the data to one or more secondary databases on another server or instance. You can then use the secondary server as a 'standby' for when your primary server is unavailable.

- Transaction log backups are performed on the database on the primary server (for example the production database).
- The backup files are copied to a shared folder that can be accessed by both servers.
- The backup files are restored to the secondary database on the standby server.

2. When to use log shipping?

Ans:

You can use log shipping when you want to maintain a standby server but you do not require automatic failover. Replication is another alternative for maintaining a standby server without automatic failover. Alternatively, you could use a failover clustering solution. This has the advantage of providing automatic failover. However, it is more difficult than log shipping to set up, requires more expensive licenses, and has other limitations such as on the locations of the servers. Database mirroring provides another alternative, but it does not support multiple standby databases, but yes ALWAYSON fulfills all requirements but again it's an expensive feature.

3. What are the advantages of using Log Shipping?

Ans:

- Log shipping doesn't require expensive hardware or software. While it is great if your standby server is similar in capacity to your production server, it is not a requirement. In addition, you can use the standby server for other tasks
- Once log shipping has been implemented, it is relatively easy to maintain.
- Assuming you have implemented log shipping correctly, it is very reliable.
- The manual failover process is generally very short, typically 15 minutes or less (Conditions Applied ☺)
- Implementing log shipping is not technically difficult. Almost any DBA with several months can successfully implement it.

4. Why you do not suggest Log Shipping for critical databases?

Ans:

Let's face it, log shipping is a compromise. It is not the ideal solution, but it is often a practical solution given real-world budget constraints. Some of the problems with log shipping include:

- Log shipping failover is not automatic. The DBA must still manually failover the server, which means the DBA must be present when the failover occurs.
- The users will experience some downtime. How long depends on how well you implemented log shipping, the nature of the production server failure, your network, the standby server, and the application or applications to be failed over.
- Some data can be lost, although not always. How much data is lost depends on how often you schedule log shipping and whether or not the transaction log on the failed production server is recoverable.
- When it comes time for the actual failover, you must do one of two things to make your applications work: either rename the standby server the same name as the failed production server (and the IP address), or re-point your user's applications to the new standby server. In some cases, neither of these options is practical.

5. What are the prerequisites for implementing Log Shipping?

Ans:

To perform log shipping using the SQL Backup Log Shipping wizard:

- You must have at least two SQL Server database engine servers or two database engine instances in your log shipping implementation.
- The database must use the full or bulk-logged recovery model.
- You must have a shared folder to copy the transaction log backups to.
- The SQL Server Agent service account of the primary server must have read/write access either to the shared folder or to the local NTFS folder. The SQL Server Agent account of the standby server must have read and delete access to the shared folder.
- The SQL Server Agent services must be running and configured with network credentials (such as a domain account) if you plan to use a network share as the shared folder.

6. What are the permissions required for configuring log shipping?

Ans:

- Access to the shared folder
- Usual SQL Server backup permissions
- Execute permissions on the SQL Backup extended stored procedure sqlbackup (for example, must be a member of the public database role in the master database)
- The user configuring the log shipping process must have SYSADMIN access to the participating servers.

7. What are the various log shipping modes available?

Ans:

The log shipping mode you select determines which operational requirement you want to use the technology for.

- *No Recovery:* If you want to use the log shipping configuration only for the standby server, choose Non-operational (No Recovery Mode); the standby database will not be available for users to query.
- *Stand By:* To allow users read-only access to the standby database, choose Read only (Standby Mode); this means you can distribute queries across the standby server to reduce the primary server's workload (but you cannot modify the data in the standby database).

8. Can you be able to technically explain the log shipping process?

Ans:

- When log shipping is running, the SQL Server Agent backup job periodically makes a backup of the transaction logs on the primary server. Each backup file is given a unique name.
- The transaction log backup files are then copied to the shared folder.
- The SQL Server Agent restore job periodically restores the completed transaction log backups on the shared folder to the standby server.
- SQL Server database engine identifies backup groups or split backups, arranges the files in sequence, and then restores each backup group sequentially.
- The transaction log backups that have been restored are then moved from the shared folder to a location that you specify for processed backups when you configure the log shipping so that they are not picked up when the restore job is next run.

9. Can you explain the fail over procedure in log shipping?

Ans:

If you need to switch from the primary database to a standby database, you must bring the standby database online manually; there is no automatic failover with the log shipping configuration.

The standby server will be inaccessible or read-only (depending upon whether you chose No Recovery Mode or Standby Mode). To make the standby database available for reading and writing, the log shipping needs to be broken and the database brought online WITH RECOVERY:

- If possible, run the SQL Server Agent backup job on the primary server to perform a final log backup on the source database. If the source database is damaged, a final log backup may fail. In this case, append NO TRUNCATE to the BACKUP LOG command in the SQL Server Agent backup job, and try running the job again.
- If there are transaction log backup files remaining in the log shipping shared folder, use SQL Backup to restore the backups to the standby database, specifying the option WITH RECOVERY when you restore the final backup. If there are no transaction log backup files remaining, recover the standby database using the native SQL Server RESTORE statement,

10. Have you ever observed the location of log shipping related SQL Agent jobs?

Ans:

- Tran log backup job lives on the Primary Server
- Tran log copy job lives on the Secondary
- Tran log restore job lives on the Secondary
- The Backup Alert job lives on the Monitor
- The Restore Alert job lives on the Monitor
- The Log Shipping Monitor lives on the Monitor

Verify each job runs without failure before sending notification to the customer.

11. Any idea what are the log shipping related system tables available?

Ans:

Primary:

log_shipping_monitor_alert: Stores alert job ID. This table is only used on the primary server if a remote monitor server has not been configured.

log_shipping_monitor_error_detail: Stores error detail for log shipping jobs associated with this primary server.

log_shipping_monitor_history_detail: Stores history detail for log shipping jobs associated with this primary server.

log_shipping_monitor_primary: Stores one monitor record for this primary database.

log_shipping_primary_databases: Contains configuration information for primary databases on a given server. It stores one row per primary database.

log_shipping_primary_SECONDARIES: Maps primary databases to secondary databases.

Secondary:

log_shipping_monitor_alert: Stores alert job ID. This table is only used on the secondary server if a remote monitor server has not been configured.

log_shipping_monitor_error_detail: Stores error detail for log shipping jobs associated with this secondary server.

log_shipping_monitor_history_detail: Stores history detail for log shipping jobs associated with this secondary server.

log_shipping_monitor_secondary: Stores one monitor record per secondary database associated with this secondary server.

log_shipping_secondary: Contains configuration information for the secondary databases on a given server. It stores one row per secondary ID.

log_shipping_secondary_databases: Stores configuration information for a given secondary database. It stores one row per secondary database.

Monitor:

log_shipping_monitor_alert: Stores alert job ID.

log_shipping_monitor_error_detail: Stores error detail for log shipping jobs.

log_shipping_monitor_history_detail: Stores history detail for log shipping jobs.

log_shipping_monitor_primary: Stores one monitor record per primary database associated with this monitor server.

log_shipping_monitor_secondary: Stores one monitor record per secondary database associated with this monitor server.

12. From your experience what are the most common reasons that causes log shipping failures?

Ans:

There might be several reasons but from my experience below are the most common reasons that causes log shipping failure.

- Space issue
- Blocking at secondary server
- Service account password changed/expired – not updated
- LSN mismatch
- Networking issues between primary and secondary
- False alerts due to disconnect between primary/secondary and monitor servers.
- New file created at primary database
- SQL Server Agent service account doesn't have proper rights on log backup folder
- Restore will fail if there is a snapshot or an active DBCC replica on the secondary database
- Orphaned Users problems: Because of different SID's between primary and secondary servers
- SQL Server Agent restarts either at Primary or Secondary may causes the LSN missing issue
- Wrong values given for "Out of Sync Alert" and "Backup Alert" thresholds.
- Huge log backups might leads to delaying the restore operation which leads to behind the time interval for restore operations

13. You found there is an issue with log shipping. What are all the things that we need to check for while troubleshooting?

Ans:

- Look through the Log Shipping Monitor for errors indicating where the failure is occurring.
- Review the log_shipping_monitor_history_detail table. This can give you a great deal of detail on what failed when and with what message.
- Go through and verify when the last successful backed-up files were copied and loaded without error.
- Verify service account password has not expired.
- Verify no users are blocking the secondary databases. Any users in the Secondary databases will block log shipping causing it to start falling behind. Kill the users in the database and monitor to see if log shipping catches up.
- Verify that none of the Disks are full or low on space.
- Verify that the servers have full contact with each other.
- Verify that there is no LSN mismatch.
- Verify if any DBCC command or a snapshot is blocking the restore operation at standby server.
- If there was a backup failure, the restore job will fail. If there is a Copy job failure, than the restore job will fail. Therefore, if you see a Restore failure verify that it is not due to a Backup or Copy failure before spending too much time on it.
- Throughout the process SQL Server job history, error log and log shipping reports from SSMS can help us in identifying the problem.
- Verify server names are registered correctly using select @@servername
- Check Date& Time on primary and secondary servers
- Check and make sure the correct values are given for these parameters "Out of Sync Alert threshold," "Backup Alert threshold"
- Check if index maintenance is happening on primary server. In most of the cases this will delay the restore operations as it generates huge log backups

14. What is WRK file in log shipping?

Ans:

".wrk" file is a temporary extension generated during the copy process and once copy completed the same file extension will be renamed to the transaction log backup (.trn) file.

The .wrk file got generate when the transaction log backups files are being copied from the backup location (Usually at Primary Server) to the secondary server by the agent job named as LS-Copy on the secondary, and when file copied completely at secondary server, they renamed to the .trn extension.

15. Why this .wrk extension required? Are there any specific usage/reason behind that?

Ans:

Yes! The temporary naming using the .wrk extension indicates/ensure that the files will not picked up by the restore job until successfully copied.

16. What is TUF file in log shipping?

Ans:

The .TUF file is the Transaction Undo File. It got generated when we configure the Log Shipping with Stand by Option. In Stand by Log Shipping option, Secondary Database is available to user in read mode. In this scenario .TUF file Keeps Pending Transaction Which are in Log File came from Primary server, and when next Log Backup will come from primary server they can be synchronized at Secondary Server.

This file contains information on all the modifications performed at the time backup is taken. The file plays vital role in Standby mode. While restoring the log backup all committed transactions are written to disk and all uncommitted transactions are recorded to the undo file. When restoring next transaction log backup SQL Server will fetch all the uncommitted transactions from undo file and check with the new transaction log backup whether committed or not. If found to be committed the transactions will be written to disk else it will be stored in undo file until it gets committed or rollback.

Log Shipping Scenarios

17. I have installed SQL Server 2012 Express edition. Is it possible to configure log shipping?

Ans:

No! Log shipping works in Enterprise, Standard, Developer, Web editions. It applies to SQL Server 2005, 2008 R2, 2012, 2014 and 2016. Note: There are other editions where Log shipping works but these are the common editions on all versions. But it doesn't work in express edition.

18. What are the most common error messages and what are the solutions worked out in your case?

Ans:

"Exclusive access could not be obtained because the database is in use"

Reason:

Secondary server restore job is failing as the database is in use

Solution: There are two solutions and one is temporary solution.

- In log shipping configuration à Secondary Database Settings à Check the box "Disconnect Users in the database while restoring backups"
- Temporary solution: Remove all connections from the database and run the restore job

"The log in this backup set begins at LSN #######, which is too recent to apply to the database"

Reason:

If we try to skip any of the log backups, then above error would be encountered. To find our missing backup, we can use MSDB backup history tables or ERRORLOG file. Both of them contain information about backup type, location etc.

Solution:

Identify the missing backup file and restore it to the secondary server manually and from the next cycle restore job will continue restoring the next log file automatically.

"Directory lookup for the file <location> failed with the operating system error 2(The system cannot find the file specified.)"

Reason:

The above error is part of the error received during restore of the transaction log backup. The error is caused when a new file is added to the primary database and the path of new file doesn't exist on a secondary server

Solution:

- Create the same path (As primary) on the secondary server where the restore is failing
- If it's not possible to recreate the path on secondary, then we need to restore the failing log backup manually using "WITH MOVE" option and move the new file to a valid location on the secondary server.

19. I have configured log shipping for my database in standby mode as our business required the secondary should be available for reporting users. Now can you tell me what the major challenge that we need to face is?

Ans:

Here the major thing is managing user access on secondary/standby database. Our standby is a read-only database and we can't directly create a user on that database. We can create a user in primary and the same user can be log shipped to secondary. But usually business policies don't allow reporting users to OLTP database.

20. Then how can we deal these users/logins problems in-case of standby server scenario in log shipping?

Ans:

Windows Authentications:

- On Primary Server create a Windows Login and map to a database user and monitor to make sure the database user copied to secondary database.
- On secondary once you confirmed that the database user is copied from primary to secondary database, create a windows login and map it with the copied user.
- On Primary drop the windows login created in first step (Only Login)

SQL Server Authentication:

- On Primary create a SQL login and map it with the required database user. Monitor to make sure the user is copied to secondary database.

- On Primary collect the SID from sys.database_principals for the created login
- On secondary create the same login by giving the SID collected from production thereof the login created with the same SID. When SID matches the database user automatically mapped to this login.
- On Primary disable the login we created on first step.

21. How to perform tail log backup on primary server in case of failover?

Ans:

If the primary database is online:

BACKUP LOG database_name TO <backup_device> WITH NORECOVERY

NORECOVERY takes the database into the restoring state. This guarantees that the database does not change after the tail-log backup.

If the primary database is damaged:

BACKUP LOG database_name TO <backup_device> WITH CONTINUE_AFTER_ERROR

It only works when log files are not damaged

22. Is it possible to log ship database between SQL 2000 & SQL 2008/2012?

Ans:

No, that's impossible, transaction log architecture is totally changed from SQL 2000 to 2008 and hence we won't be able to restore transaction log backups from SQL 2000 to SQL 2008/2012.

23. I'm getting the below error message in restoration job on secondary server, WHY?

[Microsoft SQL-DMO (ODBC SQLState: 42000)] Error 4305: [Microsoft][ODBC SQL Server Driver][SQL Server]The log in this backup set begins at LSN 9000000026200003, which is too late to apply to the database. An earlier log backup that includes LSN 8000000015100003 can be restored. [Microsoft][ODBC SQL Server Driver][SQL Server] RESTORE LOG is terminating abnormally.

Ans:

Does your SQL Server or agent restarted recently in either source or destination? Because the error states there is a mismatch in LSN. A particular transaction log was not applied in the destination as a result the subsequent transaction logs cannot be applied.

You can check log shipping monitor\log shipping tables to check the which transaction log is last applied to secondary DB, if the next consecutive transaction logs are available in the secondary server share folder you can manually restore those logs with NORECOVERY option. Once all available logs restored the log shipping jobs will work fine from the next cycle.

Incase if you are not able to find the next transaction log in secondary server shared folder, you need to reconfigure log shipping. Try the below tasks to re-establish log shipping again.

- Disable all the log shipping jobs in source and destination servers

- Take a full backup in source and restore it in secondary server using the With Standby option
- Enable all the jobs you disabled previously in step1

24. Is it possible load balance in log shipping?

Ans:

Yes of course it is possible in log shipping with conditions applied, while configuring log shipping you have the option to choose standby or no recovery mode there you select STANDBY option to make the secondary database read-only. On standby server the connection will be force closed whenever the log needs to be applied.

25. Can I take full backup of the log shipped database in primary server?

Ans:

Yes! We can take a full backup on primary server using Copy Only option. If we perform a direct full backup it breaks the log chain and effect the log shipping

26. Can I shrink log shipped database log file?

Ans:

Yes! You can shrink the log file, but we are not supposed to use WITH TRUNCATE option as it breaks the log shipping.

27. Can I take full backup of the log shipped database in secondary server?

Ans:

No! We can't run backup command against a log shipped database in secondary server.

28. I've configured Log shipping successfully on standby mode, but in the restoration job I'm getting the below error. What I do to avoid this in future?

Message:

2015-07-31 09:40:54.33 *** Error: Could not apply log backup file 'C:\Program Files\Microsoft SQL Server\MSSQL.1\MSSQL\Backup\LogShip

\TEST_20150731131501.trn' to the secondary database 'TEST'.(Microsoft.

SqlServer.Management.LogShipping) ***2015-07-31 09:40:54.33 *** Error: Exclusive access could not be obtained because the database is in use. RESTORE LOG is terminating abnormally.(.Net SqlClient Data Provider) ***

Ans:

To restore transaction logs to the secondary DB, SQL Server needs exclusive access on the database. When you configure it in standby mode, users will be able to access the database and runs query against the secondary db. Hence if the scheduled restore jobs runs at that time, the DB will have a lock and it won't allow SQL Server to restore the transaction log. If you see these errors kill active users from the standby server and run the restore job.

To prevent these errors we need to check "Disconnect users in the database when restoring backups" options in log shipping configuration wizard.

29. We are getting below error on log shipping configured database, how can I rectify this?

Ans:

[Microsoft SQL-DMO (ODBC SQLState: 42000)] Error 4323: [Microsoft][ODBC SQL Server Driver][SQL Server]The database is marked suspect. Transaction logs cannot be restored. Use RESTORE DATABASE to recover the database. [Microsoft][ODBC SQL Server Driver][SQL Server]RESTORE LOG is terminating abnormally

Ans:

We had the same issue some time ago this was related to a new file being created in a file group on the source. Restoring a backup of this new file on the secondary server solved the problem.

30. Is it possible to log ship database from SQL Server 2008 to SQL Server 2012 and vice versa?

Ans:

Yes you can log ship database from SQL Server 2008 to SQL Server 2012 this will work. However log shipping from SQL Server 2012 to SQL Server 2008 is not possible because you won't be able to restore SQL Server 2012 backup to SQL Server 2008 (downgrading version)

31. Truncate is a non-logged operation right? If I issues TRUNCATE TABLE on primary server does it effects on secondary database? If yes how?

Ans:

Truncate table command will be carried forward to the secondary server. When you run truncate command it won't delete the data's row by row hence those things will not be captured in log file. The actual process for Truncate Table is to de-allocate the pages assigned to a table, this de-allocating part will be captured in log file, when this log is shipped to secondary server the same thing will happen on redoing the log file so the table will get truncated in secondary server.

32. Have you ever encounter below error message? If yes what is the resolution?

Microsoft SQL Server, Error: 14262

ADDITIONAL INFORMATION: An exception occurred while executing a Transact-SQL statement or batch. (Microsoft.SqlServer.ConnectionInfo) The specified server name does not exist

Ans:

Need to ensure that SQL Server name is correctly. Select @@SERVERNAME will return the name. In our case it returning "NULL" as the server name entry was missing from "sysservers" the same as Windows Server name. Below steps worked out in resolving this issue.

```
sp_dropserver 'old server name'
go
sp_addserver 'new server name', local
go
```

You need to restart the SQL services for the above command to take effect.

33. Have you ever encounter below error message? If yes what is the resolution?

Error: 14420, Severity: 16, State: 1

The log shipping primary database %s.%s has backup threshold of %d minutes and has not performed a backup log operation for %d minutes. Check agent log and log shipping monitor information.

Ans:

The message 14420 does not necessarily indicate a problem with log shipping. The message indicates that the difference between the last T-log backed up file and current time on the monitor server is greater than the time that is set for the Backup Alert threshold.

- Ensure that Transaction Log backup is happening in the primary server. If the T-log backup is failing then the above error appears. You need to check the job history details of the T-log backup to identify the cause.
- You may have set an incorrect value for the Backup Alert threshold. Ideally, you must set this value to at least three times the frequency of the backup job. If you change the frequency of the backup job after log shipping is configured and functional, you must update the value of the Backup Alert threshold accordingly.
- The date or time (or both) on the monitor server is different from the date or time on the primary server. It is also possible that the system date or time was modified on the monitor or the primary server. This may also generate alert messages.
- The log shipping Copy job that is run on the primary server might not connect to the monitor server MSDB database to update the fields in the log_shipping_primaries table. This may be the result of an authentication problem between the monitor server and the primary server.

34. Have you ever encounter below error message? If yes what is the resolution?

Error: 14421, Severity: 16, State: 1

The log shipping secondary database %s.%s has restore threshold of %d minutes and is out of sync. No restore was performed for %d minutes. Restored latency is %d minutes. Check agent log and log shipping monitor information.

Ans:

The message 14421 does not necessarily indicate a problem with Log Shipping. This message indicates that the difference between the last T-log backed up file and last restored T-log file is greater than the time selected for the Out of Sync Alert threshold.

- It is possible that the Restore job on the secondary server is failing. In this case, check the job history for the Restore job because it may indicate a reason for the failure.
- You may have set an incorrect value for the Out of Sync Alert threshold. Ideally, you must set this value to at least three times the frequency of the slower of the Copy and Restore jobs. If the frequency of the Copy or Restore jobs is modified after log shipping is set up and functional, you must modify the value of the Out of Sync Alert threshold accordingly.

- The date or time (or both) on the primary server is modified such that the date or time on the primary server is significantly ahead between consecutive transaction log backups.
- Problems either with the Backup job or Copy job are most likely to result in "out of sync" alert messages. If "out of sync" alert messages are raised and if there are no problems with the Backup or the Restore job, check the Copy job for potential problems. Additionally, network connectivity may cause the Copy job to fail. If the network is very slow then the copying of T-log from primary will take longer than the threshold set for restoration. Hence it might also lead to the above error.

CHAPTER 6

SQL SERVER DATABASE MIRRORING

Interview Questions and Answers

Introduction: This chapter takes you through the SQL Server Database Mirroring related interview questions and answers. These questions are helpful for range of database administrators staring from a junior to an expert level DBA while preparing for a technical interview. These questions and answers are deals with the below topics:

- SQL Server Database Mirroring
- Database Mirroring Scenarios

SQL Server Database Mirroring

1. How database Mirroring works?

Ans:

Database mirroring does not work by sending individual transaction log backups instead it sends each individual transaction log record to the standby database. Therefore anything captured in the transaction log will be applied to the copy of the database on the other server. The action of sending transaction log records can happen synchronously or asynchronously.

2. What are the added improvements for database mirroring in SQL Server 2016?

Ans:

No Improvements! In fact from SQL Server 2012 "Database Mirroring" is in deprecated features. On SQL Server 2012/2014/2016 Microsoft advised users to shift to ALWAYSON Availability Groups.

3. Since you worked with SQL Server 2005, 2008, 2012 and 2014, did you find any improvements in Database Mirroring in any of these versions?

Ans:

Yes! Database Mirroring improved a lot in SQL Server 2008:

- *Performance Boosted:* Data compression used on the log records sent from one server to server.
- *Automatic Page Repairs:* As records are being written to the mirror, automatic page repair can occur if SQL Server finds any page that is not intact.
- Few more mirroring related performance counters and DMV added

4. Have you heard the word quorum? If yes do we see that in mirroring?

Ans:

Yes! Like clustering, the witness helps create quorum to ensure that only one of the partners currently owns the database that is used by end users and applications. Database mirroring has three types of quorum:

- FULL QUORUM
- WITNESS-TO-PARTNER QUORUM
- PARTNER-TO-PARTNER QUORUM

The quorum mechanisms used by database mirroring are not unlike the heartbeat for failover clustering. It is part of the mechanism that determines failover for a mirrored configuration. Database mirroring performs a ping across the network once every second. If ten pings are returned as missed, a failure is initiated.

5. Can you tell me what the best uses of database mirroring are?

Ans:

- Disaster Recovery and High Availability
- Migrating to New Hardware
- Reporting

6. Can you quickly explain the below in database mirroring?

Principal

Mirror

Witness

Send Queue

Redo Queue

End point

Failover

Ans:

Principal: In a database mirroring configuration, there are two copies of a single database, but only one copy is accessible to the clients at any given time. The copy of the database that the applications connect to is called the *principal database*. The server that hosts the principal database is known as the *principal server*.

Mirror: The *mirror* is the copy of the principal database. The mirror is always in a restoring state; it is not accessible to the applications. To keep this database up-to-date, the log records are transferred from the principal and applied on the mirror database. The server that hosts the mirror database is known as the *mirror server*.

Witness: The optional *witness* is an SQL Server instance in a database mirroring configuration. It is separate from the principal and mirror instances. When database mirroring is used in synchronous mode, the witness provides a mechanism for automatic failover.

Send Queue: While sending the log records from the principal to the mirror, if the log records can't be sent at the rate at which they are generated, a queue builds up at the principal. This is known as the *send queue*. The send queue does not use extra storage or memory. It exists entirely in the transaction log of the principal. It refers to the part of the log that has not yet been sent to the mirror.

Redo Queue: While applying log records on the mirror, if the log records can't be applied at the rate at which they are received, a queue builds up at the mirror. This is known as the *redo queue*. Like the send queue, the redo queue does not use extra storage or memory. It exists entirely in the transaction log of the mirror. It refers to the part of the hardened log that remains to be applied to the mirror database to roll it forward.

Endpoint: An endpoint is a SQL Server object that enables SQL Server to communicate over the network. It encapsulates a transport protocol and a port number.

Failover: When the principal database (or the server hosting it) fails, database mirroring provides a mechanism to fail over to the mirror database.

7. What is transaction safety in database mirroring?

Ans:

Database mirroring introduces the concept of transaction safety. There are two ways this can be set: **FULL (synchronous)** and **OFF (asynchronous)**. The value for transaction safety controls which mode will be used by the database mirroring session. The default value is FULL.

8. What are the different mirroring states we can see?

Ans:

A database participating in database mirroring can have one of the following *mirroring states*, or status:

- SYNCHRONIZING
- SYNCHRONIZED
- SUSPENDED
- PENDING_FAILOVER
- DISCONNECTED

9. What are the different modes in implementing database mirroring?

Ans:

Database Mirroring offers three modes of implementation. The choice you select depends on how you want to handle failover processing.

SYNCHRONOUS MODE:

- *High Availability:* This operating mode option allows you to synchronize transaction writes on both servers and enables automated failover. For this option to work, you must also have a witness server.
- *High Protection:* This option allows you to synchronize transaction write on both servers, but failover is manual. Since automated failover is not part of this option, a witness server is not used.

ASYNCHRONOUS MODE:

- *High Performance:* This option does not care if the writes are synchronized on both servers, therefore offering some performance gains. When using this option, you are just assuming that everything is going to complete successfully on the mirror. This option only allows manual failover, and a witness server is not used.

10. Does database mirroring available on all editions of SQL Server?

Ans:

No! Database Mirroring is a costly feature.

Starting from SQL Server 2008 R2 to SQL Server 2016:

- Enterprise Edition – Supports all features of mirroring
- Standard Edition – Supports Mirroring with Safety Full Only Mode
- Business Intelligence (2012 & 2014) – Supports Mirroring with Safety Full Only Mode
- Web & Express Edition – Supports Mirroring for Witness only

11. What is the quick checklist for database mirroring configuration?

Ans:

- Before a mirroring session can begin, the database owner or system administrator must create the mirror database, set up endpoints and logins, and, in some cases, create and set up certificates.
- As per Microsoft policy the two partners, that is the principal server and mirror server, must be running the same edition of SQL Server. The witness, if any, can run on any edition of SQL Server that supports database mirroring.
- For best performance, use a dedicated network interface card (NIC) for mirroring.
- Each database mirroring endpoint listens on a unique TCP port number.
- Endpoints can be used to turn on or off all mirroring functionality for the instance.
- If the computer running SQL Server has a firewall, the firewall configuration must allow both incoming and outgoing connections for the port specified in the endpoint.
- Transactions that have been prepared using the Microsoft Distributed Transaction Coordinator but are still not committed when a failover occurs are considered aborted after the database has failed over.

12. What are the limitations in database mirroring?

Ans:

- The granularity of traditional database mirroring is a database. Mirroring is configured for one database at a time. The whole instance is not mirrored.
- A mirrored database cannot be renamed during a database mirroring session.
- Database mirroring does not support FILESTREAM. A FILESTREAM FILEGROUP cannot be created on the principal server. Database mirroring cannot be configured for a database that contains FILESTREAM FILEGROUPS.

- Database mirroring is not supported with either cross-database transactions or distributed transactions.
- Two copies of the same database are involved in database mirroring, but only one database is accessible to the applications at any given time. You can create a snapshot on the mirror and use it for read-only purposes (a good solution for reporting requirements). However, you cannot directly access the mirror database or back up the mirror database.
- You cannot mirror the **master, MSDB, temp**, or **model** databases.
- Database mirroring requires that the database use the full recovery model. You can't use the simple or bulk-logged recovery models.
- One instance can serve as the principal for one database, the mirror for another database, and the witness for yet another database.
- Multiple databases in an instance can be mirrored.
- Applications that connect to a database with ADO.NET or the SQL Native Client (SNAC) can automatically redirect connections when the database fails over to the mirror.
- A database which is mirrored to another server can also be the source database for a log-shipping scenario.

13. Can you quickly explain the steps to configure mirroring by authoring through certificates?

Ans:

- BACKUP THE PRINCIPAL DATABASE AND RESTORE IT ON THE MIRROR SERVER WITH NORECOVERY
- Validate DNS entries. Add all of the participating server names (FQDN) into the Host file.
- Create a Database **Master Key on** Principal Server.
- Create a server based **certificate** which will be used to encrypt the DB Mirroring **End Point**
- Create the database Mirroring End Point for the Principal Server using the Certificate for Authorization
- Backup the certificate into a file
- Copy the certificate into Mirror and Witness Servers and place them in C Drive
- Steps 3 to 7 should be repeated on both mirror and witness server by modifying the certificate names while keeping the other configurations.
- Create a **Login** on the Principal for the mirror
- Create a User for the Login
- Associate the **Mirror certificate** with the user (We copied from mirror)
- Associate the **Witness certificate** with the user (We copied from Witness)
- Grant the connect permissions to the Login

- ➢ Repeat steps from **9** to **13** on mirror and Witness
- ➢ Prepare the **mirror server** first (Alter Database <> Set Partner= <>)
- ➢ Prepare **Principal Server** then (Alter Database <> Set Partner= <>)
- ➢ Set the **Safety Mode** on Principal Server (Alter Database <> Set Partner Safety= Full/ Off)
- ➢ Prepare the **Witness Server** (Alter Database <> Set Witness= <>)
- ➢ Validate the DB Mirroring Configuration using DB Mirroring Monitor

14. In database mirroring what are the events happens when an automatic failover occurred?

Ans:

When a failure occurs and automatic failover takes place, several events occur in the following sequence:

- ➢ *Failure occurs:* The principal database becomes unavailable. This may be caused by hardware, storage, network, or power failure on the principal server.
- ➢ *Failure is detected:* The failure is detected by the mirror and the witness.
- ➢ *Complete redo performed on mirror:* The mirror database has been in the Restoring state until now and the redo is being continuously applied on the mirror database. The remaining log in the redo queue of the mirror at the time of failure of the principal is applied on the mirror database to completely recover it.
- ➢ *Decision to fail over:* The mirror coordinates with the witness and decides that the database should now fail over to the mirror. This decision process usually takes around 1 second. If the principal comes back before the redo phase in step 3 is complete, failover is not required.
  - ✓ *Mirror becomes principal:* After all the remaining redo is applied, the mirror database is brought online and it assumes the role of the principal. The database is now available and clients can connect to the new principal and continue operation.
  - ✓ *Undo:* The uncommitted transactions in the transaction log are rolled back.

15. What is the timeframe in detecting a failure in mirroring session?

Ans:

Hard failures such as server power failure are detected quickly. Soft failures such as storage failure take a bit longer to detect. The default timeout for communication between the principal, the mirror, and the witness is 10 seconds. The timeout can be modified by using the ALTER DATABASE SET PARTNER TIMEOUT command. If the principal doesn't respond within the timeout period, it is considered to be down. If you change the timeout setting, it is a best practices recommendation to set it to 10 seconds or higher. Setting it to lower than 10 seconds may result in false failures under heavily loaded or sporadic network conditions.

16. While monitoring, have you ever used system views or CATALOGS?

Ans:

- **Mirroring state, safety level, and witness:**
  - ✓ Principal: sys.database_mirroring: Mirroring state, Safety Level etc.
  - ✓ Witness: sys.database_mirroring_witnesses
- **Endpoints:**
  - ✓ sys.database_mirroring_endpoints: Status of the end point, Encryption settings
  - ✓ sys.tcp_endpoints: Port number used by end point
- **DMV:**
  - ✓ sys.dm_db_mirroring_connections: Returns a row for each connection established for database mirroring.
  - ✓ sys.dm_db_mirroring_auto_page_repair: Returns a row for every automatic page-repair attempt on any mirrored database on the server instance
- **System Procedures:**
  - ✓ sp_dbmmonitorupdate: Updates the database mirroring monitor status table by inserting a new table row for each mirrored database, and truncates rows older than the current retention period. The default retention period is 7 days (168 hours).
  - ✓ **sp_dbmmonitorresults:** Returns the database mirroring history for the given database.

17. Have you ever used performance counters to monitor database mirroring? If yes can you describe those counters?

Ans:

To monitor the performance of database mirroring, SQL Server provides a System Monitor performance object (**SQLServer:Database Mirroring**) on each partner (principal and mirror). The **Databases** performance object on system monitor (PerfMon) provides some important information as well, such as throughput information (**Transactions/sec** counter). Following are the important counters to watch.

On the principal:

- **Log Bytes Sent/sec**: Number of bytes of the log sent to the mirror per second.
- **Log Send Queue KB**: Total kilobytes of the log that have not yet been sent to the mirror server.
- **Transaction Delay**: Delay (in milliseconds) in waiting for commit acknowledgement from the mirror. This counters reports the total delay for all the transactions in process at that time. To determine the average delay per transaction, divide this counter by the **Transactions/sec** counter. When running asynchronous mirroring this counter will always be 0.
- **Transactions/sec**: The transaction throughput of the database. This counter is in the **Databases** performance object.
- **Log Bytes Flushed/sec**: The rate at which log records are written to the disk. This is the log generation rate of the application. It plays a very important role in determining database mirroring performance. This counter is in the **Databases** performance object.

- **Disk Write Bytes/sec**: The rate at which the disk is written to. This counter is in the **Logical Disk** performance object and represents. Monitor this counter for the data as well as the log disks.

On the mirror:

- **Redo Bytes/sec**: Number of bytes of the transaction log applied on the mirror database per second.
- **Redo Queue KB**: Total kilobytes of hardened log that remain to be applied to the mirror database to roll it forward.
- **Disk Write Bytes/sec**: The rate at which the disk is written to. This counter is in the **Logical Disk** performance object and represents. Monitor this counter for the data as well as the log disks on the mirror.

18. In your production environment mirroring is configured for one of the premium database and you are asked to cross check the configuration. Can you elaborate what are all the options you would check for?

Ans:

If database mirroring is not working, check the following to make sure the configuration is correct:

- The endpoints are all started. Look at the column STATE_DESC in the CATALOG view **sys.database_mirroring_endpoints**. The default state at the time of the creation of the endpoint is STOPPED. You can start the endpoint at the time you create it by explicitly specifying the state as STARTED. Alternatively, you can use the ALTER ENDPOINT command to start the endpoint.
- The endpoints in the principal, mirror, and witness (if any) have compatible encryption settings. Look at the column IS_ENCRYPTION_ENABLED in the CATALOG view **sys.database_mirroring_endpoints** for the principal, mirror, and witness endpoints. This column has a value of either 0 or 1. A value of 0 means encryption is DISABLED for the endpoint and a value of 1 means encryption is either REQUIRED or SUPPORTED.
- The port numbers of the endpoints are the same as the corresponding port numbers specified in the SET PARTNER statements. The port number used by an endpoint is listed in the PORT column of the CATALOG view **sys.tcp_endpoints**. The port number specified in the SET PARTNER statements while establishing the database mirroring session is listed in the column MIRRORING_PARTNER_NAME of the CATALOG view **sys.database_mirroring**. Make sure that the port number in MIRRORING_PARTNER_NAME matches the port number of the corresponding endpoint.
- The endpoints have the correct type and role. The type and role of an endpoint are listed in the columns TYPE_DESC and ROLE_DESC respectively of the CATALOG view **sys.database_mirroring_endpoints**. Make sure that the type is DATABASE_MIRRORING. The role should be PARTNER if this endpoint belongs to a server that is used as the principal or mirror. The role should be WITNESS if this endpoint belongs to a server that is used as the witness.

- The user account under which the SQL Server instance is running has the necessary CONNECT permissions. If SQL Server is running under the same domain user on all the servers involved in the mirroring session (principal, mirror, witness), then there is no need to grant permissions. But if SQL Server runs under a different user on one or more of these servers, then you need to grant CONNECT permission on the endpoint of a server to the login account of the other servers.
- The remote connection through TCP/IP is enabled on all SQL Server instances involved in the database mirroring session.
- If you have a firewall between the partners and the witness, make sure the port that is used for database mirroring endpoints is opened through the firewall.

19. When we are not successful in configuring the database mirroring, what are all the things that we need to check around database mirroring? (This question is mandatory in your preparation list if you added Database Mirroring in your profile)

Ans:

When we are facing issues in configuring or when we need to troubleshoot Database Mirroring here is the master list of things that we need to check:

Accounts:

- Make sure the service accounts are having the correct permissions
- If the accounts are running in different domains or are not domain accounts, the login of one account must be created in master on the other computer. The login must be granted CONNECT permission on the end point
- If SQL Server is running as a service that is using the local system account, you must use certificates for authentication.

End Points:

- Make sure that each server instance (the principal server, mirror server, and witness, if any) has a database mirroring endpoint. (sys.database_mirroring_endpoints)
- Check that the port numbers are correct (sys.database_mirroring_endpoints and sys.tcp_endpoints)
- Make sure servers are listening on the correct ports using TELNET and netstat -ano
- Make sure that the endpoints are started (STATE=STARTED). We can check this using T-SQL statement "SELECT state_desc FROM sys.database_mirroring_endpoints." Start the end points using ALTER ENDPOINT if not started.
- Check that the ROLE is correct. We can check this using T-SQL statement "SELECT role FROM sys.database_mirroring_endpoints;"
- The login for the service account from the other server instance requires CONNECT permission on End Point.

System Address:

In database mirroring specify the instance name that can be uniquely identifiable across the network.

- **Server Name:** If all servers (principal, mirror and witness) are in same domain
- **IP Address:** Preferably static IP Address
- **FQDN:** Fully Qualified Domain Name works perfectly in all cases

Network Access:

- Each server instance must be able to access the ports of the other server instance or instances over TCP.
- This is especially important if the server instances are in different domains that do not trust each other (untrusted domains).
- Cross check servers are listening on the required ports using TELNET
- Cross check firewall settings and add exceptions for the required ports

Mirror Database Preparation:

- When you create the mirror database, make sure that you restore the full backup of the principal database specifying the same database name WITH NORECOVERY.
- Also, all log backups created after that full backup was taken must also be applied, again WITH NORECOVERY.
- Make sure file paths are same on both principal and mirror. If it is not possible include MOVE option in restore statement.
- When MOVE option specified we cannot add new files to principal without suspending the mirrir session.

Failed Create-File Operation:

- Adding a file without impacting a mirroring session requires that the path of the file exist on both servers.
- When file path is different on mirror from principal, mirroring session will be suspended.
- Mirroring session has to be removed and restore a full backup of the FILEGROUP that contains the added file.
- Then back up the log containing the add-file operation on the principal server and manually restore the log backup on the mirror database using the WITH NORECOVERY and WITH MOVE options.

Starting Mirroring – T-SQL:

- The order in which the ALTER DATABASE database_name SET PARTNER ='partner_server' statements are issued is very important.
- The first statement must be run on the mirror server. It doesn't try to contact any server but it will be instructed to wait till the principal server contact
- The second ALTER DATABASE statement must be run on the principal server. Principal Server contacts mirror and then Mirror contact back the principal server.

Cross-Database Transactions:

- We should be careful when we are using the cross database transactions on mirroring configured database.
- Database failover will not be effected but the queries that are written to interact with the other databases in the same instance or queries interact with MSDTC may file after failover in imitated.

20. What are the common reasons for failures in database mirroring?

Ans:

FAILURES DUE TO HARDWARE ERRORS:

Possible causes of hard errors include (but are not limited to) the following conditions:

- A broken connection or wire
- A bad network card
- A router change
- Changes in the firewall
- Endpoint reconfiguration
- Loss of the drive where the transaction log resides
- Operating system or process failure

FAILURES DUE TO SOFTWARE ERRORS:

Conditions that might cause mirroring time-outs include (but are not limited to) the following:

- Network errors such as TCP link time-outs, dropped or corrupted packets, or packets that are in an incorrect order.
- A hanging operating system, server, or database state
- A Windows server timing out
- Insufficient computing resources, such as a CPU or disk overload
- The transaction log filling up or the system is running out of memory or threads.
- No proper permissions given to the service accounts and end points
- Not using the FQDN (fully qualified Domain Name) to represent the principal, mirror and witness servers.

21. What are the different things to be considered when you think of a failover in database mirroring?

Ans:

- Fail the principal over to the mirror.
- Synchronize logins
- Ensure all objects that reside outside of the database are re-created on the mirror.
- Synchronize full-text indexes.

- Redirect clients to the new primary instance of SQL Server (the former mirror). If you have automatic failover configured in high safety mode, all you need to worry about are steps 2 through 5.

22. What are the various ways to monitor database mirroring?

Ans:

- Database Mirroring Monitor
- Performance Monitor
- SQL Server Profiler
- Extended Events
- Transact SQL – Views, System Views, DMV

23. Can we be able to automate the Database Mirroring monitor process? If yes can you explain in simple steps?

Ans:

There are mainly two things that we need to monitor in database mirroring:

Mirroring state:

Use the system view "master.sys.database_mirroring" to get the mirroring state description for the principal and mirror databases. Send an alert to DBA team if the state is not in synchronized or synchronizing.

Mirroring Performance:

Collect the counter values "Unsent log" and "Unrestored log" from the system view master.sys.dm_os_performance_counters and sent an alert to DBA team if either of these values are greater than the baseline value (Ex 200 MB).

Note: Alerts can be scheduled using SQL Server Agent Jobs.

Database Mirroring Scenarios

24. We have recently upgraded to SQL Server 2016 and we would like to configure database mirroring for one of our production database. As a lead DBA what is your suggestion on this?

Ans:

I would suggest use ALWAYSON Availability Groups. The reason being is Microsoft already announced that Database Mirroring will be removing from the future versions and we have to use ALWAYSON Availability Groups or Log shipping as an alternative.

25. I have a doubt, you said we should have the same version on principal and mirror but how can we use database mirroring for migrations?

Ans:

Well that's a recommendation by Microsoft! To get the full functionality of database mirroring we should have both Principal and Mirror be running the same version of SQL Server.

But when we are using mirroring for migrations for example we can have principal server on 2008 R2 and Mirror server on 2012. But once we failover from 2008 R2 to 2012 fail back is not possible.

26. We have configured mirroring for one of our database. Do we still need to perform backups for this database?

Ans:

Yes! Mirroring will increase the database availability but it's not alternative for data recovery in all the time. Regular backups are always required based on SLA (Service Level Agreement) with your business.

27. Can we configure mirroring when principal and mirror databases are in different domains?

Ans:

Yes! It is possible we have to use certificates for security between domains.

28. We have configured mirroring (Asynchronous mode) for a database in SQL Server 2012. Due to network issues we have lost connectivity between Principal and DR site (Mirror Server). But there are lots of transactions happening in principal server. We have configured log backups for every half an hour. The network connectivity fixed after 3 hours. What will happen to transactions happening on principal server?

Ans:

If you are using asynchronous mirroring mode, and the network between your principal and mirror databases fails, the log on the principal server will continue to grow until the connection is re-established.

29. When the network connection fails for 3 hours between principal and mirror database, also we have been performing log backups on principal server. When we perform log backups on principal server this truncates the log then how can it be synchronize with the mirror database once the network connect is re-established?

Ans:

When mirroring is set up, if it is paused for any reason (In our case network problem) the transaction log on principal server will not truncate with a log backup and it grow until the connection re-established.

30. Does database mirroring works across the WAN? The requirement is to configuring mirroring using high safety mode for a database where the principal and mirror databases are in 2 different geographical areas. Is this possible?

Ans:

Yes! It is possible with some limitations.

- Business should be able to accept the performance penalty
- Should be careful with witness and false alerts which leads to a unnecessary failovers

31. Index maintenance on principal server causes the huge transactions and impacts the performance of database mirroring. What do you suggest on this?

Ans:

We can't avoid the index maintenance and yes I have seen the performance issue in mirroring due to index maintenance jobs. Doing index maintenance on more frequent basis might decrease the performance impact. Also remember not just index maintenance any bulk operations on principal database should be done in batches instead of running in one go.

32. What are the consequences when we loss of the principal in mirroring?

Ans:

If the principal fails, the failover scenario depends on the transaction safety level and whether you have a witness.

Scenario 1: Safety FULL with a witness

This scenario provides the high safety with automatic failover. In the event of the failure of the principal, the mirror forms a quorum with the witness. Automatic failover will take place, thereby minimizing the database downtime. Once the last principle becomes operational, it automatically assumes the role of the mirror.

Scenario 2: Safety FULL without a witness

This scenario provides high safety, but automatic failover is not allowed. In the event of failure of the principal, the database service becomes unavailable. We need to execute the following on mirrored server to make the database service available:

```
ALTER DATABASE <database name> SET PARTNER OFF
RESTORE DATABASE <database name> WITH RECOVERY
```

Once principle becomes available, you need to re-establish the mirroring session.

Scenario 3: Safety OFF

If the safety level is OFF, there were transactions that didn't make it to the mirror at the time of the failure of the principal. These transactions will be lost. Therefore, manual failover with safety OFF involves acknowledging the possibility of data loss. We need to execute the following on mirror to make the database service available:

```
ALTER DATABASE <database_name> SET PARTNER
FORCE_SERVICE_ALLOW_DATA_LOSS
```

Once the database on principal becomes operational, it automatically assumes the role of the mirror. However, the mirroring session remains SUSPENDED, and you will need to manually RESUME the mirroring session.

33. What happens if we loss of the mirror?

Ans:

If the mirror fails, the principal continues functioning, but the mirroring state is DISCONNECTED and the principal is running exposed. Once the mirror database becomes operational, it automatically assumes the role of the mirror and starts synchronizing with the principal.

As long as the mirroring state stays DISCONNECTED, the transaction log space on the principal cannot be reused, even if you back up the transaction log. If the log file grows and reaches its maximum size limit or runs out of disk space, the complete database comes to a halt. To prevent this we have options:

- Plan for enough disk space for the transaction log to grow and bring back the mirror database before the space fills up
- Break the database mirroring session

34. What happens if we loss witness?

Ans:

If the witness server fails, database mirroring continues functioning without interruption, except that automatic failover is not possible. Once the witness becomes operational, it automatically joins the database mirroring session.

35. What happens if we lose both mirror and the witness?

Ans:

Assume you have configured database mirroring with a witness. When the mirror is unavailable, the principal runs exposed. While the mirror is unavailable, if the witness is also lost, the principal becomes isolated and can't service the clients. Even though the principal database is running, it is not available to the clients. If you attempt to connect to the database, you get the message "Database <dbname> is enabled for database mirroring, but neither the partner nor witness server instances are available: the database cannot be opened."

If the mirror or the witness cannot be brought back online quickly, then the only way to resume database service is to terminate the database mirroring session. To do this, we need to execute the following command after connecting to the master database of the principal server:

ALTER DATABASE <db_name> SET PARTNER OFF

36. Is mirroring possible in Cluster environment?

Ans:

Yes! Database mirroring setup is possible on SQL Cluster.

37. What happens if the database didn't failed but the entire cluster failed?

Ans:

Even if the cluster fails, secondary database on the Mirroring server will come online and application will point to that database for any transactions. Once the former principal server comes online, this will be become mirroring server.

38. Is it possible to implement Database Mirroring if the database being mirrored has multiple FILEGROUPS?

Ans:

Yes, it is, but you can't mirror FILESTREAM file groups. Also remember when adding a new file to a mirrored database that the underlying directory structure has to already exist on the mirror server or adding the new file will fail on the mirror.

39. In database mirroring the only mode that can result in automatic fall over is High availability. If you use the other modes the failover has to be forced from the principal. So if the principal server is destroyed for whatever reason and you are in either High Protection or High performance Mode, then the mirror is useless as you cannot force the failover. Is this correct?

Ans:

No, we can get the mirror database online. To force service in a database mirroring session

- Connect to the mirror server
- Issue the following statement:

  ALTER DATABASE SET PARTNER FORCE_SERVICE_ALLOW_DATA_LOSS

The mirror server immediately transitions to principal server, and mirroring is suspended. As the option states, any transactions that have not been updated from the (former) Principal are lost when you execute this command.

40. I have a database mirroring session where the witness and mirror servers are in one physical location, and the principal server is in another. The mirroring session is running synchronously with the witness to allow automatic failover. A disaster happens to the site where the mirror and witness are, so the principal database is unavailable. I can't seem to access the principal at all to bring it back online by removing the witness and the mirror and witness won't be available. What can I do?

Ans:

Problem:

In our database mirroring setup, witness and mirror down and immediately principal DB stops serving requests and we are even not able to access principal db.

RCA:

The behavior we're seeing (the principal database becoming unavailable) is expected. In a mirroring configuration with a witness, the principal needs to have quorum with at least one of the other partners, either the mirror, the witness, or both. If it can't see either, it doesn't know whether the witness and mirror can still see each other and the mirror may have brought itself online as the new principal. In this case though, the customer knows that the mirror and witness are actually down and so he wants to bring the principal database back online.

Resolution:

- When we were trying to get into the principal database results in the following error:

  USE <Principal DB>;

  GO

  Msg 955, Level 14, State 1, Line 1

  Database <Principal DB> is enabled for Database Mirroring, but the database lacks quorum: the database cannot be opened. Check the partner and witness connections if configured.

- This is what I'd expect. Then we tried to remove the witness:

  ALTER DATABASE <Principal DB> SET WITNESS OFF;

  GO

  Msg 1431, Level 16, State 4, Line 1

  Neither the partner nor the witness server instance for database <Principal DB> is available. Reissue the command when at least one of the instances becomes available.

- That doesn't work either because removing the witness needs to happen on one of the partners as well as the principal. The only way to get out of this situation is to break the mirroring partnership completely.

  ALTER DATABASE <Principal DB> SET PARTNER OFF;

  GO

  USE <Principal DB>;

  GO

  Command(s) completed successfully.

41. We have configured Database Mirroring with automatic failover mode. When an auto failover happens from principal to mirror what about the applications which are connecting to the principal server? Does it possible to implement the automation that allows application to connect mirror server if the given principal server doesn't respond? If yes how it is possible?

Ans:

Yes! It is possible to automating application redirects to mirror server when an automatic failover happens. This information we can provide in connection string that we need to give at application web configuration. Let's say we have configured mirroring for a database "Test_eComm." Initially principal server is 250.66.44.77,1433 and the mirror server is 250.66.44.99,1433. There are few attributes that we need to understand:

- Server: Initial Principal Server - 250.66.44.77,1433
- Failover Partner: Initial Mirror Server- 250.66.44.99,1433
- Database Name: Test_eComm
- Network: Network Type (Mostly TCP/IP): dbmssocn

Connection String looks like below:

"Server=250.66.44.77, 1433; Failover_Partner =250.66.44.99, 1433; Database=Test_eComm; Network=dbmssocn"

When the above connection string provided, the application initially try to connect to Server 250.66.44.77, 1433. When failover happen the initial principal and mirror servers switch their roles and then 250.66.44.99, 1433 becomes as mirror server. When application data access provider can't connect to the initially principal server then it tries to connect to Failover Partner which is 250.66.44.99, 1433.

42. As an experienced DBA can you explain a scenario where you resolved a database mirroring issue in production environment?

Ans:

I have seen lot of issues in mirroring but let me tell you the recent experience. I have got a new client assignment and at the very first day there was an incident raised on a database where mirroring was configured:

Problem:

- Database mirroring configured for one of our critical databases with a witness server to allow automatic failover.
- Everything has been running fine until they had a power outage on the data center.
- Database mirroring performed the failover but people reported that the application is in hung state and not responding.
- When we manually failed back, the application started worked again
- Why application is in hung state when a database failover occurred?

RCA:

We have asked few questions and verified below:

Does database Failover succeeded: Yes! Failover has been successfully initiated and the database was online on mirror server after the failover

Does application configured to auto failover when connection failed to principal: Yes! Application was using ADO.NET to connect to SQL Server and was using explicit client redirection, specifying the mirror server name in the CONNECTIONSTRING property of the SQL Connection.

Did the mirroring full functionality tested in TEST/STAGING: No! Unfortunately the full functionality was not tested. They just tested the database was failover or not but not the application.

Actual Problem Found: Application connections are not properly configured to handle the existing connection failures. The application would open a connection to SQL Server when the application initialized and would never attempt to reconnect. Mirroring server details has been explicitly given but the problem is with reconnection logic.

Solution:

We worked with the development team and recoded the connection layer in the application to cope with connection failures and implement reconnection logic. After that tested the application failover in-case of database failover and it was started working fine without any issue.

43. Have you ever encounter the Error no 1418? If yes can you explain what and when it occurs?

Ans:

- This error may occur when we try to partner the server in database mirroring.
- The server network endpoint did not respond because the specified server network address cannot be reached or does not exist.
- The original error message looks like "The server network address "TCP:SQLServer:%" cannot be reached or does not exist. Check the network address name and that the ports for the local and remote endpoints are operational (SQL Server Error: 1418)."
- We have to do a proper RCA to identify the problem and implement the solution based on RCA

CHAPTER 7

SQL Server Replication

Interview Questions and Answers

Introduction: This chapter takes you through the SQL Server Replication related interview questions and answers. These questions are helpful for range of database administrators staring from a junior to an expert level DBA while preparing for a technical interview. These questions and answers are deals with the below topics:

- SQL Server Replication
- Replication Scenarios

SQL Server Replication

1. What are the new features added in SQL Server 2008 Replication?

Ans:

- More improvements in Peer-To-Peer Transactional Replication:
    - ✓ The ability to detect conflicts during synchronization
    - ✓ The ability to add nodes to a replication topology without quisling\disabling the topology
- Improved Replication Monitor:
    - ✓ On Monitor grid now we can apply "Selection," "Sort" and "Filter" on grid columns
    - ✓ Common Jobs Tab on Publisher node has been renamed as Agents and it showcase all agents and jobs associated with the selected publisher

2. What are the new features added in SQL Server 2008 R2 Replication?

Ans:

In 2008 R2 there are no changes in Replication features.

3. What are the new features added in SQL Server 2012 Replication?

Ans:

- Replication supports ALWAYSON Availability Groups
- There 4 new system stored procedures introduced for replication support on Availability groups
- Replication supports extended events
- Replication supports up to 15000 partitions for tables and indexes

4. What are the limitations – Replication on Availability Groups on SQL Server 2012?

Ans:

- Publication database can be part of an availability group. The publication instances must share the common distributer.
- Supports Transaction, Merge and snapshot replication
- ALWAYSON Secondary can't be a publisher
- Republishing is not supported when replication is combined with ALWAYSON.
- Doesn't supports Peer-To-Peer (P2P), bi-directional, reciprocal transactional publications, and Oracle Publishing.
- A database that is enabled for Change Data Capture (CDC) and Change Tracking (CT) can be part of an availability group.

5. What are the new features added in SQL Server 2014 Replication?

Ans:

- There are no significant features added in SQL Server 2014 Replication.
- SQL Server 2014 and above does not support replication to or from SQL Server 2005 or SQL Server Compact.

6. What are the new features added in SQL Server 2016 Replication?

Ans:

- Replication supports memory-optimized tables.
- Replication is now supported to Azure SQL Database.

7. Can you define replication?

Ans:

Replication is a set of technologies for copying and distributing data and database objects from one database to another and then synchronizing between databases to maintain consistency. Using replication, you can distribute data to different locations and to remote or mobile users over local and wide area networks, dial-up connections, wireless connections, and the Internet.

8. What are the areas where the replication can be useful?

Ans:

Load balancing: Replication allows you to disseminate your data to a number of servers and then distribute the query load among those servers.

Offline processing: You may wish to manipulate data from your database on a machine that is not always connected to the network.

Redundancy: Replication allows you to build a fail-over database server which is ready to pick up the processing load at a moment's notice.

Replicating data in a server to server environment:

- Improving scalability and availability
- Data warehousing and reporting

- Integrating data from multiple sites
- Integrating heterogeneous data
- Offloading batch processing

Replicating data between a server and clients:

- Exchanging data with mobile users
- Retail point of sale (POS) applications
- Integrating data from multiple sites

9. What are the various components involved in replication?

Ans:

Publisher:

The Publisher is a database instance that makes data available to other locations through replication. The Publisher can have one or more publications, each defining a logically related set of objects and data to replicate.

Distributor:

- The "Distributor" is a database instance that acts as a store for replication specific data associated with one or more Publishers.
- Each Publisher is associated with a single database (known as a distribution database) at the Distributor.
- The distribution database stores replication status data, metadata about the publication and in some cases acts as a queue for data moving from the Publisher to the Subscribers.
- **Local Distributer:** A single database server instance acts as both the Publisher and the Distributor.
- **Remote Distributer:** Publisher and the Distributor are configured on separate database server instances

Subscribers:

- A Subscriber is a database instance that receives replicated data.
- A Subscriber can receive data from multiple Publishers and publications.
- Depending on the type of replication chosen, the Subscriber can also pass data changes back to the Publisher or republish the data to other Subscribers.

Article:

- An article identifies a database object that is included in a publication.
- A publication can contain different types of articles, including tables, views, stored procedures, and other objects.
- When tables are published as articles, filters can be used to restrict the columns and rows of the data sent to Subscribers.

Publication:

A publication is a collection of one or more articles from one database. The grouping of multiple articles into a publication makes it easier to specify a logically related set of database objects and data that are replicated as a unit.

Subscription:

A subscription is a request for a copy of a publication to be delivered to a Subscriber. The subscription defines what publication will be received, where, and when. There are two types of subscriptions: push and pull.

- *Push:* With a push subscription, the Publisher propagates changes to a Subscriber without a request from the Subscriber. Changes can be pushed to Subscribers on demand, continuously, or on a scheduled basis. The Distribution Agent or Merge Agent runs at the Distributor.
- *Pull:* With a pull subscription, the Subscriber requests changes made at the Publisher. Pull subscriptions allow the user at the Subscriber to determine when the data changes are synchronized. The Distribution Agent or the Merge Agent runs at the Subscriber.

10. What are the agents involved in replication?

Ans:

Replication uses a number of standalone programs, called agents, to carry out the tasks associated with tracking changes and distributing data.

SQL Server Agent:

SQL Server Agent hosts and schedules the agents used in replication and provides an easy way to run replication agents.

Snapshot Agent:

- The Snapshot Agent is typically used with all types of replication.
- It prepares schema and initial data files of published tables and other objects, stores the snapshot files, and records information about synchronization in the distribution database.
- The Snapshot Agent runs at the Distributor.

Log Reader Agent:

- The Log Reader Agent is used with transactional replication.
- It moves transactions marked for replication from the transaction log on the Publisher to the distribution database.
- Each database published using transactional replication has its own Log Reader Agent that runs on the Distributor and connects to the Publisher

Distribution Agent:

- The Distribution Agent is used with snapshot replication and transactional replication.
- It applies the initial snapshot to the Subscriber and moves transactions held in the distribution database to Subscribers.
- The Distribution Agent runs at either the Distributor for push subscriptions or at the Subscriber for pull subscriptions.

Merge Agent:

- The Merge Agent is used with merge replication.
- It applies the initial snapshot to the Subscriber and moves and reconciles incremental data changes that occur.
- Each merge subscription has its own Merge Agent that connects to both the Publisher and the Subscriber and updates both.
- The Merge Agent runs at either the Distributor for push subscriptions or the Subscriber for pull subscriptions.
- By default, the Merge Agent uploads changes from the Subscriber to the Publisher and then downloads changes from the Publisher to the Subscriber.

Queue Reader Agent:

- The Queue Reader Agent is used with transactional replication with the queued updating option.
- The agent runs at the Distributor and moves changes made at the Subscriber back to the Publisher.
- Unlike the Distribution Agent and the Merge Agent, only one instance of the Queue Reader Agent exists to service all Publishers and publications for a given distribution database.

11. How to monitor latency in replication?

Ans:

There are three methods.

- Replication monitor
- Replication commands
- Tracer Tokens

Replication Monitor: In replication monitor from the list of all subscriptions just double click on the desired subscription. There we find three tabs.

- Publisher to Distributor History
- Distributor to Subscriber History
- Undistributed commands

Replication Commands:

- **Publisher.SP_ReplTran:** Checks the pending transactions at p
- **Distributor.MSReplCommands and MSReplTransactions:** Gives the transactions and commands details. Actual T_SQL data is in binary format. From the entry time we can estimate the latency.
- **Distributor.SP_BrowseReplCmds:** It shows the eaxct_seqno along with the corresponding T-SQL command
- **sp_replmonitorsubscriptionpendingcmds:** It shows the total number of pending commands to be applied at subscriber along with the estimated time.

Tracer Tokens:

Available from Replication Monitor or via TSQL statements, Tracer Tokens are special timestamp transactions written to the Publisher's Transaction Log and picked up by the Log Reader. They are then read by the Distribution Agent and written to the Subscriber. Timestamps for each step are recorded in tracking tables in the Distribution Database and can be displayed in Replication Monitor or via TSQL statements.

When Log Reader picks up token it records time in MStracer_tokens table in the Distribution database. The Distribution Agent then picks up the Token and records Subscriber(s) write time in the MStracer_history tables also in the Distribution database.

Below is the T-SQL code to use Tracer tokens to troubleshoot the latency issues.

```
--A SQL Agent JOB to insert a new Tracer Token in the publication database.
USE [AdventureWorks]
Go
EXEC sys.sp_posttracertoken @publication = <PublicationName>
Go
--Token Tracking Tables
USE Distribution
Go
--publisher_commit
SELECT Top 20 * FROM MStracer_tokens Order by tracer_id desc
--subscriber_commit
SELECT Top 20 * FROM MStracer_history Order by parent_tracer_id desc
```

12. Can you quickly explain how to configure replication in a generic way?

Ans:

- Identify and configure Distributer
- Identify and configure Publisher
- **Publish Data and Database Objects:**
  - ✓ Creating a publication and defining the data and database objects in the publication, setting options, and applying filters, if necessary.
- **Subscribing to Publications:**
  - ✓ Creating PUSH and PULL subscriptions; Specify synchronization schedules and set other options.
- **Initializing Subscription:** Describes how to initialize the Subscriber
- **Synchronizing Data:** Specify options for synchronization, which occurs when the Distribution Agent or Merge Agent runs and updates are propagated between the Publisher and Subscribers

13. What are the different types in replication implementation?

Ans:

There are mainly 3 types of methodologies available in replication

- Snapshot Replication
- Merge Replication
- Transactional Replication

14. Can you brief about how Snapshot Replication works?

Ans:

The publisher simply takes a snapshot of the entire replicated database and shares it with the subscribers. There are two scenarios where snapshot replication is commonly used.

- It is used for databases that rarely change.
- It is used to set a baseline to establish replication between systems while future updates are propagated using transactional or merge replication.

15. Can you explain how Transactional Replication works?

Ans:

Transactional replication is implemented by the SQL Server Snapshot Agent, Log Reader Agent, and Distribution Agent.

Snapshot Agent: Prepares snapshot files containing schema and data of published tables and database objects, stores the files in the snapshot folder, and records synchronization jobs in the distribution database on the Distributor.

Log Reader Agent: Monitors the transaction log of each database configured for transactional replication and copies the transactions marked for replication from the transaction log into the distribution database, which acts as a reliable store-and-forward queue.

Distribution Agent: Copies the initial snapshot files from the snapshot folder and the transactions held in the distribution database tables to Subscribers. Incremental changes made at the Publisher flow to Subscribers according to the schedule of the Distribution Agent, which can run continuously for minimal latency, or at scheduled intervals.

16. Can you explain how Merge Replication works?

Ans:

- Merge Replication allows the publisher and subscriber to independently make changes to the database.
- Both entities can work without an active network connection.
- When they are reconnected, the merge replication agent checks for changes on both sets of data and modifies each database accordingly.
- If changes conflict with each other, it uses a predefined conflict resolution algorithm to determine the appropriate data.
- Merge replication is commonly used by laptop users and others who cannot be constantly connected to the publisher.

- Merge replication is implemented by the SQL Server Snapshot Agent and Merge Agent.
- *Snapshot Agent:* If the publication is unfiltered or uses static filters, the Snapshot Agent creates a single snapshot. If the publication uses parameterized filters, the Snapshot Agent creates a snapshot for each partition of data.
- *Merge Agent:* The Merge Agent applies the initial snapshots to the Subscribers. It also merges incremental data changes that occurred at the Publisher or Subscribers after the initial snapshot was created, and detects and resolves any conflicts according to rules you configure.

17. Can you be able to explain what you know about Transactional Replication with Updatable Subscriptions?

Ans:

Transactional replication supports updates at Subscribers through updatable subscriptions and peer-to-peer replication. The following are the two types of updatable subscriptions:

Immediate updating: The Publisher and Subscriber must be connected to update data at the Subscriber. When data is updated at a Subscriber, it is first propagated to the Publisher and then propagated to other Subscribers. If immediate updating is used, the changes are propagated immediately using the two-phase commit protocol.

Queued updating: The Publisher and Subscriber do not have to be connected to update data at the Subscriber. Updates can be made while the Subscriber or Publisher is offline. When data is updated at a Subscriber, it is first propagated to the Publisher and then propagated to other Subscribers. If queued updating is used, the changes are stored in a queue; the queued transactions are then applied asynchronously at the Publisher whenever network connectivity is available. Because the updates are propagated asynchronously to the Publisher, the same data may have been updated by the Publisher or by another Subscriber and conflicts can occur when applying the updates. Conflicts are detected and resolved according to a conflict resolution policy that is set when creating the publication.

18. In which replication methodology we can update at subscribers?

Ans:

- Merge replication
- Peer-to-peer transactional replication
- Transactional replication with updating subscriptions

19. Your customer given a business requirement and asked you to configure the replication topology. How do you suggest the correct replication topology?

Ans:

Before suggesting the type of replication first we need to understand these replication types and their usage.

Snapshot:

- Data changes infrequently.
- It is acceptable to have copies of data that are out of date with respect to the Publisher for a period of time.

- Replicating small volumes of data.
- A large volume of changes occurs over a short period of time.

Transactional:

- Incremental changes to be propagated to Subscribers as they occur.
- The application requires low latency between the time changes are made at the Publisher and the changes arrive at the Subscriber.
- The Publisher has a very high volume of insert, update, and delete activity.
- The Publisher or Subscriber is a non-SQL Server database, such as Oracle.

Merge:

- Multiple Subscribers might update the same data at various times and propagate those changes to the Publisher and to other Subscribers.
- Subscribers need to receive data, make changes offline, and later synchronize changes with the Publisher and other Subscribers.
- Each Subscriber requires a different partition of data.
- Conflicts might occur and, when they do, you need the ability to detect and resolve them.

20. Have you ever configured both log shipping and replication on same database? If yes can you tell me the things that we need to consider?

Ans:

No! I never implemented this scenario but we know the limitations. Replication does not continue after a log shipping failover. If a failover occurs, replication agents do not connect to the secondary, so transactions are not replicated to Subscribers. If a failback to the primary occurs, replication resumes. All transactions that log shipping copies from the secondary back to the primary are replicated to Subscribers.

21. Have you ever configured both Database Mirroring and replication on same database? If yes can you tell me the things that we need to consider?

Ans:

Yes! We have implemented both Mirroring and Replication on same database

- The principal and mirror must share a Distributor. Remote Distributor provides greater fault tolerance if the Publisher has an unplanned failover.
- Replication supports mirroring the publication database for merge replication and for transactional replication with read-only Subscribers or queued updating Subscribers
- Immediate updating Subscribers, Oracle Publishers, Publishers in a peer-to-peer topology, and republishing are not supported.
- Metadata and objects that exist outside the database are not copied to the mirror, including logins, jobs, linked servers, and so on. If you require the metadata and objects at the mirror, you must copy them manually.

22. Can you explain how snapshot agent works?

Ans:

The Snapshot Agent performs the following steps:

- *Locking:* Establishes a connection from the Distributor to the Publisher, and then takes locks on published tables if necessary:
  - ✓ For merge publications, the Snapshot Agent does not take any locks.
  - ✓ For transactional publications, by default the Snapshot Agent take locks only during the initial phase of snapshot generation.
  - ✓ For snapshot publications, locks are held during the entire snapshot generation process.
- *.SCH file:* Writes a copy of the table schema for each article to a .sch file.
- *Additional Script Files:* It generates additional script files if database objects are published, such as indexes, constraints, stored procedures, views, user-defined functions etc.
- *BCP Files:* Copies the data from the published table at the Publisher and writes the data to the snapshot folder. The snapshot is generated as a set of bulk copy program (BCP) files.
- *MSrepl_commands and MSrepl_transactions:* For snapshot and transactional publications, the Snapshot Agent appends rows to these tables in the distribution database. The entries in the **MSrepl_commands** table are commands indicating the location of .sch and .bcp files, any other snapshot files, and references to any pre- or post-snapshot scripts.
- Releases any locks on published tables.
- During snapshot generation, you cannot make schema changes on published tables. After the snapshot files are generated, you can view them in the snapshot folder using Windows Explorer.

23. Can you explain how Distribution Agent works?

Ans:

For snapshot and transactional replication, the Distribution Agent performs the following steps:

- Establishes a connection to the Distributor.
- Examines the **MSrepl_commands** and **MSrepl_transactions** tables in the distribution database on the Distributor. The agent reads the location of the snapshot files from the first table and Subscriber synchronization commands from both tables.
- Applies the schema and commands to the subscription database.

24. Can you explain how Merge Agent works?

Ans:

For an unfiltered merge replication publication, the Merge Agent performs the following steps:

- Establishes a connection to the Publisher.
- Examines the **sysmergeschemachange** table on the Publisher and determines whether there is a new snapshot that should be applied at the Subscriber.
- If a new snapshot is available, the Merge Agent applies to the subscription database the snapshot files from the location specified in **sysmergeschemachange**.

25. What is the useful system CATALOGS/tables related to Replication?

Ans:

On PUBLISHER DB:

- sysarticles
- sysarticleupdates
- syspublications
- syssubscriptions
- master..sysservers

On DISTRIBUTION DB:

- master..sysservers
- msarticles
- msdistribution_agents
- msdistribution_history
- mslogreader_agents
- mslogreader_history
- mspublication_access
- mspublications
- mspublisher_databases
- msrepl_backup_lsns
- msrepl_commands
- msrepl_errors
- msrepl_identity_range
- msrepl_transactions
- mssnapshot_agents
- mssnapshot_history
- mssubscriber_info
- mssubscriber_schedule
- mssubscriptions
- mssync_states

On SUBSCRIBER DB:

- msreplication_subscriptions
- mssubscription_agents
- mssubscription_properties

DMV:

sys.dm_repl_articles

sys.dm_repl_schemas

sys.dm_repl_tranhash

sys.dm_repl_traninfo

26. What is the useful replication related system stored procedures available?

Ans:

sp_replshowcmds:

Using sp_replshowcmds, you can view transactions that currently are not distributed (those transactions remaining in the transaction log that have not been sent to the Distributor). This stored procedure is executed at the Publisher on the publication database.

sp_repltrans:

Returns a result set of all the transactions in the publication database transaction log that are marked for replication but have not been marked as distributed. This stored procedure is executed at the Publisher on a publication database.

sp_replcmds:

Returns the commands for transactions marked for replication. This stored procedure is executed at the Publisher on the publication database.

sp_browsereplcmds:

Returns a result set in a readable version of the replicated commands stored in the distribution database, and is used as a diagnostic tool. This stored procedure is executed at the Distributor on the distribution database.

Ex:

```
sp_browsereplcmds @xact_seqno_start='0x0004453600000F8C000B',
@xact_seqno_end='0x0004453600000F8C000B',
@publisher_database_id=4,
@command_id=1 [Optional]
```

sp_browsesnapshotfolder:

Returns the complete path for the latest snapshot generated for a publication. This stored procedure is executed at the Publisher on the publication database.

27. What are the various ways to monitor replication?

Ans:

- Replication Monitor
- T-SQL Commands & system CATALOGS
- Tracer Tokens
- Performance Monitor

- Extended Events
- Verbose Logging

28. Which is the best way to monitor replication? Have you ever implemented automations in replication monitoring?

Ans:

Replication Monitor:

One of the best ways to monitor but not all the time

- It showcases the current situation to answer the question "How are things right Now?," but it doesn't baseline.
- Also replication monitor internally runs the commands to get the required details. On a busy topology it might be a performance intensive.

T-SQL Commands & system CATALOGS:

- We absolutely suggest this as it directly get only the required things
- It allows us to baseline and customizing the monitoring

Tracer Tokens:

- We don't suggest this. We have seen some scenarios where it took lot of time to respond.

Performance Monitor:

It's also a resource intensive but sometimes it might be helpful. Even for the performance counters we would suggest to use T-SQL scripts with the required DMV.

Extended Events:

We never used this method. Moreover in SQL Server 2012 Books Online Microsoft mentioned that this method is for customer support engineers (Microsoft FTE) to collect the information for troubleshooting.

Verbose Logging:

This method may not useful for monitoring replication but it's really helpful at the time of troubleshooting. Using this method we just enable Agent History profile for the detailed logging and it helps us understanding the detailed progress and error message. Make sure we are using this only for the troubleshooting as it's also a performance intensive

We suggest:

- Use a customized solution; create a list of tables to capture the replication agents, latency and pending transactions/commands details using T-SQL code.
- Define baselines for parameters
- Create scripts to capture the replication health details and store it on pre-designed tables
- Create scripts to compare the captured values with the baseline values and to send a health check report to the DBA team if there are any issues or delays

29. Can you tell me the performance counters which can help us in monitoring replication performance?

Ans:

SQLServer: Replication Agents: This group monitors the number of Log Reader and Snapshot agents currently running on the server.

SQLServer: Replication Dist: This group monitors Distribution agents' performance, including the following counters

- Dist: Delivered Cmds/Sec—Number of commands delivered to subscribers per second.
- Dist:Delivered Trans/Sec—Number of transactions delivered to subscribers per second
- Dist:Delivery Latency—Number of milliseconds it takes to deliver transactions from distributor to subscribers.

SQLServer: Replication Logreader: This group monitors Log Reader agents' performance.

- Logreader: Delivered Cmds/Sec—Number of commands delivered to subscribers per second.
- Logreader: Delivered Trans/Sec—Number of transactions delivered to subscribers per second
- Logreader: Delivery Latency—Number of milliseconds it takes to deliver transactions from publisher to distributor

SQLServer: Replication Snapshot: This group monitors the snapshot agent. Counters in this group include the following:

Snapshot: Delivered Cmds/Sec: Number of seconds delivered to the distributor

Snapshot: Delivered Trans/Sec: Number of transactions delivered to the distributor.

30. What are the things that we need to monitor periodically to know the replication health?

Ans:

There are basically three things that helps us to understand the health of replication:

- Replication Agent status
- Latency – Publisher à Distributer à Subscriber
- Outstanding commands to be subscribed

31. What recovery model is required on a replicated database?

Ans:

Replication functions properly using any of the recovery models: simple, bulk-logged, or full. Merge replication tracks change by storing information in metadata tables. Transactional replication tracks changes by marking the transaction log, but this marking process is not affected by the recovery model.

32. How do I manage constraints on published tables?

Ans:

- Transactional replication requires a primary key constraint on each published table. Merge replication does not require a primary key, but if one is present, it must be replicated. Snapshot replication does not require a primary key.
- By default, primary key constraints, indexes, and check constraints are replicated to Subscribers.
- The NOT FOR REPLICATION option is specified by default for foreign key constraints and check constraints; the constraints are enforced for user operations but not agent operations.

33. How do I manage identity columns?

Ans:

Replication provides automatic identity range management for replication topologies that include updates at the Subscriber. If a row is inserted at the Publisher and the identity value is, for example, 21, that value is replicated to each Subscriber. When replication inserts data at each Subscriber, it does not increment the identity column value in the Subscriber table; instead, the literal value 21 is inserted. Only user inserts, but not replication agent inserts cause the identity column value to be incremented.

34. What are the ports required in replication?

Ans:

Replication connections to SQL Server use the typical regular Database Engine ports (TCP port 1433 for the default instance, etc.)

Web synchronization and FTP/UNC access for replication snapshot require additional ports to be opened on the firewall. To transfer initial data and schema from one location to another, replication can use FTP (TCP port 21), or sync over HTTP (TCP port 80) or File Sharing. File sharing uses UDP port 137 and 138, and TCP port 139 if it using NetBIOS. File Sharing uses TCP port 445.

35. Does replication affect the size of the transaction log?

Ans:

Merge replication and snapshot replication do not affect transaction log size, but transactional replication can. If a database includes one or more transactional publications, the log is not truncated until all transactions relevant to the publications have been delivered to the distribution database. If the transaction log is growing too large, and the Log Reader Agent is running on a scheduled basis, consider shortening the interval between runs. Or, set it to run in continuous mode. If it is set to run in continuous mode (the default), ensure that it is running.

36. Have you ever heard the word "sync with backup" in transactional replication?

Ans:

Yes! This can be set on the distribution database and the publication database. When this option enabled transactions in the log will not be truncated until they have been backed up. The sync with backup option ensures consistency between the publication database and the distribution database, but the option does not guarantee against data loss. For example, if the transaction log is lost, transactions that have been committed since the last transaction log backup will not be available in the publication database or the distribution database. This is the same behavior as a non-replicated database.

Replication Scenarios

37. Do you have any idea how to manually remove replication? If yes what is the sequence?

Ans:

You can manually remove a replication by using system stored procedures and other Transact-SQL statements. To completely remove a replication, follow these steps:

- Drop all subscriptions that are configured for the replication
- Drop all publications that are configured for the replication.
- Drop the distributor that is configured for the replication.

38. Scenario: Transactional replication configured on a database. A transaction failed on Publication. Does the failed transaction replicated to subscriber?

Ans:

No! Only committed transactions are replicated to subscribers. We can cross check using the system procedure "sp_browsereplcmds."

39. Scenario: A transaction successfully completed on publisher but subsequently failed on subscriber. What happens to this transaction on subscriber and publisher?

Ans:

On publisher the transaction already got committed but it's failed to apply on subscriber. Transactions fails at subscriber automatically rolled back. Until the problem is fixed, the error will prevent the distribution agent from processing any separate part of the transaction - the ACID properties are maintained. Note that this is the default behavior which may be overridden

40. Scenario: There is an update statement that affects 1 Million rows on the publisher which generates 1 Million records in transaction log. Due to this large transaction we are getting Log Reader Agent timeouts. How to handle these kinds of large transactions when replication configured? Or How to deal with the Log Reader Agent and distribution Agent Time Out Errors?

(This is must question if you are showcasing replication in your experience/profile)

Ans:

When there are large transactions executed on publisher database we might see timeout errors at Log Reader Agent or Distribution Agent.

RCA:

- When update happens for 1 million records there will be 1M update statements needs to be applied at subscriber

- The log reader agent will try to read each of these commands and transfer them to the distribution database. Timeout error can stop this process and the resulting messages may include:
    - ✓ "The process could not execute 'sp_replcmds' on 'xxxxxx'."
    - ✓ "Status: 2, code: 0, text: **'Timeout expired'**"
    - ✓ "A time out occurred while waiting for memory resources to execute the query."
    - ✓ "Agent 'xxx' is retrying after an error. 0 retries attempted. See agent job history in the Jobs folder for more details."
    - ✓ "The step was cancelled (stopped) as the result of a stop job request"
- These errors are each related to the number of records marked for replication in the log which the log reader has to parse and process. There are a few profile parameters which can be used to modify the process and avoid the error:

Resolution:

When we need to deal with the larger/huge transactions we need to play with various parameters to get rid of these timeout errors:

For Log Reader Agent Timeout:

- Increase "QueryTimeout"
- Decrease "MaxCmdsInTran"
- Decrease "ReadBatchSize"
- Decrease "ReadBatchThreshold"

For Distribution Agent Timeout:

- Increase "QueryTimeout"
- Decrease "CommitBatchSize"
- Decrease "CommitBatchThreshold"

Increase "QueryTimeout": It won't decrease the latency of a big transaction, but it is often sufficient on its own to get things working again.

Decrease "MaxCmdsInTran":

- It indicates the number of commands in a transaction to be processed per batch.
- If the problem is that the transaction contains a huge amount of commands, then it could be an advantage to chop it up into several smaller transactions.
- Let's say 1 Million record update is applied in 10 transactions with each transaction having 1 lakh records.
- This will massively decrease latency and prevent associated timeouts.
- But there is a problem if one of the batches failed to update at subscriber the transaction doesn't follow ACID properties as the previous batches are already committed.

Decrease "ReadBatchSize":

- This is the maximum number of transactions read out of the transaction log of the publishing database "per processing cycle."
- The lowest this figure can prevent timeout errors when huge number of transactions causing the problem.
- But in this case it's a single transaction with 1 M commands.

Decrease "ReadBatchThreshold":

- This is very similar to the "ReadBatchSize" parameter but rather than relating to transactions, it relates to commands.
- Setting this to a small value along with increasing the QueryTimeout can help remove a backlog, especially if the problem is caused by large transactions.

Decrease "CommitBatchSize":

- The value indicates the number of transactions to be issued to the Subscriber before a COMMIT statement is issued. The default is 100.

Decrease "CommitBatchThreshold":

- The value indicates the number of replication commands to be issued to the Subscriber before a COMMIT statement is issued. The default is 1000.

41. Scenario: In transactional replication log reader agent is failing with the error message "The process could not execute 'sp_repldone/sp_replcounters' on 'Publisher'." Have you ever encountered this issue? If yes can you explain why this happens and how to resolve it?

Ans:

Yes! We had the same issue when we were working for one of the client.

RCA:

- We have checked Log Reader Agent output file for detailed error message:

  The process could not execute 'sp_repldone/sp_replcounters' on 'MyPublisher'. Repl Agent Status: 5 Status: 2, code: 18752, text: **'Another log reader is replicating the database.'**
- From this error message we could conclude two things:
  - ✓ There is an orphan Log Reader Agent that is competing with the active log reader
  - ✓ When user manually executes sp_repldone, sp_replcmds, or sp_replshowcmds against the same database and forgot to close the connection
  - ✓ Some resources on the published database are not available for the active Log Reader Agent.

Resolution:

- Check the replication monitor if any extra log reader agent is running against the given database. It mostly never showcase even an orphan log reader running

- Check the output of sp_who for specific process identification numbers (SPIDs) that are connected to the published database. Close any connections that might have run sp_repldone, sp_replcmds, or sp_replshowcmds.
- Restart the Log Reader Agent.
- Execute sp_replflush at the Publisher on the publication database, and then restart the Log Reader Agent.

42. Scenario: The log reader agent fails with this error message: "Timeout expired" How to deal with this?

Ans:

- Quickly check the network connection between publisher and distributer (if it is a remote distributer). Also cross check the service/logins are working without any issue
- If you are able to connect to the publisher, run the following query under the published database:

  ```
  sp_replcmds 1
  go
  sp_replflush
  ```
- The sp_replcmds is to Log Reader Agent will call to find out what transactions must be picked up and must be sent to the distribution database.
- If the sp_replcmds stored procedure returns data, gradually increase the parameter value of the sp_replcmds Ex. 10, 50, 100 etc. Repeat this until the same timeout expired error occurs. We can know number of transactions that the Log Reader Agent can pick up.
- Reduce the value for the "ReadBatchSize" parameter from the default of 500 transactions to the working value you found through your sp_replcmds testing.
- Increase the "QueryTimeOut" parameter from 300 seconds to 3,000 seconds
- If no record returns when you run "sp_replcmds 1," but you know that there are replication transactions that are waiting in the log then we must run DBCC CHECKDB

43. In replication setup how can we confirm that subscriber is in sync with Publisher without using GUI?

Ans:

- Check and make sure all replication agents are running without any issue
- On subscriber connect to subscriber database and run query.

  Select * from <subscriber database>.dbo.msreplication_subscriptions;
- This table contains one row for each distribution agent. From the output get the "transaction_timestamp." Ex: 0x000004570001E3FE000100000000
- Transcation_Timestamp represents the last xact_seqno/transaction got loaded in the subscription database. Ex.xact_seqno: 0x000004570001E3FE0001 (Excluded all zeros at the end)

- Connect to distribution database and run below query

  Select * from Msrepl_commands where xact_seqno > 0x000004570001E3FE0001
- If there are no rows returned from the below query, indicates the replication is in sync.

44. Replication has broken as the subscriber was down. When it comes online we were trying to reinitialize the subscription. It was failed with the error message "Cannot Reinitialize the Subscriber." Any idea how to fix this?

Ans:

RCA:

Subscription needs to be reinitialized if any snapshot needs to be applied for any broken replication. In this case Subscriptions cannot be reinitialized for non-immediate_sync publications.

Resolution:

- Connect to the subscriber database, in the Msreplication_subscriptions table; the value of immediate_sync should be changed to 1. 0 indicates non-immediate sync publications Then it allowed us to reinitialize the subscribers and we could generate snap shot from the publisher successfully.

45. In transactional replication setup Distribution agent failed with the error message "Cannot insert duplicate key row in object 'XXXX' with unique index 'PK_XXXXX'. The statement has been terminated.." Have you ever seen this kind of errors? If yes can you explain how to resolve?

Ans:

This problem occurs if when a row which is to be delivered on the subscriber already exists on the subscriber database. There are 3 ways that we can fix this:

- ***Skip the error:*** Failed transaction will be skipped and continue applying from the next transaction.
- ***Update @xact_seqno:*** To skip the specific transaction Update @xact_seqno with the help of sp_helpsubscriptionerrors and sp_setsubscriptionxactseqno
- ***Delete the row:*** Delete already existing row at subscriber

46. In transactional replication setup Distribution agent failed with the error message "The row was not found at the Subscriber when applying the replicated command." Have you ever seen this kind of errors? If yes can you explain how to resolve?

Ans:

This problem occurs if when a row which is to be deleted/updated on the subscriber on which the row is already deleted or not exists:

- ***Skip the error:*** Failed transaction will be skipped and continue applying from the next transaction.
- ***Update @xact_seqno:*** To skip the specific transaction Update @xact_seqno with the help of sp_helpsubscriptionerrors and sp_setsubscriptionxactseqno

47. How to skip Distributed Agent errors in transactional replication?

Ans:

- By default, when the Distribution Agent encounters an error, the agent stops.
- If you use the -SkipErrors parameter, and specify expected errors or errors that you do not want to interfere with replication, the agent will log the error information and then continue running.
- For example, if you want to specify that the Distribution Agent should log duplicate key violations but continue to process subsequent transactions, specify that the agent should skip errors 2601 (Cannot insert duplicate key row in object '%.*ls' with unique index '%.*ls'.) and 2627 (Violation of %ls constraint '%.*ls'. Cannot insert duplicate key in object '%.*ls'.):
- -SkipErrors 2601:2627
- The most common way to use the -SkipErrors parameter is to use the Distribution Agent profile titled Continue on Data Consistency Errors.
- The Distribution Agent will then skip errors 2601, 2627, and 20598 (The row was not found at the Subscriber when applying the replicated command).

48. How to resolve the error "Could not execute sp_MSadd_repl_commands.." Here is the full error message: "The process could not execute 'sp_MSadd_replcmds' on 'server\instance'. (Source: MSSQLServer, Error number: 1007) Cannot insert duplicate key row in object 'dbo.MSrepl_commands' with unique index 'ucMSrepl_commands'. (Source: MSSQLServer, Error number: 1007)"

Ans:

RCA:

- If any other user is executing the repl commands in the publisher and his session is quite open for a long time will produce this error.

  OR
- One of the publications receives many inserts in one transaction.
- After the transaction is committed, the Log Reader Agent starts to process and split the transaction according to the MaxCmdsInTran parameter.
- The Snapshot Agent on another publication starts before the Log Reader Agent finishes the task.
- In this scenario, the Log Reader Agent fails, and you receive the following error message:

Resolution:

- If this issue occurs 2 or 3 times, we can ignore it and simply start the logreader jobs, it will succeed.
- If it's continuing then find out the session that's causing the problem, kill the SPID and restart the agent.

- If it's frequently occurring set parameters as below
    - ✓ @sync_method <> "concurrent"
    - ✓ @immediate_sync <> "True"
    - ✓ MaxCmdsInTran = 0
- Microsoft declared it's a known issue in SQL Server 2008 R2 SP1 and SQL Server 2012. To prevent these error messages apply the required Cumulative Update Packages released after SQL Server 2012 and SQL Server 2008 R2 SP1

49. Log reader fails with "The process could not execute 'sp_replcmds' " error. How do you troubleshoot it?

Ans:

RCA:

- When we checked Snapshot Agent is also failing with the error message: "The concurrent snapshot for publication 'PUB_XXXX is not available because it has not been fully generated or the Log Reader Agent is not running to activate it"
- We checked log reader agent history and it's been failing with the error message: "The process could not execute 'sp_replcmds' on [ServerName]"
- To get the complete error details we added verbose log to the log reader agent and we have got the correct error details as: "Status: 0, code: 15517, text: 'Cannot execute as the database principal because the principal "dbo" does not exist, this type of principal cannot be impersonated, or you do not have permission.'."
- From the above error message we could identify that the current job owner is not having the DBO rights on publication database.

Resolution:

- We have given DBO rights to the job owner and then the replication agents started working without any issue.

50. How to enable replication agents for logging to output files in SQL Server?

OR

How to deal with the verbose logging in SQL Server replication?

Ans:

You can configure the SQL Server replication agents such as, the Snapshot Agent, Log Reader Agent, Queue Reader Agent, Distribution Agent, and Merge Agent to capture more information about error messages and procedure calls to a text file. To enable verbose logging you must add two parameter values to the Run Agent step of the replication agent job for which you wish to review more detailed *logging:*

- -OutputVerboseLevel [0|1|2]
- -Output [Full Output Path and File Name]
- 0: No verbose logging

- 1: Minimal Logging (Default Logging)
- 2: Detailed Logging

Verbose logging can be enabled at agent profile properties as below:

- In Replication Monitor "right-click" a Replication Agent and select "Agent Profile"
- Click on "Verbose history agent profile."
- Click the details "... "button to review the Agent Profile settings.
- Update the value to "2" for the parameter "-HistoryVerboseLevel"
- We need to restart the Replication Agent for the setting to take effect.
- After restart if you check "View Details" we can see the detailed statistics

Note: We usually do not enable detailed logging as it may impact the performance. But this is very useful while troubleshooting.

51. Have you ever encountered the error message" Subscriptions getting expired" and "subscriptions being marked as inactive"? What does it mean?

Ans:

- *Subscription Expired:* When subscriptions get expired, the subscription entries will get deleted at the publisher. So to get the replication back to sync, the subscription has to be recreated.
- *Subscription Inactive:* When subscriptions are marked as inactive, it means that the subscription can no longer receive the replicated commands and has to be re-initialized to get back to sync with the publisher.

Distribution database has a retention period of how many commands it can store (the commands to be distributed to the subscribers). If a subscriber is not able to get the commands from the distribution database within this time, then as per the retention period, the commands are removed from the distribution database by an automatic cleanup job (distribution cleanup job). Since the sequence of transactions to be applied is lost, subscriber cannot get the next available commands and hence it will be marked as inactive. Thus by re-initializing, it will get a new snapshot and the subsequent commands will be applied from the distribution database after the snapshot is created.

52. We have configured transactional replication for one of our production database (3.4 TB) which is in SQL Server 2014. Replication is running successfully and now we have a requirement to add a new article. Can we be able to add a new article without generating snapshot for all existing articles? I.e. The snapshot should be generated only for the newly added article. Is it possible? If yes can you explain how?

Ans:

Yes! It is possible. To generate snapshot only for the newly added articles we need to change two publication properties: "allow_anonymous," "immediate_sync ".

Disable Publication Properties:

```
EXEC sp_changepublication
@publication=N'<Publication Name>'
, @property=N'allow_anonymous'
, @value='false';
go
exec sp_changepublication
@publication=N'<Publication Name>'
, @property=N'immediate_sync'
, @value='false';
go
```

Add new Article: In SSMS from the publication properties add new article

Start the Snapshot Agent: right click the publication and select "View Snapshot Agent Status" and start the snapshot agent. If you check the snapshot folder you can see the snapshot generated only for the newly added article.

53. I heard that there is a problem in replication when SQL Server 2014 released. Is that true?

Ans:

Yes! Not with all topologies but yes there is a problem in dealing with snapshot replication in SQL Server 2014. But most of these problems got resolved in the service pack. Errors we encountered in SQL Server 2014 snapshot:

Error 21820 "Cannot write to the script file in the snapshot folder at the Distributor (%ls).":

- Make sure there is enough disk space available
- Crosscheck if the account under which the Snapshot Agent runs has permissions to write to the snapshot folder and its subdirectories.

Error 21331 "Unable to copy script file to the snapshot folder at the Distributor":

- Make sure there is enough disk space available
- Crosscheck if the account under which the Snapshot Agent runs has permissions to write to the snapshot folder and its subdirectories.

Error: 20690 "Cannot set up the Publisher identity range for table %s."

- To resolve this problem, you should verify that appropriate ranges were specified when the article was created, and then rerun the Snapshot Agent.

Error: 20605 "Invalidated the existing snapshot of the publication."

- To resolve this problem, we need to rerun the snapshot agent to generate a new snapshot.

Error: 14098 may occur when you try to drop Distribution Publisher

- This problem occurs when the remote Publisher is using as Distributor.
- To resolve this, you should disable publishing at the Publisher before attempting to drop this relationship.

Error: 14071 "Could not find the Distributor or the distribution database for the local server."

- To resolve this, ensure that the Distributor is installed at the publisher instance

The Distribution Agent does not deliver commands to the snapshot subscriber even when Distribution Agent is running:

- This problem occurs when you specify the Distribution Agent to use multiple subscription streams by setting the -SubscriptionStreams parameter to a value of 2 or higher.
- To resolve this set the -SubscriptionStreams parameter to a value of 1.

The replication agent jobs may fail If SQL Server Agent STARTUP account changed to a domain account using the Windows Service Control Manager:

- This problem occurs because the Windows Service Control Manager does not grant the required permissions to the new domain account.
- To resolve this problem, you can use SQL Server Configuration Manager to change the STARTUP account to a domain account.

54. My publisher is in SQL Server 2014 and we need to subscribe to SQL Server 2012 instance. Is it possible?

Ans:

Yes! It is possible with some limitations:

- When subscribing to the previous version it is limited to the functionality of that version, both in terms of replication-specific functionality and the functionality of the product as a whole.
- Merge publications use a compatibility level, which determines what features can be used in a publication and allows you to support Subscribers running previous versions of SQL Server.

55. As per the business requirement one of the articles needs to be published in two publications. Is that possible?

Ans:

Yes, but with some restrictions:

- If an article is published in a transactional publication and a merge publication, ensure that the @published_in_tran_pub property is set to TRUE for the merge article.
- An article cannot be published in both a merge publication and a transactional publication with queued updating subscriptions.
- Articles included in transactional publications that support updating subscriptions cannot be republished.
- Etc.

56. Can multiple publications use the same distribution database?

Ans:

Yes. There are no restrictions on the number or types of publications that can use the same distribution database.

57. Does replication encrypt data?

Ans:

No. Replication does not encrypt data that is stored in the database or transferred over the network.

58. How can we replicate data over the Internet?

Ans:

- A Virtual Private Network (VPN).
- The Web synchronization option for merge replication

59. Does replication resume if a connection is dropped

Ans:

Yes. Replication processing resumes at the point at which it left off if a connection is dropped.

60. Does replication work over low bandwidth connections? Does it use compression?

Ans:

Yes, replication does work over low bandwidth connections. For connections over TCP/IP, it uses the compression provided by the protocol but does not provide additional compression. For Web synchronization connections over HTTPS, it uses the compression provided by the protocol and also additional compression of the XML files used to replicate changes.

61. Are logins and passwords replicated automatically?

Ans:

No. You could create a SSIS package to transfer logins and passwords from a Publisher to one or more Subscribers.

62. Why can't I run TRUNCATE TABLE on a published table?

Ans:

TRUNCATE TABLE is a non-logged operation that does not fire triggers. It is not permitted because replication cannot track the changes caused by the operation: transactional replication tracks changes through the transaction log; merge replication tracks changes through triggers on published tables. Use DELETE command without WHERE clause.

63. What is the effect of running a bulk insert command on a replicated database?

Ans:

For transactional replication, bulk inserts are tracked and replicated like other inserts. For merge replication, you must ensure that change tracking metadata is updated properly.

64. How can we rebuild indexes in replicated databases?

Ans:

There is no specific limitation on this. We can rebuild indexes as we do in a normal database except for the primary keys on published articles. We can't drop and recreate primary keys on these tables.

65. How can we add or change indexes on publication and subscription databases?

Ans:

- Indexes can be added at the Publisher or Subscribers with no special considerations for replication.
- CREATE INDEX and ALTER INDEX are not replicated, so if you add or change an index at, for example, the Publisher, you must make the same addition or change at the Subscriber if you want it reflected there.

66. How do I drop a table that is being replicated?

Ans:

First drop the article from the publication using sp_droparticle, sp_dropmergearticle, or the Publication Properties - <Publication> dialog box, and then drop it from the database using DROP <Object>. You cannot drop articles from snapshot or transactional publications after subscriptions have been added; you must drop the subscriptions first.

67. How can we add or drop columns on a published table?

Ans:

SQL Server supports a wide variety of schema changes on published objects, including adding and dropping columns. For example, execute ALTER TABLE … DROP COLUMN at the Publisher, and the statement is replicated to Subscribers and then executed to drop the column.

CHAPTER 8

SQL SERVER FAILOVER CLUSTERING

Interview Questions and Answers

Introduction: This chapter takes you through the SQL Server Failover Clustering related interview questions and answers. These questions are helpful for range of database administrators starting from a junior to an expert level DBA for the technical interview preparation. These questions and answers are deals with the below topics:

- SQL Server Failover Clustering
- Clustering Scenarios

SQL Server Failover Clustering

1. What is Windows Cluster?

Ans:

Clustering is a technology that automatically allows one physical server to take over the tasks and responsibilities of another physical server that has failed. The goal is to ensure that users running mission-critical applications will have very less downtime when a failure occurred. A cluster is a group of independent computer systems, referred to as nodes, working together as a unified computing resource. A cluster provides a single name for clients to use and a single administrative interface, and it guarantees that data is consistent across nodes.

2. What is a Cluster Node?

Ans:

A cluster node is a server within the cluster, and it has Windows Server and the Cluster service installed.

3. What is Cluster Service?

Ans:

The cluster service manages all the activity that is specific to the cluster. One instance of the cluster service runs on each node in the cluster. The cluster service does the following

- Manages Cluster Objects and Configurations
- Manages the local restart policy
- Coordinates with other instances of the cluster service in the cluster
- Handles event notification

- Facilitates communication among other software components
- Performs failover operations

4. What is called a Resource in Windows cluster?

Ans:

A resource is a physical or logical entity, which has below properties:

- Can be brought online and taken offline
- Can be managed in the failover cluster
- Can be owned by only one node at a time

To manage resources, Cluster service communicates with a resource DLL through Resource Monitor.

5. What are the different states of a Resource in Windows cluster?

Ans:

All resources can have following states

- Offline: Resource is offline
- Offline_Pending: Offline initiated and it is in progress
- Online: Resource is currently online
- Online_Pending: Online is initiated and it is in progress
- Failed: Resource failed

6. What is a Cluster Group?

Ans:

A cluster group is a collection of logically grouped cluster resources. It may contain cluster-aware application services, such as SQL Server Group, File Server etc.

7. What is Public Network?

Ans:

A public network/External network provides client systems with access to cluster application services and IP address resources are created on networks that provide clients access to cluster services.

8. What is Private Network in windows cluster?

Ans:

A private network is also called as interconnect or heartbeat connect is a network that is setup between the nodes of the cluster and it carries only internal cluster communications. It is shared only by the cluster nodes, and is not accessible from outside the cluster. It is used by cluster nodes in order to monitor each node's status and communicate with each other.

9. What is Heartbeat in Windows cluster?

Ans:

Heartbeats are messages that Cluster Service regularly sends between the instances of Cluster Service that are on each node to manage the cluster.

10. What Failover and Failback terms mean in Windows Cluster?

Ans:

Failover: Failover is the process of moving a group of resources from one node to another in the case of a failure. For example, in a cluster where Microsoft SQL Server is running on node **A** and node **A** fails, SQL Server automatically fails over to node **B** of the cluster.

Failback: Failback is the process of returning a resource or group of resources to the node on which it was running before it failed over. For example, when node **A** comes back online, SQL Server can fail back from node **B** to node **A**.

11. What is a Quorum?

Ans:

Quorum for a cluster is the number of elements that must be online for that cluster to continue running. Each element in can cast one "vote" to determine whether the cluster continues running.

The full function of a cluster depends on:

- Quorum
- Capacity of each node to support the services and applications that fail over to that node

  Ex:

  A cluster with 7 Nodes can still have a Quorum (4 Nodes Online) after 3 node failed as majority wins

  But remember it's not just depends on Quorum also other 4 nodes should have capacity to server clients.

  - ✓ *Case 1:* On 7 Node Cluster 3 Failed and 4 Online and these 4 are capable to handle the load

    Cluster continue serving
  - ✓ *Case 2:* On 7 Node Cluster 3 Failed and 4 Online and these 4 are not capable to handle the load

    Cluster makes all nodes offline
  - ✓ *Case 3:* On 7 Node Cluster 3 Failed and 4 Online and these 4 are not capable to handle the load

    Cluster makes all nodes offline
  - ✓ *Case 4:* On 7 Node Cluster 4 Failed and 3 Online

    Cluster makes all nodes offline as majority votes are offline

12. What are the various Quorum modes available?

Ans:

Quorum Mode: Strategy to define the elements in cluster which can cast vote to make Quorum

Node Majority: Each node that is available and in communication can vote.

Node and Disk Majority: Each node plus a designated disk in the cluster storage (the "disk witness") can vote, whenever they are available and in communication.

Node and File Share Majority: Each node plus a designated file share created by the administrator (the "file share witness") can vote, whenever they are available and in communication.

No Majority: Disk Only: The cluster has quorum if one node is available and in communication with a specific disk in the cluster storage.

13. What is Node Majority model?

Ans:

This type of quorum is optimal for clusters having an odd number of nodes. In this configuration, only the nodes have votes. The shared storage does not have a vote. A majority of votes are needed to operate the cluster.

14. What is Node and Disk Majority model?

Ans:

Nodes and a shared disk get votes. This configuration allows a loss of half the nodes, providing the disk witness is available, or over half the nodes are available without the disk witness being available. This is recommended for even number of nodes in the cluster.

15. What is Node and File Share Majority model?

Ans:

This type of quorum is optimal for clusters having an even number of nodes when a shared witness disk is not an option. Other characteristics include the following:

- each node and the file share "witness" gets a vote
- it does not require a shared disk to reach a quorum
- the file share has no special requirements
- the file share should be located at a third site, making this type of quorum the best solution for geographically dispersed clusters

16. What is No Majority: Disk only mode?

Ans:

The disk witness must be available to have quorum, but the number of available nodes doesn't matter. If you have a four-node cluster and only one node is available, but the disk witness is available, you have quorum. If the disk witness isn't available, then even if all four nodes are available you can't have quorum.

17. What Quorum mode you recommend for a given cluster?

Ans:

I strongly recommend using the cluster software recommended quorum. We can see this if we run Quorum configuration wizard.

18. Can you explain how do you know the current quorum configuration on your cluster?

Ans:

Failover Cluster Manager: Manage a Cluster and choose the Cluster Name there in that summary you can see the Quorum configuration

Command Prompt: c:\cluster/quorum

19. Can we change the Quorum settings after installing the windows cluster?

Ans:

Yes, we can change the Quorum setting after the Windows Cluster installation.

20. What is Split Brain situation in Cluster?

Ans:

Cluster nodes communicate with each other over the network (port 3343). When nodes are unable to communicate with each other, they all assume the resources of the other (unreachable) nodes have to be brought online. Because the same resource will be brought online on multiple nodes at the same time, data corruption may occur. These results in a situation called "Split Brain."

21. How Spilt Brain situation is resolved?

Ans:

To prevent Split Brains we need to bring the cluster resource online on a single node (rather than multiple nodes). Each of the online node cast vote for majority and the resources come online on that group which has more votes or has majority. In case of Even number of nodes Quorum also acts as a voter to eliminate split brain situation.

22. What are the Hardware requirements for Windows Server Cluster?

Ans:

- Two windows servers (nodes)
- At least one shared disk array that supports, either SCSI or fiber channel.
- Each server must have a SCSI or fiber channel adapter to talk to the shared disk array. The shared disk array cannot use the SCSI controller used by the local hard disk or CD-ROM.
- Each server must have two PCI network cards (one for the private connection and one for the public connection)
- 1 IP Address for Windows virtual cluster name

23. Let's say a user is performing a transaction on a clustered server and failover has occurred. What will happen to the Transaction?

Ans:

If it is active/passive, there is a good chance the transaction died, but active/passive is considered by some the better as it is not as difficult to administer. I believe that is what we have on active. Still, active/active may be best depending on what the requirements are for the system.

24. How you do which node is active and which is passive. What are the criteria for deciding the active node?

Ans:

Open Cluster Administrator, check the SQL Server group where you can see current owner. So current owner is the active node and other nodes are passive.

25. What are the Hardware requirements for SQL Server Cluster?

Ans:

- 1 IP Address for MSDTC service
- 1 IP Address for SQL Server Active\Passive Instance or 2 IP address for SQL Server Active\Active Instance
- 1 IP Address for SQL Server Analysis services (if needed)

26. How many IP Addresses we require for setting up Active\Passive SQL Server cluster?

Ans:

- 2 Windows nodes – Public
- 2 Private IP Addresses – Private
- 1 Windows Virtual Cluster Name
- 1 MSDTC
- 1 SQL Server Virtual Network Name

27. How many IP Addresses we require for setting up Active\Active SQL Server cluster with Analysis services?

Ans:

- 2 Windows nodes – Public
- 2 Private IP Addresses – Private
- 1 Windows Virtual Cluster Name
- 1 MSDTC
- 1 SQL Server Virtual Network Name
- 1 SQL Server Analysis Services

28. How do you open a Cluster Administrator?

Ans:

Start Menu > Run > Cluadmin.msc

29. What is SQL Server Network Name (Virtual Name)?

Ans:

This is the SQL Server Instance name that all client applications will use to connect to the SQL Server.

30. What are the different types of SQL Server Cluster configuration?

Ans:

- Active\Passive
- Active\Active

31. What is the difference between Active\Passive and Active\Active cluster?

Ans:

Active – Passive: Active Passive cluster is a failover cluster configured in a way that only one cluster node is active at any given time. The other node, called as Passive node is always online but in an idle condition, waiting for a failure of the Active Node, upon which the Passive Node takes over the SQL Server Services and this becomes the Active Node, the previous Active Node now being a Passive Node.

Active – Active: It is a failover cluster configured in a way that both the cluster nodes are active at any given point of time. That is, one Instance of SQL Server is running on each of the nodes always; when one of the nodes has a failure, both the Instances run on the only one node until the failed node is brought up (after fixing the issue that caused the node failure). The instance is then failed over back to its designated node.

32. Difference between SQLSERVER 2005 and SQLSERVER 2008/2012 Cluster Installation?

Ans:

In sql2005 we have the option of installing SQL in remaining nodes from the primary node, But in sql2008 we need to go separately (Login to the both nodes) for installing SQL cluster

33. Is it mandatory to configure MSDTC in Windows Server 2012 cluster before installing SQL Server cluster?

Ans:

No it's not mandatory to configure MSDTC service to install SQL Server in Windows 2012 cluster. Installation will give you a warning but will not stop the installation.

34. What is the impact on cluster if the quorum disk fails in Windows Server 2008/2012 Cluster?

Ans:

Cluster continues to work but failover will not happen in case of any other failure in the active node.

35. On active directory what are the permissions required for cluster SQL Server service account?

Ans:

Clustered SQL Server Service account should have OBJECT CREATION permissions in the Active Directory.

36. Why SQL Server Services in manual mode on cluster instances?

Ans:

SQL Server services should always be in manual mode on clustered instances because these are managed by the cluster service and it's taken online on its respective owner node based on the failover.

37. What are "LooksAlive" and "IsAlive" checks?

Ans:

Windows cluster service uses "HeartBeat" process to check nodes availability for both OS and SQL Server. It performs 2 health checks:

- "LooksAlive"
- "IsAlive"

"LooksAlive" Health Check:

- It's a quick lightweight health check
- By default runs for every 5 Seconds
- It doesn't perform detailed check thereof it may not identify the services which are running but responding or in hung state.
- If incase LooksAlive check fails it calls the "IsAlive" check
- Polling interval can be changed by adjusting LooksAlivePollInterval property of Cluster service

"IsAlive" Health Check:

- It's a detailed health check
- By default runs for every 60 Seconds
- Run @@SERVERNAME to ensure that SQL Server is responding to queries
- It can't identify database failure which means it makes sure SQL Server is up, running and responding for queries but it doesn't check database level check.
- When unable to connect to SQL Server it retries for 5 times
- After continues 5 failures Windows cluster service initiate the failover to another node.
- Polling interval can be changed by adjusting IsAlivePollInterval property of Cluster service

38. On windows Cluster what are validation tests?

Ans:

Validation test is a mechanism of verifying that all the components which are participating in the Windows cluster are fine and failover is happening between the nodes.

39. What are the basics tests done by the validation tests in Windows Cluster?

Ans:

Cluster Configuration tests: Validate critical cluster configuration settings.

Inventory tests: Provide an inventory of the hardware, software, storage and server configurations.

Network tests: Validate that networks are set up properly.

Storage tests: Validate that the storage on which the failover cluster depends is behaving correctly and supports the required functions of the cluster.

System Configuration tests: Validate that the system software and configuration settings are compatible across servers.

40. Where the results of validation tests are stored?

Ans:

These reports are automatically stored for you in <WinDir>\Cluster\Reports as MHTML files.

41. We have a SQL Server cluster instance. As business required we would like to install a new database which is not critical and failover not required in-case of any issues. Can we keep this database files on local disk instead of clustered disk?

Ans:

No, it's not possible. SQL Server 2014 and all previous versions of SQL Server require databases be created on clustered resources. We can't use local drives or drives which are not part of the cluster group for holding user database files.

42. Can we configure TEMPDB database on a local drive?

Ans:

Yes! From SQL Server 2012 SQL Server cluster configuration supports TEMPDB on local disk. But make sure that the file path is same on all nodes.

43. What is SMB share?

Ans:

SMB stands for Server Message Block (SMB). SMB protocol is a network file sharing protocol that allows applications on a computer to read and write to files and to request services from server programs in a computer network. The SMB protocol can be used on top of its TCP/IP protocol or other network protocols. Windows Server 2012 introduces the new 3.0 version of the SMB protocol.

In the past, we were allowed to store data and log files into the network by activating a trace flag 1807. However, from SQL Server 2012, it is possible to store user and system databases on the network using SMB shares. This applies to both SQL Server stand-alone and SQL Server on Windows Failover Cluster.

- SMB 2.0 introduced with Windows Server 2008
- SMB 2.1 with Windows Server 2008 R2: We could see significant performance improvements like SQL OLTP workloads.
- SMB 3.0 with Windows Server 2012: Support for transparent failover of file shares providing zero downtime.
- SMB 3.02 with Windows Server 2012 R2: This is the latest version and MTU is turned on by default, which significantly enhances performance in large sequential transfers like SQL Server data warehouse.

44. What are the advantages of using SMB File Share?

Ans:

Before the advantages of SMB, SAN is always the best option for mission critical database systems on clusters.

Advantages of SMB File share:

Build low-cost clustered instances: SMB is less expensive when compare with SAN.

Use for non-productive servers: When any Non-Production environment requires cluster installation we can choose SMB

Less Operational Data Stores: For example to handle archived databases.

Temporary storage: When we need to have storage for temporary purpose.

45. How clustering is different from ALWAYSON?

Ans:

I was confused when I started learning, let me simply explain it:

ALWAYSON Availability Groups: This is an advanced feature of Database Mirroring introduced from SQL Server 2012.

ALWAYSON Failover Cluster: This is same as SQL Server Failover Cluster with some new features

46. Can you tell me the best feature in SQL Server 2012 ALWAYSON Failover Cluster when compared to SQL Server 2008 R2 Failover Cluster?

Ans:

In SQL Server 2012 ALWAYSON Failover Clusters we can have cluster nodes on different subnets.

47. In a Failover Cluster what are the elements should be matched between nodes?

Ans:

To get the fully functional failover all nodes in a Failover Cluster should have:

- Similar hardware configuration
- Identical software configuration
- Operating system version and patch level
- SQL Server version and patch level
- SQL Server components
- Instance name

48. What are the different services managed by Windows Server Failover Cluster (WSFC) service?

Ans:

The WSFC service manages

- Server cluster configuration
- Quorum configuration
- Failover policy
- Failover operations

- Virtual Network Name (VNN)
- Virtual IP addresses

49. What are the various failures that cause Cluster Failover from one node to other?

Ans:

- Hardware failures
- Operating System failures
- Application/Service failures
- Planned/Manual Failover

50. What are the primary elements of a failover cluster?

Ans:

WSFC Resource Group:

A SQL Server FCI runs in a WSFC resource group. Each node in the resource group maintains a synchronized copy of the configuration settings and check-pointed registry keys to ensure full functionality of the FCI after a failover, and only one of the nodes in the cluster owns the resource group at a time known as active node.

SQL Server Binaries:

The product binaries are installed locally on each node of the Failover Cluster Instance

Storage:

Contrary to the Always On availability group, an FCI must use shared storage between all nodes of the FCI for database and log storage. The shared storage can be in the form of WSFC cluster disks, disks on a SAN, or file shares on an SMB.

Network Name:

The VNN (Virtual Network Name) for the FCI provides a unified connection point for the FCI. This allows applications to connect to the VNN without the need to know the currently active node. When a failover occurs, the VNN is registered to the new active node after it starts. This process is transparent to the client or application connecting to SQL Server and this minimize the downtime the application or clients experience during a failure.

Virtual IPs:

In the case of a multi-subnet FCI, a virtual IP address is assigned to each subnet in the FCI. During a failover, the VNN on the DNS server is updated to point to the virtual IP address for the respective subnet. Applications and clients can then connect to the FCI using the same VNN after a multi-subnet failover.

51. When a failover initiated what is the approximate time for cluster failover?

Ans:

It depends on various factors. When your SQL Server instance last performed a checkpoint operation, there can be a substantial amount of dirty pages in the buffer cache. Consequently, failovers last as long as it takes to write the remaining dirty pages to disk. Beginning with Microsoft

SQL Server 2012, the FCI can use indirect checkpoints to throttle the amount of dirty pages kept in the buffer cache.

52. Do you see any observations in health monitoring between SQL Server 2008 R2 and 2012?

Ans:

- WSFC service monitors both the health of the underlying WSFC cluster, as well as the health of the SQL Server instance.
- Microsoft SQL Server 2012, the WSFC service uses a dedicated connection to poll the active SQL Server instance for detailed component diagnostics through a system stored procedure which helps in preventing false failovers.
- The detailed component diagnostics makes it possible to configure a more flexible failover policy, whereby you can choose what failure conditions trigger failovers and which failure conditions do not.
- Also it makes easier the Root Cause Analysis

Cluster Scenarios

53. Can you quickly describe the events occurs when a failover happens? Let's say we have Node 1 and Node 2. Node 1 is active and Node 2 is passive and virtual network name is VirtualNode1.

Ans:

- Steps performed by Failover Cluster Manager when a failover occurred:
- Stops the SQL Server Agent service and any services dependent on the SQL Server service
- All dirty pages in the buffer cache are written to disk
- Stops the SQL Server service
- Releases Node A's hold on the IP address and network name for VirtualNode1
- Releases Node A's hold on the shared storage
- Tells Node B to take control of the shared storage
- Tells Node B to take control of the IP address and network name for VirtualNode1
- Starts the SQL Server service on Node B
- Starts the SQL Server Agent service and any services dependent on the SQL Server service
- Client application connection requests are automatically directed to the new active node using the same virtual network name (VNN)

Case 1: Manual Failover: Performs all above steps

Case 2: Node1 down/failure: Once cluster manager identifies that SQL Server is down/failed on Node-A then steps starts from 6 and performs till step 10.

Case 3: SQL Server service is running but not responding: Failover cluster manager can't note that SQL Server is not available until its "keep alive" check fails. Once it determines SQL Server is not responsive, it tries to perform all steps from 1 to 10 thereof in this case we might see the longer failover times.

54. How to add a new node to existing SQL Server Cluster?

Ans:

We'll talk about 2008 R2 and 2012.

- It's as simple as installing a new SQL Server instance.
- Run SQL Server Setup
- Select "Add node to SQL Server Failover Cluster"
- Next give all required details
- On Cluster Node Configuration Page Name on the node will automatically populated
- Again continue with the next steps and finally "Add Node Progress"
- After successfully adding node we need to make sure the node is working as expected
- Manually Move/Failover SQL Server Service to newly installed node
- After moving cross check all services are online on newly added node.

55. How to apply service pack on Active/Passive cluster on 2008 and 2012?

Ans:

- Freeze the service groups on Node A (active node).
- Confirm all SQL services are stopped on Node B.
- Upgrade the SQL Server 2008 instance on Node B.
- Reboot node B.
- Unfreeze the service group on node A.
- Fail over the service group to Node B.
- After the service group comes online, freeze the service group on Node B.
- Confirm all SQL services are stopped on Node A.
- Upgrade the SQL Server 2008 instance on Node A.
- Reboot Node A.
- Unfreeze the service group on node B.
- Fail back the service group to Node A.

56. Have you ever applied a service pack on SQL Server 2005 Active/Passive cluster?

Ans:

- Login to the Console on the target node
- Copy the Service Pack to a local drive on the target node
- Move all instances to the target node
- You can only install on the Active Node.
- Move the Cluster Resource to the target node

- Move the MSDTC Resource to the target node
- Verify all users are logged out from all other nodes (RDP and Console sessions)
- Start the Service Pack install
  - ✓ Use a domain account with admin rights to all servers.
  - ✓ Ignore locked files
- Reboot current server
- You should not need to perform the install on any other nodes, nor reboot them. The service pack will update the passive nodes first.

57. You find SP is not applied on all the nodes across the cluster. How to apply SP only on required nodes?

Ans:

If you find that the product level is not consistent across all the nodes, you will need to fool the 2005 patch installer into only patching the nodes that need updating. To do so, you will have to perform the following steps:

1. Fail Instance, Cluster, and MSDTC groups to an unpatched node
2. Remove any successfully patched nodes from failover candidates of the SQL Server Service of the instance group (do this using Cluster Admin tool)
3. Run the patch
4. After the patch installs successfully, add the Nodes removed in Step 2 back to the SQL Server Service of the Instance group

Why do you need to do this? Well when the patch installer determines that not all nodes in the cluster are at the same patch level, a passive node operation will fail and will prevent you from moving forward with any further patching.

58. How to change the SQL Server service account in a cluster environment?

Ans:

Method 1: (No failover required)

- Freeze the service group on active node from cluster administrator, change the service account and then restart the service.

Method 2:

- Offline the SQL resources
- Update the service account at SSCM and restart the service as needed
- Add the SQL resources back to online
- Note: Don't forget to update service account at the remaining nodes on the cluster.

Method 3:

- Node 2 (inactive node) change the SQL start-up account
- Fail over the SQL service group from node 1 to node 2.
- Node 1 (now the inactive node) change the SQL start-up account

59. How to apply service pack on Active/Active cluster Nodes?

Ans:

- Make a note of all node names (and/or IP addresses), SQL Server virtual names along with preferred nodes. If there are more than three nodes you may need to also take note of possible owners for each SQL resource group. For my example assume that I have a cluster with node1 and node2, SQL1 normally lives on node1 and SQL2 normally lives on node2.
- To start with a clean slate and ensure any previous updates are completed both nodes should be restarted if possible. Choose the physical node that you want to patch second and restart that node (in this example node2).
- Restart the node you want to patch first (node1). This will mean that both active SQL instances are now running on node2. Some restarts will be essential, but you could avoid the first two restarts if you need to keep downtime to a minimum and just fail SQL1 over to node2. The main point here is to always patch a passive node.
- In cluster administrator remove node1 from the possible owners lists of SQL1 and SQL2. This means that neither SQL instance can fail over to node1 while it is being patched.
- Run the service pack executable on node1.
- Restart node1.
- Add node1 back into the possible owners lists of SQL1 and SQL2 and fail both instances over to node1.
- Repeat steps 4 – 6 on node2.
- Add node2 back into the possible owners lists of SQL1 and SQL2 and fail both instances over to node2. Check that the build level is correct and review the SQL Server error logs.
- Fail SQL1 over to node1. Check build levels and SQL Server error logs

60. You had a request to install SQL Server 2008 failover cluster on Windows Server 2012 R2. Windows failover cluster is already ready. SQL Server 2008 installation failed at setup support files and the installation was failed for the rule "Cluster Service Verification". How do you resolve this issue?

Ans:

RCA:

- When verifies log file "InstallFailoverClusterGlobalRules" it's clearly saying that SQL couldn't verifies the cluster service.
- We verified and confirmed windows cluster service is online but SQL couldn't access the cluster service
- We tried installing SQL Server from command line by skipping the rules: Not worked and ended with the same error.
- "Setup/SkipRules=Cluster_VerifyForErrors/Action=InstallFailoverCluster"
- While searching for the solution we found that the problem is expected and the root cause is SQL Server setup is trying to check windows cluster service using the deprecated feature in Windows 2012 R2.

- Deprecated features: Failover Cluster Command Interface (cluster.exe) and Failover Cluster Automation Server.
- Since these are deprecated features these are not enabled by default in Windows 2012 R2

Solution:

- Check the windows Cluster Installation using PowerShell command:
- "Get-WindowsFeature RSAT-Cluster*"
- It showcase all windows cluster features installed/enabled status
- If you observe "Failover Cluster Automation Server" and "Failover Cluster Command Interface" are Available but not installed.
- Install the feature "Failover Cluster Automation Server" using the PowerShell command
- "Install-WindowsFeature -Name RSAT-Clustering-AutomationServer"
- After you see the feature is got installed successfully, try installing SQL Server and you should get succeed at this time.

61. We need to install and configure SQL Server 2012 Active/Passive cluster on Windows Server 2012 R2. Windows cluster is ready. Now can you tell me how do you install SQL Server Failover Cluster? I don't want you to explain step by step but tell me the most important points that we need to take care during the installation?

Ans:

Since Windows Server Failover Cluster is ready will start with the next step:

- Configure MSTDC Role
  - ✓ Go to Failover Cluster Manager → Roles → Configure Role
  - ✓ Select Distributed Transaction Coordinator (DTC)
- **Client Access Point:** Name and IP address required. Make sure that your logged in account should have an appropriate rights on Active Directory (AD) as this creates a computer object on Active Directory with the given name.
- We need a dedicated drive at least with 2 GB free space for MSDTC, assign that drive to this role
- After this configuration you should be able to see MSDTC is up and running under Roles in Failover Cluster Manager.
- **Install SQL Server on Node -1**
  - ✓ Run SQL Server Installer
  - ✓ Select "New SQL Server Failover Cluster Instance"
  - ✓ **On Instance Configuration Page:**
  - ✓ **SQL Server Network Name:** Careful while giving this name as this is the name that applications will use to connect to the database. Clients can identify this SQL instance using this name.

- ✓ **Instance Root Directory:** Need not change this. Remember this is the path where SQL binaries available not your databases.
- ✓ **Important Note:** Your account which are using for SQL Server Cluster Installation should have proper rights on Active Directory as a new object will be created at AD with this network name.
- ✓ **Cluster Resource Group:** Give a suitable name for Cluster Resource Group
- ✓ Cluster Disk Selection: Select the cluster volumes/disks that are going to be used for storing SQL databases.
- ✓ **Cluster Network Configuration:** Give the ipv4 ip address
- ✓ **Server Configuration:** Give service account under which SQL Server will run. As Microsoft recommended we need to use a Domain/AD account.
- ✓ Continue with the next page and complete the installation on Node-1

➢ **Install SQL Server on Node -2**

- ✓ On Node-2 and start SQL Server installer
- ✓ Select "Add node to SQL Server Failover Cluster"
- ✓ Same steps as we followed on Node-1
- ✓ We need not give Resource Group Name, IP Address and Service Accounts
- ✓ Give password for service accounts
- ✓ Continue with the remaining steps as it is and finish the installation.

➢ Then connect to Failover Cluster Manager and try to failover SQL Server resource from Active (Node 1) to passive (Node 2) to make sure failover is working as expected.

62. Can you tell me few T-SQL commands that you use to quickly know the cluster status?

Ans:

```
/*** To find the current instance is Clustered or not ***/
SELECT CASE WHEN SERVERPROPERTY('IsClustered') = 0 THEN 'Non-clustered' ELSE 'Clustered' End;
GO
/*** If clustered - Returns Node Name on which SQL Server Instance is Currently running***/
/*** If Non-clustered - Returns the hostname***/
SELECT SERVERPROPERTY ('ComputerNamePhysicalNetBIOS') AS [Current_NodeName];
/** Find all cluster Nodes information and status ****/
SELECT * FROM fn_virtualservernodes ()
--OR
SELECT * FROM sys.dm_os_cluster_nodes
```

```
/** Find SQL Server Cluster Shared Drive Names ***/
SELECT * FROM fn_servershareddrives ()
--OR
SELECT * FROM sys.dm_io_cluster_shared_drives
```

63. **Any SQL DBA who works on cluster instances should have a minimum knowledge on using PowerShell. Do you know any PowerShell commands which can be useful in knowing the cluster status?**

Ans:

Yes! We use PowerShell commands to get the cluster instance details and also most of the times PS is the only way to fix problems in clustered environment. There are 2 things should be done while using PowerShell:

- Start PowerShell with "Run as Administrator"
- Import the "FailoverClusters" module
- To Import the module FailoverClusters

  PS C:\> Import-Module FailoverClusters

Most common cmdlets we use:

Get-ClusterGroup:

- To know the status of all cluster groups in our cluster: Cluster Name "SQLCUST01"
- PS C:\> Get-ClusterGroup -Cluster SQLCLUSTER
- Get-ClusterResource & Where-Object & Sort-Object:
- Get-ClusterResource: Get all clustered resources information
- Where-Object: Filter only SQL Server Group resources
- Sort-Object: Sort based on the Group name
- Ex:

  ```
  PS C:\> Get-ClusterResource -Cluster SQLCLUSTER |
          Where-Object {$_.OwnerGroup -like "SQL Server*"} |
          Sort-Object -Property OwnerGroup
  ```

Start-ClusterResource:

- To start a cluster resource SQL Server Input Cluster Name and Resource Name
- Ex: PS C:\> Start-ClusterResource -Cluster SQLCLUSTER -Name "SQL Server (INST1)"

Stop-ClusterResource:

- To stop a cluster resource SQL Server Input Cluster Name and Resource Name
- Ex: PS C:\> Stop-ClusterResource -Cluster SQLCLUSTER -Name "SQL Server (INST1)"

Move-ClusterGroup:

- It can move an entire resource group from one node to other in a cluster we need to input Resource Group Name, Cluster Name and Node to which the group has to be moved
- PS C:\> Move-ClusterGroup "SQL Server (INST1)" -Cluster SQLCLUSTER -Node SQLNODE02

Note:

Also we can run T-SQL commands at PowerShell to do that we need to import the module sqlps

PS C:\> Import-Module sqlps

Now check SQL Server ERRORLOG using Powershell:

PS SQLSERVER:\> Invoke-Sqlcmd -Query "EXEC master.dbo.XP_READERRORLOG 0, 1, N'error', `

null,null,null, N'desc'" -ServerInstance "SQL1\INST1"

64. I have a 2 Node Active/Passive cluster. On Active Node there are 3 SQL Agent jobs are scheduled. Now a failover initiated and SQL Server Resource group moved to Node 2. My question is "does these jobs are also replicated to Node 2? Or we need to manually create them again on Node 2?

Ans:

All Jobs and Maintenance Plans are taken care by failover procedure. We need not move/create SQL Jobs/Maintenance Plans on other node. The logic is simple all these jobs and maintenance plans are stored on system database MSDB and the failover just starts using the SQL Service on Node 2 but the datasource (All databases physical file location) is same as it access from Node 1.

65. I have 2 node Active/Passive failover cluster on SQL Server 2012 built on Windows Server 2012 R2. Now on active node SQL instance one of the databases is not coming online due to a page corruption. Can you get it online by initiating a manual failover to other node?

Ans:

No way! Let me give you a clarity on clustering, failover clustering is to give 24X7 support for your Services (Ex SQL Server) not for your data.

- When you have 2 node Active Passive cluster:
- 2 Different SQL Server installed on 2 Nodes
- Both nodes access data/data files from a single shared disk.
- That means if a user database "EmpDB.MDF" is stored on disk E:
- When Node A is active: SQL Server on A access data file from disk E
- When Failover to Node B: SQL Server on A disconnect the session to datafile "EmpDB.MDF" on E drive and a new session starts from SQL Server on Node B to E drive.
- When there is a page corruption on Datafile it can't be resolved by initiating a failover.

66. I need a solution for both my services and data what will be the best solution available in SQL Server?

Ans:

There are few ways:

SQL Server 2008 R2: SQL Server Failover Cluster + Database Mirroring/Log shipping/ Replication

SQL Server 2012/2014: ALWAYSON Failover Clusrering + ALWAYSON Availability Groups/ Log shipping/Replication

SQL Server 2008 R2/2012/2014: Geo-Clustering/Multisite Failover/Active-Active Cluster configuration: In this we need not use a central storage and we can use individual disks. But we need a disk level replication solution. We can use a third party solution for replicating data between disks Ex: DataKeeper Cluster Edition. Also the nodes can be in different subnets this is the new feature added in SQL Server 2012.

67. Can I install all SQL Server components on my cluster?

Ans:

No! SQL Server Integration Services is not "cluster-aware" and can't fail back and forth with your cluster. SSRS also not a cluster aware service but there is an indirect way to installing SSRS on cluster instance.

68. How to know the approximate time require for failover?

Ans:

There are lots of factors that involve in failover time. Ex: SQL Server databases recovery time and buffer cache that needs to be written to disk etc.

I would recommend:

- Create a test load (Should match with peak load) on your server and capture the failover time.
- To make sure the failover time matching with you service level agreement, have a look into indirect checkpoint.

69. Can we implement clustering on a virtualized server?

Ans:

Yes, we can create failover clusters with virtual servers with VMware or Hyper-V and try SQL Server clustering. But it is not recommended for premium production applications.

70. You have an incident on one of the premium server due to a cluster failover. While fixing that what is your recommendation? Will you use cluster management console or PowerShell?

Ans:

- I always recommend using PowerShell script.
- Most of the times Cluster Management Console will respond very slowly in case of failures and failovers.

- Make sure you are prepared with the all require PS commands to fix production issues.
- Also you should run PS in admin mode

71. Can we be able to make Cluster Node online without Quorum?

Ans:

We were not able to connect to SQL Server. We tried to connect to Cluster Manager Console even it's not responding for a long time. We found that SQL Server Instance is offline and Windows Failover Cluster Instance is offline too.

RCA:

- 2 Node Active/Passive Cluster
- Node 1 - Active is having 1 vote
- Node 2 - Stand By is having 1 vote
- Quorum Disk is have 1 vote
- Standby node and Quorum Disk went offline
- Windows Failover Cluster Instance (WFCI) checks that majority of votes are offline
- WFCI is also went to offline
- Of course SQL Server too went offline

Resolution:

- We tried to make Windows Failover Cluster Instance Online without Quorum
- Connect to the current Active Node and make sure Cluster Service is not running from services.msc
- If it is running stop it
- Connect to Power shell console with Admin rights and import required module "FailoverClusters"
- Start the cluster node using the below command to start cluster node without the quorum
- Start-ClusterNode –Name "WSCLUSTER-Premium" -FixQuorum
- Once the WSFC has been brought online, make sure that the cluster node is guaranteed as a voting member by setting the NodeWeight
- (Get-ClusterNode –Name "WSCLUSTER-Premium").NodeWeight = 1
- Once the WSFC is online, the SQL Server failover clustered instance is automatically brought online
- Then fix the issues on Quorum Disk
- Try to bring the other cluster node online

Note: From SQL Server 2012 and above we can skip the NodeWeight setup step as it will be adjusted dynamically based on the configuration.

72. SQL Server configured on 2 nodes Active/Passive cluster. Now the requirement is to add SSRS feature to the existing SQL Instance then we can get the same failover functionality for our SSRS. Can you explain how to do this?

Ans:

Since SSRS is not a cluster aware service there is no straight forward method to do this. But yes we can achieve this as below:

Installing SSRS:

- If we try to add SSRS feature to existing SQL clustered instance it fails at rules page and doesn't allow you to install SSRS.
- This can be resolved by skipping the rules using below command: Issue the below command at cmd

  Setup.exe/SkipRules=StandaloneInstall_HasClusteredOrPreparedInstanceCheck/Action=Install
- It starts SQL Server installer and bypass the cluster instance check installation rule
- We can be able to add SSRS feature for the existing SQL Server instance
- Once it is done on Active node repeat the same process on passive node.

Configuring SSRS:

- Now configure SSRS using SSRS configuration manager
- Most important part is while giving SQL instance path use the SQL Server failover cluster network/virtual name instead of node name.
- If we use node name while configuring, after failover report manager failed to locate the SQL Server instance.
- Once SSRS configured on active node do the same on passive node.
- Now your SSRS is installed and configured on clustered instance. Failover SQL Server from Active node to Passive node and test SSRS functionality on passive node.

73. We have been using SQL Server cluster instances for our applications. Now our client required a name change for SQL Server Network name which is being used by our applications to connect to SQL Server cluster instance. How do you change SQL Server network name?

Ans:

Before changing the Network Name:

- Check the current SQL Server Network/Virtual name
- Using T-SQL statement: SELECT @@Servername or
- Failover Cluster Manager: Name under Server Name
- List out all clients which are using this SQL Server i.e. Applications, third party tools, reporting tools etc.

Change the SQL Server Network Name:

- From Failover Cluster Manager Right click on Server Name à Properties
- On General tab you can see the column DNS Name which is nothing but the network/virtual name.
- Change the DNS name with the required new name and click on Apply
- It takes few seconds to change the name

Post changing the Network Name:

- Check the Server name as we did in first step. Now you should see the new name
- Recycle the resources and services: On failover cluster manager right click on Server Name à Take offline and Bring Online.
- Now try to connect to SQL Server instance using the new network/virtual name
- Now Failover SQL Server service from Active node to Passive Node and test the connectivity
- Once you confirm all working fine then inform the clients to update their connection string to sue the newly changed network name to connect to Failover Cluster SQL Server instance.

74. Have you ever removed a SQL Server cluster node from failover cluster configuration? Can you explain the procedure?

Ans:

Yes!

- Let's say we have 2 node cluster and we are going to remove Node2.
- Connect to the node2 instance
- Mount SQL Server installation setup
- Run setup.exe as administrator
- Go to tab "Maintenance" and select "Remove Node from SQL Server Failover Cluster"
- After that it checks the rules and takes you through the removal steps.
- Mostly no inputs required from us
- A successful cluster node removal, you can verify at Failover Cluster Manager or using DMV "sys.DM_OS_Cluster_Nodes"

75. We have a SQL Server 2012 cluster setup. On active instance one of the DBA members was trying to remove SYSADMIN accounts. He was assisted to remove SYSADMIN role from all existing logins and add a new login "SQL12Admin" with SYSADMIN rights. Accidentally he removed all logins from SYSADMIN role but not able to add "SQL12Admin" to SYSADMIN role as he doesn't have rights to do that. Also SA account was disabled as a part of security policy. Now tell me how do you get their SYSADMIN rights back for at least one login "SQL12Admin"?

Ans:

Usually if we have the same situation on standalone server this problem can be resolved by restarting SQL Server in single user mode and we can add a login to SYSADMIN role. But in this case we need to deal with the cluster instance.

- On active node open Failover Cluster Manager and expand to the clustered SQL Server group within services and applications. Right-click and select "Take this service or application offline"
- Along with SQL Server cluster disk and IP address is also offline. Bring the clustered disks and the IP address back online by right-clicking those resources and choosing "Bring this resource online."
- Open command prompt and start SQL Server in single user mode

  "net start mssqlserver/m"
- SQL Server starts in single user mode. However it prevents us to connect from SSMS.
- In CMD connect to SQL Server instance using SQLCMD

  sqlcmd -S 192.168.1.102
- On a successful connection add the login "SQL12Admin" to SYSADMIN role:

  "sp_addsrvrolemember 'SQL12Admin', 'SYSADMIN'"
- Stop SQL Server

  "net stop mssqlserver"
- Open Failover Cluster Manager and Right Click on SQL Server group and "Bring this service or application online."
- Now you should be able to login using "SQL12Admin" with SYSADMIN rights

76. What are the various log files that helps us in troubleshooting issues and in Root Cause Analysis?

Ans:

SQL Server error logs: Check SQL Server error logs to find out the errors

Windows Event Viewer (System/Application): As usual check this place to find if anything suspicious

Failover Cluster Manager:

We can see the high level details from Cluster Wizard Summary page. Also we can see events and logs by filtering the required events.

Cluster Log Files:

Generate Cluster Log files Using Cluster.exe:

To generate Cluster.log issue below command from CMD:

C:\> cluster/cluster log/g

Generate Cluster Log files Using PowerShell:

- Cluster.exe is in deprecated features from SQL Server 2012 thereof we can use Powershell command to get the Cluster.log:
- PS C:\Import-Module FailoverClusters
- PS C:\get-clusterlog
- To get cluster log on required location

  PS C:\get-clusterlog –destination C:\Temp
- To get Cluster log for last 30 Min

  PS C:\get-clusterlog -TimeSpan 30

Failover Cluster Instance Diagnostics Log using T-SQL:

- Start Diagnostic Logging
- ALTER SERVER CONFIGURATION SET DIAGNOSTICS LOG ON;
- Set Diagnostic File Location:
- ALTER SERVER CONFIGURATION SET DIAGNOSTICS LOG PATH = 'C:\logs';
- Specifying the maximum size of each diagnostic log
- ALTER SERVER CONFIGURATION SET DIAGNOSTICS LOG MAX_SIZE = 30 MB;
- Stop Diagnostic Logging
- ALTER SERVER CONFIGURATION SET DIAGNOSTICS LOG OFF;
- To read Diagnostic log file:

  SELECT

  xml_data.value ('(event/@name)[1]','VARCHAR(max)') AS 'Name'

  ,xml_data.value ('(event/@package)[1]','VARCHAR(max)') AS 'Package'

  ,xml_data.value ('(event/@timestamp)[1]','datetime') AS 'Time'

  ,xml_data.value ('(event/data[@name="state"]/value)[1]','int') AS 'State'

  ,xml_data.value ('(event/data[@name="state_desc"]/text)[1]','VARCHAR(max)') AS 'State Description'

  ,xml_data.value('(event/data[@name="failure_condition_level"]/value)[1]','int') AS 'Failure Conditions'

  ,xml_data.value('(event/data[@name="node_name"]/value)[1]','VARCHAR(max)') AS 'Node_Name'

  ,xml_data.value('(event/data[@name="instancename"]/value)[1]','VARCHAR(max)') AS 'Instance Name'

  ,xml_data.value('(event/data[@name="creation time"]/value)[1]','datetime') AS 'Creation Time'

,xml_data.value('(event/data[@name="component"]/value)[1]','VARCHAR(max)') AS 'Component'

,xml_data.value('(event/data[@name="data"]/value)[1]','VARCHAR(max)') AS 'Data'

,xml_data.value('(event/data[@name="info"]/value)[1]','VARCHAR(max)') AS 'Info'

FROM

(SELECT object_name AS 'event'

,CONVERT(xml,event_data) AS 'xml_data'

FROM sys.fn_xe_file_target_read_file('C:\Program Files\Microsoft SQL Server\MSSQL11.MSSQLSERVER\MSSQL\Log\SQLNODE1_MSSQLSERVER_SQLDIAG_0_129936003752530000.xel',NULL,NULL,NULL)

)

AS XEventData

ORDER BY Time;

- Stop Diagnostic Logging
- ALTER SERVER CONFIGURATION SET DIAGNOSTICS LOG OFF;

77. What is the default location for storing cluster logs? What are the limitations of cluster log files?

Ans:

- Cluster logs located in %windir%\Cluster\Reports directory on each node of the cluster
- The log files are stored in an *.etl format.
- Naming Format in Windows Server 2008
  - ✓ ClusterLog.etl.001
  - ✓ ClusterLog.etl.002
  - ✓ ClusterLog.etl.003
- Naming Format in Windows Server 2008 R2
  - ✓ Microsoft-Windows-FailoverClustering Diagnostic.etl.001
  - ✓ Microsoft-Windows-FailoverClustering Diagnostic.etl.002
  - ✓ Microsoft-Windows-FailoverClustering Diagnostic.etl.003
- The default size of these logs is 100MB each. You can change it as per your requirements.
- We can have maximum 3 *.etl files.
- The ETL.001 file is the active file being used by the live cluster service to write debug entries.
- File rollover happens only on reboot. On reboot, new ETL.001 will be created & last file will be deleted.
- In case, Latest ETL.001 file reach to MAX size, Data inside the file will start truncating on basis of FIFO (First In First Out). But file rollover happen only on reboot.

78. How to revalidate your cluster?

Ans:

- Failover Cluster Console select Failover Cluster Management and click on validate a configuration
- Follow the wizard instructions and on Summary page click on "View Report"
- The same report will be stored on folder
  "%SystemRoot%\Cluster\Reports\Validation Report date and time.html"

79. Can you quickly tell me few problems you faced while working with SQL Server clustering instances?

Ans:

Problem 1: SQL Server cannot log on to the network after it migrates to another node

RCA:

- There might be two reasons
- SQL Server service accounts are unable to contact a domain controller.
- SQL Server service account passwords are not identical on all cluster nodes

Resolution:

- Check your event logs for signs of networking issues such as adapter failures or DNS problems. Verify that you can ping your domain controller.
- Update service account passwords correctly on all nodes

Problem 2: Failure of a SQL Server service causes failover

RCA:

- Failure of specific service may cause the SQL Server group to fail over
- For example full text service is failed for some reason and it initiates a failover for SQL Server Group

Resolution:

- For services which should not initiate entire SQL Server Group failover in case of failures should be configured accordingly.
- For example when Full Text Service is failed but DB engine is running fine, this full text failure should not initiate a failover. To achieve this uncheck the property "**Affect the Group**" from full text service advanced properties.

Problem 3: SQL Server Setup fails on a cluster with error 11001

RCA:

- An orphan registry key in
  [HKEY_LOCAL_MACHINE\SOFTWARE\Microsoft\Microsoft SQL Server\MSSQL.X\Cluster]

Resolution:

- Make sure the MSSQL.X registry hive is not currently in use, and then delete the cluster key.

Problem 4: Cluster Setup Error: "The installer has insufficient privileges to access this directory: <drive>\Microsoft SQL Server. The installation cannot continue. Log on as an administrator or contact your system administrator"

RCA:

- This error is caused by a SCSI shared drive that is not partitioned properly.

Resolution:

Re-create a single partition on the shared disk:

- Delete the disk resource from the cluster and delete all partitions on the disk.
- Verify in the disk properties that the disk is a basic disk
- Create one partition on the shared disk, format the disk, and assign a drive letter to the disk.
- Add the disk to the cluster
- Run SQL Server Setup.

Problem 5: Applications fail to enlist SQL Server resources in a distributed transaction

RCA:

- Microsoft Distributed Transaction Coordinator (MS DTC) is not completely configured in Windows
- This might affect Linked Servers, Distributed Queries and Remote Stored Procedures

Resolution:

- Fully enable MS DTC services on the servers where SQL Server is installed and MS DTC is configured.
- From control panel change Logon account for MSDTC as "NT AUTHORITY\NetworkService"

Problem 6: Unable to failover SQL Instance to one of the node and it's failing with the error "The action Move didn't complete Error Code: 0x80071398"

RCA:

- The node on which the failover is failing, that node may not be checked in "Possible Owners" list.

Resolution:

- From the Failover Cluster Manager, check Possible Owners list from resources Advanced Properties and make sure the NODE is checked.
- In our case the issue was with "IP Address" resource, when we checked the Possible Owners list the required NODE was unchecked. After enabling that node in possible owners list we could be able to successfully failover to that node.

CHAPTER 9

SQL SERVER ALWAYSON

Interview Questions and Answers

Introduction: This chapter takes you through the SQL Server ALWAYSON related interview questions and answers. These questions are helpful for range of database administrators starting from a junior to an expert level DBA for the technical interview preparation. These questions and answers are deals with the below topics:

- SQL Server ALWAYSON
- AlwaysOn Scenarios

SQL Server AlwaysOn

1. What is ALWAYSON in SQL Server?

Ans:

ALWAYSON Availability Groups feature is a high-availability and disaster-recovery solution that provides an enterprise-level alternative to database mirroring. Introduced in SQL Server 2012, ALWAYSON Availability Groups maximizes the availability of a set of user databases for an enterprise. An availability group supports a failover environment for a discrete set of user databases, known as *availability databases* that fail over together. An availability group supports a set of read-write primary databases and one to four sets of corresponding secondary databases. Optionally, secondary databases can be made available for read-only access and/or some backup operations.

2. What are Availability Groups?

Ans:

A container for a set of databases, availability databases, that fails over together. Let's consider a scenario where a set of 3 databases are interlinked based on application requirement. Now we need to setup HA for these 3 databases. If we choose mirroring we need to have a separate mirroring setup for these 3 databases where as in ALWAYSON Availability Groups easier the job by grouping all these 3 databases.

3. What are Availability Databases?

Ans:

It's a database that belongs to an availability group. For each availability database, the availability group maintains a single read-write copy (the primary database) and one to four read-only copies (secondary databases).

4. Which SQL/Windows Server Editions include ALWAYSON Availability Group functionality?

Ans:

SQL Server Enterprise Edition and Windows Enterprise Edition

5. How many replicas can I have in an ALWAYSON Availability Group?

Ans:

SQL Server 2012: 1 Primary and up to 4 Secondary's

SQL Server 2014: 1 Primary and up to 8 Secondary's

6. What are the ALWAYSON improvements added in SQL Server 2014?

Ans:

Enhanced Availability for Read-Only Replicas:

With SQL Server 2014, the availability of secondary replicas has been enhanced to allow read workloads to continue to run even in the case of lengthy network failures or the loss of quorum for the Windows Server Failover Cluster.

Increased Number of Replicas:

SQL Server 2012 supported a maximum of four secondary replicas. With SQL Server 2014, ALWAYSON Availability Groups now supports up to eight secondary replicas.

Integration with Windows Azure:

On-premises SQL Server instances can use the new Windows Azure configuration options in the ALWAYSON Availability Group wizard to create one or more asynchronous secondary replicas on Windows Azure Infrastructure as a Service (IaaS) services.

SQL Server 2014 ALWAYSON Availability Groups can provide high availability for SQL Server databases hosted in Windows Azure.

Enhanced Diagnostics:

SQL Server 2014 ALWAYSON Availability Groups diagnostic and troubleshooting message display has been improved to offer more specific information. Additional columns have also been made more discoverable in the ALWAYSON Dashboard.

7. What are the ALWAYSON improvements in SQL Server 2016?

Ans:

Round-robin load balancing in readable SECONDARIES:

In SQL Server 2014 redirecting activity to the secondary replicas happens through read-only routing list. But the first replica in the list gets the most activity because it's the one that is always tried first. In SQL Server 2016, the list of readable secondary replicas offers up connection information on a round robin basis. Also, each replica has its own read-only routing list so that read-only balancing via the availability group listener could route traffic to secondary replicas.

Increased number of auto-failover targets:

In SQL Server 2014, there can be three synchronous replicas, but only two of those can be designated as automatic failover targets. In SQL Server 2016, all three synchronous replicas can now be designated as failover targets.

Distributed Transaction Coordinator support:

SQL Server 2016 ALWAYSON Availability Groups supports the Distributed Transaction Coordinator (DTC) to manage transactions across multiple databases and instances. Remember to get this support SQL Server should be in Windows Server 2016 or 2012 R2 with the latest rollup patch.

Failover on database health:

In 2014 and 2012 failover is depends on SQL Server instance health but starting from 2016 failover can be based on database health. Ex: One of the databases is offline in an instance:

- **2014/2012:** Since instance and other databases are running fine it doesn't trigger a failover
- **2016:** We can control the failover behavior based on database health; in this case all databases within the affected AG would failover.

Enhanced log replication throughput and redo speed:

Microsoft has worked to streamline the pipeline between the synchronous replicas to gain better log-data throughput when utilizing SQL Server ALWAYSON Availability Groups.

Support for group-managed service accounts:

A group Managed Service Account (gMSA) is a type of security account released in Windows Server 2012 and improved in SQL Server 2016. If the instance is part of an AG, setting up and maintaining permissions to access common resources such as file shares often becomes complex as security provisions need to be established for the service account from each instance within the AG. The group account provides similar security capabilities as a local managed service account on an individual server, but it has a domain scope. gMSA can automatically manages password synchronization across all nodes.

8. How many ALWAYSON Availability Groups can be configured in Always ON?

Ans:

Up to 10 availability groups is the recommendation, but it's not enforced

9. How many databases can be configured in an ALWAYSON Availability Group?

Ans:

Up to 100 is the recommendation, but it's not enforced

10. What are the Restrictions on Availability Groups?

Ans:

- Availability replicas must be hosted by different nodes of one WSFC cluster
- Unique availability group name: Each availability group name must be unique on the WSFC cluster. The maximum length for an availability group name is 128 characters.

- Availability replicas: Each availability group supports one primary replica and up to four secondary replicas. All of the replicas can run under asynchronous-commit mode, or up to three of them can run under synchronous-commit mode.
- Maximum number of availability groups and availability databases per computer: The actual number of databases and availability groups you can put on a computer (VM or physical) depends on the hardware and workload, but there is no enforced limit. Microsoft has extensively tested with 10 AGs and 100 DBs per physical machine.
- Do not use the Failover Cluster Manager to manipulate availability groups.

11. What are the minimum requirements of a database to be part of the Always ON Availability Group?

Ans:

- Availability groups must be created with user databases. Systems databases can't be used.
- Databases must be read-write. Read-only databases aren't supported.
- Databases must be multiuser databases.
- Databases can't use the AUTO_CLOSE feature.
- Databases must use the full recovery model, and there must be a full backup available.
- A given database can only be in a single availability group, and that database can't be configured to use database mirroring.

12. How many read-write and read only databases replica can be configure in SQL Server 2012 and 2014?

Ans:

- SQL Server 2012 supported a maximum of four secondary replicas.
- With SQL Server 2014, ALWAYSON Availability Groups now supports up to eight secondary replicas.

13. Is it possible to setup Log Shipping on a database which is part of Availability Group?

Ans:

Yes, it can be configured.

14. Is it possible to setup Replication on a database which is part of Availability Group?

Ans:

Yes, it is possible.

15. Does FILESTEAM, Change Data Capture and Database Snapshot supported are supported by Availability Group?

Ans:

Yes, all these features are supported by ALWAYSON Availability Group.

16. Can system database participate in AG?

Ans:

No.

17. What version of Windows do I need for ALWAYSON AGs?

Ans:

We highly recommend Windows Server 2012R2 and above.

18. Can I have different indexes or tables on my replicas?

Ans:

No, the replica database contents will be exactly the same as the primary.

19. What is Availability mode in Always ON?

Ans:

The availability mode is a property of each availability replica. The availability mode determines whether the primary replica waits to commit transactions on a database until a given secondary replica has written the transaction log records to disk (hardened the log). ALWAYSON supports below modes:

Asynchronous-commit mode: Primary replica commits the transaction on a database without waiting for the conformation from the secondary replica.

Synchronous-commit mode: Primary replica does not commit the transaction on a database until it gets the confirmation (written the transaction log records to disk on secondary) from secondary replica.

20. What is the Difference between Asynchronous-commit mode and Synchronous-commit mode?

Ans:

Asynchronous-commit mode:

An availability replica that uses this availability mode is known as an asynchronous-commit replica. Under asynchronous-commit mode, the primary replica commits transactions without waiting for acknowledgement that an asynchronous-commit secondary replica has hardened the log. Asynchronous-commit mode minimizes transaction latency on the secondary databases but allows them to lag behind the primary databases, making some data loss possible.

Synchronous-commit mode:

An availability replica that uses this availability mode is known as a synchronous-commit replica. Under synchronous-commit mode, before committing transactions, a synchronous-commit primary replica waits for a synchronous-commit secondary replica to acknowledge that it has finished hardening the log. Synchronous-commit mode ensures that once a given secondary database is synchronized with the primary database, committed transactions are fully protected. This protection comes at the cost of increased transaction latency.

21. What is called Primary replica?

Ans:

The availability replica that makes the primary databases available for read-write connections from clients is called Primary Replica. It sends transaction log records for each primary database to every secondary replica.

22. What is called Secondary replica?

Ans:

An availability replica that maintains a secondary copy of each availability database, and serves as a potential failover targets for the availability group. Optionally, a secondary replica can support read-only access to secondary databases can support creating backups on secondary databases.

23. What is Availability Group listener?

Ans:

Availability Group Listener is a server name to which clients can connect in order to access a database in a primary or secondary replica of an ALWAYSON availability group. Availability group listeners direct incoming connections to the primary replica or to a read-only secondary replica.

24. What are Readable Secondary Replicas?

Ans:

The ALWAYSON Availability Groups active secondary capabilities include support for read-only access to one or more secondary replicas (readable secondary replicas). A readable secondary replica allows read-only access to all its secondary databases. However, readable secondary databases are not set to read-only. They are dynamic. A given secondary database changes as changes on the corresponding primary database are applied to the secondary database.

25. What are the benefits of Readable Secondary Replicas?

Ans:

Directing read-only connections to readable secondary replicas provides the following benefits:

- ➢ Offloads your secondary read-only workloads from your primary replica, which conserves its resources for your mission critical workloads. If you have mission critical read-workload or the workload that cannot tolerate latency, you should run it on the primary.
- ➢ Improves your return on investment for the systems that host readable secondary replicas.
- ➢ In addition, readable SECONDARIES provide robust support for read-only operations, as follows:
    - ✓ Temporary statistics on readable secondary database optimize read-only queries. For more information, see Statistics for Read-Only Access Databases, later in this topic.
    - ✓ Read-only workloads use row versioning to remove blocking contention on the secondary databases. All queries that run against the secondary databases are automatically mapped to snapshot isolation transaction level, even when other transaction isolation levels are explicitly set. Also, all locking hints are ignored. This eliminates reader/writer contention.

26. How many synchronous secondary replicas can I have?

Ans:

We can have up to 2 synchronous replicas, but we are not required to use any. We could run all SECONDARIES in asynchronous mode if desired

27. Can we use a secondary for reporting purpose?

Ans:

Yes. An active secondary can be used to offload read-only queries from the primary to a secondary instance in the availability group.

28. Can we use secondary replicas to take the DB backups?

Ans:

Yes. An active secondary can be used for some types of backups

29. What all types of DB backups are possible on Secondary Replicas?

Ans:

- **BACKUP DATABASE** supports only copy-only full backups of databases, files, or FILEGROUPS when it is executed on secondary replicas. Note that copy-only backups do not impact the log chain or clear the differential bitmap.
- Differential backups are not supported on secondary replicas.

30. What is "Failover" in ALWAYSON?

Ans:

Within the context of a session between the primary replica and a secondary replica, the primary and secondary roles are potentially interchangeable in a process known as failover. During a failover the target secondary replica transitions to the primary role, becoming the new primary replica. The new primary replica brings its databases online as the primary databases, and client applications can connect to them. When the former primary replica is available, it transitions to the secondary role, becoming a secondary replica. The former primary databases become secondary databases and data synchronization resumes.

31. How many types of Failover are supported by Always ON?

Ans:

Three forms of failover exist—automatic, manual, and forced (with possible data loss). The form or forms of failover supported by a given secondary replica depends on its availability mode.

32. What are the Failover types supported by Synchronous-commit mode?

Ans:

- **Planned manual failover** (without data loss)
- **Automatic failover** (without data loss)

33. What is planned manual failover?

Ans:

A manual failover occurs after a database administrator issues a failover command and causes a synchronized secondary replica to transition to the primary role (with guaranteed data protection) and the primary replica to transition to the secondary role. A manual failover requires that both the primary replica and the target secondary replica are running under synchronous-commit mode, and the secondary replica must already be synchronized.

34. What is Automatic failover?

Ans:

An automatic failover occurs in response to a failure that causes a synchronized secondary replica to transition to the primary role (with guaranteed data protection). When the former primary replica becomes available, it transitions to the secondary role. Automatic failover requires that both the primary replica and the target secondary replica are running under synchronous-commit mode with the failover mode set to "Automatic." In addition, the secondary replica must already be synchronized, have WSFC quorum, and meet the conditions specified by the flexible failover policy of the availability group.

35. What are the Failover types supported by under asynchronous-commit mode?

Ans:

Only form of failover is forced manual failover (with possible data loss), typically called **forced failover. Forced failover** is considered a form of manual failover because it can only be initiated manually. Forced failover is a disaster recovery option. It is the only form of failover that is possible when the target secondary replica is not synchronized with the primary replica.

36. What is the use of ALWAYSON Dashboard?

Ans:

Database administrators use the ALWAYSON Dashboard to obtains an at-a-glance view the health of an ALWAYSON availability group and its availability replicas and databases in SQL Server 2012. Some of the typical uses for the ALWAYSON Dashboard are:

- Choosing a replica for a manual failover.
- Estimating data loss if you force failover.
- Evaluating data-synchronization performance.
- Evaluating the performance impact of a synchronous-commit secondary replica

37. What is availability group wizard?

Ans:

Availability Group Wizard is a GUI using SQL Server Management Studio to create and configure an ALWAYSON availability group in SQL Server 2012.

38. Suppose primary database became in suspect mode. Will AG have failover to secondary replica?

Ans:

Issues at the database level, such as a database becoming suspect due to the loss of a data file, deletion of a database, or corruption of a transaction log, do not cause an availability group to failover.

39. Can we have two primary availability replicas?

Ans:

No, it is not possible.

40. Does AG support automatic page repair for protection against any page corruption happens?

Ans:

Yes, it automatically takes care of the automatic page repair.

41. How to add a secondary database from an availability group using T-SQL?

Ans:

```
ALTER DATABASE Db1 SET HADR AVAILABILITY GROUP = <AGName>;
```

42. How to remove a secondary database from an availability group?

Ans:

```
ALTER DATABASE <DBName> SET HADR OFF;
```

43. SQL Server 2012 ALWAYSON supports encryption and compression?

Ans:

SQL Server 2012 ALWAYSON Availability Group supports row and page compression for tables and indexes, we can use the data compression feature to help compress the data inside a database, and to help reduce the size of the database. We can use encryption in SQL Server for connections, data, and stored procedures; we can also perform database level encryption: Transparent data encryption (TDE). If you use transparent data encryption (TDE), the service master key for creating and decrypting other keys must be the same on every server instance that hosts an availability replica for the availability group

44. Does AG support Bulk-Logged recovery model?

Ans:

No, it does not.

45. Can a database belong to more than one availability group?

Ans:

No. It's not allowed.

46. What is session timeout period?

Ans:

Session-timeout period is a replica property that controls how many seconds (in seconds) that an availability replica waits for a ping response from a connected replica before considering the connection to have failed. By default, a replica waits 10 seconds for a ping response. This replica property applies only the connection between a given secondary replica and the primary replica of the availability group.

47. How to change the Session Timeout period?

Ans:

```
ALTER AVAILABILITY GROUP <AG Name>
MODIFY REPLICA ON '<Instance Name>' WITH (SESSION_TIMEOUT = 15);
```

48. What are different synchronization preferences are available?

Ans:

As part of the availability group creation process, we have to make an exact copy of the data on the primary replica on the secondary replica. This is known as the initial data synchronization for the Availability Group.

49. How many types of Data synchronization preference options are available in Always ON?

Ans:

There are three options- Full, Join only, or Skip initial data synchronization.

50. Is it possible to run DBCC CHECKDB on secondary replicas?

Ans:

Yes.

51. Can I redirect the read-only connections to the secondary replica instead of Primary replica?

Ans:

Yes, we can specify the read_only intent in the connection string and add only SECONDARIES (not the primary) to the read_only_routing list. If you want to disallow direct connections to the primary from read_only connections, then set its allow_connections to read_write.

52. If a DBA expands a data file manually on the primary; will SQL Server automatically grow the same file on SECONDARIES?

Ans:

Yes! It will be automatically expanded on the Secondary replica.

53. Is it possible to create additional indexes on read-only secondary replicas to improve query performance?

Ans:

No, it is not possible.

54. Is it possible to create additional statistics on read-only SECONDARIES to improve query performance?

Ans:

No. But we can allow SQL Server to automatically create statistics on read-only secondary replicas.

55. Can we manually fail over to a secondary replica?

Ans:

Yes. If the secondary is in synchronous-commit mode and is set to "SYNCHRONIZED" you can manually fail over without data loss. If the secondary is not in a synchronized state then a manual failover is allowed but with possible data loss

56. What is read intent option?

Ans:

There are two options to configure secondary replica for running read workload. The first option 'Read-intent-only' is used to provide a directive to ALWAYSON secondary replica to accept connections that have the property ApplicationIntent = ReadOnly set. The word 'intent' is important here as there is no application check made to guarantee that there are no DDL/DML operations in the application connecting with 'ReadOnly' but an assumption is made that customer will only connect read workloads.

57. Does ALWAYSON Availability Groups repair the data page corruption as Database Mirroring?

Ans:

Yes. If a corrupt page is detected, SQL Server will attempt to repair the page by getting it from another replica.

58. What are the benefits of Always on feature?

Ans:

- Utilizing database mirroring for the data transfer over TCP/IP
- providing a combination of Synchronous and Asynchronous mirroring
- providing a logical grouping of similar databases via Availability Groups
- Creating up to four readable secondary replicas
- Allowing backups to be undertaken on a secondary replica
- Performing DBCC statements against a secondary replica
- Employing Built-in Compression & Encryption

59. How much network bandwidth is required for a successful AlwaysOn AG setup?

Ans:

For a really rough estimate, sum up the amount of uncompressed transaction log backups that you generate in a 24-hour period. You'll need to push that amount of data per day across the wire. Things get trickier when you have multiple replicas – the primary pushes changes out to all replicas, so if you've got 3 replicas in your DR site, you'll need 3x the network throughput. Calculating burst requirements is much more difficult – but at least this helps you get started.

60. What's the performance overhead of a synchronous replica?

Ans:

From the primary replica, ping the secondary, and see how long (in milliseconds) the response takes. Then run load tests on the secondary's transaction log drive and see how long writes take. That's the minimum additional time that will be added to each transaction on the primary. To reduce the impact, make sure your network is low-latency and your transaction log drive writes are fast.

61. How far behind will my asynchronous replica be?

Ans:

The faster your network and your servers are, and the less transactional activity you have, the more up-to-date each replica will be. I've seen setups where the replicas are indistinguishable from the primary. However, I've also seen cases with underpowered replicas, slow wide area network connections, and heavy log activity (like index maintenance) where the replicas were several minutes behind.

62. What's the difference between AGs in SQL 2012 and SQL 2014?

Ans:

SQL Server 2014's biggest improvement is that the replica's databases stay visible when the primary drops offline – as long as the underlying cluster is still up and running. If I have one primary and four secondary replicas, and I lose just my primary, the SECONDARIES are still online servicing read-only queries. (Now, you may have difficulties connecting to them unless you're using the secondary's name, but that's another story.) Back in SQL 2012, when the primary dropped offline, all of the SECONDARIES' copies immediately dropped offline – breaking all read-only reporting queries.

63. How do I monitor ALWAYSON Availability Groups?

Ans:

That's rather challenging right now. Uptime monitoring means knowing if the listener is accepting writeable connections, if it's correctly routing read-only requests to other servers, if all read-only replicas are up and running, if load is distributed between replicas the way you want, and how far each replica is running behind. Performance monitoring is even tougher – each replica has its own statistics and execution plans, so queries can run at totally different speeds on identical replicas.

AlwaysOn Scenarios

64. Can we configure Automatic failover of Availability Groups with SQL Server Failover cluster instances?

Ans:

SQL Server Failover Cluster Instances (FCIs) do not support automatic failover by availability groups, so any availability replica that is hosted by an FCI can only be configured for manual failover.

65. Can we take Transaction log backups on the secondary replicas?

Ans:

Yes, we can take transaction log backups on the secondary replicas without COPY_ONLY option.

66. Do we need SQL Server Cluster instances to configure Always ON?

Ans:

No we don't need SQL Server Cluster instances to configure Always ON.

67. Do we need shared storage to configure Always ON?

Ans:

No, we don't need shared storage.

68. How does licensing work with ALWAYSON Availability Groups in SQL 2012 and 2014?

Ans:

All replicas have to have Enterprise Edition. If you run queries, backups, or DBCCs on a replica, you have to license it. For every server licensed with Software Assurance, you get one standby replica for free – but only as long as it's truly standby, and you're not doing queries, backups, or DBCCs on it.

69. Can I use ALWAYSON Availability Groups with Standard Edition?

Ans:

Not at this time, but it's certainly something folks have been asking for since database mirroring has been deprecated.

70. Do ALWAYSON AGs require shared storage or a SAN?

Ans:

No, you can use local storage, like cheap SSDs.

71. Do Availability Groups require a Windows cluster?

Ans:

Yes, they're built atop Windows failover clustering. This is the same Windows feature that also enables failover clustered instances of SQL Server, but you don't have to run a failover clustered instance in order to use ALWAYSON Availability Groups.

72. Do I need a shared quorum disk for my cluster?

Ans:

No

73. If I fail over to an asynchronous replica, and its behind, how do I sync up changes after the original primary comes back online?

Ans:

When I go through an AG design with a team, we talk about the work required to merge the two databases together. If it's complex (like lots of parent/child tables with identity fields, and no update date stamp field on the tables), then management agrees to a certain amount of data loss upon failover. For example, "If we're under fifteen minutes of data is involved, we're just going to walk away from it." Then we build a project plan for what it would take to actually recover >15 minutes of data, and management decides whether they want to build that tool ahead of time, or wait until disaster strikes.

74. We have got an alert "WSFC cluster service is offline." What is your action plan?

Ans:

This alert is raised when the WSFC cluster is offline or in the forced quorum state. All availability groups hosted within this cluster are offline (a disaster recovery action is required).

Possible Reasons:

This issue can be caused by a cluster service issue or by the loss of the quorum in the cluster.

Possible Solutions:

Use the Cluster Administrator tool to perform the forced quorum or disaster recovery workflow. Once WFSC is started you must re-evaluate and reconfigure NodeWeight values to correctly construct a new quorum before bringing other nodes back online. Otherwise, the cluster may go back offline again.

Reestablishment may require if there are any High Availability features (ALWAYSON Availability Groups, Log Shipping, Database Mirroring) using on effected nodes.

75. How to force a WSFC (Windows Server Failover Cluster) Cluster to start without a quorum?

Ans:

This can be done using

- Failover Cluster Manager
- Net.exe
- PowerShell

Here we'll see how this can be done using FCM (Failover Cluster Manager)

- Open a Failover Cluster Manager and connect to the desired cluster node to force online.
- In the Actions pane, click Force Cluster Start, and then click Yes – Force my cluster to start.
- In the left pane, in the Failover Cluster Manager tree, click the cluster name.
- In the summary pane, confirm that the current Quorum Configuration value is: Warning: Cluster is running in Force Quorum state.

76. We have got an alert "Availability group is offline." Can you explain about this warning and your action plan?

Ans:

This alert is raised when the cluster resource of the availability group is offline or the availability group does not have a primary replica.

Possible Reasons:

- The availability group is not configured with automatic failover mode. The primary replica becomes unavailable and the role of all replicas in the availability group become RESOLVING.
- The availability group is configured with automatic failover mode and does not complete successfully.
- The availability group resource in the cluster becomes offline.
- There is an automatic, manual, or forced failover in progress for the availability group.

Possible Solutions:

- If the SQL Server instance of the primary replica is down, restart the server and then verify that the availability group recovers to a healthy state.
- If the automatic failover appears to have failed, verify that the databases on the replica are synchronized with the previously known primary replica, and then failover to the primary replica. If the databases are not synchronized, select a replica with a minimum loss of data, and then recover to failover mode.
- If the resource in the cluster is offline while the instances of SQL Server appear to be healthy, use Failover Cluster Manager to check the cluster health or other cluster issues on the server. You can also use the Failover Cluster Manager to attempt to turn the availability group resource online.
- If there is a failover in progress, wait for the failover to complete.

77. We have got an alert "Availability group is not ready for automatic failover." Can you explain about this warning and your action plan?

Ans:

This alert is raised when the failover mode of the primary replica is automatic; however none of the secondary replicas in the availability group are failover ready.

Possible Reasons:

The primary replica is configured for automatic failover; however, the secondary replica is not ready for automatic failover as it might be unavailable or its data synchronization state is currently not SYNCHRONIZED.

Possible Solutions:

- Verify that at least one secondary replica is configured as automatic failover. If there is not a secondary replica configured as automatic failover, update the configuration of a secondary replica to be the automatic failover target with synchronous commit.
- Use the policy to verify that the data is in a synchronization state and the automatic failover target is SYNCHRONIZED, and then resolve the issue at the availability replica.

78. In your environment data inserted on Primary replica but not able to see that on secondary replica. When you check that Availability is in healthy state and in most cases data reflects in a few minutes but in this case it's didn't happen. Now you need to check for the bottleneck and fix the issue. Can you explain your views and workaround in this situation?

Ans:

Possible Reasons:

- Long-Running Active Transactions
- High Network Latency or Low Network Throughput Causes Log Build-up on the Primary Replica

- Another Reporting Workload Blocks the Redo Thread from Running
- Redo Thread Falls behind Due to Resource Contention

Possible Workaround:

- Use DBCC OPENTRAN and check if there are any oldest transactions running on primary replica and see if they can be rolled back.
- A high DMV (sys.dm_hadr_database_replica_states) value log_send_queue_size can indicate logs being held back at the primary replica. Dividing this value by log_send_rate can give you a rough estimate on how soon data can be caught up on the secondary replica.
- Check two performance objects SQL Server:Availability Replica > Flow Control Time (ms/sec) and SQL Server:Availability Replica > Flow control/sec. Multiplying these two values shows you in the last second how much time was spent waiting for flow control to clear. The longer the flow control wait time, the lower the send rate.
- When the redo thread is blocked, an extended event called sqlserver.lock_redo_blocked is generated. Additionally, you can query the DMV sys.dm_exec_request on the secondary replica to find out which session is blocking the REDO thread, and then you can take corrective action. You can let the reporting workload to finish, at which point the redo thread is unblocked. You can unblock the redo thread immediately by executing the KILL command on the blocking session ID. The following query returns the session ID of the reporting workload that is blocking the redo thread.

  Transact-SQL

  ```
  Select session_id, command, blocking_session_id, wait_time, wait_type, wait_resource
  from sys.dm_exec_requests
  where command = 'DB STARTUP'
  ```
- When Redo Thread Falls Behind Due to Resource Contention; a large reporting workload on the secondary replica has slowed down the performance of the secondary replica, and the redo thread has fallen behind. You can use the following DMV query to see how far the redo thread has fallen behind, by measuring the difference between the gap between last_redone_lsn and last_received_lsn.

  Transact-SQL

  ```
  Select recovery_lsn, truncation_lsn, last_hardened_lsn,
          last_received_lsn, last_redone_lsn, last_redone_time
  from sys.dm_hadr_database_replica_states.
  ```

  If you see thread is indeed failing behind, do a proper investigation and take the help of resource governor and can control the CPU cycles

Note: Have a look at MSDN sites and try to understand these solutions because when you say possible solutions, immediately you might be asked about resolutions.

79. You perform a forced manual failover on an availability group to an asynchronous-commit secondary replica; you find that data loss is more than your recovery point

objective (RPO). Or, when you calculate the potential data loss of an asynchronous-commit secondary replica using the method in Monitor Performance for ALWAYSON Availability Groups, you find that it exceeds your RPO. What are the possible reasons that causes data loss is more than your recovery point objective?

Ans:

There are mainly two reasons:

- **High Network Latency or Low Network Throughput Causes Log Build-up on the Primary Replica.** The primary replica activates flow control on the log send when it has exceeded the maximum allowable number of unacknowledged messages sent over to the secondary replica. Until some of these messages have been acknowledged, no more log blocks can be sent to the secondary replica. Since data loss can be prevented only when they have been hardened on the secondary replica, the build-up of unsent log messages increases potential data loss.
- **Disk I/O Bottleneck Slows Down Log Hardening on the Secondary Replica.** If the log file and the data file are both mapped to the same hard disk, reporting workload with intensive reads on the data file will consume the same I/O resources needed by the log hardening operation. Slow log hardening can translate to slow acknowledgement to the primary replica, which can cause excessive activation of the flow control and long flow control wait times.

80. After an automatic failover or a planned manual failover without data loss on an availability group, you find that the failover time exceeds your recovery time objective (RTO). Or, when you estimate the failover time of a synchronous-commit secondary replica (such as an automatic failover partner) using the method in Monitor Performance for ALWAYSON Availability Groups, you find that it exceeds your RTO. Can you explain the possible reasons which causes the failover time exceeds defined RTO?

Ans:

- *Reporting Workload Blocks the Redo Thread from Running:* On the secondary replica, the read-only queries acquire schema stability (Sch-S) locks. These Sch-S locks can block the redo thread from acquiring schema modification (Sch-M) locks to make any DDL changes. A blocked redo thread cannot apply log records until it is unblocked. Once unblocked, it can continue to catch up to the end of log and allow the subsequent undo and failover process to proceed.
- *Redo Thread Falls Behind Due to Resource Contention:* When applying log records on the secondary replica, the redo thread reads the log records from the log disk, and then for each log record it accesses the data pages to apply the log record. The page access can be I/O bound (accessing the physical disk) if the page is not already in the buffer pool. If there is I/O bound reporting workload, the reporting workload competes for I/O resources with the redo thread and can slow down the redo thread.

81. Let's say you have configured Automatic failover on SQL Server 2012 ALWAYSON environment. An automatic failover triggered but unsuccessful in making secondary replica as PRIMARY. How do you identify that failover is not successful and what are the possible reasons that causes an unsuccessful failover?

Ans:

If an automatic failover event is not successful, the secondary replica does not successfully transition to the primary role. Therefore, the availability replica will report that this replica is in Resolving status. Additionally, the availability databases report that they are in Not Synchronizing status, and applications cannot access these databases.

Possible Reasons for Unsuccessful Failover:

- *"Maximum Failures in the Specified Period" value is exhausted:* The availability group has Windows cluster resource properties, such as the Maximum Failures in the Specified Period property. This property is used to avoid the indefinite movement of a clustered resource when multiple node failures occur.
- *Insufficient NT Authority\SYSTEM account permissions:* The SQL Server Database Engine resource DLL connects to the instance of SQL Server that is hosting the primary replica by using ODBC in order to monitor health. The logon credentials that are used for this connection are the local SQL Server NT AUTHORITY\SYSTEM login account. By default, this local login account is granted the following permissions: 1.Alter Any Availability Group, 2.Connect SQL, 3.View server state. If the NT AUTHORITY\SYSTEM login account lacks any of these permissions on the automatic failover partner (the secondary replica), then SQL Server cannot start health detection when an automatic failover occurs. Therefore, the secondary replica cannot transition to the primary role. To investigate and diagnose whether this is the cause, review the Windows cluster log.
- *The availability databases are not in a SYNCHRONIZED state:* In order to automatically fail over, all availability databases that are defined in the availability group must be in a SYNCHRONIZED state between the primary replica and the secondary replica. When an automatic failover occurs, this synchronization condition must be met in order to make sure that there is no data loss. Therefore, if one availability database in the availability group in the synchronizing or not synchronized state, automatic failover will not successfully transition the secondary replica into the primary role.

82. Have you ever seen the Error 41009?

Ans:

Yes! This error might occur when you try to create multiple availability groups in a SQL Server 2012 ALWAYSON failover clustering environment. This issue can be resolved by applying Cumulative Update Package 2.

83. Let's say you added a new file to a database which is a part of ALWAYSON Availability Groups. The add file operation succeeded on primary replica but failed in secondary replica. What is the impact and how you troubleshoot?

Ans:

This might happens due to a different file path between the systems that hosts primary and secondary replica. Failed add-file operation will cause the secondary database to be suspended. This, in turn, causes the secondary replica to enter the NOT SYNCHRONIZING state.

Resolution:

- Remove the secondary database from the availability group.
- On the existing secondary database, restore a full backup of the FILEGROUP that contains the added file to the secondary database, using WITH NORECOVERY and WITH MOVE (Specify the correct file path as per secondary).
- Back up the transaction log that contains the add-file operation on the primary database, and manually restore the log backup on the secondary database using WITH NORECOVERY and WITH MOVE. Restore the last transaction log file with NO RECOVERY.
- Rejoin the secondary database to the availability group.

84. Can you write T-SQL statement for joining a replica to availability group? (AG name "ProAG"

Ans:

Connect to the server instance that hosts the secondary replica and issue the below statement:

ALTER AVAILABILITY GROUP ProAG JOIN;

The same operation can be done using SSMS or using Power Shell

85. Data synchronization state for one of the availability database is not healthy. Can you tell me the possible reasons?

Ans:

If this is an asynchronous-commit availability replica, all availability databases should be in the SYNCHRONIZING state. If this is a synchronous-commit availability replica, all availability databases should be in the SYNCHRONIZED state. This issue can be caused by the following:

- The availability replica might be disconnected.
- The data movement might be suspended.
- The database might not be accessible.
- There might be a temporary delay issue due to network latency or the load on the primary or secondary replica.

86. Let's say we have a premium production server and it is in ALWAYSON Availability Group. You observe that CPU utilization is hitting top at a specific time in a day. You did an RCA and found that CPU utilization reaches top and most CPU is from backup process due to backup compression is on. Now what do you suggest? Do we have any features for backup?

Ans:

Yes! There is an option to perform backup from secondary replicas. We can set this from Availability Group properties we can find "Backup Preferences" and from that we can choose one of the options from:

Preferred Secondary: Backups performed on Secondary if there is no secondary configured performed from primary

Secondary Only: Backups should be done from secondary only

Primary: Must occur on Primary Replica

Any Replica: Can occur from any replica in Availability Group

87. Is there any specific limitations if we need to perform auto backups from secondary backups?

Ans:

Yes! There are few:

- Only Copy_Only backup allowed from secondary replica
- Differential backups not allowed from secondary replica.
- Log backups can be performed from different secondary replicas but all these backups maintains a single log chain (LSN sequence). It might help in some of the situations

88. Have you ever applied patches/CU/service packs on ALWAYSON Availability Groups? Did you face any issues while applying?

Ans:

Yes! I have applied CU and service packs on SQL Server 2012 SP2 Cumulative Update 4

I had a bad experience with ALWAYSON AG:

After CU4 applied we saw that ALWAYSON Availability Groups are in Non- Synchronizing state.

After RCA we found that there was a huge blocking between user sessions and a unknown session, CHECKPOINT with command running as "DB_STARTUP."

Through of the MSDN SITE we found that Microsoft declared it's a bug and the solution chosen as below:

- We had to open an outage:
- Disable Automatic Failover
- Restart the SQL Server on Primary Replica
- Re-enable automatic failover.
- This worked and fixed the issue.

89. Can you explain any difficult issue you have faced recently on High Availability Groups?

Ans:

Sure! We are configuring ALWAYSON AG on SQL Server 2014.

We have taken backup from Primary replica and restored on secondary replica

When we are trying to add secondary replica to availability group to our surprise SQL Server got shut down and we found the error message:

(Error: 3449, Severity: 21, State: 1.

SQL Server must shut down in order to recover a database (database ID 1). The database is either a user database that could not be shut down or a system database. Restart SQL Server. If the database fails to recover after another STARTUP, repair or restore. SQL Trace was stopped due to server shutdown. Trace ID = '1'. This is an informational message only; no user action is required.)

Cause:

We did RCA and found the below.

- Service broker is enabled at Primary Replica
- We have taken a full backup from Primary Replica
- Restored on Secondary Replica where Service Broker is not enabled
- When we try to add secondary replica to AG, Service Broker is enabled, the same GUID on availability database is detected which causes an silent error 9772:
- "The Service Broker in database "<dbname>" cannot be enabled because there is already an enabled Service Broker with the same ID."
- This results into error 3449 and shut down the SQL Server unexpectedly.

Solution:

This has been fixed by applying the CU1 on SQL Server 2014.

90. Replica is in "resolving" status? What does it mean?

Ans:

A replica is into "RESOLVING" state when an auto failover is not successful.

Additionally the availability databases reports that they are in non-synchronizing state and not accessible.0

91. What are the top reasons that cause an unsuccessful failover?

Ans:

- Auto failovers in a specific period may crossed the value "Maximum Failures in the Specified Period"
- Insufficient NT Authority\SYSTEM account permissions
- The availability databases are not in a SYNCHRONIZED state

92. Create Availability Group Fails with Error 35250 'Failed to join the database'. Have you ever encountered this kind of error? What are the possible reasons and solutions for this error?

Ans:

Yes! I faced this failure when attempting to create an availability group. Here are the possible reasons that cause the failure:

Inbound Port 5022 Traffic is blocked: By default, ALWAYSON configures the database mirroring endpoints to use port 5022. Make sure the inbound traffic is enabled for this port on windows firewall and TELNET the server to make sure the server is listening on 5022.

Endpoint is not created or not started: Check the End Point status on all replicas using the query "select name, state_desc, port from sys.tcp_endpoints where type_desc='DATABASE_MIRRORING' ". If End point is not available or not started, create an end point and start it.

- To create an endpoint:

  Create endpoint [Hadr_endpoint] state=started

  as tcp (listener_port = 5022, listener_ip = all)

  for database_mirroring (role = all, authentication = windows negotiate, encryption = required algorithm aes)

- To Start an End Point:

  Alter endpoint [Hadr_endpoint] state = started

Note: Sometimes sys.tcp_endpoints.state_desc may incorrectly report the endpoint as STARTED when it is not started. Try to execute ALTER ENDPOINT and start it

Endpoint permissions issue:

If database mirroring endpoints are configured to use Windows authentication, ensure that the SQL Server instances hosting your availability replicas run with a SQL Server STARTUP account are domain accounts. Also make sure SQL Service account has CONNECT permission on the end_point.

GRANTCONNECTONENDPOINT::[Hadr_endpoint]TO[DOMAINACCOUNT$]

SQL Server is not listening on port 5022:

To determine if SQL Server is listening on port 5022, review the SQL Server error log. You should find the following message(s) in the SQL Server error log:

Server is listening on ['any' <ipv6> 5022].

Server is listening on ['any' <ipv4> 5022].

SQL Server may not be able to listen on port 5022 if another application is already listening on the port. Run 'netstat -a' to determine what application is using the port:

93. Any idea about error 19471 error while creating Microsoft SQL Server 2012 ALWAYSON availability group listener?

Ans:

There might be two common reasons that cause to occur 19471. In this case SQL Server doesn't give the much information instead we can get it from cluster log.

We cannot create a group listener because of domain policy restriction: For example an Active Directory policy is defined that allows authenticated users in a domain that are assigned the "Add workstations to a domain" user permission and can create up to 20 computer accounts in the domain. We received the error 19471 because we have exceeded the limit.

You cannot create a listener because of cluster name account permissions: This might be the reason when the cluster name account is not having sufficient permissions to create computer object on Active Directory.

CHAPTER 10

SQL SERVER CONCURRENCY & LOCKING

Interview Questions and Answers

Introduction: This chapter takes you through the SQL Server Concurrency and Locking related interview questions and answers. These questions are helpful for range of database administrators and SQL Developers starting from a junior to an expert level DBA for the technical interview preparation. These questions and answers are deals with the below topics:

- Deadlocks
- Transactions
- Locking
- Isolation Levels

Deadlocks

1. What is a deadlock and what is a LIVELOCK?

Ans:

DEADLOCK: Deadlock is a situation when two processes, each having a lock on one piece of data, attempt to acquire a lock on the other's piece. Each process would wait indefinitely for the other to release the lock, unless one of the user processes is terminated. SQL Server detects deadlocks and terminates one user's process.

LIVELOCK: A LIVELOCK is one, where a request for an exclusive lock is repeatedly denied because a series of overlapping shared locks keeps interfering. SQL Server detects the situation after four denials and refuses further shared locks. A LIVELOCK also occurs when read transactions monopolize a table or page, forcing a write transaction to wait indefinitely.

2. Can deadlocks occur on resources other than database object?

Ans:

YES.

3. What are the different types of resources that can deadlock?

Ans:

Deadlock is a condition that can occur on any system with multiple threads, not just on a relational database management system, and can occur for resources other than locks on database objects. Here are the resources:

Locks: Waiting to acquire locks on resources, such as objects, pages, rows, metadata, and applications can cause deadlock.

Worker threads: A queued task waiting for an available worker thread can cause deadlock. If the queued task owns resources that are blocking all worker threads, a deadlock will result

Memory: When concurrent requests are waiting for memory grants that cannot be satisfied with the available memory, a deadlock can occur.

Parallel query execution-related resources: Coordinator, producer, or consumer threads associated with an exchange port may block each other causing a deadlock usually when including at least one other process that is not a part of the parallel query. Also, when a parallel query starts execution, SQL Server determines the degree of parallelism, or the number of worker threads, based upon the current workload. If the system workload unexpectedly changes, for example, where new queries start running on the server or the system runs out of worker threads, then a deadlock could occur.

Multiple Active Result Sets (MARS) resources: Resources used to control interleaving of multiple active requests under MARS, including:

- *User resource:* When a thread is waiting for a resource that is potentially controlled by a user application, the resource is considered to be an external or user resource and is treated like a lock
- *Session Mutex:* The tasks running in one session are interleaved, meaning that only one task can run under the session at a given time. Before the task can run, it must have exclusive access to the session mutex.
- *Transaction Mutex:* All tasks running in one transaction are interleaved, meaning that only one task can run under the transaction at a given time. Before the task can run, it must have exclusive access to the transaction mutex.

4. Can you be able to explain how deadlock detection algorithm works in SQL Server?

Ans:

- Deadlock detection is performed by a lock monitor thread that periodically initiates a search through all of the tasks in an instance of the Database Engine.
- The default interval is 5 seconds.
- If the lock monitor thread finds deadlocks, the deadlock detection interval will drop from 5 seconds to as low as 100 milliseconds depending on the frequency of deadlocks.
- If the Lock Monitor thread stops finding deadlocks, the Database Engine increases the intervals between searches to 5 seconds.
- Deadlock monitor identifies the resource on which the thread is waiting on. Identifies the owner of that resource and it continues the search till it finds a cycle.
- After Deadlock is detected the database engine ends a deadlock by choosing one of the threads as a deadlock victim.
- The batch related to the victim thread will be terminated and the internal transaction will be roll backed which releases the locks on resources.

- This allows the transactions of the other threads to become unblocked and continue.
- It returns 1205 error message to the application.

5. As we know that deadlock detector identify the locking chains when found a deadlock situation it kills one of the processes which is known as victim. My question is on which basis it chooses a transaction to be killed or be a victim?

Ans:

Choosing a victim in deadlock is depends on depends on each session's deadlock priority:

Both Sessions with the Same Deadlock Priority: If both sessions have the same deadlock priority, the instance of SQL Server chooses the session that is less expensive to roll back as the deadlock victim. **Example:** Session 1 and Session 2 Deadlocked.

Session 1: Deadlock Priority: High; Transaction completion Status: 40%; Rollback Time: 130 Sec

Session 1: Deadlock Priority: High; Transaction completion Status: 80%; Rollback Time: 370 Sec

Now based on the rollback time Victim will be Session 1

Both Sessions with Different Deadlock Priority: If the sessions have different deadlock priorities, the session with the lowest deadlock priority is chosen as the deadlock victim.

Example: Session 1 and Session 2 Deadlocked.

Session 1: Deadlock Priority: High; Transaction completion Status: 40%; Rollback Time: 130 Sec

Session 1: Deadlock Priority: Low; Transaction completion Status: 80%; Rollback Time: 370 Sec

Now based on the Deadlock priority setting victim will be Session 2

6. What is deadlock priority and how to change this value?

Ans:

- DEADLOCK_PRIORITY option dictates how the spids are handled when a deadlock occurs. The default deadlock priority is NORMAL.
- SET DEADLOCK_PRIORITY allows a process to determine its priority for being chosen as the victim using one of 21 different priority levels, from –10 to 10.
- We can also use LOW(-5), NORMAL (0) and HIGH (5)
- Default setting is NORMAL (0).
- DEADLOCK_PRIORITY setting is considered at run time, not at the parse time

  Syntax: SET DEADLOCK_PRIORITY [HIGH/LOW/[-10 to 10]];

7. What is a deadlock and how is it different from a standard block situation?

Ans:

A deadlock occurs when two or more tasks permanently block each other by each task having a lock on a resource which the other tasks are trying to lock. In a deadlock situation, both transactions in the deadlock will wait forever unless the deadlock is broken by an external process – in a standard blocking scenario, the blocked task will simply wait until the blocking task releases the conflicting lock scenario.

8. Did you remember the deadlock error message? Also can you explain all the possible ways to get the deadlock information?

Ans:

Error:

Transaction (Process ID 52) was deadlocked on lock resources with another process and has been chosen as the deadlock victim. Rerun the transaction.

Ways to Identifying Deadlocks:

- Enabling Trace Flag
- Extended Events
- System Health
- Windows Performance Monitor
- SQL Profiler

Enabling a Trace Flag:

- By default Deadlocks are not written into SQL Server error log, to do so we have to enable a trace flag.
- Trace Flag 1204 – Data is captured in node level
- Trace Flag 1222 – Data is captured in XML format
- Syntax: DBCC TRACEON (1222, -1)

  Note: -1 indicates trace should run for all sessions

Extended Events:

Extended Events are eventually going to replace the SQL Server Profiler all together (i.e. SQL Server Profiler is on the Deprecated Feature list). It produces the same XML graph as SQL Server Profiler, and is lighter in performance impact. We need to choose XML_DEADLOCK_REPORT event.

Till SQL Server 2008 R2 the X-events must be created using scripts. From SQL Server 2012 we can configure extended events using GUI.

System Health:

By default the system health event will log the deadlock information for the instance. We can use the below sample query to list out deadlock events from the system health.

```
SELECT
xed.value('@timestamp', 'datetime') as Creation_Date,
xed.query('.') AS Extend_Event
FROM
(
SELECT CAST([target_data] AS XML) AS Target_Data
FROM sys.dm_xe_session_targets AS xt
```

```
INNER JOIN sys.dm_xe_sessions AS xs
ON xs.address = xt.event_session_address
WHERE xs.name = N'system_health'
AND xt.target_name = N'ring_buffer'
) AS XML_Data
CROSS APPLY
Target_Data.nodes('RingBufferTarget/event[@name="xml_deadlock_report"]') AS
XEventData(xed)
ORDER BY Creation_Date DESC
```

Windows Performance Monitor:

- Performance Monitor Counter Details:
  - ✓ **Object:** SQLServer:Locks
  - ✓ **Counter:** Number of Deadlocks/sec
  - ✓ **Instance:** _Total
- We can also get these details using DMV:

```
SELECT cntr_value AS NumOfDeadLocks
FROM sys.dm_os_performance_counters
WHERE object_name = 'SQLServer:Locks'
AND counter_name = 'Number of Deadlocks/sec'
AND instance_name = '_Total'
```

Using Profiler:

- SQL Server Profiler/Server Side Trace **Event Class:** Locks **Event Name:** Deadlock Graph. It gives a XML graph with all the required details

9. **We have a production environment and recently we identified deadlocks are occurring on very frequent basis. You are assigned to implement the best practices to prevent deadlocks. Can you list out few things which can prevent deadlocks?**

Ans:

- While updating have the application access server objects in the same order each time.
- During transactions, don't allow any user input. Collect it before the transaction begins.
- Keep transactions as short as possible. To accomplish this when your application does need to read the same data more than once, cache it by storing it in a variable or an array, and then re-reading it from there, not from SQL Server.
- Reduce lock time. Develop your application to grab locks at the latest possible time, and then releases them at the very earliest time.
- If appropriate, reduce lock escalation by using the ROWLOCK or PAGLOCK.

- Consider using the NOLOCK hint to prevent locking if the data being locked is not modified often.
- If appropriate, use low level isolation level according to the possibilities
- Look for other opportunities to improve the efficiency of the queries
- If both deadlock participants are using the same index, consider adding an index that can provide an alternate access path to one of the spids.

10. Let's say we have enabled a trace flag to log deadlock information in SQL Server error log. What kind of information we can get from the log?

Ans:

DBID: Database ID from which the transaction initiated

SPID: Which is nothing but connection ID from which the actual query completed/killed

Victim: The process which killed by Victor

Victor: The process which won the deadlock means completed successfully

Proc Name: Name of the procedure if in case the transaction initiated from a procedure

SQL Handle: SQL Handle and also input buffer QUERY also displayed

Page Info:

We can also get page information which causes the deadlock (This we can get when trace flag 1204 is enabled). There is a code to understand about the page.

- If IndId = 0:
  - ✓ Data Page if there is no clustered index on that table
  - ✓ Clustered index leaf page is there is a clustered index available on that table
- If IndId = 1:
  - ✓ Non-Leaf page of the Clustered Index
- If IndId = 255:
  - ✓ Text Image Page
- If IndId = Other value:
  - ✓ Non Clustered Secondary Index

From SPID itself we can get maximum information, we can use DBCC INPUTBUFFER (SPID) to get corresponding command/transaction details. But it restricts on command length thereof we can use below command.

```
SELECT
        LTRIM (RTRIM (a.text)) AS 'SQL',
        LTRIM (RTRIM (spid)) AS 'SPID',
        LTRIM (RTRIM (blocked)) AS 'Blocked',
        LTRIM (RTRIM (cpu)) AS 'CPU',
        db_name (LTRIM (RTRIM (s.dbid))) DBName,
```

```
        LTRIM (RTRIM (login_time)) AS 'Login_Time',
        LTRIM (RTRIM (last_batch)) AS 'Last_Batch',
        LTRIM (RTRIM (status)) AS 'Status',
        LTRIM (RTRIM (loginame)) AS 'LoginName',
        LTRIM (RTRIM (hostname)) AS 'HostName',
        LTRIM (RTRIM (program_name)) AS 'ProgramName',
        LTRIM (RTRIM (cmd)) AS 'CMD'
FROM sys.sysprocesses s
CROSS APPLY sys.dm_exec_sql_text(s.sql_handle)a
WHERE spid = <SPID>
```

11. What are the different cases which causes deadlocks?

Ans:

Table Insertions in Opposite Order:

Description: This means that Inserting data into two or more tables in opposite order in different transactions.

Transaction 1 inserts data into Table A

Transaction 2 inserts data into Table B

Transaction 1 trying to insert data into Table B à Now T1 is blocked by T2

Transaction 2 trying to insert data into Table A à Now T2 is blocked by T1

Deadlock occurs as T2 is trying to insert data on same page where T1 is already hold that page same happened in wise versa.

Solution: Always follow the same sequence in table insertions across the application/Database

Insertions to different parts of the same Table:

Description: This deadlock can occur when two connections insert into different parts of the same table in opposite order when rows share pages. For example Table A has a column "ID" and a clustered index defined on this. Inserting rows with same ID's will fall on to the same page. From this we can understand there is a possibility of deadlock when data insertion happens from different transactions.

Solution: This can be avoided by enabling IRL (Insert Row Lock)

```
sp_tableoption 'example1', 'insert row lock', true
```

Insertions Using IRL:

Description: IRL allows two or more users to share a page when they do only insert operations, which often results in better throughput. However, enabling IRL will not always reduce deadlocks. In some cases, IRL may introduce deadlocks.

When IRL enabled it can reduce deadlocks when only inserts happening in transactions. If in case update statements issued from transactions which issue an "Exclusive Page Lock" and thereof this again leads to Deadlock.

Solution: Isolate updates from inserts in transactions, if it is not possible disable "IRL" option.

Inserting and updating on same page:

Description: Inserting and updating on the same page from different transactions my lead to deadlock

Solution: Create a cluster index with high fill factor, so it reduces number of rows in a page which reduces deadlocks.

Index Traversing:

Deadlocks may occur with RLOCK and XRLOCK locks, which are acquired during index traversing.

Non Clustered Indexes:

Description: In some cases, non-clustered secondary indexes may introduce deadlocks. Let's say we created a Non-Clustered index on a column "C" in a table A. There are 2 transactions inserting data into table and updating the column "C" in a same sequence. In this case deadlock may occur.

Solution: Either that secondary non clustered index has to be dropped or isolate updates from inserts

12. What kind of locks we can see while checking through Deadlock log?

Ans:

SH_INT and EX_INT:

Intent locks that are taken on a higher-level item (for example, a table) before lower-level locks (for example, a page) can be taken, because the lock manager is unaware of the relationship between different types of items (in this case, pages and tables). If an EX_INT lock was not taken on the table before taking EX_PAG locks on the pages, another user could take an EX_TAB lock on the same table and the lock manager would not know that a conflict existed. Currently, SQL Server has intent locks only on tables. There are two kinds of intent locks: shared (SH_INT) and exclusive (EX_INT) locks.

EX_PAGE:

This is an exclusive page lock that is taken when a page is updated due to a DELETE, UPDATE, or INSERT statement with insert row-level locking (IRL) disabled.

UP_PAGE:

This is an update page lock that is taken in place of a shared-page lock when a page is scanned and the optimizer knows that the page will be updated (or the UPDLOCK hint is used).

PR_EXT, NX_EXT, UPD_EXT, and EX_EXT:

These locks are taken when allocating or de-allocating disk space. UPD_EXT is taken when allocating or de-allocating a page from an existing extent and the others are used when allocating or de-allocating entire extents.

IX_PAGE and LN_PAGE:

These are IRL locks. IX_PAGE is an intent-to-do-row-locking lock on a page. LN_PAGE is taken when a page on which IRL is being done needs to be split.

RLOCK and XRLOCK:

These short-term locks are taken when traversing an index b-tree. There are two types of this kind of lock: shared (RLOCK) and exclusive (XRLOCK). Shared locks are taken during scan, while exclusive locks are taken on index pages during an update.

EX_TAB:

This is an exclusive table lock that occurs when the SQL Server optimizer determines that a table scan is the most efficient way to solve an update query (for example, when there are no indexes on a table). EX_TAB locks also appear when you lock the table with TABLOCKX hint or when SQL Server escalates the page locks on a table to a table lock.

SH_TAB:

This is a shared table lock that is used when the optimizer assumes that most of the table will be scanned (or page locking escalates) or the TABLOCK hint is used.

Transactions

13. What are the properties of a transaction?

Ans:

There are 4 properties called ACID.

Atomicity: All changes to data are performed as if they are a single operation. That is, all the changes are performed, or none of them are.

Example: In an application that transfers funds from one account to another, the atomicity property ensures that, if a debit is made successfully from one account, the corresponding credit is made to the other account.

Consistency: Data is in a consistent state when a transaction starts and when it ends.

Example: In an application that transfers funds from one account to another, the consistency property ensures that the total value of funds in both the accounts is the same at the start and end of each transaction.

Isolation: The intermediate state of a transaction is invisible to other transactions. As a result, transactions that run concurrently appear to be serialized.

Example: in an application that transfers funds from one account to another, the isolation property ensures that another transaction sees the transferred funds in one account or the other, but not in both, nor in neither.

Durability: After a transaction successfully completes, changes to data persist and are not undone, even in the event of a system failure.

Example: in an application that transfers funds from one account to another, the durability property ensures that the changes made to each account will not be reversed.

14. Have you ever used Transaction Initiation modes? What are those?

Ans:

Transaction Initiation mode determines how a transaction should be opened when running a query or a batch. There are 4 modes:

Auto Commit: This is a default mode. When you run a query or DML statement a transaction opens internally and closed automatically one the statement successfully completed.

Explicit: User explicitly opens a transaction using BEGIN TRAN. This transaction should be closed externally using either COMMIT or ROLLBACK.

Implicit: Forcibly opens a transaction using the set option "SET IMPLICIT_TRANSACTION ON." This means when we execute a DML statement we have to code to commit/rollback the transaction based on conditions. To simplify this it opens an implicit transaction but closing should be taken care by developer.

AUTOMIC BLOCK: This is helpful when we deal with In-Memory objects. All statements in ATOMIC blocks, which are required with natively compiled stored procedures, always run as part of a single transaction

15. How distributed transactions works in SQL Server?

Ans:

Distributed transactions are the transactions that worked across the databases, instances in the given session. Snapshot isolation level does not support distributed transactions.

We can explicitly start a distributed transaction using "BEGIN DISTRIBUTED TRANSACTION <TranName>"

For example, if BEGIN DISTRIBUTED TRANSACTION is issued on Server A, the session calls a stored procedure on Server B and another stored procedure on Server C. The stored procedure on Server C executes a distributed query against Server D, and then all four computers are involved in the distributed transaction. The instance of the Database Engine on Server A is the originating controlling instance for the transaction.

When a distributed query is executed in a local transaction, the transaction is automatically promoted to a distributed transaction if the target OLE DB data source supports **ITransactionLocal**. If the target OLE DB data source does not support **ITransactionLocal**, only read-only operations are allowed in the distributed query. In order to work with these transactions, make sure below settings are done.

- MSDTC must be running on all supported instances
- Choose the option "No authentication required" from MSDTC properties

Turn on random options at linked server properties like "RPC," "RPC Out," "Data Access" etc.

16. I have been using SQL Server backup statement inside an explicit transaction. If I rollback the transaction what will happen to my backup?

Ex: BEGIN TRAN

BACKUP DATABASE TEST TO DISK = <>......;

ROLLBACK

Ans:

We can't include BACKUP command inside an explicit transaction. If you try to include a backup statement in a transaction it fails with an error message "Cannot perform a backup or restore operation within a transaction."

17. Can we include DDL inside a transaction? Does it works if it rollbacks?

Ans:

Yes! We can use DDL commands inside a transaction and these DDL commands also follow the transaction ACID properties. For example if we create a table inside a transaction and the transaction rolled back then the table will also be dropped.

18. What are the other statements that can't be included inside an explicit transaction?

Ans:

You can use all Transact-SQL statements in an explicit transaction, except for the following statements:

- ALTER DATABASE
- CREATE FULLTEXT INDEX
- ALTER FULLTEXT CATALOG
- DROP DATABASE
- ALTER FULLTEXT INDEX
- DROP FULLTEXT CATALOG
- BACKUP
- DROP FULLTEXT INDEX
- CREATE DATABASE
- RECONFIGURE
- CREATE FULLTEXT CATALOG
- RESTORE

19. Can we use UPDATE STSTISTICS inside a transaction?

Ans:

Yes and No! Yes we can use UPDATE STSTISTICS inside a transaction but it doesn't follow ACID properties means a rollback can't impact statistics update.

Locking

20. What are the different types of lock modes in SQL Server?

Ans:

- Shared
- Update
- Exclusive
- Schema (modification and stability)
- Bulk Update
- Intent (shared, update, exclusive)
- Key Range (shared, insert, exclusive)

21. Can you explain scenarios where each type of lock would be taken?

Ans:

SHARED: Used for read operations that do not change or update data, such as a SELECT statement.

UPDATE: Update locks (U) are acquired just prior to modifying the data. If a transaction modifies a row, then the update lock is escalated to an exclusive lock; otherwise, it is converted to a shared lock. Only one transaction can acquire update locks to a resource at one time. Using update locks prevents multiple connections from having a shared lock that want to eventually modify a resource using an exclusive lock. Shared locks are compatible with other shared locks, but are not compatible with Update locks.

EXCLUSIVE: Used for data-modification operations, such as INSERT, UPDATE, or DELETE. It ensures that multiple updates cannot be made to the same resource at the same time.

INTENT: Used to establish a lock hierarchy. The types of intent locks are: intent shared (IS), intent exclusive (IX), and shared with intent exclusive (SIX). (Another question in the difficult level section expands on this)

SCHEMA: Used when an operation dependent on the schema of a table is executing. The types of schema locks are: schema modification (Sch-M) and schema stability (Sch-S).

BULK UPDATE: Used when bulk copying data into a table and when the TABLOCK hint is specified.

KEY RANGE: Protects the range of rows read by a query when using the serializable transaction isolation level. It ensures that other transactions cannot insert rows that would qualify for the queries of the serializable transaction if the queries were run again.

22. What is the lock escalation in SQL Server?

Ans:

The process of converting many fine-grained locks into fewer coarse-grained locks is known as Lock Escalation. Escalation reduces system resource consumption/overhead while increasing the possibility of concurrency conflicts. To simplify this there is a lot of resource required to maintain a larger number of locks. Lock escalation escalates/converts lower level locks to higher level locks.

To escalate locks, the Database Engine attempts to change the intent lock on the table to the corresponding full lock, for example, changing an intent exclusive (IX) lock to an exclusive (X) lock, or intent shared (IS) lock to a shared (S) lock). If the lock escalation attempt succeeds and the full table lock is acquired, then all heap or B-tree, page (PAGE), key-range (KEY), or row-level (RID) locks held by the transaction on the heap or index are released. If the full lock cannot be acquired, no lock escalation happens at that time and the Database Engine will continue to acquire row, key, or page locks.

23. When Lock Escalation is triggered?

Ans:

Lock escalation is triggered at either of these times:

- When a single Transact-SQL statement acquires at least 5,000 locks on a single table or index.
- When the number of locks in an instance of the Database Engine exceeds memory or configuration thresholds.
- If locks cannot be escalated because of lock conflicts, the Database Engine periodically triggers lock escalation at every 1,250 new locks acquired.

24. Can we be able to disable the "Lock Escalation" in SQL Server Instance?

Ans:

Yes! Lock Escalation can be deactivated using the below trace flags:

1211: Disables Lock Escalation completely. Allows to use 60% of the allocated memory if 60% of memory is used and more locking is needed it throws an out-of-memory error.

1224: Disables Lock Escalation until the memory threshold of 40% allocated memory is reached. When memory threshold reached 40% the Lock Escalation will be enabled.

25. My requirement is to disable lock escalation only for a specific table. Is it possible?

Ans:

Yes! It is. Till 2008 we don't have this option but from 2008 we can do this using ALTER TABLE. Also from 2008 Locks can be escalated to partition level if table is partitioned.

```
ALTER TABLE <Table Name> SET (LOCK_ESCALATION = { AUTO | TABLE | DISABLE } )
```

- **AUTO:**
  - ✓ If table is partitioned the locks will be escalated to the partition-level
  - ✓ If table is not partitioned the locks will be escalated to the table-level
- **TABLE:**
  - ✓ Default behavior
  - ✓ Locks are escalated to the table-level
- **DISABLE:**
  - ✓ Lock escalation to the table-level is deactivated in most cases
  - ✓ In some necessary cases it's allowed to escalate to the table-level

26. Can locks ever be de-escalated?

Ans:

No, locks are only escalated, never de-escalated.

27. Name as many of the lockable resources as possible in SQL Server?

Ans:

- RID (single row on a heap)
- KEY (single row (or range) on an index)
- PAGE

- ➢ EXTENT
- ➢ HOBT (heap or b-tree)
- ➢ TABLE (entire table, all data and indexes)
- ➢ FILE
- ➢ APPLICATION
- ➢ METADATA
- ➢ ALLOCATION_UNIT
- ➢ DATABASE

28. What requirements must be met for a BULK-UPDATE lock to be granted, and what benefit do they server?

Ans:

The Database Engine uses bulk update (BU) locks when bulk copying data into a table, and either the TABLOCK hint is specified or the table lock on bulk load table option is set. Bulk update (BU) locks allow multiple threads to bulk load data concurrently into the same table while preventing other processes that are not bulk loading data from accessing the table.

29. What is the least restrictive type of lock? What is the most restrictive?

Ans:

The least restrictive type of lock is a shared lock. The most restrictive type of lock is a schema-modification

30. Does a WITH NOLOCK issues any lock?

Ans:

Yes! NO LOCK means this lock is compatible with all shared, update and exclusive locks. But the NO LOCK is ignored with INSERT and UPDATE statements. Also when there is a schema change happening it doesn't allow NO LOCK queries to access that resource.

31. In what circumstances will you see key-range locks, and what are they meant to protect against?

Ans:

You will only see key-range locks when operating in the SERIALIZABLE isolation level.

- Key-range locks protect a range of rows implicitly included in a record set being read by a Transact-SQL statement. The serializable isolation level requires that any query executed during a transaction must obtain the same set of rows every time it is executed during the transaction. A key range lock protects this requirement by preventing other transactions from inserting new rows whose keys would fall in the range of keys read by the serializable transaction.
- Key-range locking prevents phantom reads. By protecting the ranges of keys between rows, it also prevents phantom insertions into a set of records accessed by a transaction.

32. Explain the purpose of INTENT locks?

Ans:

The Database Engine uses intent locks to protect placing a shared (S) lock or exclusive (X) lock on a resource lower in the lock hierarchy. Intent locks are named intent locks because they are acquired before a lock at the lower level, and therefore signal intent to place locks at a lower level. Intent locks serve two purposes:

- To prevent other transactions from modifying the higher-level resource in a way that would invalidate the lock at the lower level.
- To improve the efficiency of the Database Engine in detecting lock conflicts at the higher level of granularity.

33. What is the size of a lock structure?

Ans:

96 bytes

34. Can you demonstrate "Locking," "Blocking" and "Deadlock"?

Ans:

Here I am giving basic details about Locking; there is a lot to learn about locking. Remember I am not talking about ISOLATION LEVELS. Below examples considers the default ISOLATION level "READ COMMITTED"

Locking:

Lock: Basically when we talk about relational database, data is stored in tables. Internally a Table is represented using Pages. A lock is a memory structure which is issued by a transaction/session on a resource. Here the resource might be a Table/Page/Row/Index etc. There are 3 types of locks that you should understand.

Shared Lock: Shared Lock issued when a read operation required.

Update Lock: Update lock is an intermediate lock between shared and exclusive lock. When a DML (Update, Delete and Insert) operation required it has to be issued an exclusive lock. But Exclusive lock is not compatible with other locks, means when an exclusive lock is hold on a table it doesn't allow any other locks. It's initially acquire a Update Lock wait till all shared locks released and upgrade to exclusive lock.

Exclusive Lock: Exclusive Lock issued while updating data.

Example:

- Transaction 1: Issued a command "SELECT * FROM EMPLOYEE" - "Shared Lock"
- Transaction 1: Issued a command "UPDATE EMPLOYEE SET SAL = SAL+1000 WHERE SAL <10000":
    - ✓ "Shared Lock" migrates to "Update Lock"
    - ✓ It waits till all shared locks released on table Employee.
    - ✓ "Update Lock" migrates to "Exclusive Lock"

Blocking:

A connection places a lock on a Table/page/index and the other connection is waiting on first connection to release lock. Now the Connection 2 is blocked by connection 1.

Ex:

- Transaction 1: Issued a SELECT command on Table "Emp"
- Transaction 1: Issued UPDATE command on Table "Emp" and processing data, no ROLLBACK or COMMIT happened
- Transaction 2: Issued a SELECT command on Table "Emp."
- Transaction 2: It waits till Transaction 1 releases locks by issuing COMMIT/ROLLBACK

Here Transaction 2 is blocked by Transaction 1.

DEADLOCK:

Process 1 holds Table 1 and waiting for Table 2. Process 2 holds Table 2 and waiting for Table 1 is called deadlock. To simplify say that Process 1 and Process 2 are blocked each other.

Ex:

- Transaction 1: Update table Employee
- Transaction 2: Update table Employee_Details
- Transaction 1: Update table Employee_Details (Waiting to hold a lock on Employee_Details which is already locked by Transaction 2)
- Transaction 2: Update table Employee (Waiting to hold a lock on Employee which is already locked by Transaction 1)

Transaction 1 and Transaction 2 are in Deadlock situation. Here SQL Server chooses one of the Transaction as "Victor"(Continue Processing) and the other one becomes "Victim" (Will be killed forcibly). Victor will be decided by the amount of work completed. Also we can control this using Deadlock Priority.

35. What is the difference between pessimistic and optimistic locking?

Ans:

Pessimistic Locking:

- The pessimistic approach is a user thinking "I'm sure someone will try to update this row at the same time as I will, so I better ask the database server to not let anyone touch it until I'm done with it."
- Issues locks to block the resource. It doesn't allow more than one user at a time when updating/modifying the same piece of data.
- Readers block writer, writers block readers and writers.

Optimistic Locking:

- The optimistic approach is a user thinking "I'm sure it's all good and there will be no conflicts, so I'm just going to remember this row to double-check later, but I'll let the database server do whatever it wants with the row."

- It doesn't lock anything but it asks transaction to remember (Row Versioning) what are the rows it's going to work with and it simply validate while updating back. There might be conflicts as it allows more than one user at a time to work with the same piece of data.
- Readers do not block writers and writers do not block readers, but, writers can and will block writers.

36. Explain how the database engine manages the memory footprint for the lock pool when running in a dynamic lock management mode.

Ans:

When running in dynamic management mode (i.e. if the server is started with locks configuration option set to 0), the lock manager acquires sufficient memory from the Database Engine for an initial pool of 2,500 lock structures. As the lock pool is exhausted, additional memory is acquired for the pool. The dynamic lock pool does not acquire more than 60 percent of the memory allocated to the Database Engine. After the lock pool has reached 60 percent of the memory acquired by an instance of the Database Engine, or no more memory is available on the computer, further requests for locks generate an error.

37. What is your experience in handling blocking alerts in your current working environment?

Ans:

We have a monitoring job for blocking processes. We do get a blocking alert if there is any process blocked for more than 10 min.

- We'll immediately capture the blocking information and will wait for the next 10 min
- There are multiple ways to capture blocking information but mostly we use "sys.sysprocesses" and "sp_who2," "DBCC INPUTBUFFER"
- To get the blocking and blocked queries information we use "sys.sysprocesses," "sys.dm_exec_requests" with "sys.dm_exec_sql_text()"
- We usually quickly identify the below parameters for both blocking and blocked processes:
  - ✓ SPID
  - ✓ SQL Query
  - ✓ DBID
  - ✓ LOGIN_TIME
  - ✓ LAST_BATCH
  - ✓ STATUS,
  - ✓ LOGIN_NAME
  - ✓ HOST_NAME
  - ✓ PROGRAM_NAME

- As per SLA the wait time is 20 Min. If the process is still blocked after 20 min then we need to open an incident and we'll notify the user/application owner who is running the command.
- If in-case of any known issue similar to data porting and huge data feed jobs we will be requested to wait till the process gets completed.
- If we get approval then we go ahead and kill that blocking SPID using KILL <SPID>;
- Sometimes blocking doesn't clear even if we kill the blocking process. We can check the rollback status using KILL <SPID> WITH STATUSONLY.
- If it returns "Estimated rollback completion: 0%. Estimated time Remaining 0 seconds" which indicates this process is initiated other process and we need to kill that sub process too.
- Usually we can see these situations when a remote distributed query initiated the blocking process.
- If we see blocking on the same resource very often then we have to identify the root cause using "SP_LOCK" and "SYS.DM_TRAN_LOCKS"

Isolation Levels

38. What are the concurrent problems occur in accessing a database?

Ans:

TR – Transaction

R - Resource

Uncommitted dependency/dirty reads:

TR1 → Updates Data → R1

TR2 → Reads Data → R1

TR1 → Rollback the Update Operation → R1

Now TR2 has the inconsistent data or wrong data.

Inconsistent Analysis/non-repeatable reads:

TR1 → Reads Data → R1

TR2 → Updates Data → R1

TR1 → Again reads the same data → R1

Wrong match between first TR1 and second time TR1

Phantom reads (via insert/delete):

TR1 → Reads Data (Result Contains 10 Records → R1

TR2 → Insert/Delete Data (insert 6 new delete 1 Record)→ R1

TR1 → Again reads the same data → R1

In Second time TR1 we found 6 New Records and we can't find a record which retrieves in first time.

39. What are the different isolation levels available?

Ans:

- Read Uncommitted Isolation Level
- Read Committed Isolation Level
- Repeatable Read Isolation Level
- Serializable Isolation Level
- Snapshot Isolation Level
- Read Committed Snapshot Isolation Level

40. Demonstrate Isolation levels?

Ans:

- *Read Uncommitted:* This is the lowest isolation level. It only isolates transactions and activities to ensure that physically corrupt data is never read. It allows dirty reads, non-repeatable reads, and phantom reads.
- *Read Committed:* This isolation level does not permit dirty reads, but does allow non-repeatable reads and phantom reads. This is the default isolation level for SQL Server, and is used for each connection to SQL Server unless one of the other isolation levels has manually been set for a connection.
- *Repeatable Read:* This isolation level does not permit dirty reads or non-repeatable reads, but does allow phantom reads.
- *Serializable Read:* This is the highest isolation level and ensures that all transactions and statements are completely isolated from each other. It does not allow dirty reads, non-repeatable reads, or phantom reads.
- *READ_COMMITTED_SNAPSHOT (statement level):*

  READ_COMMITTED_SNAPSHOT is a variation of the default READ_COMMITTED isolation level. It uses row versioning, instead of locking, to provide read consistency at the SQL Server statement level. When a statement runs that specifies the READ_COMMITTED isolation level, and the READ_COMMITTED_SNAPSHOT option is turned on at the database level, all statements see a snapshot of the data as it existed at the start of any current transaction. It uses the row-versioned snapshot of the row to return data, and no locking is needed by the statement, which is normally the case. The biggest benefit of this isolation level is that reads do not block writes and writes do not block reads. Writes can still block writes, but this is necessary to prevent data corruption.
- *ALLOW_SNAPSHOT_ISOLATION (transaction level):*

  ALLOW_SNAPSHOT_ISOLATION is similar to READ_COMMITTED_SNAPSHOT, but it is based at the transaction level, not the statement level. When the ALLOW_SNAPSHOT_ISOLATION is turned on at the database level *and* the TRANSACTION ISOLATION LEVEL SNAPSHOT isolation level is turned on for the transaction (using the SET command), all statements see a snapshot of the data as it existed at the start of the transaction.

41. Are you using In-Memory OLTP? Any Idea what are the ISOLATION LEVELS supports for memory optimized tables?

Ans:

Yes we tried In-Memory on Pre-Prod (2014) but due to lot of limitations we stopped thinking of it. In-Memory OLTP is improved well in SQL Server 2016. However Memory optimized tables supports ISOLATION LEVELS as below:

- READ UNCOMMITTED: Doesn't support
- READ COMMITTED: Supports only when AUTOCOMMIT mode is on
- SNAPSHOT: Supports
- REPEATABLE READ: Supports
- SERIALIZABLE: Supports

42. The Serializable and Snapshot isolation both protect data against dirty reads, non-repeatable reads, and phantom reads. Then what is the difference between them?

Ans:

Yes! That's true they both isolation levels achieves the same results but we can know the differences in WRITE operations instead of READ. For example we are trying to update a table from two different transactions.

With the Serializable isolation level, the database engine issues a shared lock on the accessed data and holds that lock until the transaction is completed. As a result, no other transactions can modify the data as long as the current transaction is active. Transaction 2 will be waiting till the Transaction 1 completes.

With the Snapshot isolation level, the database engine does not lock the data. Other transactions can update the data at the same time as the current transaction, resulting in update conflicts. When transaction1 updates data and the transaction2 also trying to update the same row with different value, the operation will be aborted by throwing an update conflict error.

43. What is the MEMORY_OPTIMIZED_ELEVATE_TO_SNAPSHOT?

Ans:

The MEMORY_OPTIMIZED_ELEVATE_TO_SNAPSHOT option is specific to memory-optimized tables, new in SQL Server 2014. When the option is enabled, the database engine uses Snapshot isolation for all interpreted T-SQL operations on memory-optimized tables, whether or not the isolation level is set explicitly at the session level.

44. There is an application connecting to my database and the application is using an ISOLATION LEVEL set in application side. How can we know which isolation level the application is using?

Ans:

We can get this information using a DMV:

First identify any of the session ID using for that application. Below query gives us the isolation level which is using by the application:

```
SELECT transaction_isolation_level
FROM sys.dm_exec_sessions
WHERE session_id = @@SPID;
```

- 0 - Unspecified
- 1 - Read Uncommitted
- 2 - Read Committed
- 3 - Repeatable
- 4 - Serializable
- 5 - Snapshot

45. What is the difference between "READ UNCOMMITTED" isolation level and "NOLOCK" table hint?

Ans:

Their job is same but the difference comes in scope. They both request Database Engine to not issue any shared locks when requested for data. And both options ignored when we specify it for WRITE/DML operations.

READ UNCOMMITTED: It works in session level, once we set this option the same isolation level applies all queries running under that session.

WITH NOLOCK: It works only for the specific query/table

46. What are the Pessimistic and Optimistic ISOLATION levels?

Ans:

- Serializable: Pessimistic
- Repeatable Read: Pessimistic
- Read Uncommitted: Pessimistic
- Read Committed: It supports both Optimistic and Pessimistic (Default)
- Snapshot: Optimistic

47. Within the READ_COMMITTED isolation level, during a read operation how long are locks held/retained for?

Ans:

When SQL Server executes a statement at the read committed isolation level, it acquires short lived share locks on a row by row basis. The duration of these share locks is just long enough to read and process each row; the server generally releases each lock before proceeding to the next row. Thus, if you run a simple select statement under read committed and check for locks, you will typically see at most a single row lock at a time. The sole purpose of these locks is to ensure that the statement only reads and returns committed data. The locks work because updates always acquire an exclusive lock which blocks any readers trying to acquire a share lock.

48. Within the REPEATABLE_READ and SERIALIZABLE isolation levels, during a read operation and assuming row-level locking, how long are locks held/retained for?

Ans:

Within either of these isolation levels, locks are held for the duration of the transaction, unlike within the READ_COMMITTED isolation level as noted above.

49. Describe the differences between the pessimistic SERIALIZABLE model and the optimistic SNAPSHOT model in terms of transactional isolation (i.e., not the concurrency differences, but instead how the exact same transactional modifications may result in different final outcomes).

Ans:

There is a bag containing a mixture of white and black marbles. Suppose that we want to run two transactions.

Serializable:

- First transaction turns each of the white marbles into black marbles.
- The second transaction turns each of the black marbles into white marbles.
- If we run these transactions under SERIALIZABLE isolation, we must run them one at a time. The first transaction will leave a bag with marbles of only one color. After that, the second transaction will change all of these marbles to the other color.
- There are only two possible outcomes: a bag with only white marbles or a bag with only black marbles.

Snapshot:

- If we run these transactions under snapshot isolation, there is a third outcome that is not possible under SERIALIZABLE isolation.
- Each transaction can simultaneously take a snapshot of the bag of marbles as it exists before we make any changes.
- Now one transaction finds the white marbles and turns them into black marbles. At the same time, the other transactions finds the black marbles - but only those marbles that where black when we took the snapshot - not those marbles that the first transaction changed to black - and turns them into white marbles. In the end, we still have a mixed bag of marbles with some white and some black. In fact, we have precisely switched each marble.

50. Any idea about row versioning?

Ans:

The concept of row versioning is not new to SQL Server, as SQL Server has been using it for years with triggers. For example, when a DELETE trigger is executed for a row, a copy of that row is stored in the "deleted table" just in case the trigger is rolled back and the deleted row needs to be "undeleted." In a sense, the row is versioned, and if need be, can be reused.

Row versioning for isolation levels is very similar, though not identical to row versioning for triggers. When a row versioning-based isolation level (which includes the two new ones we are now discussing) is enabled at the database level, the database engine maintains versions of each row that is modified (for an entire database). Whenever a transaction modifies any row, an image of the row before the modification is copied into a page of what is called the version store. The version store is located in the TEMPDB database and is used for temporary storage of versioned rows for all of the databases on a single SQL Server instance.

51. A small conversation on ISOLATION Levels?

Ans:

Interviewer: What do you know about ISOLATION levels?

Me: Explained about all available isolation levels

Interviewer: What is the default Isolation level?

Me: Read Committed

Interviewer: What is the problem with Read Committed isolation level?

Me: Non-repeatable Reads and Phantom Reads still exists in READ COMMITTED

Interviewer: Have you ever used "WITH NOLOCK" query hint?

Me: Yes! Explained about it

Interviewer: Ok, so do you mean that when specifies NO LOCK, there is no lock is being issued on that table/row/page?

Me: No! It still issues a lock but that lock is totally compatible with other low level locks (UPDATE, EXCLUSIVE).

Interviewer: Are you sure that is true? Can you give me an example?

Me: Yes I am sure let me give you an example. Let's say we have a table T with a million rows. Now I issued a command "SELECT * FROM T" and immediately in other window I executed a command "DROP TABLE T." DROP TABLE will wait till the first executed select statement is completed. So it is true that there is lock on that table which is not compatible with the schema lock.

Interviewer: What is the impact "DELETE FROM T WITH (NOLOCK)"?

Me: Database engine ignores NOLOCK hint when using in from clause with UPDATE and DELETE

CHAPTER 11

SQL SERVER PERFORMANCE TUNING

Interview Questions and Answers

Introduction: This chapter takes you through the SQL Server Performance Tuning related interview questions and answers. These questions are helpful for range of database developers and administrators starting from a junior to an expert level for the technical interview preparation. These questions and answers are deals with the below topics:

- Indexes
- Statistics
- Performance Monitoring
- Query Tuning
- Performance Tuning Scenarios
- Partitions
- In-Memory OLTP
- TEMPDB
- Miscellaneous

Indexes

1. What are the different indexes available in SQL Server?

Ans:

Clustered Index: A clustered index sorts and stores the data rows of the table or view in order based on the clustered index key. The clustered index is implemented as a B-tree index structure that supports fast retrieval of the rows, based on their clustered index key values.

Non Clustered Index: A non-clustered index can be defined on a table or view with a clustered index or on a heap. Each index row in the non-clustered index contains the non-clustered key value and a row locator. This locator points to the data row in the clustered index or heap having the key value. The rows in the index are stored in the order of the index key values, but the data rows are not guaranteed to be in any particular order unless a clustered index is created on the table.

Unique Index: An index that ensures the uniqueness of each value in the indexed column. If the index is a composite, the uniqueness is enforced across the columns as a whole, not on the individual columns. For example, if you were to create an index on the FirstName and LastName columns in a table, the names together must be unique, but the individual names can be duplicated. A unique index is automatically created when you define a primary key or unique constraint:

- *Primary key:* When you define a primary key constraint on one or more columns, SQL Server automatically creates a unique, clustered index if a clustered index does not already exist on the table or view. However, you can override the default behavior and define a unique, non-clustered index on the primary key.
- *Unique:* When you define a unique constraint, SQL Server automatically creates a unique, non-clustered index. You can specify that a unique clustered index be created if a clustered index does not already exist on the table.

Covering Indexes: A non-clustered index that is extended to include non-key columns in addition to the key columns is called covering index. They are not considered by the Database Engine when calculating the number of index key columns or index key size. Need to use INCLUDE clause while creating index. This is mostly used to cover all columns in most frequently used queries in OLTP.

Full Text Indexes: A special type of token-based functional index that is built and maintained by the Microsoft Full-Text Engine for SQL Server. It provides efficient support for sophisticated word searches in character string data.

Spatial Indexes: A spatial index provides the ability to perform certain operations more efficiently on spatial objects (spatial data) in a column of the geometry data type. The spatial index reduces the number of objects on which relatively costly spatial operations need to be applied.

Filtered Index: An optimized non-clustered index especially suited to cover queries that select from a well-defined subset of data. It uses a filter predicate to index a portion of rows in the table. A well-designed filtered index can improve query performance, reduce index maintenance costs, and reduce index storage costs compared with full-table indexes. Use where clause in create index statement.

Composite index: An index that contains more than one column. Both clustered and non-clustered indexes can be composite indexes.

XML Indexes: A shredded, and persisted, representation of the XML binary large objects (BLOBs) in the xml data type column.

2. How to choose the correct (Clustered/Non- Clustered) index on a column?

Ans:

Selecting Clustered Index:

- Clustered indexes are ideal for queries that select by a range of values or where you need sorted results. Examples of this include when you are using BETWEEN, <, >, GROUP BY, ORDER BY, and aggregates such as MAX, MIN, and COUNT in your queries.
- Clustered indexes are good for queries that look up a record with a unique value (such as an employee number) and when you need to retrieve most or all of the data in the record.
- Clustered indexes are good for queries that access columns with a limited number of distinct values, such as columns that holds country or state data. But if column data has

little distinctiveness, such as columns with a yes or no, or male or female, then these columns should not be indexed at all.

- Avoid putting a clustered index on columns that increment, such as an identity, date, or similarly incrementing columns, if your table is subject to a high level of INSERTS.

Selecting Non - Clustered Index:

- Non-clustered indexes are best for queries that return few rows (including just one row) and where the index has good selectivity (above 95%).
- If a column in a table is not at least 95% unique, then most likely the SQL Server Query Optimizer will not use a non-clustered index based on that column. For example, a column with "yes" or "no" as the data won't be at least 95% unique.
- Keep the "width" of your indexes as narrow as possible, especially when creating composite (multi-column) indexes. This reduces the size of the index and reduces the number of reads required to read the index, boosting performance.
- If possible, try to create indexes on columns that have integer values instead of characters. Integer values have less overhead than character values.
- If you know that your application will be performing the same query over and over on the same table, consider creating a covering index on the table. A covering index includes all of the columns referenced in the query.
- An index is only useful to a query if the WHERE clause of the query matches the column(s) that are leftmost in the index. So if you create a composite index, such as "City, State," then a query such as "WHERE City = 'Houston'" will use the index, but the query "WHERE STATE = 'TX'" will not use the index.

3. How to design indexes for a database? Or

What are the index creation best practices?

Ans:

- Understand the characteristics of the database (OLTP/OLAP)
- Understand the characteristics of the most frequently used queries.
- Understand the characteristics of the columns used in the queries.
- Choose the right index at the right place. For example, creating a clustered index on an existing large table would benefit from the ONLINE index option.
- Determine the optimal storage location for the index. A non-clustered index can be stored in the same FILEGROUP as the underlying table, or on a different FILEGROUP. If those FILEGROUPS are in different physical drives it will improve the performance.

Database Considerations:

- Avoid over indexing
- Use many indexes to improve query performance on tables with low update requirements, but large volumes of data.

- Indexing small tables may not be optimal
- Indexes on views can provide significant performance gains when the view contains aggregations and/or table joins. The view does not have to be explicitly referenced in the query for the query optimizer to use it

Column considerations:

- Keep the length of the index key short for clustered indexes. Additionally, clustered indexes benefit from being created on unique or non-null columns.
- Columns that are of the ntext, image, VARCHAR (max), NVARCHAR (max), and VARBINARY (max) data types cannot be specified as index key columns. However, VARCHAR (max), NVARCHAR (max), VARBINARY (max), and xml data types can participate in a non-clustered index as non-key index columns
- Consider using filtered indexes on columns that have well-defined subsets
- Consider the order of the columns if the index will contain multiple columns. The column that is used in the WHERE clause in an equal to (=), greater than (>), less than (<), or BETWEEN search condition, or participates in a join, should be placed first.

Index Characteristics: Determine the right index depends on the business need

- Clustered versus non-clustered
- Unique versus non-unique
- Single column versus multicolumn
- Ascending or descending order on the columns in the index
- Full-table versus filtered for non-clustered indexes
- Determine the Fill Factor

4. What is fill factor? How to choose the fill factor while creating an index?

Ans:

The Fill Factor specifies the % of fullness of the leaf level pages of an index. When an index is created or rebuilt the leaf level pages are written to the level where the pages are filled up to the fill factor value and the remainder of the page is left blank for future usage. This is the case when a value other than 0 or 100 is specified. For example, if a fill factor value of 70 is chosen, the index pages are all written with the pages being 70 % full, leaving 30 % of space for future usage.

5. When to choose High or Low Fill factor Value?

Ans:

You might choose a high fill factor value when there is very little or no change in the underlying table's data, such as a decision support system where data modification is not frequent, but on a regular and scheduled basis. Such a fill factor value would be better, since it creates an index smaller in size and hence queries can retrieve the required data with less disk I/O operations since it has to read fewer pages. On the other hand if you have an index that is constantly changing you would want to have a lower value to keep some free space available for new index entries. Otherwise SQL Server would have to constantly do page splits to fit the new values into the index pages.

6. What is Online Indexing?

Ans:

Online indexing means performing index maintenance operations (reorganizing or rebuilding) in background while the data still available for access. Before SQL Server 2005 indexing operations were usually performed as a part of other maintenance tasks running during off-peak hours. During these offline operations, the indexing operations hold exclusive locks on the underlying table and associated indexes. During online index operations, SQL Server eliminates the need of exclusive locks

7. How Online Indexing works?

Ans:

The online index operation can be divided into three phases:

- ➢ Preparation
- ➢ Build
- ➢ Final

The Build phase is a longest phase of all. It is in this phase where the creation, dropping, or rebuilding of indexes take place. The duration of the Build phase depends on the size of the data and the speed of the hardware. Exclusive locks are not held in this phase, so concurrent DML operations can be performed during this phase. The Preparation and Final phases are for shorter durations. They are independent of the size factor of the data. During these two short phases, the table or the indexed data is not available for concurrent DML operations.

8. What are the primary differences between index reorganization and an index rebuild?

Ans:

- ➢ Reorganization is an "online" operation by default; a rebuild is an "offline" operation by default
- ➢ Reorganization only affects the leaf level of an index
- ➢ Reorganization swaps data pages in-place by using only the pages already allocated to the index; a rebuild uses new pages/allocations
- ➢ Reorganization is always a fully-logged operation; a rebuild can be a minimally-logged operation
- ➢ Reorganization can be stopped mid-process and all completed work is retained; a rebuild is transactional and must be completed in entirety to keep changes

9. During an index reorganization operation, if the index spans multiple files, will pages be allowed to migrate between files

Ans:

No - pages will not migrate between files during index reorganization.

10. If you need to REBUILD a non-clustered index that is 10GB in size and have 5GB of free data-file space available with no room to grow the data file(s), how can you accomplish the task?

Ans:

When rebuilding an existing non-clustered index, you typically require free space that is approximately equivalent to 2.2 times the size of the existing index, since during a rebuild operation, the existing index is kept until the rebuilt structure is complete and an additional approximately 20% free space for temporary sorting structures used during the rebuild operation

- In this case, you would require at least an additional 10+ GB of free space for the rebuild operation to succeed, since the index itself is 10GB in size.
- Using SORT_IN_TEMPDB would not suffice in this case, since only the temporary sort tables are stored in TEMPDB in this case, and at least 10 GB of free space would still be required in the database data files.

11. What is the Covering Index?

Ans:

If you know that your application will be performing the same query over and over on the same table, consider creating a covering index on the table. A covering index, which is a form of a composite non clustered index, includes all of the columns referenced in SELECT, JOIN, and WHERE clauses of a query. Because of this, the index contains the data you are looking for and SQL Server doesn't have to look up the actual data in the table, reducing logical and/or physical I/O, and boosting performance. On the other hand, if the covering index gets too big (has too many columns), this could actually increase I/O and degrade performance.

12. What is the difference between composite index and covering index?

Ans:

Both Covering and Composite indexes are used for different scenarios.

Composite Index: An index created on more than one column.

- If a composite clustered index is defined on 2 columns Col1 Col2:
  - ✓ B-Tree Non-Leaf Nodes: Values for Col1 and Col2
  - ✓ B-Tree Leaf Nodes: Values for Col1, Col2, Col3 .....Col N
- If a composite non-clustered index is defined on 2 columns:
  - ✓ B-Tree Non-Leaf Nodes: Values for Col1 and Col2
  - ✓ B-Tree Leaf Nodes: Values for Col1, Col2 and Row Pointers to Clustered Index/Heap

Covering Index: Covering Index is used to remove KEY or RID Lookups. When we design a query on OLTP where the query usage frequency is very high and every time the query is issuing KEY/RID lookups then we can get benefit by creating covering index. Covering Index is an index contains all columns used in a targeted query. A covering index Without INCLUDE clause is same as composite index.

- If a covering clustered index is defined on 4 columns Col1 Col2 and INCLUDE (Col3, Col4):
  - ✓ No Way: We can't create covering index as clustered

- If a covering non-clustered index is defined on 4 columns Col1 Col2 and INCLUDE (Col3, Col4):
  - ✓ B-Tree Non-Leaf Nodes: Values for Col1 and Col2
  - ✓ B-Tree Leaf Nodes: Values for Col1, Col2, Col3 and Col4

13. While creating the covering index on which basis we should determine adding a column in Index main part and in INCLUDE clause?

Ans:

- Columns that used for searching should be on main part of the Index which means columns that appear in JOINS, WHERE, GROUP BY and ORDER BY should be on Index main part.
- Columns which are returned but not used in any search should be in INCLUDE part which means columns that appear in SELECT and HAVING should be in INCLUDE part.

14. Do we need to create a covering index for all queries? If not on which basis we have to create covering index?

Ans:

Is strictly No! There are few parameters that we need to consider while designing/suggesting a covering index. Below are the cases:

- How frequently this query is going to be executed?
- What is the frequency of Inserts and Updates on this table?
- Is the current response time is ok for your business

Example 1: Let's say your query is getting 6 columns from a table and in execution plan you are seeing key lookups. Current execution time is 2 sec. So this is usually acceptable in any environment. But here in this case the same query is getting executed for 200 to 250 times in 5 min. In this case creating a covering index will surely help in improving the performance.

Example 2: if we create a covering index on a table where there is huge number of inserts and updates expected, this covering index will negatively impact the performance.

15. Any idea about filtered index? Why indexed views when we can achieve the same with filtered index?

Ans:

Filtered index and indexed views are looks similar in some of the cases. But here are the differences.

Filtered Index:

- Created on column of a single base table
- No complex logic allowed in where clause. For example LIKE is not allowed
- Can be rebuilt online
- Computed columns are not supported
- Can be created as a non-unique index

Indexed View:

- Can be created on columns from multiple base tables
- Complex logic is allowed in where clause
- Can't be rebuilt online
- Computed columns are supported
- Can only be created as a unique index

16. Can we disable an index?

Ans:

Yes! We can.

17. What is the difference between disable and drop an index?

Ans:

Disable:

- It retains the metadata, statistics as is in sys.dm_db_index_usage_stats.
- Index will not be considered by query optimizer
- Query will fail if incase the index is used in any query hint.
- Foreign key constraints are disabled
- To enable back we have to rebuild the index using "ALTER INDEX <index name> ON SCHEMA.TABLE REBUILD"

Drop:

- Removes all metadata, statistics, index pages
- To enable back we have to recreate the index using CREATE INDEX statement

18. Is there any difference between disabling CLUSTERED and NON-CLUSTERED Index?

Ans:

Yes!

Disable Non-Clustered:

- De-allocate the index pages and freed up the space in database

Clustered:

- Data is still available in table but cannot be accessible except for DROP or REBUILD.
- All related non-clustered indexes, views and foreign key constraints are also disabled.
- We cannot query the table.

19. "ALTER INDEX <INDEXNAME> ON <TABLENAME> ENABLE" is this the correct statement to enable a disabled index?

Ans:

No!

To enable back we have to rebuild the index using "ALTER INDEX <index name> ON SCHEMA.TABLE REBUILD"

20. When you call an index is a duplicate index?

Ans:

When an index is called as duplicate when

- The index key values are same as other index on the same table columns.
- The Order of the columns is also same if it is a composite index
- ASC/DESC specification is also the same for both the indexes.
- The INCLUDED columns are also same (if any. Order doesn't matter for included)

21. Is there any benefit by creating duplicate indexes?

Ans:

As per my knowledge NO! There is no benefit from duplicate indexes. In fact there are problems in having duplicate indexes. Only one of the duplicate indexes will be used by the optimizer but the index maintenance has to be done for both the indexes. Means both indexes have to be updated when doing DML operations, fragmentation needs to be removed through index rebuilds/reorganize jobs etc. which leads to low performance.

22. There is a non-clustered index IX_1 available on table T. I have created a duplicate index IX_2. Now can you tell me which is the index is chosen by query optimizer and why?

Ans:

I am sure the optimizer choses IX_2 and never go for IX_1. I am confident on this as I had a situation earlier where I came to know "Optimizer is always choosing the latest index if duplicates are available."

Reason: When optimizer find two same indexes with different name it chooses the index with the latest statistics. If statistics are also same for both indexes then it chooses the index with the latest metadata that means it always chooses the last created duplicate index not the old one.

23. Can we create a Non-Clustered index on a Clustered indexed column? What is the benefit?

Ans:

Yes! It is possible. You can create it if you clearly understand how B-Tree forms for clustered and Non-Clustered indexes. However from my knowledge here are the benefits by having Clustered and Non-Clustered indexes on same column:

- Scanning Non-Clustered index leaf nodes is easier than clustered index leaf nodes as Clustered Index leaf node is having actual rows and Non-clustered index leaf nodes are having only Index Columns. So it can help in improving the queries like SELECT COUNT(<Indexed Column>) as it simply scans the non-clustered index instead of clustered index.

- ➢ The other case where you have queries that require only indexed columns, here again scanning the non-clustered index is faster than clustered index.

Note: Having Non-Clustered on Clustered index column might help you in improving the performance for some queries but it will surely increase the Index maintenance which in-turn to more I/O and disk space usage

24. What happens to non-clustered index when we drop a clustered index?

Ans:

When a table is having Clustered Index: Non-Clustered Indexes leaf nodes have key values to point out to clustered index.

When a table is a HEAP: Non-Clustered index leaf node is point to RID (Row ID – Physical Location File à Page à Record No).

When a Clustered Index dropped: All non-clustered indexes on that table should be rebuilt to repoint their leaf nodes values from clustered index key to RID. That is the reason dropping clustered index takes longer time on huge tables.

25. What is the impact on non-clustered index when a clustered index created on a table where already some non-clustered indexes available?

Ans:

Creating a clustered index on a heap impacts the non-clustered indexes if there are any. All Non-Clustered indexes should be reorganized to point out to clustered Index keys instead of RID.

26. Let's say I have a table like: Tab (Col1, Col2, Col3, Col4, Col5, Col6, Col7). I created a clustered index and a non-clustered index like Clustered On (Col1, Col2) and Non-Clustered index on (Col1, Col2). Can you explain the B-Tree structure?

Ans:

Clustered Index Structure:

- ➢ Intermediate Levels (Searching & Navigation): Col1, Col2
- ➢ Leaf Level (Data): Col1, Col2, Col3, Col4, Col5, Col6, Col7

Non-Clustered Index Structure:

- ➢ Intermediate Levels (Searching & Navigation): Col1, Col2
- ➢ Leaf Level (Data): Col1, Col2

This is the narrowest index we can create and it improves the performance in some of the scenarios ex: SELECT COUNT (*) FROM Tab; Because for counting number of rows in a table optimizer choses the index with the least number of pages at leaf level. So a non-clustered index usually has a small number of pages than clustered. And this having an entry for each row it gives the accurate result.

27. We have a table T (Col1, Col2, Col3, Col4, Col5, Col6, Col7).

Index [1]: Col1 – Primary Key

Index [2]: Col2, Col3 – Unique Non-Clustered Index

Index [3]: Col4 – Non-Unique Non-Clustered Index

Index [4]: Col5 – Non-Unique Non-Clustered Index with INCLUDE columns as (Sol6 and Col7)

Now can you be able to quickly explain the B-Tree structure for these indexes.

Ans:

Index [1]:

- Intermediate Levels: Col1
- Leaf Level (Data): Col1, Col2, Col3, Col4, Col5, Col6, Col7

Index [2]:

- Intermediate Levels: Col2, Col3
- Leaf Level: Col1, Col2, Col3

Index [3]:

- Intermediate Levels: Col1, Col4 (For non-unique non-clustered indexes clustered index key also attached at intermediate levels as well)
- Leaf Level: Col1, Col4

Index [4]:

- Intermediate Levels: Col1, Col5
- Leaf Level: Col1, Col5, Col6, Col7

28. What are Density, Selectivity and Depth of an index?

Ans:

Density:

- It's a measure to identify uniqueness of a column. It tells optimizer how often duplicate values occur in that column:
- Density Formula: 1/[Number of distinct values in that columns] .
- Density Values range from 0 to 1.0
- High Density à Less Unique values; Low Density à High number of Unique Values
- I have a column where the value is same for all rows. The column density is: 1/1 = 1.0 which is the highest possible density.
- I have a unique column now the density is: 1/Rowcount
- Better Performance: Low Density

Selectivity:

- It's also a measure to identify uniqueness of a column
- Selectivity formula: [Total rows qualified in predicate or filter]/[Total rows in the table]

- Let's say in a table T total rows are 12000. Now we'll see the SELECTIVITY
  - ✓ When all rows from the table are passed in the filter SELECTIVITY: [12000]/[12000] = 1.0
  - ✓ When all rows are disqualified at filter SELECTIVITY: [0]/[12000] = 0
- High Selectivity: Huge rows are filtering through the predicate
- Low Selectivity: Less number of rows filtering through the predicate
- Better Performance: High Selectivity

Depth:

- Indexes are represented in the form of B-Trees. To find a record in leaf page the storage engine starts at "ROOT" and navigates down to the each level to find the correct "Leaf Page." This is called traversing the index using binary search.
- The number of levels in an index binary tree is called the Index **Depth.**
- Leaf level starts with 0 and increase by 1 up to the root page of the index
- Number of levels increased (More Depth) à More traversing à Low Performance
- Choose a small index keys which can reduce the index depth by holding more keys. When the index key is small "Fan-Out" (Number of index records per page in non-leaf node) will be higher.
- Better Performance: Less Depth

29. What is fragmentation?

Ans:

Fragmentation can be defined as any condition that cause more than optimal amount of disk I/O to be performed in accessing a table or cause the longer disk I/O. Optimal performance comes for the SELECT queries when the data pages of tables are contiguous or fully packed. Fragmentation can happen in two levels, file system level fragmentation which is called as Logical/Physical Disk Fragmentation and Index level fragmentation.

30. What are the different types of index fragmentations?

Ans:

- Internal Fragmentation
- Logical Fragmentation
- Extent Fragmentation

Internal Fragmentation (Inside Page): When pages are less than fully used, the part of each page that is unused constitutes a form of fragmentation, since the table's or index's rows are no longer packed together as tightly as they could be. This is known as Internal Fragmentation

Logical Fragmentation (Between Pages): SQL Server uses 8KB Pages to store data on disk. When a clustered index is created on a table, SQL Server creates a b-tree data structure for the index and links all data pages at the leaf level of the tree in a logical order by using a doubly linked list. Logical fragmentation occurs when the pages in this doubly linked list are not contiguous in the index, meaning that indexes have pages in which the logical ordering of pages, which is based on the key value, does not match the physical ordering inside the data file.

Extent Fragmentation: Extent fragmentation occurs when the extents of a table or index are not contiguous with the database leaving extents from one or more indexes intermingled in the file.

31. What are the reason that leads to Internal, logical and extent fragmentation?

Ans:

Internal Fragmentation:

- Random deletes resulting in empty space on data pages
- Page-splits due to inserts or updates
- Shrinking the row such as when updating a large value to a smaller value
- Using a fill factor of less than 100
- Using large row sizes

Logical Fragmentation:

- Page-splits due to inserts or updates
- Heavy deletes that can cause pages be removed from the page chain, resulting in dis-contiguous page chain

Extent Fragmentation:

- Random deletes, which could leave some of the pages in an extent unused while the extent itself is still reserved as part of the table's space allocation. Think of it like Internal fragmentation, but in extents instead of pages
- Deletes on ranges of contiguous rows within the table, causing one or more entire extents to become de-allocated, thus leaving a gap between the surrounding extents of the table or index
- Interleaving of a table's data extents with the extents of other objects

32. How to monitor the fragmentation and how to resolve it?

Ans:

We can use DMF sys.dm_db_index_physical_stats:

There are two columns that give us the fragmentation information:

- Avg_fragmentation_in_percent – depicts logical fragmentation
- Avg_page_space_used_in_percent – depicts internal fragmentation

Also this DMF can be run with three different options as below:

- DETAILED – reads all data and index pages. Be careful with using this options since it causes the entire index be read into memory and may result in IO/Memory issues
- SAMPLED: reads 1% of the pages if more than 10,000 pages
- LIMITED: only reads the parent level of b-tree (same as DBCC SHOWCONTIG WITH FAST). Limited option doesn't report page density, since it does not read the leaf level pages

Solutions to Resolve Fragmentation issues:

- Recreate: CREATE INDEX WITH DROP_EXISTING
- Rebuild – ALTER INDEX ... REBUILD
- Reorganize – ALTER INDEX ... REORGANIZE
- To reduce the extent fragmentation of a heap, create a clustered index on the table and then drop the index

33. How to know unused indexes in a table.

Ans:

By using a DMV we'll find the unused indexes details. We have a DMV called "sys.dm_db_index_usage_stats" which retrieves the statistics of indexes, if an index id is not in that dmv then we can say that index is not been using from a long time.

34. On which basis we will create computed indexes?

Ans:

For composite indexes, take into consideration the order of the columns in the index definition. Columns that will be used in comparison expressions in the WHERE clause (such as WHERE FirstName = 'Charlie') should be listed first. Subsequent columns should be listed based on the uniqueness of their values, with the most unique listed first.

35. Can we create index on table variables?

Ans:

Yes, Implicitly. We can create but these can't be useful as statistics are not created or considered by optimizer. Creating an index on a table variable can be done implicitly within the declaration of the table variable by defining a primary key and creating unique constraints. The primary key will represent a clustered index, while the unique constraint a non-clustered index.

```
DECLARE @Users TABLE
(
UserID INT PRIMARY KEY,
UserName VARCHAR(50),
UNIQUE (UserName)
)
```

The drawback is that the indexes (or constraints) need to be unique. One potential way to circumvent this however is to create a composite unique constraint:

```
DECLARE @Users TABLE
(
UserID INT PRIMARY KEY,
UserName VARCHAR (50),
FirstName VARCHAR (50),
UNIQUE (UserName, UserID)
```

)

You can also create the equivalent of a clustered index. To do so, just add the clustered reserved word.

```
DECLARE @Users TABLE
(
UserID INT PRIMARY KEY,
UserName VARCHAR (50),
FirstName VARCHAR (50),
UNIQUE CLUSTERED (UserName, UserID)
)
```

36. What is the Heap Table?

Ans:

- A table without any index created on it
- Data is not stored in any particular order
- Specific data cannot be retrieved quickly, unless there are also non-clustered indexes
- Data pages are not linked, so sequential access needs to refer back to the index allocation map (IAM) pages
- Since there is no clustered index, additional time is not needed to maintain the index
- Since there is no clustered index, there is not the need for additional space to store the clustered index tree
- These tables have a index_id value of 0 in the sys.indexes CATALOG view

37. How to get the index usage information?

Ans:

"sys.dm_db_index_usage_stats" binds with "sysobjects":

This view gives you information about overall access methods to your indexes. There are several columns that are returned from this DMV, but here are some helpful columns about index usage:

- user_seeks - number of index seeks
- user_scans- number of index scans
- user_lookups - number of index lookups
- user_updates - number of insert, update or delete operations

"sys.dm_db_index_operational_stats" binds with sysindexes:

This view gives you information about insert, update and delete operations that occur on a particular index. In addition, this view also offers data about locking, latching and access methods. There are several columns that are returned from this view, but these are some of the more interesting columns:

- leaf_insert_count - total count of leaf level inserts
- leaf_delete_count - total count of leaf level inserts
- leaf_update_count - total count of leaf level updates

```
SELECT
DB_NAME (DATABASE_ID) AS DATABASENAME,
OBJECT_NAME (B.OBJECT_ID) AS TABLENAME,
INDEX_NAME = (SELECT NAME FROM SYS.INDEXES A WHERE A.OBJECT_
ID = B.OBJECT_ID AND A.INDEX_ID = B.INDEX_ID),
USER_SEEKS,
USER_SCANS,
USER_LOOKUPS,
USER_UPDATES
FROMSYS.DM_DB_INDEX_USAGE_STATS B
INNER JOIN SYS.OBJECTS C ON B.OBJECT_ID = C.OBJECT_ID
WHERE DATABASE_ID = DB_ID(DB_NAME()) AND C.TYPE <> 'S'
```

38. What methods are available for removing fragmentation of any kind on an index in SQL Server?

Ans:

Before SQL Server 2005:

```
DBCC INDEXDEFRAG
DBCC DBREINDEX
CREATE INDEX…DROP EXISTING (cluster)
DROP INDEX; CREATE INDEX
```

SQL Server 2005, 2008, 2012, 2014, 2016:

```
ALTER INDEX...REORGANIZE
ALTER INDEX...REBUILD
CREATE INDEX...DROP EXISTING (cluster)
DROP INDEX; CREATE INDEX
```

39. How to make forcefully use an index in a query? Or what table hint needs to be specified to forcefully use an index in a query?

Ans:

We can specify "Index" table hint in a query to forcefully use an index.

```
Ex: SELECT Emp_ID, Name FROM Emp WITH (INDEX (NIX_NAME_EMP))
```

40. While creating an index if I mention "PAD INDEX" what does it mean?

Ans:

Ok, PAD INDEX impacts the option FILL FACTOR. Usually when we give FILL FACTOR it applies only to the bottom layer (Leaf Nodes) of the given Index, if we mention PAD INDEX option means that apply FILL FACTOR to all layers of Index.

41. Can we be able to remove fragmentation on a heap? If yes can you explain how?

Ans:

From SQL Server 2008 onwards we can use REBUILD command to remove fragmentation from heap.

```
ALTER TABLE <Table Name> REBUILD
```

42. What are the benefits of "COLUMNSTORE" index?

Ans:

The benefits of using a non-clustered "COLUMNSTORE" index are:

- Only the columns needed to solve a query are fetched from disk
- It is easier to compress the data due to the redundancy of data within a column
- Buffer hit rates are improved because data is highly compressed and frequently accessed parts of commonly used columns remain in memory, while infrequently used parts are paged out.

43. How can you identify for which columns we have to include to non-clustered index or what are the columns for which we can create the covering index?

Ans:

Usually we can choose covering indexes to improve the performance of a query. To remove key lookup/rid lookup we can create a covering index. To identify the columns which are leading to bookmark lookup just check in execution plan move the mouse pointer over "Key Lookup" and note down the columns mentioned in "Output List" section.

44. When a clustered index scan happens?

Ans:

Clustered index scan is almost equals to Table Scan. Usually index scan happens when there is no "WHERE" condition specified in select query or when dealing with VARCHAR columns. For example in below example

```
"SELECT * FROM EMPLOYEE"
"SELECT * FROM EMPLOYEE WHERE FIRST_NAME LIKE '%A%'"
```

If there is no clustered index available on that table there would be a table scan happens if there is a clustered index available "Index Scan" happens.

45. Can you explain what Indexed views are?

Ans:

- This is also known as materialized views.
- A view is a virtual table and it contains just a SQL query but an indexed view is just like a table and it physically stores data on disk.

- An indexed view can have one clustered index and more than one non clustered index.
- It must be created with "Schema Binding" option. Hence no modification possible for base tables until the view is being altered or dropped.
- In developer and Enterprise editions the optimizer automatically uses indexes created on views even though it doesn't referencing the indexed view.
- To explicitly use indexes created on view, specify "WITH (NOEXPAND)" query hint.
- To forcefully use the base table indexes specify the query hint "WITH EXPAND VIEWS"

46. What are the various limitations with Indexed views?

Ans:

Limitations with Indexed View:

- There are lots of limitations like we can't use any aggregate function except COUNT_BIG(*)
- All functions and expressions used in indexed view must be deterministic.
  - ✓ Deterministic: Always returns the same output for the same given input EX: DATEADD()
  - ✓ Non-Deterministic: Output would be changing from time to time for the same given input Ex: GETDATE()
- Certain database SET options have required values if we wish to create any indexed views in that database – for example, ANSI_NULLS, ANSI_PADDING, ANSI_WARNINGS, ARITHABORT, CONCAT_NULL_YIELDS_NULL, and QUOTED_IDENTIFIER must be ON; NUMERIC_ROUNDABORT must be OFF.
- All columns referenced in the view must be deterministic – that is, they must return the same value each time.
- We cannot include certain aggregate functions in an indexed view – COUNT, DISTINCT, MIN, MAX, TOP, and more.
- You can't have a self-join or an outer join, an OUTER APPLY or a CROSS APPLY.

47. On which basis query optimizer decides to use indexes on views or base tables?

Ans:

If the data in the indexed view covers all or part of the SQL statement, and the query optimizer determines that an index on the view is the low-cost access path, the query optimizer will choose the index regardless of whether the view is referenced by name in the query. And also in some cases even though the query covers all data from view and still the optimizer uses indexes from base tables when dealing with the tiny datasets.

48. I have an indexed view, now base table data has been modified, does the modified data reflected in view automatically?

Ans:

Once a view is indexed, the data is kept in sync with the base tables by incorporating the changes to the view in the query plan which updates the base table. So, a query which adds a row to a table referenced by an indexed view will have additional operators added to the end of the plan to maintain the view.

49. Can we be able to create a clustered index on a column with duplicate values?

Ans:

Yes! It is possible. But we are not supposed to create a clustered index on a column with duplicate values.

50. Why clustered index shouldn't be created on a column when it's having duplicates?

Ans:

Let me explain how clustered index is internally organized when we create it on a non-unique column.

When database engine find a duplicate on clustered index column it adds a four byte integer (unique identifier) to that duplicate value so that it can uniquely identify all rows in the table. This causes an extra processing and it will impact the performance when there is lot of duplicate values and the column is used in foreign key relationship.

51. Creating indexes always improves the performance. Do you agree on this statement?

Ans:

No! I don't agree below are the reasons:

- Creating unnecessary, duplicate indexes can cause extra index maintenance
- Creating too many indexes on a table where more inserts and updates happening leads to an extra resource utilization and can easily hurts the performance
- Creating covering index on a infrequently used queries leads to an extra maintenance
- Etc.

Statistics

52. What are the index statistics?

Ans:

Index statistics contain information about the distribution of index key values. By distribution, I mean the number of rows associated with each key value. SQL Server uses this information to determine what kind of execution plan to use when processing a query.

53. When are index statistics updated?

Ans:

The AUTO_UPDATE_STATISTICS database setting controls when statistics are automatically updated. Once statistics have been created, SQL Server then determines when to update those statistics based on how out-of-date the statistics might be. SQL Server identifies out of date statistics based on the number of inserts, updates, and deletes that have occurred since the last time statistics were updated, and then recreates the statistics based on a threshold. The threshold is relative to the number of records in the table. (Enable the properties – "auto create statistics" and "auto update statistics" for OLTP)

54. Explain database options "Auto Update Statistics" and "Auto Update Statistics Asynchronous"?

Ans:

Auto Update Statistics: If there is an incoming query but statistics are stale then SQL Server first update the statistics before building the execution plan.

Auto Update Statistics Asynchronous: If there is an incoming query but statistics are stale then SQL Servers uses the stale statistics, builds the execution plan and then update the statistics.

55. How to update statistics manually?

Ans:

If you want to manually update statistics, you can use either sp_updatestats or UPDATE STATISTICS <statistics name>

56. What are the various types of statistics available?

Ans:

There are three different types of statistics available.

- Statistics created due to index creation.
- Statistics created by optimizer.
- User defined statistics created from "CREATE STATISTICS"

57. How to find out when statistics updated last time?

Ans:

A simple logic is, run the query and observes the values for both "estimated rows" and "actual rows," if they both are close to each other you need not worried about the statistics. If you find big difference between them then you need to think about updating statistics.

In general we can find out last statistics updated info from below query

```
SELECT object_name (object_id) as table_name
        , name as stats_name
        , stats_date (object_id, stats_id) as last_update
FROM sys.stats
WHERE objectproperty(object_id, 'IsUserTable') = 1
ORDER BY last_update
```

58. In "SQL Server" do we have Statistics on Table and Statistics on Index? Or both are same?

Ans:

Yes! We have two different statistics Table and Index. But there is no essential differences expect the point they created and source.

- ➢ Statistics on Index are initially created as a part of Index creation. When we create an index on pre-existing data, a full scan happens and creates the statistics as a part of index creation.
- ➢ Statistics on table column are initially created when the columns referred on filtering conditions such as "WHERE," "JOIN ON" etc. But the scan happens on sample data not with the full scan.
- ➢ Also both statistics are created when issued a manual CREATE STATISTICS.

59. Did you hear the term cardinality estimation?

Ans:

Yes! Query optimizer needs to calculate the estimated number of rows by taking the help from statistics and histogram. This process is known as cardinality estimation.

60. Query optimizer will take the help of statistics/histogram right. Now can you tell me what kind of information that query optimizer gets from the statistics/histogram?

Ans:

Let's say a query with search criteria is submitted. Now Query Optimizer looks into the statistics and seeks for the answers for below questions

- ➢ Is it possible that this set of statistics containing this value which is specified in search condition?
- ➢ If it does contain the value, what will be the estimated row count for the matching rows?

Histogram contains 5 columns:

RANGE_HI_Key: Represents the top data distributed values based on index or previous executed search conditions.

RANGE_Rows: When optimizer can't find the exact match but nearby values. It captures the number of rows between the given nearby values.

EQ_ROWS: Number of rows exactly matching the search condition.

DISTINCT_Range_Rows: When optimizer can't find the exact match but nearby values. It captures the number of distinct rows between the given nearby values.

AVG_RANGE_ROWS: When optimizer can't find the exact match it still gets the estimated row count by using the formula: [Range_Rows]/[Distinct_Range_Rows]

61. Can you be able to take an example and how histogram works in cardinality estimates?

Ans:

Let's say we have a table called ITEMS and there is an index on ID column. Below is the histogram:

Example 1:

```
SELECT * FROM [DBO].[ITEMS] WHERE ID = 569
```

Here is the histogram for the column **"ID":**

From the histogram it is clear that there are total 1879 rows which are matching the value ID = 569. Thereof "Estimated Row Count: 1879"

RANGE_HI_KEY	RANGE_ROWS	EQ_ROWS	DISTINCT_RANGE_ROWS	AVG_RANGE_ROWS
555	0	12	0	1
558	130	112	6	21.66666667
559	0	1234	0	1
566	240	311	5	48
567	0	133	0	1
568	0	431	0	1
569	0	1879	0	1

Fig 11.1

Now we'll see another example.

Example 2:

SELECT * FROM [DBO].[ITEMS] WHERE ID = 565;

- From the histogram you can see there is no value listed under RANGE_HI_KEY for the value 565.
- But there is other nearby values: 559 and 566 with the RANGE_ROWS = 240.
- This means there are 240 rows in the table with the ID's between (>559 & <566). I.e these 240 rows should belongs to any of these ID's (560, 561, 562, 563, 564 or 565).
- Next it checks the column DISTINCT_RANGE_ROWS for 566 and the value is 5. That means from the available 240 rows there are 5 unique **ID** available.
- That mean we are not exactly sure how many rows under the each ID but we can get the estimated row count by AVG the value: 240/5 = 48.
- 48 is the estimated row count when ID = 565.

RANGE_HI_KEY	RANGE_ROWS	EQ_ROWS	DISTINCT_RANGE_ROWS	AVG_RANGE_ROWS
555	0	12	0	1
558	130	112	6	21.66666667
559	0	1234	0	1
566	240	311	5	48
567	0	133	0	1
568	0	431	0	1
569	0	1879	0	1

Fig 11.2

62. Can we be able to see this histogram using T-SQL?

Ans:

Yes! We can get the available histogram.

```
DBCC SHOW_STATISTICS ('<Table_Name>',<Index_Name>);
```

63. Let's say an index is created on composite column. Does the histogram maintained for all columns?

Ans:

No! Histogram shows only for the first column. SQL Server generates histogram only for the first index key column that is part of your index. For all subsequent index key columns SQL Server only stores the selectivity of the column in the Density Vector. Therefore you should always make sure that the column with the highest selectivity is the first one in your composite index key.

64. If I ask you to find number of modifications (INSERT/UPDATE/DELETE) happened on a table column after the last statistics update. What is your approach? Is there any way that we can find this value?

Ans:

Yes! There is a way that we can find the number of modifications occurred on a column since last statistics update. Column "RowModCtr" from "sys.sysindexes" will be updated when the corresponding column modified. When a statistics update happens this counter will be set to 0. Below example explains it in a better way.

Code:

```
SET NOCOUNT ON;
-- Update statistics on non-clustered index defined on SAL column
UPDATE STATISTICS [DBO].[EMP](NON_CLIX_SAL_1);
--check the count for RowModCtr
SELECT RowModCtr FROM sys.sysindexes WHERE name = 'NON_CLIX_SAL_1';
-- UPDATING 200 ROWS
UPDATE [dbo].[emp] SET sal = sal+10 WHERE ID between 1001 and 1200;
-- DELETING 3 ROWS
DELETE [dbo].[emp] WHERE ID BETWEEN 10001 AND 10003
--Now check again the count for RowModCtr
SELECT rowmodctr FROM sys.sysindexes WHERE name = 'NON_CLIX_SAL_1';
```

Note: Before 2005 this value is at table level and from 2008, 2012, 2014 and 2016 this implies on column level.

65. I have a query here, let's say I just updated statistics for a column C1 and then RowModCtr becomes ZERO. Then I started a transaction updated 300 rows and I did a Rollback. Then what happens to RowModCtr does the value modified as 300 or it still remains the same as ZERO as no transaction is yet committed after last stat update?

Ans:

It's 300 for sure as RowModCtr will be updated for each and every modification. It doesn't care whether the transaction committed or rollback. Just like a transaction log; if you update 300 rows and rollback then the entire operation will be written to log file right.

66. In your system AUTO UPDATE STATISTICS is on and can you tell me on which basis "UPDATE STATISTICS" triggered?

Ans:

UPDATE STATISTICS are triggered by SQL Server database engine based on below conditions:

- Cardinality of a table is less than six and the table is in the TEMPDB database, auto update after every six modifications to the table.
- Cardinality of a table is greater than 6, but less than or equal to 500, update statistics after every 500 modifications.
- Cardinality of a table is greater than 500, update statistics when (500 + 20 percent of the table) changes have occurred.
- For table variables, a cardinality change does not trigger an auto–update of the statistics.

Note: Cardinality as you know this is the estimated row count from that table and the number of modifications can get from "RowModCtr" from "sys.sysindexes"

67. Let's say you had a situation where you need showcase to your customer when "UPDATE STATS" triggering. What are the ways and where we can get this information?

Ans:

There are various ways that can showcase statistics are updating:

- We can get the last statistics update date from DBCC SHOW_STSTISTICS
  - ✓ Ex: DBCC SHOW_STATISTICS ('EMP',NON_CLIX_SAL_1);
- We can get the same information using STAT_DATE() function
  - ✓ Ex: SELECT name AS index_name, STATS_DATE(OBJECT_ID, index_id) AS StatsUpdated FROM sys.indexes WHERE name = 'NON_CLIX_SAL_1';
- If the column RowModCtr is ZERO means that statistics are up to date
- We can trace this information using profiler events SP:StmtCompleted and SP:StmtStarted. We can see the code like below when statistics updated:
  - ✓ Ex:
```
SELECT StatMan([SC0])
    FROM (
    SELECT TOP 100 PERCENT <COLUMN> AS [SC0]
    FROM [dbo].<TABLE> WITH (READUNCOMMITTED)
    ORDER BY [SC0] ) AS _MS_UPDSTATS_TBL
```
- Enabling the trace 205 or 8721 will write this information to SQL Server error log.

68. You are assigned to handle a very large database (6.5 TB). What is your approach in updating statistics?

Ans:

- Make sure AUTO UPDATE STATS - Asynchronous is ON
- Identify top transactional tables which needs an update statistics with FULL scan

- Switch off Auto Update Statistics using "WITH NORECOMPUTE" for the tables identified in the step 2.
- Configure a process for updating statistics for the tables selected in step 2. This we can use our own logic based on RowModCtr.
- Monitor the time taking, I/O, memory usage for the manual statistics update and adjust the schedule times.

69. What are the most common mistakes in updating statistics from the environments you worked?

Ans:

Below are the most common mistakes happens in dealing with statistics:

Updating Statistics after Index Rebuilds: Since statistics update (Even Auto Update is turned off using WITH NORECOMPUTE) is a part of Index Rebuild, doing the same again causes an extra I/O which may leads to low performance.

Relaying on SQL Server default Auto Update: Auto Update follows the default configurations which means statistics update triggered when 500+20% of rows modified. Just imagine if your table is having 40 million rows then next statistics update when there is 20% rows modified (Insert/Delete/Update) on that table. That means statistics will be updated after 8 Million row modifications which might put your queries in trouble.

Running Statistics Update Without specifying the sample size: It might kill the performance I have seen lot of incidents where running update statistics without specifying the sample rows or resample. When we specify resample it considers the same value as previous. We need the accurate statistics to gain the best performance. If you run update statistics with default sample it update statistics with a fraction of total row count in a table. It applies the same percentage for all tables in your database which causes a sudden performance down on your database system. Best way is use a proper sample and use the resample based on your table size.

Updating Statistics too frequently: This may leads to two things. Cost increased for running UPDATE STATISTICS and the other one is your queries recompiles frequently, you know what the problem here ☺

70. Can we switch off AUTO UPDATE statistics for a specific index/column?

Ans:

Yes! It can be done using "WITH NORECOMPUTE" in UPDATE STATISTICS command.

We can turn off Auto Update Stats for a selective index as below:

Ex: UPDATE STATISTICS [DBO].[EMP](NON_CLIX_SAL_1) WITH NORECOMPUTE ;

It means database engine does not update statistics for the given index automatically. We should have a maintenance plan/job that take cares of manual statistics update based on the value RowModCtr.

71. I have switched off AUTO UPDATE using NORECOMPUTE. How can I re-enable it?

Ans:

When you next time UPDATE STATS on that column just run without the clause "WITH NORECOUMPUTE." That's all it starts updating the statistics automatically.

72. Does SQL Server get any statistics when using a dataset through linked server?

Ans:

No. No statistics are provided through linked server, to get statistics on dataset load data into local table/temp table and then create an index.

73. Can we import/Export statistics from/to SQL Server?

Ans:

Yes! From "Generate and Publish Scripts" wizard we can choose "Script Statistics and Histogram" from "Advanced scripting options" window.

74. Can we save some space by removing the statistics for unused indexes?

Ans:

We actually need not worry about the apace occupied by the statistics. It doesn't take much space to store the statistics of a column/index. For example histogram stores only up to 200 rows, by clearing that 200 rows we might save some space in kb's which is too small and can be ignored.

75. Do we need to UPDATE STATISTICS after Index Rebuild/Reorganize?

Ans:

Index Rebuild: No statistics update required as update statistics is also a part of rebuild

Index Reorganize: Statistics are not updated as a part of reorganize but we can setup a process that can take care of this based on RowModCntr value.

76. Does these two operations are equal? "UPDATE STATISTICS WITH FULL SCAN" and "Statistics Update during the index rebuild"?

Ans:

Yes!

77. Can we create custom statistics in SQL Server like we do in Oracle?

Ans:

In oracle we can create custom statistics all the way down to creating our own Histogram. There is not much control provided in SQL Server but here we have filter statistics which can help us in creating custom statistics which in turn helpful for optimizer in creating the more optimized execution plans. There are certain scenarios where these filter statistics are useful in:

- When data is widely distributed
- There are a lot of null values
- Working with partitioned data

78. Can we have statistics on a view?

Ans:

No! But yes.

No: We can't have statistics on a view.

Yes: When a view is an indexed/materialized

79. Can we have statistics on temporary table?

Ans:

- Yes! Just like permanent table we can have statistics on temporary table.
- When the columns in temp table used in T-SQL where clause a set of statistics get created
- But the disadvantage is these statistics creation causes the statements recompile. It might impact the larger queries.

80. Can we have statistics on table variable?

Ans:

No!

81. How does partitioning affect the statistics usage?

Ans:

Let's say we have a clustered index on partitioned table.

- On a partitioned table we may not see accurate statistics.
- Statistics can help optimizer in choosing the correct partition based on the search criteria
- But within partition we might see INDEX SCAN when there is a chance to INDEX SEEK.
- It is always suggested to create filter/manual statistics on partition level.

Performance Monitoring

82. What are the bottlenecks that affect the performance of your application/database?

Ans:

Here is the list of parameters which may affect the performance of an application or database:

- Database Design\Database Code
- Application Design\Application Code
- Blocking/Deadlocks
- CPU
- Memory
- IO
- NETWORK
- Server/Database Configurations

Database Design\Database Code:

- **Indexes:**
  - ✓ Remove Unused and duplicate Indexes
  - ✓ Create the missing indexes based on usage
  - ✓ Take care of index maintenance
  - ✓ Choose the correct fill factor based on OLTP/OLAP
- **Statistics:** Configure the correct way for updating statistics
- **Joins:**
  - ✓ Make sure columns used for joins are having indexes
  - ✓ Joining on columns with same data type gains performance
  - ✓ Too many joins on frequently used queries may impact the performance
  - ✓ Generally, frequent operations requiring 5 or more table joins should be avoided by redesigning the database
- **Cursors:** Avoid using cursors instead try using the alternative solutions
- Do not use the conversion/system/user defined functions in where clause
- Too much of normalization
- Choose the Appropriate Data Types
- Use Triggers Cautiously
- Don't Access More Data Than You Need
- **Stored Procedures:** Encapsulate Your Code in Stored Procedures
  - ✓ Try to put all your T-SQL code in stored procedures which reduces the network traffic by just calling the proc from application and reduces the I/O overhead by using the compiled execution plan
  - ✓ Always SET the required options Ex: "SET NOCOUNT ON"
- Isolate OLTP and OLAP instances
- For Delete operation use soft delete which means marking data as deleted and apply the actual delete operation when traffic is low

Application Design/Application code:

Application Design issues:

- Perform as many data-centered tasks as possible on SQL Server in the form of stored procedures. Avoid manipulating data at the presentation and business services tiers.
- Don't maintain state (don't store data from the database) in the business services tier. Maintain state in the database as much as possible
- Don't create complex or deep object hierarchies. The creation and use of complex classes or a large number of objects used to model complex business rules can be resource intensive and reduce the performance and scalability of your application. This is because the memory allocation when creating and freeing these objects is costly.

- Consider designing the application to take advantage of database connection pooling and object pooling using Microsoft Transaction Server (MTS). MTS allows both database connections and objects to be pooled, greatly increasing the overall performance and scalability of your application.
- If your application runs queries against SQL Server that by nature are long, design the application to be able to run queries asynchronously. This way, one query does not have to wait for the next before it can run. One way to build in this functionality into your n-tier application is to use the Microsoft Message Queue Server (MSMQ).

Application Code:

- **Use OLE DB to Access SQL Server:**
  - ✓ You can access SQL Server data using either ODBC or OLE DB. For best performance, always select OLE DB. OLE DB is used natively by SQL Server, and is the most effective way to access any SQL Server data.
- **Use DSN-less in Connection String:**
  - ✓ While creating an ADO connection to SQL Server, you can either use a DSN in the connection string, or you can use a DSN-less connection. For optimal performance, use DSN-less connections. Using them prevents the need for the OLE DB driver to look up connection string information in the registry of the client the application code is running on, saving some overhead.
- **Encapsulate your DML (Data Manipulation Language) in Stored Procedures**
  - ✓ ADO allows you three different ways to SELECT, INSERT, UPDATE, or DELETE data in a SQL Server database. You can use ADO's methods, you can use dynamic SQL, or you can use stored procedures. For better performance prefer Stored Procedures
- **Encapsulate Your ADO Code in COM Components**
  - ✓ Put the ADO code that accesses SQL Server data into COM components. This gives you all the standard benefits of COM components, such as object pooling using MTS. And for ASP-based applications, it provides greater speed because the ADO code in COM objects is already compiled, unlike ADO code found in ASP pages. How you implement your data manipulation code in COM components should be considered when the application is first designed.
  - ✓ For optimum performance, COM objects should be compiled as in-process DLLs (which is required if they are to run under MTS). You should always employ early binding when referencing COM objects, and create them explicitly, not implicitly.

CPU:

- Signal waits > 25% of total waits

  (See sys.dm_os_wait_stats for Signal waits and Total waits. Signal waits measure the time spent in the runnable queue waiting for CPU. High signal waits indicate a CPU bottleneck.)

- Plan re-use < 90%

  (Compare SQL Server SQL Statistics: batch requests/sec to SQL compilations/sec. Compute plan re-use as follows: Plan re-use = (Batch requests - SQL compilations)/ Batch requests)

Memory:

- Consistently low average page life expectancy. (MSSQL$Instance: Buffer Manager\Page Life Expectancy:)

  (See Average Page Life Expectancy Counter which is in the Perfmon object SQL Server Buffer Manager (this represents is the average number of seconds a page stays in cache). For OLTP, an average page life expectancy of 300 is 5 minutes. Anything less could indicate memory pressure, missing indexes, or a cache flush)

- Consistently low SQL Cache hit ratio. (MSSQL$Instance: Plan Cache\Cache Hit Ratio:)

  (OLTP applications should have a high cache hit ratio. Since OLTP transactions are small, there should not be big drops in SQL Cache hit rates or consistently low cache hit rates < 90%. Drops or low cache hit may indicate memory pressure or missing indexes.)

Disk I/O:

- High average disk seconds per read.

  (When the IO subsystem is queued, disk seconds per read increases. See Perfmon Logical or Physical disk (disk seconds/read counter). Normally it takes 4–8ms to complete a read when there is no IO pressure. When the IO subsystem is under pressure due to high IO requests, the average time to complete a read increases, showing the effect of disk queues. Periodic higher values for disk seconds/read may be acceptable for many applications. Sustained high values for disk seconds/read (>15ms) does indicate a disk bottleneck.)

- High average disk seconds per write.

  (Sustained high values for average disk seconds/write is a reliable indicator of a disk bottleneck.)

Blocking/Deadlocks:

- High average row lock or latch waits.
- Top wait statistics
- High number of deadlocks.
- To prevent deadlocks design queries/procedures:
  - ✓ Access tables in the same order throughout all modules
  - ✓ Collect all inputs before the transaction begins
  - ✓ Keep transaction short with in a batch
  - ✓ Use the correct isolation level

Network bottleneck:

- High network latency coupled with an application that incurs many round trips to the database.

- Network bandwidth is used up.

  (See counters packets/sec and current bandwidth counters in the network interface object of Performance Monitor)

Server/Database Configurations:

Collect real time data in your environment and design a standard for configuring Server and Database level settings. Example:

- Min Server Memory
- Max Server Memory
- Max Degree of Parallelism
- Fill Factor
- Priority Boost
- Affinity Mask
- Cost threshold Parallelism
- Instant File Initialization
- Lock Pages in Memory
- Data and Log File Growth
- Backup compression

83. What is the process of tuning the Performance?

Ans:

- *Identification:* Use native tools like Execution Plans, DMV, Extended Events, Query Tuning Advisor, Activity Monitor, system stored procedures, DBCC, custom stored procedures or third party tools etc.
- *Analysis:* Analyze the data to determine the core problems
- **Providing Solution:**
  - ✓ Creating new index on appropriate columns
  - ✓ Altering the complex quires to make them use the existing indexes.
  - ✓ By Updating Statistics for Tables and Views.
  - ✓ By rebuilding or reorganizing indexes.
  - ✓ By Resolving blocking problems.
  - ✓ By preventing Deadlocks
  - ✓ Resolving parameter sniffing issues
  - ✓ Using the proper SET options
  - ✓ Changing the Database/Server configurations
  - ✓ Recoding to troubleshoot the performance bottleneck
  - ✓ Enabling trace flags

- *Testing:* Test the various options to ensure they perform better and do not cause worse performance in other portions of the application
- *Knowledge sharing:* Share your experience with the team to ensure they understand the problem and solution, so the issue does not occur again, also document the problem and the possible solutions on central repository.

84. What are the tools available for SQL Server performance tuning/monitoring?

Ans:

- *Execution Plans:* There are three types Graphical, Text and XML.
- *Live Query Statistics (2016):* Just like execution plan Live Query Statistics shows the live execution of the active/running query. We can see how data is processing from operator to operator in an execution plan. We can get valuable statistics include number of rows produced, elapsed time, operator progress, etc.
- *DMV:* Dynamic management views shows the current state of the SQL Server
- *Resource Governor:* Allows us to limit and control the resource utilization.
- *Activity Monitor:* It displays graphically about Processes, Resource Waits, Datafile I/O, Recent expensive Quires.
- *PerfMon:* Windows native tool to view/monitor the performance of both SQL and windows servers
- *Database Tuning Advisor (DTA):* Recommend indexes
- *Profiler:* Can run traces and find out the expensive/long running quires/transactions
- *Extended Events:* Can be used for collecting data
- *Error Logs:* Error logs can help us in troubleshooting performance issues
- *System SP:* Ex: SP_WHO, SP_LOCK, SP_SPACEUSED, SP_MONITOR
- *DBCC:* Ex: DBCC SHOW_STATISTICS, DBCC SQLPERF() etc
- *Built-in Functions:* Ex: @@CPU_BUSY, @@PACKET_ERRORS And @@ CONNECTIONS etc.
- *Trace Flags:* Sometimes enabling trace flags can help us in improving the performance and troubleshooting. Ex: 3205 disable the hardware compression for tape drivers. 1224: Disables lock escalation based on the number of locks. However, memory pressure can still activate lock escalation.
- *Windows Task Manager and event viewer:* Both Task Manager and Event Viewer helps us in monitoring resource utilization and troubleshooting.
- *Third Party:* Quest, Apex, Redgate, Idera, SQL Power etc. providing advanced monitoring tools

85. What are all the parameters we need to check when a stored procedure is running slow?

Ans:

- Check if there is any blocking or deadlocks during the execution

- Execution Plan
  - ✓ Bookmark/RID/KEY Lookup
  - ✓ Sort
  - ✓ Table Scan/Index Scan
  - ✓ Data/Line Density
  - ✓ HASH/Nested Loop/Merge Joins
  - ✓ Tables/Index statistics
  - ✓ Warning Signs
  - ✓ Logical Reads
  - ✓ Number of Executions
  - ✓ Query Statistics – Logical and Physical Reads
  - ✓ Cardinality Estimates, Histogram
- Check if there are any temp objects using and can be replaced by any other best option
- Check how data processing happening. Apply all required data filters before applying/joining with other data sets.
- Check if there are any user defined functions using in select or where clause and think of alternatives if possible.
- Check if there are any query hints using and see if those are really required.
- Check if there are any proper SET options can help

86. What are the top memory related performance counters?

Ans:

Memory: Available Bytes:

- **High:** Good Health
- **Low:** Low Value Indicates Shortage of Memory
- Available Bytes counter indicates how many bytes of memory are currently available for use by processes.

Memory: Pages/sec:

- **High:** Indicates excessive paging
- **Low:** Good Health
- Pages/sec counter indicates the number of pages that either were retrieved from disk due to hard page faults or written to disk to free space in the working set due to page faults.

SQL Server: Buffer Manager: Buffer Cache Hit Ratio:

- **High > 90%:** Good Health
- **Low < 90%:** More requests are getting data from physical disk instead of data cache

Minimum Server Memory:

- Minimum amount of memory which is initially allocated to SQL Server. Default value 0

Maximum Server Memory:

- Maximum Server Memory that SQL Server can use up to. Make sure you are having a proper statistics and future plan before making any changes. Default value is set to 2 Peta Bytes. To determine this value first we need to know the memory required for OS and memory required for any other applications/services. Maximum Server Memory = Total Physical Memory – (Memory Required for OS + Memory Required for Other Applications);

Memory Manager:Total Server Memory (KB):

- Shows how much memory SQL Server is using. The primary use of SQL Server's memory is for the buffer pool, but some memory is also used for storing query plans and keeping track of user process information.

Memory Manager:Target Server Memory (KB):

- This value shows how much memory SQL Server attempts to acquire. If you haven't configured a max server memory value for SQL Server, the target amount of memory will be about 5MB less than the total available system memory.
- **Total Server Memory is almost same as Target Server Memory** - Good Health
- **Total Server Memory is much smaller than Target Server Memory** – There is a Memory Pressure or Max Server Memory is set to too low.

Page Life Expectancy:

- **High**: Good Health
- **Low:** Memory Pressure or Max Server Memory is not allocated properly
- Number of seconds a page is staying on buffer cache. Usually we do calculate based on the Memory allocated to SQL Server Instance. For 4 GB ram the PLE is supposed to be 300 sec/5 Min.
- 4 GB – (4/4) * 300 = 300 Sec = 5 Min
- 16 GB – (16/4) * 300 = 1200 Sec = 20 Min
- 32 GB – (32/4) * 300 = 2400 Sec = 40 Min
- This is to set an estimated health benchmark for PLE. One can follow their own formula based on their environment and experience.

87. Can you tell me few significant configuration options that we can check when you are dealing with memory performance?

Ans:

There are four significant properties of SQL Server.

Max server memory and Min server memory:

Use the two server memory options, min server memory and max server memory, to reconfigure the amount of memory (in megabytes) that is managed by the SQL Server Memory Manager for a SQL Server process used by an instance of SQL Server. By default Min Memory is set to be 0 and Max Memory is set to be 2147483647 MB (2 Petabytes). Never leave these two settings as default. Depends on the memory available and other applications running on windows Server, change these two settings.

For example we have 24 GB available and the settings can be like this:

Min Memory: 1 GB

Max Memory: 16 GB

Remember total max memory of all instances should not exceeds the actual physical memory available

Priority boost: By default, the priority boost setting is 0, which causes SQL Server to run at a normal priority. If you set priority boost to 1, the SQL Server process runs at a high priority.

Lightweight pooling: Switch on this parameter when you want to make SQL Server use the fiber mode facility. Unless there is a real need and environment (Large multi-processor servers) available we should not use this option at production servers.

88. On which basis you would determine the Max Server Memory Setting for SQL Server?

Ans:

Max Server Memory is the maximum amount of memory reserved for SQL Server. There are few things needs to be considered:

- Applications sharing the host with SQL Server and required average memory for those Apps
- Total Physical memory is less than 16 GB leave 1 GB for OS for each 4 GB
- Total Physical memory is greater than 16 GB leave 1 GB for OS for each 8 GB
- Monitor Memory\Available Mbytes counter and check the status
- Ex: If no user application is sharing with SQL Server
  - ✓ Total Physical Memory = 8 GB: 2 GB for OS and Apps + (6 GB – Max Server Memory)
  - ✓ Total Physical Memory = 16 GB: 4 GB for OS and Apps + (12 GB – Max Server Memory)
  - ✓ Total Physical Memory = 96 GB: 12 GB for OS and Apps + (84 GB – Max Server Memory)

Remember in 64 bit machine we need to consider Non-Buffer Pool object memory region while leaving memory for OS. This is just a baseline that we followed while setting up new environments. We are strictly supposed to monitor the memory usage in peak hours and adjust the settings.

89. Can you quickly tell me the most commonly used performance counters to monitor SQL Server performance?

Ans:

MEMORY: Page/Sec: It indicates number of pages read from or written to disk per second. High value indicates a problem/bottleneck. Ex: > 50 may indicate memory pressure.

MEMORY: Available MBytes: <10 MB—There should be an issue

Physical Disk: Disk Time: 50% - Medium || >80%: Serious issue

Physical Disk\Avg. Disk Queue Length: Check for disk bottlenecks: if the value exceeds 2 then it is likely that a disk bottleneck exists.

Processor: Process Time: > 80% is a problem

System: Processor queue length: >2 means there is a bottleneck. Waiting I/O processes are not greater than double of total available disks.

High percentage of Signal Wait: Signal wait is the time a worker spends waiting for CPU time after it has finished waiting on something else (such as a lock, a latch or some other wait). Time spent waiting on the CPU is indicative of a CPU bottleneck. Signal wait can be found by executing DBCC SQLPERF (waitstats) or by querying sys.dm_os_wait_stats.

Network Interface: Total Bites per Sec: If network Bandwidth is 100 MB, this value not should be < 50

SQLServer: Buffer Manager: Buffer Cache Hit Ratio: number of time SQL hits buffer for a page. It should be more than 90%.

SQLServer: Buffer Manager: Page life expectancy: Minimum a Page should stay at least 300 sec (5 Min) per every 4GB memory in buffer if not there is a memory pressure. If you have 64 GB then PLE benchmark can be define (64/4) X 300 = 16 X 300 = 4800 Sec = 1 Hr 20 Min.

SQLServer: SQL Statistics: Batch Requests/Sec: Number of Transact-SQL command batches received per second. High batch requests mean good throughput.

SQL Server: General Statistics: User Connections: Counts the number of users currently connected to SQL Server.

MSSQL$Instance: General Statistics\Processes Blocked: Long blocks indicate contention for resources.

SSIS: Buffers Spooled: The number of buffers currently written to the disk. If the data flow engine runs low on physical memory, buffers not currently used are written to disk and then reloaded when needed. High value indicates the memory pressure.

Process/Private Bytes (DTEXEC.exe): The amount of memory currently in use by Integration Services.

Process/Working Set (DTEXEC.exe): The total amount of allocated memory by Integration Services.

ReportServer$<instance_name>:Service: Memory Pressure State: "High pressure" and "Exceeded pressure" values indicates low memory

ReportServer$<instance_name>:Service: Requests/sec: The number of requests that are processed per second. This value represents the current throughput of the application

90. You have given a new environment with SQL Server installed with default values. Your manager asked you to check the configuration settings and do require changes as per your business requirement. What are the top 5 settings that you would first look into?

Ans:

MAXIMUM DEGREE OF PARALLELISM (MAXDOP):

- Default: Use all available CPU's
- Change: Limit to number of cores in a single CPU socket.
- Ex: 2 CPU Sockets, 4 Core Each Socket – MAXDOP should be 4

COST THRESHOLD FOR PARALLELISM:

- The optimizer uses that cost threshold to figure out when it should start evaluating plans that can use multiple threads.
- Default: 5
- Change: Let's make it to 20 and we can tune based on performance

INSTANT FILE INITIALIZATION:

- Default: Disabled
- Change: Give "Perform volume maintenance tasks" permission to the SQL Server process account

BACKUP COMPRESSION:

- Default: Disabled
- Change: Enable it for smaller backups and faster restores

REMOTE DAC (Dedicator Admin Connection):

- Default: Disabled
- Change: Enable it. If there is any damage happens this will be the only hope.

Data and Log File growth:

- Default: Data File 1MB and Log File 10%
- Change: Pre-allocate to estimated size for the next month/quarter/year and give a decent percentage

Maximum Server Memory:

- Default: More than 2 peta bytes
- Change: Maximum server memory setting plays a vital role, if SQL Server is not sharing the host
- Total Memory < = 16 GB: Leave 1 GB to OS for Each 4 GB
- Total Memory > 16 GB: 4GB + Leave 1 GB to OS for Each 8 GB

Lock Pages in Memory:

- Default: It's not enabled
- Change: Enable it to SQL Server service account

91. What are the useful DMV's we generally use to monitor the performance?

Ans:

CPU – Usage:

- **DM_OS_SCHEDULERS:** Runnable task counts show high values CPU bottleneck
- **DM_OS_RING_BUFFERS:** CPU usage and memory changes

I/O – Usage:

- **DM_IO_VIRTUAL_FILE_STATS:** I/O total writes and reads. Statistics for MDF, LDF
- **DM_IO_PENDING_IO_REQUESTS:** I/O requests pending in SQL Server side

Memory – Usage:

- **DM_OS_SYS_INFO:** Buffer Pool Usage
- **DM_OS_PERFORMANCE_COUNTERS:** Server and database related counters
- **DM_OS_SYS_MEMORY:** Total and Available physical memory
- **DM_OS_SYS_MEMORY:** Physical_Memory_In_Use etc
- **DM_OS_MEMORY_CLERKS:** Memory allocated through AWE
- **DM_OS_BUFFER_DESCRIPTORS:** Database and object level memory usage

Index – Usage:

- **DM_INDEX_PHYSICAL_STATS:** AVG FRAGMENTATION % (Logical Frag), AVG PAGE SPACE USED (Internal Frag)
- **DM_INDEX_USAGE_STATS:** No of user seeks/scans/lookups/updates. If any indexid is not in this means it's not using from long time
- **DM_INDEX_OPERATIONAL_STATS:** No of inserts/deletes/updates at index leaf level
- **DM_DB_MISSING_INDEX_COLUMNS:** Indexes that the query optimizer would use, if they were available.
- **DM_DB_MISSING_INDEX_DETAILS:** Missing indexes, including the table, columns used in equality operations, columns used in inequality operations and columns used in include operations.

Database – Usage:

- **DM_DB_FILE_SPACE_USAGE:** Temdb Database space usage information
- **DM_DB_SESSION_SPACE_USAGE:** Pages allocated and de-allocated by each session for the database.
- **DM_DB_PARTITION_STATS:** Page and row-count information for every partition in the current database.

Connectivity – Information:

- **DM_EXEC_SESSIONS:** Session details. Equals to sp_who2 or sys.sysprocesses
- **DM_EXEC_ CONNECTIONS:** Connection information Ex: Client IP address, port
- **DM_EXEC_REQUESTS:** Requests from each connection Ex: Wait info, Transaction info etc

Other:

- **DM_EXEC_SQL_TEXT:** To get actual sql from sql_handle
- **DM_OS_WAIT_STATS:** Wait Stats information

92. Window's task manager is not showing the correct memory usage by SQL Server. How to identify the exact memory usage from SQL Server?

Ans:

To know the exact memory usage relay on column "physical_memory_in_use_kb" from DMV "sys.dm_os_process_memory." Using performance counters also we can find the usage.

- Performance object: Process
  - ✓ Counter: Private Bytes
  - ✓ Instance: sqlservr
- Performance object: Process
  - ✓ Counter: Working Set
  - ✓ Instance: sqlservr

The Private Bytes counter measures the memory that is currently committed. The Working Set counter measures the physical memory that is currently occupied by the process.

For 64-bit SQL Server we can also check the current memory usage using the below performance counter.

Performance object: SQL Server:Memory Manager

Counter: Total Server Memory (KB)

93. How do you know how much memory has been allocated to SQL Server using AWE?

Ans:

We can use DBCC MEMORYSTSTUS command to know the memory allocation information. But it's trick to understand the results.

We can use a DMV called "sys.DM_OS_Memory_Clerks." Sample query to calculate total AWE memory allocated is:

"SELECT SUM(awe_allocated_kb) FROM sys.dm_os_memory_clerks"

From 2008 onwards we can get all memory related information using DMV "sys.dm_os_process_memory."

94. How to identify the CPU bottlenecks and how to resolve it?

Ans:

Identify SQL Server CPU utilization:

Firstly we have to confirm that SQL Server - CPU utilization is high. DMV sys.dm_os_ring_buffers can get the detailed report on CPU utilization for the last N minutes.

```
DECLARE @ts BIGINT;
DECLARE @lastNmin TINYINT;
```

```
SET @lastNmin = 10;
SELECT @ts =(SELECT cpu_ticks/(cpu_ticks/ms_ticks) FROM sys.dm_os_sys_info);
SELECT TOP(@lastNmin)
        SQLProcessUtilization AS [SQLServer_CPU_Utilization],
        SystemIdle AS [System_Idle_Process],
        100 - SystemIdle - SQLProcessUtilization AS
[Other_Process_CPU_Utilization],
        DATEADD(ms,-1 *(@ts - [timestamp]),GETDATE())AS [Event_Time]
FROM (SELECT record.value('(./Record/@id)[1]','int')AS record_id,
record.value('(./Record/SchedulerMonitorEvent/SystemHealth/SystemIdle)[1]','int')AS
[SystemIdle],
record.value('(./Record/SchedulerMonitorEvent/SystemHealth/ProcessUtilization)
[1]','int')AS [SQLProcessUtilization],
[timestamp]
FROM (SELECT[timestamp], convert(xml, record) AS [record]
FROM sys.dm_os_ring_buffers
WHERE ring_buffer_type =N'RING_BUFFER_SCHEDULER_MONITOR'AND
record LIKE'%%')AS x )AS y
ORDER BY record_id DESC;
```

Output:

- SQLServer_CPU_Utilization: % CPU utilized from SQL Server Process
- System_Idle_Process: % CPU Idle - Not serving to any process
- Other_Process_CPU_Utilization: % CPU utilized by processes otherthan SQL Server
- Event_Time: Time when these values captured

Identify Database Wise CPU utilization in an Instance:

If you really see CPU utilization is high from SQL Server then we have to do further analysis. Now we have to find the database which is causing the high CPU usage. The column Total_Worker_Time from the DMV "sys.dm_exec_query_stats" can help us to list out the database wise CPU utilization.

Identify Query Wise CPU utilization in a database:

From the above we found one of the databases is causing the high CPU utilization then find out the top queries which are causing the high CPU from that database. To get this information we can use these DMV's sys.dm_os_ring_buffers, sys.dm_exec_sessions.

95. Did you remember any system CATALOG or view that you used to quickly know the performance bottleneck?

Ans:

Yes. Lot many times I used "sysprocesses." We may not confirm that it is the only bottleneck but at least we can find the bottleneck. **Lastwaittype** column with **waittime** plays a vital role in identifying the issue. This is a very interesting column because it can tell you what the offending query is waiting for to complete.

Network_IO: There is too much of traffic in Network

Cxpacket: Your process is waiting on other parallel processes to complete.

SOS_SCHEDULER_YIELD: CPU bound. We may not have enough CPU in your box

IO_Completion: Disk issue. We may not have enough disk space or running on corrupted disk array.

96. What Are SQL Server Waits?

Ans:

Instead of measuring activity of CPU, storage, or memory, we can ask what SQL Server has been waiting on when executing queries. In general there are three categories of waits that could affect any given request:

- *Resource waits* are caused by a particular resource, perhaps a specific lock that is unavailable when the requested is submitted.
- *External waits* occur when SQL Server worker thread is waiting on an external process
- *Queue waits* normally apply to internal background tasks, such as ghost cleanup, which physically removes records that have been previously deleted.

97. What are the main events and columns helpful in troubleshooting performance issues using profiler?

Ans:

Events:

- **Event Group: Performance**
  - ✓ **Event:** ShowPlan_ALL (BinaryData column must be selected)
  - ✓ **Event:** ShowPlan_XML
- **Event Group: T-SQL**
  - ✓ **Event:** SQL:BatchStarted
  - ✓ **Event:** SQL:BatchCompleted
- **Event Group: Stored Procedures**
  - ✓ **Event:** RPC:Completed
- **Event Group: Locks**
  - ✓ **Event:** Lock: Deadlock Graph
  - ✓ **Event:** Lock: Lock Deadlock Chain (Series of events that leaads to a deadlock)
- **Event Group: Sessions**
  - ✓ **Event:** Existing Connection

- **Event Group: Security Audit**
  - ✓ **Event:** Audit Login
  - ✓ **Event:** Audit Log Out

Columns:

Below are the most common columns that help us in understanding the trace file to troubleshoot the problems.

- TextData
- ApplicationName
- NTUserName
- LoginName
- CPU
- Reads
- Writes
- Duration
- SPID
- StartTime
- EndTime
- Database Name
- Error
- HostName
- LinkedServerName
- NTDomainName
- ServerName
- SQLHandle

All these columns need not be available for all of the events, but depends on the event select we have to choose the appropriate columns.

Filters:

- ApplicationName
- DatabaseName
- DBUserName
- Error
- HostName
- NTUserName
- NTDomainName

Query Tuning

98. How to read the graphical execution plan? What are the key elements that can help us in finding the bottlenecks?

Ans:

The plan should be read from right to left

- Check the Graphical execution plan of a stored procedure/Query
  - ✓ *Table Scan:* Index is missing
  - ✓ *Index Scan:* Proper indexes are not using
  - ✓ *BookMark/RID/Key Lookup:* Limit the number of columns in the select list
  - ✓ *Filter:* Remove any functions from where clause, May require additional indexes
  - ✓ *Sort:* Does the data really need to be sorted? Can an index be used to avoid sorting? Can sorting be done at the client more efficiently?
  - ✓ *DataFlow Arrow:* High density: Sometimes you find few rows as outcome but the arrow line density indicates the query/proc processing huge number of rows
  - ✓ *Cost:* Can easily find out which table/operation taking much time
  - ✓ *Sort and other warnings:* It's a dangerous sign that tells us that the SORT operation required paging
  - ✓ *Join Type:* Based on the dataset size and available indexes make sure the suitable join operator is being used from HASH/Nested Loop/Merge Joins
  - ✓ *Logical Reads:* Huge number of logical reads indicates memory pressure due to wrong indexes or poor query design
  - ✓ *Actual and Estimated Row Counts:* When there is huge difference then it's a problem with statistics update
- From the execution plan we can find out the bottleneck and give the possible solution to avoid the latency

99. Why the Actual and Estimated Execution Plans Might Differ

Ans

When Statistics are Stale:

The main cause of a difference between the plans is differences between the *statistics* and the actual data. This generally occurs over time as data is added and deleted.

When the Estimated plan is invalid:

When the batch contains temporary tables or T-SQL statements or dynamic SQL which may refers some of the objects that are not currently existed in the database, but will be created once the batch is run.

100. What are the permissions required to view execution plans?

Ans:

User must be mapped to one of these roles SYSADMIN, db_owner, db_creator or the user will be granted the permission "Show Plan."

GRANT SHOWPLAN TO [username]

101. What are the parameters to be considered by database engine while designing execution plan?

Ans:

Database engine considers Statistics and Histogram which answers the below questions:

- Rows in the table
- Rows matching the search condition
- Rows matching the Join condition
- Available indexes
- How index ordered
- Index density

102. What are the different types of hints available in SQL Server?

Ans:

There are three types of hints available in SQL Server to control the query optimization. These are

- *Query Hints:* Control execution plan design for entire given query
- *Join Hints:* Tell optimizer to use the forced join
- *Table Hints:* Tell optimizer to use specific or given index

103. Can you explain the query hints you implemented?

Ans:

EXPAND VIEWS: When we are dealing with materialized views/indexed views, query uses index on view instead of the index on internal table. This hint will help when you want to let your query use indexes from internal tables instead of indexed views without rewriting queries.

Ex: OPTION (EXPAND VIEWS)

OPTIMIZE FOR: The OPTIMIZE FOR hint allows you to instruct the optimizer to optimize query execution for the particular parameter value that you supply. This is more useful in dealing with bad parameter sniffing when data distribution changes frequently

OPTION (OPTIMIZE FOR (@Area = 'North USA'))

OPTIMIZE FOR UNKNOWN: This hint directs the query optimizer to use the standard algorithms it has always used if no parameters values had been passed to the query at all. In this case the optimizer will look at all available statistical data to reach a determination of what the values of the local variables used to generate the query plan should be, instead of looking at the specific parameter values that were passed to the query by the application.

RECOMPILE: When your query is creating an execution plan which is performing well only for few parameters and the plan is performing bad with the most of the input parameters then use this hint. This hint forces optimizer to design a new execution plan every time the procedure called/ executed. This option we have used in procedures where we were using dynamic SQL. Creating execution plan every time is a CPU intensive and also we lose reuse of execution plan benefits.

OPTION (RECOMPILE)

MAXRECURSION: Recursive queries are easier with CTE this hint "MAXRECURSION" hint places an upper limit on the number of recursions within a query. Valid values are between 0 and 32,767. Setting the value to zero allows for infinite recursion.

OPTION (MAXRECURSION 50)

MAXDOP: It helps us to use the property MAX DEGREE OF PARALLELISM at query level. We had a problem with one of my query which was running fine but some of the times it was running dead slow. When we investigated we found 2 execution plans for that query. One is for when the query running faster and the other one for which the query was running very slow. The slow running query has been utilizing parallelism whereas the faster one not. The reason is when the query is executing in parallel streams it's been taking time for taking data from single stream to multiple streams and again bringing all back together at end. We used MAXDOP query hint to switch off parallelism for this specific query.

OPTION (MAXDOP 1)

FAST n: This query hint force optimizer to design an execution plan to get FIRST n rows faster. Overall result-set may take more time than normal execution. This we can apply when the application requires the first n records should be returned first without any wait.

Ex: OPTION (FAST 10)

104. What are the join hints?

Ans:

LOOP/MERGE/HASH join hints: These are the **join hints** can this hint can force query optimizer to use one of the three join methods LOOP, MERGE OR HASH.

Ex: "LEFT LOOP JOIN"

105. What are the various Table Hints you implemented?

Ans:

NOLOCK: When we use this option it means that using READUNCOMMITED isolation level at query level. NOLOCK is doesn't mean that it will not issue any locks instead it is compatible with other locks except schema lock. Remember if we are using this means we are not working on correct dataset and we are ok to work with dirty pages.

EX: WITH (NOLOCK)

READPAST: Unlike NOLOCK table hint it returns all rows/pages which are not locked. There is no blocking and dirty reads in the returned result set but the rows which are currently locked by other transactions are not returned.

EX: WITH (READPAST)

NOEXPAND: Specifies that any indexed views are not expanded to access underlying tables when the query optimizer processes the query. The query optimizer treats the view like a table with clustered index. NOEXPAND applies only to indexed views.

Ex: WITH (NOEXPAND)

INDEX (): Force optimizer to use the specific index while designing the execution plan. If a clustered index exists, INDEX (0) forces a clustered index scan and INDEX (1) forces a clustered index scan or seek. If no clustered index exists, INDEX (0) forces a table scan and INDEX (1) is interpreted as an error.

Ex: WITH (INDEX (0))

FORCESEEK: Specifies that the query optimizer use only an index seek operation as the access path to the data in the table or view. Starting with SQL Server 2008 R2 SP1, index parameters can also be specified.

Ex: WITH (forceseek (Index_Name(col1, col2….Col N)))

FORCESCAN: Introduced in SQL Server 2008 R2 SP1, this hint specifies that the query optimizer use only an index scan operation as the access path to the referenced table or view. The FORCESCAN hint can be useful for queries in which the optimizer underestimates the number of affected rows and chooses a seek operation rather than a scan operation. When this occurs, the amount of memory granted for the operation is too small and query performance is impacted.

Ex: WITH (FORCESCAN)

These are the most common hints that we use enterprise database environments. Apart from these there are lot of other hints:

Lock hints: PAGLOCK, NOLOCK, READCOMMITTEDLOCK, ROWLOCK, TABLOCK, UPDLOCK, XLOCK.

Isolation level hints: HOLDLOCK, NOLOCK, READCOMMITTED, REPEATABLEREAD and SERIALIZABLE.

106. Can we use more than one hint at a time?

Ans:

Of course yes!

Ex: FROM t WITH (TABLOCK, INDEX (<Index Name>)) ;

107. I have used a hint FORSESEEK with some parameters and let's say it's difficult to design an execution plan with those parameters. Does query optimizer ignore these hints and generate an execution plan?

Ans:

No! Especially for FORCESEEK make sure we are using the correct parameter or mention it without parameters to get the best possible execution plan. There are lot of limitations with FORCESEEK hint and it may cause an execution error "Plan cannot be generated."

108. If I apply both FORCESCAN and FORCESEEK on the same query what will happen?

Ans:

Microsoft knows it sometimes DBA's are intelligent than optimizer that's why they have added some limitations.

FORCESEEK can't be used with another FORCESEEK, INDEX () and FORCESCAN hints.

We can't use the "COLUMNSTORE" Index name as a parameter in FORCESEEK

109. Join operators will be chosen only when we use joins in our query! Is it right?

Ans:

No! A join operator is an algorithm which is chosen by query optimizer while joining data sets using joins (Implicit/Explicit/Outer), IN/NOT IN, EXISTS/NOT EXISTS, CROSS/OUTER Apply, Correlated Subqueries, Grouping, Aggregations, INTERSECT/UNION/MINUS, Duplicate Removal.

110. What are the different types of Hash Joins?

Ans:

There are three different types of Hash Joins:

- *In-Memory:* Build Input size is less than available memory, hash matching happens in memory
- *Grace:* Build Input size is greater than available memory, data spool out to disk, partitions required. Large Build Input is partitioned into smaller partitions and match will happen with the probe input.
- *Recursive:* Hash Match proceeds in several steps, each step has a build and probe phase. A lot of partitions and sorting required. Hence a single thread might require lot of I/O.
- *Hybrid:* If Build Input is slightly larger than memory, In-Memory and Grace Hash join combined and performs Hash Match. This is known as hash bailout.

Note: Optimizer doesn't know whether the Build Input can be fit in memory or not thereof SQL Server initially starts with In-Memory and later on transits to Grace and Recursive has join.

111. On which basis query optimizer choose the join operator?

Ans:

Choosing of a join operator is depends on Estimated Rows from input data sets, Indexes, Statistics, type of operation (Ex: =, <> etc).

112. Can you explain how these join operator works?

Ans:

Before understanding join operator functionality we should know about "Outer Input" and "Inner Input." In an execution plan the operator/table/dataset on top right of "Join Operator" is called "Outer Input" and the operator just below the outer input is called "Inner Input."

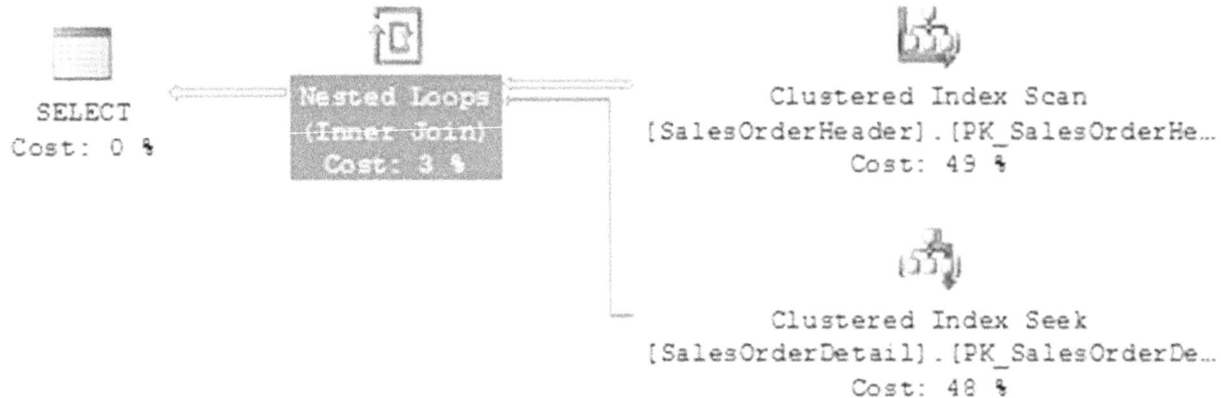

Fig 11.3

Here in above figure:

Outer Input: SalesOrderHeader

Inner Input: SalesOrderDetail

Nested Loops:

- For each record from "Outer Input" it finds matching rows in "Inner Input."
- We can clearly observe this through these points:
  - ✓ Outer Input: "Number of Executions: 1" and "Index Scan"
  - ✓ Inner Input: "Number of Executions: X" and "Index Seek." This X is number of rows from Outer Input.
- Complexity: O(NLogM). N is the number of rows from Outer Input where LogM is the complexity of each seeks in Inner Input.
- "Nested Loops" is the best operator when:
  - ✓ Outer Input is small
  - ✓ Inner Input has proper index defined on the join key column
  - ✓ Statistics are up to date

Note: Be cautious when statistics are not up to date. If optimizer wrongly considers the "Output Input" is having 1000 rows when the actual count is 1200000 rows, this operator might become as the costliest operator. 1000 times index seek is nothing like performing 1200000 Index seeks.

Merge:

- Perform a join between two large data sets which are in sorted order and joined on a key with "Equality Operator/=" operator in the ON clause.
- The Merge Join simultaneously reads a row from each input and compares them using the join key. If there's a match, they are returned. Otherwise, the row with the smaller value can be discarded because, since both inputs are sorted, the discarded row will not match any other row on the other set of data.

- This repeats until one of the tables is completed. Even if there are still rows on the other table, they will clearly not match any rows on the fully-scanned table, so there is no need to continue.
- We can clearly observe this through these points:
  - ✓ Outer Input: "Number of Executions: 1" and "Index Scan"
  - ✓ Inner Input: "Number of Executions: 1" and "Index Scan."
- Complexity: O(N+M). N is the number of rows from Outer Input where M is the number of rows from Inner Input.
- "Merge" is the best operator when:
  - ✓ Both Outer Input and Inner Input are the large data sets
  - ✓ Both are in same sorted order
  - ✓ Joining on a common key using "=" operator

Note: Optimizer will not choose "Merge" when all matches but the data sets are not in sorted order. There is an extra "Sort" operation performed by optimizer when we force to use "Merge" operator on non-sorted datasets.

Hash Match:

- There are few things we should know before understanding Hash Match operator:
  - ✓ Hashing Function: An algorithm that converts one or more values into a single numeric value.
  - ✓ Hash Table: A Data structure that divides all rows into equal sized buckets and each bucket is represented with a Hash value.
  - ✓ Build Input: The operator on top right of Hash Match is called Build Input. Smaller table is chosen.
  - ✓ Probe Input: The operator just below Build Input is called Probe Input. Larger table is chosen.
- The hash join first scans or computes the entire build input and then builds a hash table in memory. Each row is inserted into a hash bucket depending on the hash value computed for the hash key. This build phase is followed by the probe phase. The entire probe input is scanned or computed one row at a time, and for each probe row, the hash key's value is computed, the corresponding hash bucket is scanned, and the matches are produced.
- The two inputs (Build and Probe) are executed only once.
- We can clearly observe this through these points:
  - ✓ Build Input: "Number of Executions: 1" and "Index Scan"
  - ✓ Probe Input: "Number of Executions: 1" and "Index Scan."
- Complexity: O (N*hc + M*hm + J). N is smaller dataset/Build Input, M is larger dataset/Probe Input, hc is the complexity of hash table, hm is the complexity of the hash match function and "J" (Joker) complexity of dynamic creation and calculation of hash function.

- This operator is chosen when:
  - ✓ The scenario is not favoring any of the other operators.
  - ✓ Tables are very large and not ordered
  - ✓ No proper indexes defined
  - ✓ A complex scenario where the optimizer doesn't find any other way except Hash Match

Note: As long as the smaller table (Build Input) is very small, this algorithm can be very efficient. But if both tables are very large, this can be a very costly execution plan. Also there is a higher chance to have wrong cost estimations as the Hash Functionality is dynamic and optimizer cannot predict at the time of compilation.

113. What are the operators which may have negative performance impact on your SQL Query?

Ans:

- Like/Not Like
- NOT IN
- NOT EXISTS
- EXCEPT
- FUNCTIONS – (SELECT and WHERE Clause)

114. How "Like" and "Not Like" impacts the performance?

Ans:

Like operator works well with a small dataset but it impact the performance in a negative way when dataset increased to millions. When we use like operator the query may not get benefit from the Index.

Example:

- *Name Like '%han%'*: Clustered Index scan happens. Means it scan entire table to fetch the result
- *Name Like 'Chan%':* Index seek with Key Lookup happens. It traverses the tree based on the first four letters and get all strings which starts with "Chan."
- *Name Like 'Chan%kar':* Index seek with Key Lookup happens. It traverses the tree based on the first four letters and get all strings which starts with "Chan" and then filtered out the words ends with "kar."

Not Like: A scan needs to be happen on dataset. We are not supposed to use this operator unless we don't find any other alternatives.

Note: Simple example that showcase how difficult to do a Like or Not Like: You are given a telephone directory and asked you to find the phone numbers for all the names that starts with "CHAN." What do you do? Yes, you do have a look on Index page and turn into the C page and scan through few lines to find out the names starts with Chan, isn't it? And If I ask you to find out the names that ends with "Kar" can we find an easy way other than scanning the entire book?

115. What is the alternative to "Like" operator?

Ans:

- LIKE cannot be avoided but do a prefix search (LIKE '<first few letters>%'). Usually most of the business scenarios required prefix and a wild card search.
- We can use a CONTAINS if FULLTEXT search is enabled. But it's totally a different story as it requires the change in query.
- Apply "LIKE" on final result set: When we don't have a way to avoid LIKE '%<text>%'. Apply all other filters if there are any and then apply the LIKE predicate on final result set.

116. NOT IN, NOT EXISTS and EXCEPT. Which is the best clause from performance prospective?

Ans:

NOT IN: It returns all the values from the left hand table that does not appear in the right hand table.

NOT EXISTS: It returns all the values from the left hand table that does not appear in the right hand table.

EXCEPT (NOT EXISTS + DISTINCT): It filters the distinct values from the left hand table that do not appear in the right hand table.

Remember for all these operations there should be an index/table scan happens as to check non matching rows it needs to traverse entire index/table. Also remember if there is no clustered index defined on table, EXCEPT causes an extra SORT operation.

117. What is the alternative way for NOT IN/NOT EXISTS/EXCEPT?

Ans:

Yes! We can use LEFT JOIN + IS NULL in place of above 3 clauses. Or if we are using any of these clauses to fix orphan data, we can use MERGE clause.

Example:

EXCEPT:

```
SELECT ID FROM EMP
EXCEPT
SELECT ID FROM EMP_Details
```

NOT IN:

```
SELECT ID FROM EMP WHERE ID NOT IN(SELECT ID FROM EMP_Details);
```

NOT EXISTS:

```
SELECT ID FROM EMP WHERE NOT EXISTS(SELECT ID FROM EMP_Details);
```

➔ Here in this case NOT EXISTS does not works.

LEFT JOIN + IS NULL:

```
SELECT E1.ID AS EMP1, E2.ID AS EMP2,E1.NAME
```

```
FROM EMP E1
LEFT JOIN EMP_Details E2 ON E1.ID = E2.ID
WHERE E2.ID IS NULL;
```

Note: When we use LEFT JOIN + IS NULL we can clearly see the difference in execution time if we can test it with huge data set.

118. Does these objects stored in Memory or TEMPDB? CTE, Temp Table, Table Variable

Ans:

Temp Table and Table Variable are stored on TEMPDB and CTE stored on Memory.

119. How scalar user defined functions impact the performance?

Ans:

When I was being working with one of my customer I came across a long running stored procedure which was actually using for a reporting purpose. We couldn't find anything suspicious on primary verification. Found the real problem after deep investigation, the problem was the extensive use of user defined function. There is while loop from which the function is being called and for every single iteration there were 200 calls which couldn't be catch until we have gone through the code. I restructured the procedure, removed the use of scalar user defined function and used a XML method which performs the same functionality in a single go. Finally the restructured procedure execution time came down to 4 Min from 69 min.

120. Can you explain few reasons and convince why SQL Server scalar functions are bad?

Ans:

Functions are useful to reduce the code redundancy but scalar functions impact the performance. There are few reasons:

- Scalar functions act like cursors, causing row-by row processing. This itself can explain how performance impacts when number of rows increased.
- Scalar functions don't allow queries to benefit from parallelism.
- Scalar functions may lead to an incorrect cost estimation resulting in suboptimal execution plans.
- Hidden Bottlenecks: Tough to understand the performance impact by going through execution plan.

121. What is a predicate?

Ans:

A predicate is an expression/condition that qualifies/filters rows.

There are 3 types of predicates:

- WHERE clause
- JOIN...ON
- HAVING clause

122. What is Density Vector?

Ans:

The best example as given at "msdn," the query optimizer uses densities to enhance cardinality estimates for queries that return multiple columns from the same table or indexed view. The density vector contains one density for each prefix of columns in the statistics object. For example, if a statistics object has the key columns CustomerId, ItemId, Price, density is calculated on each of the following column prefixes.

- [CustomerId]: Rows with matching values for CustomerId
- [CustomerId, ItemId]: Rows with matching values for CustomerId and ItemId
- [CustomerId, ItemId, Price]: Rows with matching values for CustomerId, ItemId and Price

123. What is SARG?

Ans:

SARG is a shortcut to represent Search Arguments. To be simply said that SARG represents your query search condition. Based on SARG query optimizer gets the estimated row outcome and designs the execution plan.

124. What are foldable and non-foldable expressions?

Ans:

Foldable Expressions: Expressions which can be evaluated as a constant at the time of optimization then it is called a foldable expression. Ex: "Id = 16758," Name = 'Jason' etc.

Non-foldable Expressions: Expressions which can't be evaluated as at the time of optimization are known as non-foldable expressions. Ex: Value = ABS(-68).

Note: We know the benefit of having a constant in search clause results into a best suited execution plan.

125. Any idea what is "contradiction detection" by query optimizer?

Ans:

Contradiction detection is a technic used by query optimizer. If you write a query in such way that it never return any rows at all then query optimizer identifies that and use a "Constant Scan" operator when next time it finds the same query it doesn't go to the table and simply result zero rows.

Example: No employees exists to match the filter in below query

```
SELECT * FROM Emp WHERE ID BETWEEN 10000 AND 9000;
```

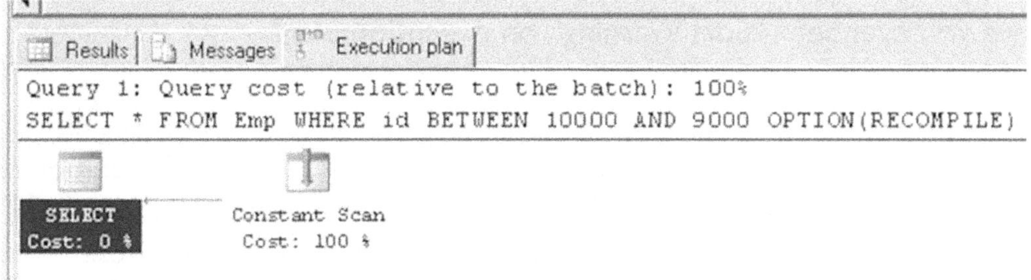

Fig 11.4

Note: Option recompile prevents considering parameters in generating execution plan.

126. Does query optimizer get benefit from a CHECK constraint in any way?

Ans:

Yes! Just like the foreign key constraint query optimizer utilizes the check constraint when there is a situation where the written query returns 0 rows always. Let's say we have a column called age and a check constraint defined on that column like (Age > 26). Now the below query returns 0 rows:

"SELECT * FROM EMP WHERE Age < =25 option (recompile)"

Query optimizer need not scan/seek through the table as there is already check constraint defined on that column and from that logic (Age>26) itself QO can identify the estimated row count is 0. Again a "Constant Scan" happens which saves the execution plan design and index traversing time.

Note: Query Optimizer considers only trusted CHECK constraints (sys.check_constraints). Also using Recompile it tells QO to not use parameterized execution plan and do a constant scan as long as the given values are out of CHECK constraint.

127. We have a table called Tab1 (Col1, col2, col3), Now Col1 is the primary key and there is a non-clustered index defined on Col3. Now tell me what are the steps taken when you update a value on Col3?

Ans:

- Locate the value needs to be updated on clustered index
- Update the value in clustered index leaf level
- Locate the value needs to be updated on Non-Clustered Index
- Update the value in Non-Clustered Index.

128. If we update the column with the same existing value (Current value is 18345 I am updating this value with the same 18345), what is the impact? Does it gone through all the processes and update the value again on Non-Clustered index or is there any specific methodology it follows?

Ans:

Query optimizer is talented enough to identify if we are trying to update with the same value as existed in that row. When it identifies it doesn't update it again and simply skip the update. You can observe this using INDEX_OPERATIONAL_STATS DMV.

129. Have you ever seen "Sort Warning" on execution plan?

Ans:

Yes! Sort warning indicates that the SORT operator is using TEMPDB to spill out the data during the execution. Let me explain what actually happens when a SORT operation required in query execution. It uses memory to sort the dataset but when it is not possible to hold the entire dataset in memory it starts spilling out to TEMPDB which is nothing but disk this is why we see the SORT warning in execution plan. As from my experience SORT WARNING is a serious sign which might kill the performance. Sort warning looks like a SORT operator with a warning sign.

Remember that sort warning might create a lot of problems if incase "TEMPDB" is not placed on a proper storage. In that case we might experience a very low I/O and response time. To avoid SORT warning utilize a clustered index column on your query if the base table is heap then you can create one.

130. When SORT operator requested for some extra memory why doesn't SQL Server request for memory grants?

Ans:

Did someone say that SQL Server doesn't request Memory grants for SORT operator? It actually asks for memory grants when SORT operator required more memory with conditions applied. SQL Server asks for Memory Grants when SORT operation required while creating an INDEX. But it doesn't ask for the memory grants when the SORT required for user queries.

131. So if there is no warning and only a SORT operator showing in execution plan. Is this a good sign?

Ans:

No! SORT it ways require some extra processing and there is no good SORT operation. Best practice suggests that "Avoid SORT operator where it is possible."

132. Can you quickly explain what is the bad parameter sniffing?

Ans:

As we know that parameter sniffing becomes bad when the same execution plan is used for different values which results into a bad execution plan.

Simple example:

- Procedure executed with the parameter @p = 1
- Then the query optimizer creates an execution plan based the parameter value @p = 1
- Let's say when @p = 1 there are 20 rows then it considers the estimated rows are 20 and then designs the execution plan with clustered index seek.
- This execution plan stored in cache and the same plan used when the next time the same procedure called irrespective of the parameter value.
- Let's say this time @p = 8 and when @p = 8 there are 3 lakh records.
- But the same execution plan (the plan that created based on @p = 1) is used for @ p = 8.
- Does 20 seeks is equal to 3 lakh seeks? Absolutely no right now this will create the problem and causes the sudden performance slowdown of your query.

133. What are the various ways to handle the bad parameter sniffing?

Ans:

There are few ways that can help us in situations where bad parameter sniffing causes the performance slowdown.

Use local Variables instead of directly using the parameters:

Map procedure parameters to the local variables and use local variables instead. Use these local variables in queries so that optimizer generates a generic execution plan instead of a parameter based execution plan. Remember generic plan may not be the best plan.

Use the SQL Server Hint OPTION OPTIMIZE FOR:

When we use OPTIMIZE FOR UNKNOWN it also acts as the same like using local variables. To reduce the code modification complexity this option added on 2008. It also uses the generic execution plan for all parameter values.

Stored Procedure WITH RECOMPILE:

Every time when a new call initiated the stored procedure get compiled and generates a new execution plan which causes an extra CPU loads. Sometimes this might improve the performance for a temporary purpose but it surely impact the overall performance in long running.

SQL Server query hint RECOMPILE:

Sometimes we may not find any other way except the option 'RECOMPILE' in this we can use the query level option "RECOMPILE" instead of compiling entire stored procedure.

Disable parameter sniffing at the instance level:

It's a bad option we never suggest this but to just listing out here to showcase there is an option to do that. We can do this by enabling the trace flag 4136.

Disable Parameter Sniffing for a Specific SQL Query:

This is also not a good option as it might work temporary basis but it will create problems in near future when data increases. This can be done using the query hint OPTION (QUERYTRACEON 4136).

134. I understand SQL Server query optimizer generates a generic plan when we use local variables or OPTIMIZE FOR UNKNOWN option right? But can you tell me why it doesn't generate the best plan? And on which basis it generates the generic plan?

Ans:

The same doubt I have got when the first time I got to know about this generic plan. Ok let's come to this point:

- Query optimizer generates the best suited plan when we use procedure parameter directly into query as the optimizer can see the value at the compile time hence it can utilize the histogram to get the estimated row counts.
- Query optimizer generates a generic plan when we use local variables as it cannot see the value of a local variable at the time of compile time thereof it cannot use the histogram and generates a generic plan.

Now we'll see how the generic plan is designed.

- As we know that density is defined as: [1]/[Total number of distinct records].

- Let's say the column "ItemID" is having 320 distinct records then the density = [1]/[320] = 0.003125.
- SQL Server uses "Uniformity Assumption" from "Statistics Mathematical Model." It says that data is distributed equally for all distinct values.
- This means the estimated row count is calculated using: [Total Row Count] *[Density]
- Same can be calculated using: [Total Row Count]/[Total Number of Distinct values]
- In this case let's say total row count for "ItemID" is 86500 now the estimated row count is: 86500 * 0.003125 = 270.3125 = 86500/320.
- For any given ItemID it generates the same plan and considers the same estimated row count.

135. Then when do we need to go for the option OPTIMIZE FOR UNKNOWN"?

Ans:

There is no direct answer for this, but yes if your query is troubling due to bad parameter sniffing yes we can go with this option when most of the arguments are getting the benefit from the generic plan.

136. While analysing SQL queries apart from execution plan, statistics what else you observer in advance level?

Ans:

- Waits and queues/Wait Stats
- Latches
- Spinlocks

137. That's interesting; can you explain what "Wait Stats" is?

Ans:

If you understand the SQL Server architecture the actual operation is being taken care by "Threads/ Fibers." Now let's understand these terms:

Waits – Queues/Wait Stats: By analyzing these values we can understand where the bottleneck is means for what (Resource/Thread/CPU) the SQL Server is waiting on. This means that we can identify where the delay is and from that we can take or tune the system to make it more optimized database.

For any given request the execution life cycle is:

- Running
- Suspended: If resource is not available otherwise it immediately goes to runnable state
- Runnable
- Running

"Total Wait Time": Time between Running and Running

"Signal Wait Time": Time spent on the runnable queue.

"Resource Wait Time": Time spent on SUSPEND state. Means time waited to get the requested resource.

138. Can you explain the top 3 wait stats which should be considered while tuning the system?

Ans:

PAGEIOLATCH_SH: This wait occurs when a thread is waiting for a data page to be read into memory from disk. Possible causes:

- When buffer pool under memory pressure.
- When the required resources are not fit into the memory (Lot of index scans).

PAGEIOLATCH_SH: This wait occurs when there is huge TEMPDB coextension or Insert hotspot.

- Multiple concurrent threads creating and dropping temp tables combined with a small number of TEMPDB files and no trace flag 1118 enabled.
- Lots of concurrent threads inserting small rows into a clustered index with an identity value, leading to contention on the index leaf-level pages

SOS_SCHEDULER_YIELD: This wait occurs when a thread exhausting its scheduling quantum (4ms) and heavily recurring instances.

- Workload is memory resident and there is no contention for resources
- Ex: Scanning an index/table. All the index pages are in memory thereof it doesn't require any resource that other thread hold or not required any waiting to lock, no memory allocation required etc.

WRITELOG: This wait occurs when the I/O subsystem not being able to keep up with the rate of log flushing combined with lots of tiny transactions forcing frequent flushes of minimal-sized log blocks.

CXPACKET: This wait occurs when parallelism happens and threads having unbalanced work load.

- Control thread might be waiting for other threads to complete their tasks
- Sometimes when threads finished their tasks early also causes this wait type.

ASYNC_NETWORK_IO: This wait occurs when RBAR (Row-By-Agonizing-Row) processing is happening at client instead of caching the results at client side and by asking SQL Server to send more rows.

Note: Remember we can't decide which is good or bad just seeing the wait type. But if you see the same wait type is happening frequently with longer times there we need to have a look with an in-depth analysis

139. What is a latch?

Ans:

- In concurrent programming code path is called as the critical section.
- This critical section should always run single threaded.
- Latch is a specialized version of this critical section that allows multiple threads.
- It allows multiple threads to read a shared resource

- It allows one thread at a time to write on a resource.
- Latch is used to coordinate the physical level concurrent execution where as a lock is used to coordinate the logical level concurrent execution.

140. What is the difference between locks and latches?

Ans:

Locks:

- Controls transactions
- We can influence locks through ISOLATION Level or lock hints
- Protects the database content
- During the entire transaction
- Primary locks includes Shared, Update, Exclusive and Intention
- Kept in lock manager Hash-table

Latches:

- Control Threads
- We can't influence latches
- Protects the critical session – code path
- Primary latches includes Keep, Shared, Update, Exclusive and Destroy
- Kept in protected Data Structure

141. What are the types of latches?

Ans:

I/O Latches: Control the concurrency when read/write from/to the storage subsystem. Ex: PAGEIOLATCH_*.

Buffer Latches: Control the concurrency on resources which are on buffer pool. Ex: PAGELATCH_*.

Non-Buffer Latches: Non-Buffer Latches to protect shared data structures besides the buffer pool itself. Ex: Latch_*

142. What are the DMV's that can help us in analysing these latches and wait stats?

Ans:

sys.dm_os_wait_stats

sys.dm_os_waiting_tasks

sys.dm_os_latch_stats

sys.dm_os_spinlock_stats – Undocumented

143. What is a spin lock?

Ans:

In SQL Server architecture if you see there are few data structures which are really hot on which lot of reads and writes happens very frequently. If it stats keeping a latch on these objects it kills the performance as every time when it is required it has to go through the life cycle (Running, Suspended, Runnable and Running). That's the reason SQL Server introduced SpinLock to control the concurrency for the very frequently used data structures (Ex Lock Manager, Buffer free lists) etc.

144. While designing a new execution plan what are all the elements considered by database engine? Can you quickly list out as much as components you remember?

Ans:

- Estimated row Counts
- Available Hardware
- Configuration Options
- Query Hints
- Indexes
- Partitions
- File groups and Files
- Requested and Available Memory
- Statistics
- Histogram
- Cardinality Estimates
- Join Order
- Parallelism

145. What is RID Lookup\Bookmark Lookup?

Ans:

RID lookup will be seen when you use non-clustered indexes with join queries.

In order to understand the RID look up we need to first understand how non-clustered indexes work with clustered indexes and heap tables. Non-clustered indexes also use the B-tree structure fundamental to search data. In non-clustered indexes the leaf node is a 'Rowid' which points to different things depending on two scenarios:-

Scenario 1: If the table which is having the primary key in the join has a clustered index on the join key then the leaf nodes i.e. 'rowid' will point to the index key of clustered index hence a clustered index seek happens

Scenario 2: if the table which is having the primary does not have a clustered index then the non-clustered index leaf node 'rowid' will point to actual row on the heap table. As the data is stored in a different heap table, it uses the lookup (i.e. RID lookup) to get to the actual row hence an Index seek (Non clustered) with RID lookup happens

146. Does query plans generated only for stored procedures? If No, what are the various database objects for which Query Plans get generated?

Ans:

It's No! Below is the database objects for which query plan is generated.

- Stored procedures
- Scalar user-defined functions
- Multi-step table-valued functions
- Triggers

147. Does query plan is generated for Inline Table Functions and Views?

Ans:

No

148. We have a stored procedure and we are passing the parameters to the query inside the procedure. Now can you tell me how query plan got generated for below scenarios?

Using constant value in Query; Ex: WHERE Age < 25

Using the Stored Procedure Parameter directly; Ex: WHERE is_eStore = 1

Assigning SP parameter into local variable and using the local variable in query; Ex SET @ Age_Var = @Age; Query……WHERE Age < @Age_Var;

Ans:

Constant: When a query includes a constant, SQL Server can use the value of the constant with full trust, and even it get benefited from constraints and foreign keys. For example if there is a CHECK constraint on Age column with condition Age>27 then for the given query it need not search the table as the check constraint itself saying it's not possible to have rows with Age < 25.

Stored Procedure Parameter: SQL Server does not know the run-time value, but it "sniffs" the input value when compiling the query. It generates an execution plan to match the given parameter value. Sometimes it's might become as a bad parameter sniffing. Let's say

When is_eStore = 1 – Actual row count 6K

When is_eStore = 0 – Actual Row count 5 Lakh

Initially stored procedure executed with is_eStore = 1 and plan generated accordingly and stored in cache. When next time procedure is called with is_eStore = 0 the same plan will be used which may leads to a wrong execution plan for 80K rows.

Local Variable:

Local variables: For a local variable, SQL Server has no idea at all of the run-time value, and applies standard assumptions. It generates a generic execution plan which may works for any parameter. It determines the data distribution using: Total Number of Rows/Number of Unique Values which gives a generic row count for any given parameter.

149. What are the cases when a stored procedures execution plan removed from cache?

Ans:

Stored procedures execution plan stays in the cache, until some event forces the plan out of the cache.

There are three main conditions that cause execution plan removed from cache:

- More memory is required by the system
- The "age" of the plan has reached zero
- The plan isn't currently being referenced by an existing connection

There are other scenarios causes removing plan from cache:

- Altering procedure using ALTER PROCEDURE
- Executing sp_recompile on the procedure
- DBCC FREEPROCCACHE which clears the entire plan cache.
- Restarting SQL Server
- Changing certain configuration options

There are other events that do not cause the entire procedure plan to be evicted from the cache, but which trigger recompilation of one or more individual statements in the procedure.

- Changing the definition of a table that appears in the statement.
- Dropping or adding an index for a table appearing in the statement. This includes rebuilding an index with ALTER INDEX or DBCC DBREINDEX.
- New or updated statistics for a table in the statement with the commands CREATE STATISTICS and UPDATE STATISTICS.
- Running sp_recompile on a table referred to in the statement.
- Combining DDL and DML operations
- Modifying SET options

150. Does modifying SET options can cause a stored procedure recompilation?

Ans:

Yes! Below are the few examples for SET options which might causes creating a new query plan:

- DATEFORMAT
- ANSI_PADDING
- ANSI_WARNINGS,
- ANSI_NULLS,
- QUOTED_IDENTIFIER,
- ARITHABORT

151. Can you tell me any one issue from which you learnt something new?

Ans:

In our production application one of the pages was running slow and I was asked to look into that. I found that there is a procedure which was causing the slowness and when I tried to execute it from server surprisingly the stored procedure running faster. What we found is the same procedure is getting executed faster when executing from SSMS but it's running slow from application.

RCA:

- I was really not sure till this issue comes that the SET option can cause a stored procedure to behave differently in different places.
- Default Values:
  - ✓ SET ARITHABORT ON – SSMS
  - ✓ SET ARITHABORT OFF – Front end Application
- From SSMS when I switched off ARITHABORT option I could reproduce the same issue, the procedure started running slow
- That's because of a bad parameter sniffing with one of the bit parameter.
- When the parameter @P = 1 – 300 rows and when @P = 0 there are 7.5 lakh records
- Initially plan created by considering the value @p = 1 and using the same plan for @p= 0 too

Resolution:

The bad parameter sniffing issue can be resolved using different options:

- Using local variables
- OPTIMIZE FOR hint
- WITH RECOMPILE query option

152. As we know that dynamic SQL should always be executed using "sp_executesql" so that it can reuse the execution plan from cache. I believe you aware of this. Here is my question, how SQL Server can identify plan from cache in-case of dynamic SQL? We know that stored procedure can be identified by its name in the cache but how this dynamic SQL submitted through SP_EXECUTESQL is identified from cache?

Ans:

When SQL Server looks up a stored procedure in the cache, it uses the name of the procedure. But that is not possible with dynamic SQL, as there is no name. Instead, SQL Server computes a hash from the query text – including any parameter list and uses this hash as a key in the plan cache. And here is something very important: this hash value is computed without any normalization whatsoever of the batch text. Comments are not stripped. White space is not trimmed or collapsed. Case is not forced to upper or lowercase, even if the database has a case-insensitive collation. The hash is computed from the text exactly as submitted, and any small difference will yield a different hash and a different cache entry. That means even for a small change in submitted SQL it creates a new execution plan. The change might be lower to uppercase or even an extra space.

153. What are the different types of execution plan formats available in SQL Server?

Ans:

Execution plan can be viewed in three different formats

Graphical Plans: Easy to read but less information available.

This is the easiest way to view the execution plan in graphical format. It can be on by using Ctrl+M or there is a direct i-con available in SSMS.

Text Plans: Hard to read but more detailed information retrieved.

- SET SHOWPLAN_ALL ON/OFF: Shows estimated execution plan for the query
- SET SHOWPLAN_TEXT ON/OFF: Shows a very limited set of estimated data for use with tools like osql.exe.
- SET STATISTICS PROFILE ON/OFF: similar to SHOWPLAN_ALLexcept it represents the data for the Actual execution plan.

XML Plans: Hard to read but maximum detailed information retrieved

- SET SHOWPLAN_XML ON/OFF: Estimated execution plan
- STATISTICS XML ON/OFF: Actual execution plan

154. From the execution plan point of view what are the logical and physical operators?

Ans:

Logical Operators:

Logical operators describe the relational algebraic operation used to process a statement. It describes conceptually what operation needs to be performed.

Physical Operators:

Physical operators implement the operation described by logical operators. Each physical operator is an object or routine that performs an operation. For example, some physical operators access columns or rows from a table, index or view. Other physical operators perform other operations such as calculations, aggregations, data integrity checks or joins. Physical operators have costs associated with them. The physical operators initialize, collect data, and close.

- *Init ():* The Init () method causes a physical operator to initialize itself.
- *GetNext ():* The GetNext () method causes a physical operator to get the first, or subsequent row of data.
- *Close ():* The Close () method causes a physical operator to perform some clean-up operations and shut itself down. The number of times it is called appears as ActualRows in the Showplan output.

155. Can you explain any 5 operators that you have most seen in tuning SQL queries using execution plans?

Ans:

Sort: Ordering the rows. Sort operation can be avoided by using the correct clustered index. Also more than one sort operation indicates bad signs.

Clustered Index Seek: Searching the clustered index, it's the best operator when the result set is small.

Clustered Index Scan: Just like table scan and scan row by row. It's useful when majority of table data retrieved. Cross check if any unnecessary data retrieving and apply a proper filter.

Non-clustered Index Scan/Index Scan: Scans the non-clustered index

Non-clustered Index Seek/Index Seek: Seeks the non-clustered index

Table Scan: Scans the entire table row by row. This can be ok if table is a small dataset. But we need to create required indexes if the table is joining with huge tables and hurting performance.

Key Lookup: When a non-clustered index seeks happens it may or may not get all required data from the non-clustered index. If the index is not covering all columns then it should go to clustered index to get the remaining columns data, this lookup process is known as Key-Lookup. Try to create a covering index if the query is more frequently using and if you can see some performance gain by adding covering index.

RID Lookup: Just like the key lookup but the table is a heap means the Non-clustered index has to go lookup the direct table instead of clustered index. Create a clustered index on base table and create a covering index to cover the more frequent queries.

Nested Loops: This is a join operator and most suited when joining small datasets/tables, indexes are properly designed and statistics are up to date. Its might be a bad sign when this operator is happening between huge tables. Try to tune the query or use the proper query hints to use the correct join operator.

Merge Join: This is a join operator and most suited when joining large datasets/tables, both datasets ordered/sorted and joining on a common key. Optimizer will not choose "Merge" when all matches but the data sets are not in sorted order.

Hash Match: Relatively bad sign and this operator is chosen when datasets are large, not in any order, no proper indexes available, statistics are not up to date or a complex scenario where the other join operators can't be performed. Try to analyse the input datasets and cross check if any of other join operators can replace the "Hash Match" by altering the query or creating proper indexes.

Top: If it appears in SELECT execution plan means we are using "TOP" in query. If it appears in UPDATE execution plan which means there is a row count limit restricting to use TOP.

Compute Scalar: This represents an operation of evaluating an expression to produce a computed single defined value/scalar value. Ex: Emp_firstName+Emp_Last_Name AS "Name."

Constant Scan: The Constant Scan operator introduces one or more constant rows into a query. A Compute Scalar operator is often used after a Constant Scan to add columns to a row produced by the Constant Scan operator.

Filter: By adding the HAVING clause, the Filter operator has been added to the execution plan. This Filter is applied in last stage after all aggregations which might hurt the performance. If possible we should try to restrict/filter rows at initial stage using WHERE clause or in join.

Spool: The Spool operator saves an intermediate query result to the TEMPDB database

Stream Aggregate: The Stream Aggregate operator groups rows (Group By) by one or more columns and then calculates one or more aggregate expressions returned by the query. The output of this operator can be referenced by later operators in the query, returned to the client, or both. The Stream Aggregate operator requires input ordered by the columns within its groups. The optimizer will use a Sort operator prior to this operator if the data is not already sorted

Distribute Streams: The Distribute Streams operator is used only in parallel query plans. The Distribute Streams operator takes a single input stream of records and produces multiple output streams. Each record from the input stream appears in one of the output streams.

Gather Streams: The Gather Streams operator is only used in parallel query plans. The Gather Streams operator consumes several input streams and produces a single output stream of records by combining the input streams.

156. What is the Bitmap operator in SQL Server execution plan? (Asked in 8 interviews)

Ans:

- SQL Server uses the Bitmap operator to implement bitmap filtering in parallel query plans.
- Bitmap filtering speeds up query execution by eliminating rows with key values that cannot produce any join records before passing rows through another operator such as the Parallelism operator.
- A bitmap filter uses a compact representation of a set of values from a table in one part of the operator tree to filter rows from a second table in another part of the tree.
- By removing unnecessary rows early in the query, subsequent operators have fewer rows to work with, and the overall performance of the query improves.
- The optimizer determines when a bitmap is selective enough to be useful and in which operators to apply the filter. "Bitmap" is a physical operator for the logical operator "Bitmap Create"

157. How to clear the procedure cache from the given SQL Server instance?

Ans:

DBCC FREEPROCCACHE: Removes all elements from the plan cache for all the databases in the given SQL Server instance.

158. How to clear the plan cache for a specific database?

Ans:

DBCC FLUSHPROCINDB (<Database ID>): Get the database ID and substitute, it clears plan cache for the given specific database ID.

159. How to clear the plan cache for a specific query?

Ans:

DBCC FREEPROCCACHE (<Plan_Handle>): Get the query/procedure plan handle from sys.dm_exec_cached_plans and substitute in <Plan_Handle>. It clears the given plan from the cache.

160. Have you ever used DBCC FREESYSTEMCACHE?

Ans:

Yes! It releases all unused cache entries from all caches. The SQL Server Database Engine proactively cleans up unused cache entries in the background to make memory available for current entries. However, you can use this command to manually remove unused entries from all caches or from a specified Resource Governor Pool cache.

There are different types of cache available in SQL Server instance. This clears all types of cache from the instance. The below statement list out all available caches:

> "SELECT 'DBCC freesystemcache ('+'"'+name+'"'+')' from sys.dm_os_memory_clerks group by name;"
>
> For example we can clear the cache for:
>
> DBCC freesystemcache ('Log Pool')
>
> DBCC freesystemcache ('TEMPDB')
>
> DBCC freesystemcache ('Temporary Tables & Table Variables')
>
> DBCC freesystemcache ('Transactions')...etc

161. What is the option DBCC FREESESSIONCACHE?

Ans:

This DBCC is used to flush the distributed query connection cache used by distributed queries against an instance of Microsoft SQL Server.

Performance Tuning Scenarios

162. Here is a scenario: When we are monitoring memory usage by one of the SQL Server instance, surprisingly SQL Server is using more memory than Max Server Memory configuration. Any idea why it's happing?

Ans:

- Yes! It is expected as Memory is allocated for SQL Server: BPool + Non-Bpool.
- BPool can be controlled by the Max Server Memory Setting but not the Non-BPool memory.
- Also Lock Pages in Memory can control BPool memory but still Non-BPool pages are paged to disk

163. When I have been checking for buffer usage one of the stored procedure is using large number of Logical Reads. Does this impact performance? What are the most possible reasons for a large number of logical reads?

Ans:

Yes! Large number of logical reads leads to memory pressure. There are few common reasons that cause more logical reads:

- *Unused Indexes:* Indexes should be built on the basis of data retrieval process. If indexes defined on columns and those columns are not being used in queries that leads to huge number of logical reads.
- *Wide Indexes:* Indexing on the large number of columns will leads to high logical reads.
- *Poor Fill Factor/Page Density:* When a less fill factor is specified large number of page needed to qualify a simple query which leads to High Logical Reads.

- *Poor Query Design:* If query leads to index scan, Hash Join when Merge Join is possible, not using indexes etc. causes the more number of logical reads.

164. **We recently had to cancel a long-running update. After the operation rolled back, the next daily transaction log backup was huge. My question is the operation got roll backed and nothing had changed in the database. But why we were getting huge log backups?**

Ans:

The huge transaction/differential backup expected after rollback the long running update. Even when an operation is rolled back, the database is still changed. All backups need to reflect those changes.

- Any time SQL Server makes a change to the database, two things happen:
  - ✓ It generates transaction log records that describe the change.
  - ✓ For any data file pages modified by the change, the corresponding bit is set in a differential bitmap. This signifies those pages should be backed up by the next differential backup.
- Each change performed during rollback is really just another database change and for every change to the database, there must be a transaction log record.
- So even changes made during a rollback must be properly logged. This means a large operation rollback will generate not only transaction log records for the forward part of the operation, but also for the rollback.
- While initially running update statement it causes the differential bitmap to have bits set because portions of the database have changed, and we can't clear those bits in the differential bitmap. It doesn't matter whether the change was eventually rolled back. The data file pages have still been changed and so must be backed up by the differential backup.

165. **I have a huge database and there are few tables which are holding huge datasets. These tables are partitioned. Recently we have added a new partition and we need to update statistics to include these new partitions. What is your approach? Can we apply UPDATE STATISTICS WITH FULL SCAN and entire table?**

Ans:

Not exactly, we are not supposed to trigger "update statistics with full scan" on large tables without knowing the impact. Let me explain a situation where we handled the similar kind of scenario.

We had a table with 6 TB data and 11 TB Indexes with 98 partitions. On this table if we do UPDATE STATISTICS WITH FULL SCAN, it will take 52 hours which is a very longer operation. From SQL Server 2014 we have an option called INCREMENTAL STATS. Be default it is off we can set it to ON. The incremental option creates and stores statistics on a per partition basis, and when updated, only refreshes statistics on those partitions that need new statistics.

This INCREMENTAL option doesn't support for the following statistics types:

- Indexes which are not partition-aligned with the base table
- Read-only databases

- ➢ Filtered indexes
- ➢ Views
- ➢ Internal tables
- ➢ Spatial indexes or XML indexes

166. You are writing a query and as per the requirement you need to use "IN" clause. But your manager suggested using INNER JOIN instead of IN clause. What is your choice? Why?

Ans:

First thing I would check the expected row count in query inside IN clause.

First let me tell you the experience that I had with IN clause. I asked to check a query which was written to pull out a report and there was a timeout error from front end. When I checked, there is an IN clause with a sub query inside IN clause. I replaced it with an INNER JOIN and the query execution time turns into 8 sec from 350 sec.

I don't blindly suggest using INNER JOIN instead of IN clause. That depends on the row count that the query is going to deal with. IN clause also works very well when there are only few values or constants. There are certain scenarios where IN clause is perfectly apt for the situation and faster as well.

167. We have a scenario: We have a huge transactional table on which insert/delete operations happens heavily also the same table they would like to use for reporting purpose. We need to suggest best practices for INSERT/DELETE operations and reporting operations. Can you quickly tell me few best practices?

Ans:

We should remember few things in designing the solution for this:

- ➢ No longer transactions
- ➢ No huge number of locks
- ➢ No Deadlocks
- ➢ Future support

Solutions:

- ➢ Reporting:
  - ✓ Use Transactional Replication to report tables from master/transactional table
  - ✓ 3 tier data moment: Queue changes based on timestamp into staging and program to move from stag to report table.
  - ✓ At the time of data movement use with NOLOCK option while querying from Transaction table
- ➢ Use Bulk inserts method
- ➢ Soft Delete: Add a bit column and soft delete rows and program to delete all these rows when the traffic is low.

168. See we have a simple table with 1000 rows and a simple select statement is taking longer time. Just say "SELECT COL1, COL2, COL3 from Tab" is taking more than a minute. What might be the reason and how do you troubleshoot it?

Ans:

I cannot say one direct solution but I can do analyze and go with the possible reasons and solutions by answering the below questions.

- What is the table size?
- Does the table is having any LOB (VARBINARY (Max)/ntext/image/XML etc.) data columns?
- Did we check if there is any blocking?
- Any triggers and constraints defined on the table (Useful to analyze DML operations)
- Did we check the I/O response time?
- Did you check the table fragmentation?
- Did we check last wait type and time?
- Any chances for page corruption?

Answering these questions can help us in designing the solution.

Before that let me tell you a similar experience I had.

We had a database (600 GB). In that there is a table T1 with 16 million rows and the other table T2 with 1800 rows. Now the problem is a simple select/Delete statement on T2 is taking 40 sec time whereas running a search criteria on T1 (The bigger table) is getting the result in 3 sec.

Analysis:

- T1 is a very small table (35MB)
- It does not have any LOB object columns
- No blocking during the SELECT
- The table is a HEAP
- From "sys.dm_exec_requests" we could find Wait_Type and Last_wait_type are: PAGEIOLATCH_EX and wait_time is high. This wait_type indicates that the process is waiting to have an exclusive lock on a page which is not currently in Memory and needs to get from the disk.
- Occasionally records are inserting/deleting
- The table is being used on all module (Application) related queries and stored procedures by joining with a key column.
- Table had a fragmentation: 91% (It shouldn't be a serious problem as there were only 350 pages)

Solution:

- We have created a clustered index on the key column.
- Still the problem exists.

- We have copied the data to other table and dropped and recreated the table with the clustered index.
- Now the problem got solved and the select statement executed in less than a sec.

169. **What kind of search criteria (Scan/seek) happens on two tables (Emp, Dept) in below query and why?**

Ans:

Dept (Id, Name) – ID – Primary Key

Emp (Id, Name, Dept_ID) – Dept_ID – Foreign Key

"SELECT E.ID, E.NAME, E.Dept_ID

FROM EMP E

INNER JOIN DEPT D ON D.ID = E.Dept_ID;"

Emp: Clustered Index Scan

Dept: Nothing will happen. Query optimizer doesn't touch the table Dept. Because there is already a foreign key relationship which means Dept_ID from Emp will have only values from Dept.ID. This is one of the good features that save the execution time. But remember optimizer consider only trusted foreign keys.

170. **I have seen some of the developers creating views on complex queries and create the queries by joining all those views to create the end result. To simply say that they simplify the end result query by joining nested views instead of using complex queries. Do you suggest this or you see any issue here?**

Ans:

We strongly oppose applying JOIN on nested views. Here are the reasons:

- SQL Server query optimizer estimate the number of rows returned from each table in the query.
- When there are nested views using it doesn't get that much of time to get estimates from each level.
- Once the nesting go beyond 3 levels optimizer just stops giving costs and assumes the internal objects returns 1 record.
- The same issue happens when we use Multi statement table valued user defined functions and table variables.
- Optimizer assumes that these functions returns 1 record and design the execution plan accordingly.
- From 2014 this value changed to 100 rows so now from 2014 optimizer assumes the internal objects from nested views or Multi statement user defined functions will returns 100 rows.
- These wrong estimates might result in a bad execution plan.

171. **We have a query which is running fine in development but facing performance issues at production. You got the execution plan from production DBA. Now you need to compare with the development execution plan. What is your approach?**

Ans:

As we know compare to development production systems are having high configurations. Thereof we can actually export statistics from production and load them into development. But still it doesn't give the same results as production as these systems differs in hardware configurations.

In this scenario we can look into an undocumented DBCC command DBCC OPTIMIZER_WHATIF. Using this command we can set the number of CPU's, Memory and other system parameters. These values will be used by optimizer while designing the execution plan. See for example we have 4 GB RAM in dev but in production it's 64 GB. Using this command we can hypothetically set the RAM as 64GB, it doesn't affect anything on your windows system but just showcase the RAM as 64 GB to optimizer.

172. **Let's say we have a table called "Employee" having columns ID, Name, Age and Salary. Basically it's a heap and I would like to ask you few questions on this. Please answer inline**

Ans:

- **Initially for any select operation what kind of operation happens?**
  - ✓ Table Scan
- **Let's say we have created a non-clustered index on "ID" column then:**
  - ✓ Where ID = 100989 -- Index Seek with Heap Lookup
  - ✓ Where ID Between 1009 AND 1990 -- Table Scan
  - ✓ Where Name = 'Emp-Name' -- Table Scan
  - ✓ Where Name Like '%A%' -- Table Scan

  -- Drop that non clustered index
- **Let's say we have created a clustered index on "ID" column then:**
  - ✓ Where ID = 100989 -- Clustered Index Seek
  - ✓ Where ID Between 1009 AND 1990 -- Clustered Index Seek
  - ✓ Where Name = 'Emp-Name' -- Clustered Index Scan
  - ✓ Where Name Like '%A%' -- Clustered Index Scan
- **Let's say we have created a Non-clustered index on "Name" column then:**
- **Now we have two indexes defined. Clustered on ID and Non-Clustered on Name**
  - ✓ Where ID = 100989 -- Clustered Index Seek
  - ✓ Where ID Between 1009 AND 1990 -- Clustered Index Seek
  - ✓ Where Name = 'Emp-Name' -- Clustered Index Scan
  - ✓ Where Name Like '%A%' -- Clustered Index Scan

173. Can you tell me any one performance issue with partitioned tables?

Ans:

Yes! When I was working for an insurance client and assigned to tune stored procedures. One of the stored procedure, it was taking long time, from the primary investigation there is a hash match happening between two datasets. When I looked into those tables both are having clustered index defined and both tables are related using PRIMARY – FOREIGN keys. Moreover clustered index key column is using on join condition. There should be a merge join happens but it was Hash Match. The only hint I found was the order of columns in JOIN "ON" clause is suspicious (Comparing 2 non key columns and then comparing the clustered index column as a 3rd condition).

But from my knowledge it shouldn't impact the execution plan. Further investigated into the table properties found those 2 are partitioned tables and then I have got a help from one of the msdn blogs. Finally this is an optimizer bug in SQL Server 2008. When we are joining partitioned tables joining order is really matters. We should use the clustered index column first then only optimizer knows that the input datasets are in sorted order. There was a Trace flag given to prevent this issue and this issue got fixed in SQL Server 2008 R2.

174. From your experience can you tell me what are the top most issues that cause performance issues?

Ans:

From my experience below are the top issue that causes the performance issues most of the time:

- Bad Parameter Sniffing
- Scalar User Defined functions using in a query or with a loop
- TEMPDB PAGELATCH contention
- The CXPACKET WAIT TYPE
- Locking and Blocking
- Poorly written queries
- Poorly designed Indexes
- Wrongly configuring Server/Database options

Bad parameter sniffing: Usually in any environment when first time code written and tested it will be on smaller datasets but the problem comes when data growing. I faced lot of performance issues on production systems due to bad parameter sniffing.

Scalar User Defined functions using in a query or with a loop: This is one of the most dangerous areas which can create a lot of problems. Also troubleshooting is not easy when user defined functions causing the performance issues. For example: A scalar user defined function is using in simple query where clause. The query returns 1000 records and the query is been placed inside a while loop with 100 iterations. Now can you guess how many times the function is executed: 1000 * 100 = 100000 times.

TEMPDB PAGELATCH contention: This is also the problem we face most of the times. To resolve this we should follow the best practices in designing the TEMPDB database.

The CXPACKET WAIT TYPE: Just seeing this wait type may not be the problem but sometimes getting this wait type for longer times may require some root cause analysis. We can handle these issues by using the correct configuration for MAXDOP.

Locking and Blocking: As we know this is one of the reasons that cause queries running slow. Follow the best practices in writing queries and batches. Ex: Always access tables in the same order, use required query hints while selecting data from reporting purpose, make transaction as small as possible, use the correct isolation level based on business requirement etc.

Poorly written queries: Define a standard check list and make sure each and every procedure/ function or any other SQL batch follows the checklist. We defined a checklist and we do a detailed code review before committing to the production. Ex: Apply data filters at initial level, don't use "select *" when required only few columns, use clustered indexed column to avoid sort operation, dynamic SQL should always be executed using sp_executesql, SET NOCOUNT ON when not required the row counts etc.

Poorly designed Indexes: Design and maintain indexes well. Ex: Make sure all tables are having aligned with the proper indexes, use covering indexes for most frequently used queries, remove unused, unnecessary or duplicate indexes and maintain indexes (Reorganise/Rebuild) based on fragmentation levels.

Wrongly configuring Server/Database options: Leaving default values or configuring wrong values for some of the server and database level settings may impact the performance seriously. Ex: MAXDOP, Maximum Server Memory etc.

Partitions

175. What is the table partitioning in SQL Server?

Ans:

- Table partitioning allows tables or indexes to be stored in multiple physical locations.
- A partitioned index is made of multiple small indexes that hold the range values of a same column.
- Partitioning is a transparent feature, means it doesn't require the code change in the calling application.

176. Can we partition a table when it is a heap or having clustered indexes or non-clustered indexes?

Ans:

Yes! A table can be partitioned when it's a heap or a clustered/non-clustered index defined on it

177. What is the primary usage of a partitioning a table and where it is used?

Ans:

- SWITCHING-IN and SWITCHING-OUT (Data archiving) is the primary usage of partitioning a table.
  - ✓ **SWITCHING-IN:** Switch/Load an entire partition from table A to Table B- Data loading is faster when doing switch-in.

- ✓ **SWITCHING-OUT:** Switch/Move an entire partition from Table B to Archive.
- ✓ This is very useful in dealing with frequent ETL/Data feeds.

Apart from Switching we can get the benefits:

- ➢ Performance gain by keeping your file groups on different drives
- ➢ More concurrency
- ➢ Index maintenance can be easier
- ➢ Through read only file-groups we can have some options to optimize backup/restore

178. What are the most common problems/limitations in SWITCHING-IN and SWITCHING-OUT a partition?

Ans:

- ➢ An exclusive lock Sch-M/schema modification lock will be held during the SWITCH which never allow any other transaction to access data
- ➢ All enabled non-clustered indexes must be partition aligned, means partition key must be a part of all indexes which is not possible on OLTP systems.
- ➢ This is not a problem but a caution: While switching the destination table partition should be empty.
- ➢ To switch partitions between tables, those partitions must share the same file group.

179. What is the partition elimination?

Ans:

When your table is partitioned query optimizer may direct the query to a specific partition or few partitions or to entire table. Considering few partitions rather than entire table and designing execution plan is known as partition elimination.

180. Does partition elimination happens by default?

Ans:

No! Histogram doesn't showcase the partition level statistics thereof optimizer may not consider partitions while designing execution plan. To get the best execution plan it is supposed to use the partitioned key in search/filter criteria.

181. When do you go for partitioning a table?

Ans:

Usually people (DBA/Architect) look for partitioning when they are having a problem scaling up their databases. Below are the signs:

- ➢ Queries returning large amounts of data and running slow.
- ➢ Queries returning small amounts of data and running slow.
- ➢ Data loading got slower.
- ➢ Frequent blocking between writes and reads.
- ➢ Long running index maintenance jobs.

- Using the same database as transactional and reporting purpose.

Note: Table partition is really an awesome feature but remember partitioning a table means a table is having a major surgery. My suggestion is to figure out all problems and bottlenecks. Do have a proper investigation and RCA before making the major changes.

182. What are the things needs to be considered before going for a partitioning?

Ans:

- List out all current problems that forcing you to have partitioning.
- Check the overall system (Database/Server) health and see if there is any other parameter which is causing the slowness.
- List out all frequent queries which are going to get benefit by partitioning the table.
- Tune as many queries as you can and also list out number of queries which can be tuned by partitioning.
- You should know estimates on expected data growth/Number of records loading per day etc.
- Know the limitations
- Know it's an enterprise feature and consider the budget if not yet using enterprise edition

183. What are the basic limitations we should know before implementing partitions?

Ans:

- In SQL Server 2008 individual partitions can be rebuilt offline only. Rebuilt can be done online for the entire partitioned index.
- Setting a file group read-only doesn't avoid lock management overhead that is only true when a entire database is in read-only
- Switching-IN and Switching-Out requires a Schema modification Lock during the operation.
- Partitioning is not cheap as it requires enterprise edition for production implementation.

Caution: Portioning is introduced for loading/moving huge datasets between tables. There are high chances that performance might degrade when querying without using portioned key in search criteria.

184. Can we be able to do online rebuild for a single partition in SQL Server 2012?

Ans:

No! Till SQL Server 2012 we can't do online rebuild only for the single partition. But 2014 it's a great improvement that allows us to perform online rebuild for a single partition.

185. Can you tell me any partition improvements in SQL Server 2016?

Ans:

Yes! There is an improvement which is really helpful in dropping/deleting a specific partition in a table.

Truncate Single Partition: SQL Server 2016 allows us to TRUNCATE a single partition in a partitioned table. Ex: TRUNCATE TABLE dbo.Test WITH (PARTITIONS (5));

Partition Limit Increased: SQL Server 2016 supports up to 15,000 partitions by default whereas in 2012 it's 1000 by default.

186. Can we use more than one column as a partition key?

Ans:

No! But Yes! We cannot use more than one column as partition key explicitly but we can use a composite column as a partition key.

187. Can you quickly tell me the steps to partition a table?

Ans:

- *Partition Key:* On which basis table values got partitioned.
- *Partition Function:* It defines partition boundary values (It doesn't directly split the values but define the range for partitions).
- *Range Left:* Boundary value belongs to its left partition and the given value is the last value in the left partition.
- *Range Right:* Boundary value belongs to its right partition and the given value is the first value in the right partition.
- *Partition Schema:* Maps the logical partitions to physical file groups. All partitions into a single file group or we can map into individual file group.

Steps to Partition a Table:

- ✓ Create a partition function
- ✓ Create a partition schema
- ✓ Create a table on partition schema
- ✓ Create indexes on partitioned table

188. How to do a switch a partition between two tables (Stage and Destination)?

Ans:

- Let's say we have a stag table and loaded with the 2015 data in partition 15.
- Make sure Meta data (Data type length and all indexes) is same between these 2 tables (Stag and Destination).
- Make sure destination partition is empty.
- Start switching partition:
- "ALTER TABLE [dbo].[stag] SWITCH PARTITION 15 TO [dbo].[destination] PARTITION 15;"

Result: Data moved to Destination - Partition 15 from Stag - Partition 15. We can see the rowcount is zero @ stage and can see the total rows matches with 2015 data on destination.

189. What exactly happens when a partition switch happens? Does really rows copied/ duplicated?

Ans:

No! Internally Meta data including indexes will be mapped between stag and destination table. That is the reason mete data should match between tables.

190. Can we switch a partition to a non-partitioned table?

Ans:

Yes! We can do that. Data will be switched by giving a warning. And we need not mention the destination partition number while switching. Also after switching the non-partitioned table still remains the same (non-partitioned)

191. I am looking for improving the performance, can I think of partitioning?

Ans:

Partitioning is introduced to help warehouse people to do a bulk data loads and deletes by SWITCHING partitions between tables. Yes partitioning a table might improve the performance but at the same time it might decrease the performance in most of the cases. If you are looking for the performance let's have a look at index design and query tuning, do follow best practices and do have best configurations at both database and server level that matches your business requirement.

192. Let's say we have an ETL task. If you need to partition a table which table do you choose and why? "Source," Staging" and "Archive"?

Ans:

I do partition Staging and Destination.

Reason: So that I can simply switch the partition from Stag to Archive. Also in most of the cases we can have control on Stag and Destination not on source system.

In-Memory OLTP

193. What is In-Memory OLTP?

Ans:

In-Memory OLTP is Microsoft's latest in-memory processing technology. In-Memory OLTP is optimized for Online Transaction Processing (OLTP) and integrated into SQL Server's Database Engine. In-Memory OLTP originally introduced in SQL Server 2014 and it mainly features two new data structures:

- Memory-Optimized Tables
- Natively-Compiled Stored Procedures

194. What are Memory-Optimized Tables?

Ans:

Memory-optimized tables store their data into memory using multiple versions of each row's data. This technique is characterized as 'non-blocking multi-version optimistic concurrency control' and eliminates both locks and latches thereof allowing the best concurrency control which leads to the significant performance improvement. The main features of Memory-Optimized Tables are:

- The entire table resides in memory
- Rows in the table are read from, and written to, memory
- Multiple versions of rows can be managed In-Memory
- Eliminates locks and latches
- The option of durable & non-durable data
- Data in memory-optimized tables is only read from disk during database recovery

195. What is the difference between durable and non-durable memory optimized tables?

Ans:

Durable: Data is recovered in-case of any failure.

Non-Durable: Data is not recovered in-case of any failure.

There are certain things that we should understand before defining a table as Durable or Non-Durable.

- Memory Optimized tables are Durable by default which means data is recovered from transactional log file in-case of any failure.
- We can also define a Memory Optimized Table as non-durable in this case the table data is not recovered when there is a failure.
- Transactions don't require any Disk I/O for Non-Durable tables thereof we can see faster turnaround time.
- Use Durable when dealing with the permanent tables
- We can use the option Non-Durable when we are working with a staging/temporary datasets.
- Defining the option for DURABILITY:
  - ✓ Durable: WITH (MEMORY_OPTIMIZED = ON, DURABILITY = SCHEMA_AND_DATA);
  - ✓ Non-Durable: WITH (MEMORY_OPTIMIZED = ON, DURABILITY = SCHEMA_ONLY);

196. Can we define indexes on Memory-Optimized tables?

Ans:

Yes! With below limitations:

- Memory-Optimized tables doesn't support clustered indexes
- Memory-Optimized tables only supports Non-clustered indexes (Up to 8)
- Along with the index specification we need to specify the BUCKET_COUNT.
- BUCKET_COUNT has to be defined as 1.5 or 2 times of the unique rows. When your tables is going to hold 1000 unique rows means Bucket_Count = 2000.

197. For a Memory Optimized Table, since I keep entire table in memory does indexes really required?

Ans:

Yes! Even in memory to get your data quickly indexes required.

- Let's say we have created a Memory Optimized table T1 with 60000 rows.
- For Range operations (<. >, <=, >=, BETWEEN) it performs a scan when there is no index.
- If an index (Non-Clustered) defined on the same table can give you faster results with an efficient seek operation.
- When an SQL UPDATE statement modifies data in a memory-optimized table, corresponding changes to its indexes are not written to the log.
- The entries in a memory-optimized index contain a direct memory address to the row in the table.

198. What are the phases in creating and using a Memory Optimized Table?

Ans:

When we create memory optimized tables below are the phases in which the table created and available for usage:

- Memory Optimized Table Creation using DDL
- Code Generation and Compilation
- Table DLL produced
- Table DLL Loaded Into Memory
- Access and manipulate data from the Memory Optimized Table
- Use below query to identify the loaded modules:

  SELECT name, description FROM sys.dm_os_loaded_modules where description = 'XTP Native DLL';

199. What are Natively-Compiled stored procedures?

Ans:

A natively-compiled stored procedure is a SQL Server object that can access only memory-optimized data structures such as memory-optimized tables, table variables, etc. Features of a natively-compiled stored procedure:

- It is compiled to native code (DLL) upon its creation
- It can only interact with memory-optimized tables
- Aggressive optimizations take time at compile time
- The call to a natively-compiled stored procedure is actually a call to its DLL entry point

200. What are the clauses required to define a Natively-Compiled Stored Procedure?

Ans:

- The WITH NATIVE_COMPILATION clause is used

- The SCHMABINDING clause to bound the stored procedure to the schema of the objects it references
- The BEGIN_ATOMIC clause is required because the stored procedure must consist of exactly one block along with the Transaction Isolation Level.

201. What are the phases in creating and using a Natively-Compiled Stored Procedure?

Ans:

When we create a Natively-Compiled Stored Procedure below are the phases in which the procedure is created and available for usage:

- Natively-Compiled Stored Procedure using DDL
- Query Optimization
- Code Generation
- Compilation
- Native Stored Procedure DLL get produced
- Native Stored Procedure DLL get Loaded into Memory
- Call/Execute the stored procedure
- The parser extracts the name and stored procedure parameters
- The In-Memory OLTP runtime locates the DLL entry point for the stored procedure
- The DLL executes the procedure logic and returns the results to the client
- Use below query to identify the loaded modules:

  SELECT name, description FROM sys.dm_os_loaded_modules where description = 'XTP Native DLL';

202. One of your clients is using SQL Server 2008 R2 and they want to upgrade it to 2014 just because they liked the feature "In-Memory OLTP" and they thought "In-Memory OLTP" adds a lot of value to their business by improving the performance. What would you suggest them?

Ans:

I don't recommend upgrading from SQL Server 2008 R2 to 2014 just to because of the feature "In-Memory OLTP." There are 100 more features improved in 2014 when compared to 2008 R2. Before all that I need to explain why we can't use In-Memory OLTP right now:

There are lot of limitations kept me stay back from using In-Memory OLTP on 2014.

Memory Optimized Tables - Limitations:

- In-Memory OLTP doesn't support Foreign Keys
- When you define a Hash Index, you always have to specify the Hash Bucket count during the table creation.
- We need to predict the future data growth by the time of memory optimized table creation.
- We can't use UNIQUE, CHECK and DEFAULT constraints.

- In Memory Tables always uses a BIN collation and are case sensitive for this reason. It requires code changes.
- Triggers doesn't work with Memory Optimized Tables
- No partition support
- Doesn't support computed columns
- No Identity key support we have to sequences
- No Table changes allowed
- No Index changes allowed
- Row size limit to 8060 bytes

Native-Compiled Stored Procedure - Limitations:

- We can't see the actual execution plan which is very tough in situations where we need to tune the performance.
- These stored procedures don't support many native T-SQL functions. Ex: REPLACE
- Compiles and optimized initially when we create it. But the same plan may not suitable when there is a huge change happens in data distribution.
- Huge amount of RAM required. Microsoft recommends an amount of RAM which is double what your Memory Optimized Table is in size, e.g. 100 GB RAM for a table size of 50 GB.
- Doesn't support cross database queries
- UNION, UNION ALL, CONTAINS, INTERSECT, EXCEPT, LEFT & OUTER JOIN, PIVOT, UNPIVOT, APPLY and lot many native T-SQL functionality doesn't support in Native-Compiled Stored Procedures.

In-Memory OLTP is one of the best features for sure when it supports maximum native features. I would suggest wait for few more months and upgrading to SQL Server 2016.

203. One of your servers is upgraded to SQL Server 2014 Enterprise edition. You are asked to suggest where we can use the feature "In-Memory OLTP"? After all limitations what do you suggest?

Ans:

Even with all these limitations bigger organizations are using this feature for mission critical applications for the performance improvements.

- Dealing with large/huge temporary tables
- Dealing with staging tables where data is non-durable

204. What are all the In-Memory OLTP features that doesn't supported by 2014 but supported in 2016?

Ans:

As I said earlier there is lot of limitations in using In-Memory OLTP on SQL Server 2014. But all these limitations are handled on SQL Server 2016. Here is the list of In-Memory OLTP features which are not supported in 2014 but supported in 2016.

- Durable Table size is increased to 2 TB in 2016 where is in 2014 it's 250 GB
- Altering Memory Optimized Tables
- Altering Natively-Compiled Stored Procedures
- Parallel plan for operations accessing memory-optimized tables
- Transparent Data Encryption
- Natively-compiled, scalar user-defined functions
- Collation support: SQL Server 2014 supports only *_BIN2 collation where in SQL Server 2016 it fully supports all collations.
- Indexes on null able columns
- Multiple Active Result Sets (MARS)
- Large Objects (LOBs) i.e. VARCHAR(MAX), NVARCHAR(MAX), VARBINARY(MAX);
- Below native features doesn't supported in 2014 Native-Compiled Stored Procedures, but supports in 2016:
  - ✓ UNION and UNION ALL
  - ✓ SELECT DISTINCT
  - ✓ LEFT and RIGHT OUTER JOIN
  - ✓ OR and NOT operators
  - ✓ Subqueries in all clauses of a SELECT statement
  - ✓ Nested stored procedure calls
  - ✓ All built-in math functions

205. Does DBCC PINTABLE command is same as SQL Server 2014 Memory Optimized Tables?

Ans:

No! These are two different features and are based on two different architectures.

DBCC PINTABLE:

- When a table is marked with DBCC PINTABLE command, this table related pages are not removed/flushed from memory.
- First time the page has to be picked from the disk as normal page but when the second time the same page required it is available in memory.
- Once these pages are placed in memory they can't be released to disk even when there is a memory pressure.
- When there is a huge table pinned with DBCC PINTABLE there are chances that the entire table might be pulled into memory which means it utilize the entire buffer pool and doesn't allow other requests to use buffer pool.
- Pin tables required the same level of latching, locking and logging with the same index structures as traditional disk based tables.
- DBCC PINTABLE feature is deprecated from SQL Server 2005

In-Memory OLTP:

- In-memory OLTP architecture is a separate component of the database engine which allows you to create memory optimized tables.
- These memory optimized tables have a completely different data and index structure.
- Once a table is marked as Memory Optimized the entire table is being kept and managed in memory based on durability setting.
- No locking or latching is required when you access these tables
- There are no data pages, index pages or buffer pool for memory optimized tables.
- Data for the memory optimized table gets stored in the memory in a completely different structure

206. Does Meta data for a memory optimized table is stored in SQL Server CATALOGS?

Ans:

Yes! Meta data for memory optimized tables are stored on SQL Server Catalogues as like Meta data of disk based tables.

207. I have started using memory optimized tables and I have added my database to ALWAYSON Availability Group. Does failover works for Memory Optimized Tables?

Ans:

Yes! Memory optimized tables will fail over in the same manner as disk based tables.

208. Can we be able to apply operations on both disk based and memory optimized tables in the same transaction?

Ans:

Yes! We can issue DML operations (INSERT, SELECT, DELETE, UPDATE) on disk based and memory optimized tables in the same transaction. These transactions are known as "Cross-container Transactions."

209. Do you know what is Interop refers to in in-Memory OLTP?

Ans:

The interpreted Transact-SQL that references memory-optimized tables is known as interop

210. How to deal with Parameter Sniffing in natively compiles stored procedures?

Ans:

Parameter sniffing is not used for compiling natively compiled stored procedures. All parameters to the stored procedure are considered to have UNKNOWN values.

TEMPDB

211. TEMPDB is filling up drastically, what might be the activity that filling up the TEMPDB?

Ans:

Usually, TEMPDB fills up when you are low on disk space, or when you have set an unreasonably low maximum size for database growth.

Many people think that TEMPDB is only used for #temp tables. But in fact, you can easily fill up TEMPDB without ever creating a single temp table. Some other scenarios that can cause TEMPDB to fill up:

- Any sorting that requires more memory than has been allocated to SQL Server will be forced to do its work in TEMPDB
- DBCC CheckDB ('any database') will perform its work in TEMPDB -- on larger databases, this can consume quite a bit of space
- DBCC DBREINDEX or similar DBCC commands with 'Sort in TEMPDB' option set will also potentially fill up TEMPDB
- Large resultsets involving unions, order by/group by, cartesian joins, outer joins, cursors, temp tables, table variables, and hashing can often require help from TEMPDB
- Any transactions left uncommitted and not rolled back can leave objects orphaned in TEMPDB
- Use of an ODBC DSN with the option 'create temporary stored procedures' set can leave objects there for the life of the connection
- Table value functions that pull large data sets hold their data in TEMPDB
- If you are using Snapshot isolation on a database with a high number of transactions the snapshot data is stored in TEMPDB

212. How to analyse the TEMPDB usage?

Ans:

- Run the below command

  ```
  USE TEMPDB
  GO
  SELECT table_name FROM information_schema.tables
  ```

  If you have a few tables, then you are most likely dealing with a large set issue. If you have a very large number of tables, then there is a runaway process or an unclosed process.
- Find the size of the tables. Shortlist the biggest tables and depends on the type of table we can find out the source.
- Make sure that disk space is not full and capacity settings for TEMPDB (low size for max growth)

  Also with queries that fail to use an index on large tables can cause this from time to time. Do you have autoshrink turned on for TEMPDB
- You could check in on your record locking strategies for your executable sessions and/or records might not be getting released properly. Use the query optimizer tools maybe
- Check for index rebuilding jobs, data pulling jobs/triggers blocking sessions, long running transactions
- Use profiler/perfmon/dbcc commands to find the bottlenecks

- You can use Profiler to watch for events like database file auto grow and log file auto grow. If this is happening often, then you know that the space you've allocated to TEMPDB is not sufficient.
- You can also watch performance monitor's counter for PhysicalDisk: CurrentDiskQueueLength on the drive where TEMPDB exists. If this number is consistently greater than 2, then there is likely a bottleneck in disk I/O.

213. How to fix the TEMPDB filling issue?

Ans:

Short-Term Fix:

- Shrink TEMPDB: We can shrink the DB using ShrinkDatabase, DBCC ShrinkFile. If you can't shrink the log, it might be due to an uncommitted transaction.
    - ✓ See if you have any long-running transactions with the following command "DBCC OPENTRAN(TEMPDB)"
    - ✓ Check the oldest transaction (if it returns any), and see who the SPID is "DBCC INPUTBUFFER(SPID)"
    - ✓ Query will help you determine if you want to end this process with "KILL SPID"
- Restarting SQL Server will re-create TEMPDB from scratch, and it will return to its usually allocated size. In and of itself, this solution is only effective in the very short term; assumedly, the application and/or T-SQL code which caused TEMPDB to grow once will likely cause it to grow again.

Long-Term Prevention:

- Make sure that TEMPDB is set to AUTOGROW -- do *NOT* set a maximum size for TEMPDB. If the current drive is too full to allow AUTOGROW events, then buy a bigger drive, or add files to TEMPDB on another device (using ALTER DATABASE) and allow those files to AUTOGROW.
- For optimal performance, make sure that its initial size is adequate to handle a typical workload (AUTOGROW events can cause performance to suffer as it allocates new extents).
- If possible, put TEMPDB on its own physical disk, array or disk subsystem
- To prevent TEMPDB log file growth, make sure TEMPDB is in simple recovery mode
- Try to make sure you have covering indexes for all large tables that are used in queries that can't use a clustered index/index seek.
- In general, try to make your code as efficient as possible... avoid cursors, nested loops, and #temp tables if possible.
- Make sure all the transactions are having the corresponding Commit and Rollback

214. The most common argument I heard is table variables are in-memory structures (stored in memory not on TEMPDB) not like temporary tables. Is that true? How can you justify?

Ans:

It's actually a wrong assumption; both table variables and temp tables are stored in TEMPDB. A DMV "sys.dm_db_session_space_usage" can help us to make sure these objects use Temdb. On a development machine restart the SQL Server and select data from above DMV as below.

```
SELECT session_id,
database_id,
user_objects_alloc_page_count
FROM sys.dm_db_session_space_usage
WHERE session_id > 50;
```

Initially user_objects_alloc_page_count is shown as 0.

Create a simple temporary table and insert test data and now check the same DMV, we can see the page_count as 1.

Then create a table variable and insert a row and we can see the page_count increased to 2.

215. What database objects are stored in TEMPDB?

Ans:

There are three different types of objects stored in TEMPDB.

Internal Objects:

- Intermediate runs for sort.
- Intermediate results for hash join and hash aggregates.
- XML variables or other large object (LOB) data type variables. (text, image, ntext, VARCHAR(max), VARBINARY(max))
- Queries that need a spool to store intermediate results.
- Keyset cursors to store the keys.
- Static cursors to store a query result.
- Service Broker to store messages in transit.
- INSTEAD OF triggers to store data for internal processing.
- DBCC CHECK internally uses a query that may need to spool intermediate results.
- Query notification and event notification use Service Broker.

Note:

Page allocations on internal objects and Updates to internal objects do not generate log records.

Does not appear in CATALOG views such as sys.all_objects

Version Store:

- Snapshot Isolation/Read Committed Snapshot Islotaion
- Triggers (After Triggers). Instead of triggers doesn't generate versions.
- MARS (Multiple Active Result Sets)
- Index Rebuilds

Note:

Inserts into version stores do not generate log records.

Does not appear in CATALOG views such as sys.all_objects

User Objects:

- User defined tables and indexes
- Local and global temporary tables, bulk insert and BCP intermediate results
- Index rebuilds with "SORT IN TEMPDB" option.

Note:

Most of the operations under this category are bulk logged.

Appear in CATALOGue views such as sys.all_objects.

216. What is TEMPDB PAGELATCH Contention?

Ans:

Before understanding the TEMPDB Latch Contention first we should have some knowledge on below things:

Latch: A latch is a short-term synchronization lock used by SQL Server to protect physical page

PFS (Page Free Space): Stores 1 byte for page to indicate type of page and free space available in that page. The 1 page on any database data file is always a PFS page.

GAM (Global Allocation MAP): Stores 1 bit for extent to indicate which extents are in use and which are empty. The 2 page on any database data file is always a GAM page.

SGAM (Shared Global Allocation MAP): Stores 1 bit for extent to indicate whether the extent is a mixed extent with free space or a full extent. SQL Server reads this page to find a mixed extent with free space to allocate space to a small object. The 3 page on any database data file is always a SGAM page.

These pages can be identified as below:

2:1:1 → Database ID -2 (TEMPDB), Datafile ID -1 (Data file), Page ID – 1 (PFS)

2:1:2 → Database ID -2 (TEMPDB), Datafile ID -1 (Data file), Page ID – 2 (GAM)

2:1:3 → Database ID -2 (TEMPDB), Datafile ID -1 (Data file), Page ID – 3 (SGAM)

When Application is creating a Temp table:

- To determine where in TEMPDB to create your table, SQL Server will read the SGAM page (2:1:3) to find a mixed extent with free space to allocate to the table.
- QL Server takes out an exclusive latch on the SGAM page while it's updating the page and then moves on to read the PFS page to find a free page within the extent to allocate to the object.
- An exclusive latch will also be taken out on the PFS page to ensure that no one else can allocate the same data page, which is then released when the update is complete.
- The problem comes in when the number of users increased and trying to create many temp objects on TEMPDB creates a PAGELATCH wait, with 2:1:1 (PFS) or 2:1:3 (SGAM).
- This is known as TEMPDB Page Latch Contention

217. How to identify the TEMPDB contention?

Ans:

Paul S.Randal has given an excellent explanation on this.

Run below query:

```
SELECT
[owt].[session_id],
[owt].[exec_context_id],
[owt].[wait_duration_ms],
[owt].[wait_type],
[owt].[blocking_session_id],
[owt].[resource_description],
CASE [owt].[wait_type]
WHEN N'CXPACKET' THEN
RIGHT ([owt].[resource_description],
CHARINDEX (N'=', REVERSE ([owt].[resource_description])) - 1)
ELSE NULL
END AS [Node ID],
[es].[program_name],
[est].text,
[er].[database_id],
[eqp].[query_plan],
[er].[cpu_time]
FROM sys.dm_os_waiting_tasks [owt]
INNER JOIN sys.dm_exec_sessions [es] ON
[owt].[session_id] = [es].[session_id]
INNER JOIN sys.dm_exec_requests [er] ON
[es].[session_id] = [er].[session_id]
OUTER APPLY sys.dm_exec_sql_text ([er].[sql_handle]) [est]
OUTER APPLY sys.dm_exec_query_plan ([er].[plan_handle]) [eqp]
WHERE
[es].[is_user_process] = 1
ORDER BY
[owt].[session_id],
[owt].[exec_context_id];
GO
```

Analyze Result Set:

If you see lot of rows with the below values then we can confirm the TEMPDB is having PAGELATCH contention.

Wait_Type: PAGELATCH_UP or PAGELATCH_EX; Update or Exclusive locks

Resource Description: 2:1:1 (TEMPDB - PFS) Or 2:1:3 (TEMPDB SGAM)

218. How to resolve the TEMPDB contention issue?

Ans:

There are three ways to resolve TEMPDB Contention issue and increase the throughput of the overall workload:

- Reduce using Temp Tables
- Enable start up Trace flag 1118
- Create multiple TEMPDB data files

Reduce Using the Temp tables: No way, we can't control this.

Enable Start up Trace Flag 1118:

Up to SQL Server 2014 we have Trace Flag 1118 which is used to allocate a Uniform Extent instead of Mixed Extents to minimize contention in extent allocation. If this trace flag is enabled, then the first 8 data pages for tables are also Uniform Extents rather than Mixed Extents.

In SQL Server 2016, this uniform extent allocation is the default behavior and we can change this behavior if required by using an ALTER DATABASE command, however we cannot change the behavior for the TEMPDB database.

Create multiple TEMPDB data files:

Creating multiple TEMPDB data files will help to remove the PFS page contention, by spreading the allocation workload over multiple files, thus reducing contention on the individual, per-file PFS pages.

219. How many data files have to be created for TEMPDB?

Ans:

As per the Microsoft assistance, if you have more than 8 logical cores, create 8 data files. If still seeing PFS contentions then add more in chunks of 4.

Ex:

2 CPU, 2 Physical Cores each and "Hyper Threading" enabled

Total Logical Cores = (2 CPU X 4 Cores) X 2 "Hyderthreading" = 16

Total TEMPDB Data files can be created = 8

Note: Most important thing is all data files should be equally sized. SQL Database Engine will follow Round Robin algorithm in storing data/objects on data files when all data files are created with same size. It spreads loads equally across all the data files means when a new object needs to be created it chooses the datafile with least data filled with

Miscellaneous

220. Can you explain step by step process in receiving, compiling, optimizing and executing a query submitted from an application to SQL Server database engine?

Ans:

To avoid the duplication I am just redirecting to the Chapter "SQL Server Architecture." Please have a look at the detailed answer given in that chapter (Question 29).

221. There is a major change happened in Query Optimizer in SQL Server 2014. Do you have any clue on that?

Ans:

Yes! Starting from SQL Server 7.0 and continued in SQL Server 2000, 2005, 2008, 2008 R2 even in 2012 used the same cardinality estimator. SQL Server 2014 introduces the first major redesign of the SQL Server Query Optimizer cardinality estimation process since version 7.0. The goal for the redesign was to improve accuracy, consistency and supportability of key areas within the cardinality estimation process, ultimately affecting average query execution plan quality and associated workload performance.

- Increased Correlation Assumption for Multiple Predicates
- Join Estimate Algorithm
- Distinct Value count Estimation

222. What are the performance improvements in SQL Server 2014?

Ans:

Resource Governor: First introduced in 2008 but now in 2014 we can throttle I/O operations

Buffer Pool Extensions: expand the Buffer Pool with a paging file that is stored on very fast storage, like SSD drives. The Buffer Pool Extensions are coming quite handy, if you don't have the ability to physically add more additional RAM to your database server.

Lock Priorities: Server 2014 introduces Lock Priorities, where we can control how SQL Server should react if a blocking situation occurs.

Clustered "COLUMNSTORE" Indexes: SQL Server 2014 introduced Clustered "COLUMNSTORE" Indexes, which is an amazingly new way concept how to deal with COLUMNSTORE data in SQL Server. And in addition the Clustered COLUMNSTORE Index can be also changed directly without using tricks like Partition Switching.

Cardinality Estimation Redesigned: After SQL Server 7.0 this is the first version in which the cardinality estimator is totally redesigned from the scratch for the more accurate estimations.

In-Memory OLTP: SQL Server introduced In-Memory OLTP which allows us to hold the entire table into memory and pre-compiled stored procedures to use these tables. Everything is now stored directly in the memory, without touching your physical storage anymore. And in addition In-Memory OLTP is based on so-called Lock Free Data Structures, means locking, blocking, latching, and spin locking is gone. But there are lot of side effects and limitations.

223. Do you know any performance improvements in SQL Server 2016?

Ans:

Live Query statistics: If you are a DBA or developer, there must have been situations where a query takes a long time to execute and "actual" query plan can only be seen once execution is completed. Live Query Statistics introduced in SQL Server 2016 which allows us to view live execution plan which displays overall query progress and run-time execution statistics such as elapsed time, operator progress, number of rows processed etc. while the query is executing.

Compare Execution Plans: One of the best features is "Compare Showplan" which allows us to compare two execution plans. It's very helpful while debugging and tuning queries.

Improvements in Cardinality Estimator: SQL Server 2016 improved the CE which was newly designed in 2014 for more accurate estimates.

Query Store: The Query Store feature maintains a history of query execution plans with their performance data, and quickly identifies queries that have gotten slower recently, allowing administrators or developers to force the use of an older, better plan if needed.

Multi-threaded Inserts: Insert operation can also be "multi-threaded or can have a parallel plan."

In-Memory improvements: Even though In-Memory introduced in 2014 we can't fully implement that in 2014 because of its limitations. But now in 2016 we can start implementing In-Memory OLTP.

- Optimized accessing algorithms
- Concurrency control increased
- Lock free objects that eliminates all physical locks and catches
- etc.

Statistics:

- *More frequent updates when working with large tables:* In the past, the threshold for amount of changed rows that triggers auto update of statistics was 20%, which was inappropriate for large tables. Starting with SQL Server 2016 (compatibility level 130), this threshold is related to the number of rows in a table. For example, if a table had 1 billion rows, under the old behavior it would have taken 200 million rows to be changed before auto-stats update kicks in. In SQL Server 2016, it would take only 1 million rows to trigger auto stats update.
- *Multi-threading for Statistics:* Statistics are now "sampled by a multi-threaded process" when using compatibility level 130

Joins and Foreign Key Constraints: If a row is modified and it is potentially referenced by a foreign key constraint, checks need to be done to ensure the constraint isn't violated.

In SQL Server 2014, this check would be conducted by joining to each table that references the table in question. As you can imagine, this can quickly become quite expensive. To address this, SQL Server has introduced a new Referential Integrity Operator which can quickly perform the violation rules on referencing tables.

Database Scoped Configurations:

SQL Server 2016 introduced Database Scoped Configurations which can allows us to control certain settings from database level instead of instance level.

- MAXDOP
- LEGACY_CARDINALITY_ESTIMATION – ON/OFF
- ONLINE_OPERATION_DEFAULT – ON/OFF
- PARAMETER_SNIFFING – ON/OFF
- QUERY_OPTIMIZER_HOTFIXES – ON/OFF
- MIXED_PAGE_ALLOCATION - ON/OFF

TEMPDB SGAM Contention Behavior:

In 2016 no needs to enable trace flag 1118 to reduce TEMPDB Contention. In SQL Server 2016, this uniform extent allocation is the default behavior and we can change this behavior if required by using an ALTER DATABASE command, however we cannot change the behavior for the TEMPDB database.

224. What happens when a checkpoint occurs?

Ans:

- Checks if there are any dirty pages (Pages marked as modified after last checkpoint) on buffer
- Writes all log records from buffer to disk (It should be done before pushing modified page into disk so that it helps in recovering. This is called WriteAhead logging)
- Writes all dirty pages from buffer to disk
- Simple Recovery: It checks if there are any VLF's that can be inactive

225. What are the different types of checkpoints?

Ans:

Automatic (Server Level): These are issued automatically in background as per Recover Interval server level setting. Initially it is 0 and checkpoint happens for every one minute.

Indirect (Database Level – 2012/2014/2016): We can set a checkpoint Target Recovery Time which overrides server level recovery interval. It works like automatic checkpoints but this setting can be done at database level.

Manual (Database Level): This can be issued manually just like a T-SQL statement

Internal: We don't have control on this type of checkpoint. It issued by various server operations. Ex: Databases are added, removed using Alter, Backup, snapshot, shutdown, changing recovery model etc.

226. Does all dirty pages written to disk when an automatic checkpoint occurs?

Ans:

Yes it writes all dirty pages from buffer to disk. But "TEMPDB" is an exception where data pages are not written to disk as a part of checkpoint.

227. Any idea why TEMPDB is an exception for checkpoint?

Ans:

Because SQL Server need not recover TEMPDB in case of any disaster.

228. Can you describe the differences between checkpoint and lazy writer?

Ans:

Checkpoint:

- Checkpoint it used to keep database recovery time in check
- Checkpoint can be controlled by user
- Either a manual or automatic checkpoint, it marks an entry into Transaction Log before it executes
- To check Checkpoint occurrence:

  SELECT * FROM ::fn_dblog (null,null) WHERE operation LIKE '%CKPT';
- Checkpoint only checks if page is dirty or not
- Checkpoint is affected by:
  - ✓ Checkpoint duration: How long it run for
  - ✓ Recovery Interval: How often it runs
- Checkpoint runs based on defined frequency
- Checkpoint tries to write as many pages at the maximum possible speed
- Checkpoint process doesn't put the buffer page back on the free list
- We can find last checkpoint occurrence in boot page
- Auto frequency can be controlled using the setting "Recovery Interval"
- Checkpoint can be affected by database recovery model

Lazy writer:

- Lazy writer is used to make sure there is enough memory left in SQL buffer pool to accommodate new pages
- Lazy writer can't be controlled by user
- Lazy writer doesn't make any entry in Transaction Log
- To check the Lazy writer occurrence we can use performance monitor counter: SQL Server Buffer Manager: Lazy writes\sec
- Lazy write clears any page from memory when it satisfies below conditions:
  - ✓ A object requested for memory and available memory is full
  - ✓ Cost factor of the page is zero
  - ✓ Page is not currently referenced from any connection
- Lazy writer effected by:
  - ✓ Memory pressure
  - ✓ Page reference counter in memory

- Lazy writer runs when system encounters memory pressure
- Lazy writer tried to write as few pages as necessary
- Lazy writer scans the buffer cache and reclaim unused pages and put it in free list
- Lazy writer doesn't write to boot page
- Frequency can't be controlled, it uses clock algorithm
- There is no database recovery model impact on lazy writer

229. Did you ever observe the query running status? Can you explain the various statuses and their meaning?

Ans:

Yes! There are various types of statuses all these indicates how the request is getting executed internally. There are components involved in handling the query execution that includes processor/ CPU, threads/fibers, Scheduler, Lock Managers, Resources (Page/Row etc).

Pending: The request is waiting for the thread

Suspended: The thread is assigned but it is not currently active as it's been waiting for the required resource to be available.

Runnable: Once the required resource is available it sends to a queue (First In First Out) and change the status from SUSPENDED to RUNNABLE. Once the turn comes processor picks the thread and start executing by changing the status to running.

Running: Thread is running on the processor

Sleeping: There is no work to be done.

Background: It represents a background thread, that's might be a deadlock or resource monitor.

230. What is the option "Lock Pages in Memory"?

Ans:

Lock Pages in Memory is a setting that can be set on 64-bit operating systems that essentially tell Windows not to swap out SQL Server memory to disk. By default, this setting is turned off on 64-bit systems, but depends on various conditions this option needs to be turned on. We must be very careful in dealing with this option. One can enable this after a detailed analysis of current environment.

Following issues may rise when "Lock Pages in Memory" is not turned on:

- SQL Server performance suddenly decreases.
- Application that connects to SQL Server may encounter timeouts.
- The hardware running SQL Server may not respond for a short time periods.

231. What is the recommended setting for MAXDOP?

Ans:

The Microsoft SQL Server max degree of parallelism (MAXDOP) configuration option controls the number of processors that are used for the execution of a query in a parallel plan. This option determines the computing and threads resources that are used for the query plan operators that perform the work in parallel.

By default, SQL Server will use all available CPUs during query execution. While this is great for large queries, it can cause performance problems and limit concurrency. A better approach is to limit parallelism to the number of physical cores in a single CPU socket.

Example: We have a configuration 2 CPU sockets and 4 Cores then the MAXDOP = 4

Generic Setting for MAXDOP:

- MAXDOP should not be 0 and should not be greater than 8.
- Schedulers can be seen by running this query and would be the rows that have a scheduler_id < 255:
- If we get more than 8 schedulers visible then we can maximum set the value to 8.
- SELECT * FROM sys.dm_os_schedulers WHERE scheduler_id < 255;

232. Why Shrink files/Shrink DB/Auto Shrink is really bad?

Ans:

In the SHRINKFILE command, SQL Server isn't especially careful about where it puts the pages being moved from the end of the file to open pages towards the beginning of the file.

- The data becomes fragmented, potentially up to 100% fragmentation, this is a performance killer for your database;
- The operation is slow - all pointers to/from the page/rows being moved have to be fixed up, and the SHRINKFILE operation is single-threaded, so it can be *really* slow (the single-threaded nature of SHRINKFILE is not going to change any time soon)

Recommendations:

- Shrink the file by using Truncate Only: First it removes the inactive part of the log and then perform shrink operation
- Rebuild/Reorganize the indexes once the shrink is done so the Fragmentation level is decreased

233. What are the best RAID levels to use with SQL Server?

Ans:

Before choosing the RAID (Redundant Array of Independent Disks) we should have a look into usage of SQL Server files.

As a basic thumb rule "Data Files" need random access, "Log files" need sequential access and "TEMPDB" must be on a fastest drive and must be separated from data and log files.

We have to consider the below factors while choosing the RAID level:

- Reliability
- Storage Efficiency
- Random Read
- Random Write

➢ Sequential Write

➢ Sequential Write

➢ Cost.

As an Admin we have to consider all of these parameters in choosing the proper RAID level. Obviously the choice is always between RAID-5 and RAID-10

234. I wanted to know what are the maximum worker threads setting and active worker thread count on SQL Server. Can you tell me how to capture this info? What's the default value for max thread count?

Ans:

We can check the current settings and thread allocation using the below queries.

➢ *Thread setting:* select max_workers_count from sys.dm_os_sys_info

➢ *Active threads:* select count(*) from sys.dm_os_threads

➢ *Default value* is 255.

Increasing the number of worker threads may actually decrease the performance because too many threads causes context switching which could take so much of the resources that the OS starts to degrade in overall performance.

235. What is data compression in a SQL Server database?

Ans:

SQL Server 2012 supports row and page compression for tables and indexes. You can use the data compression feature to help compress the data inside a database, and to help reduce the size of the database. In addition to saving space, data compression can help improve performance of I/O intensive workloads because the data is stored in fewer pages and queries need to read fewer pages from disk. However, extra CPU resources are required on the database server to compress and decompress the data, while data is exchanged with the application.

236. What all database objects can be configured with Data compression?

Ans:

Data compression can be configured for the following database objects:

➢ A whole table that is stored as a heap

➢ A whole table that is stored as a clustered index

➢ A whole non-clustered index

➢ A whole indexed view

➢ For partitioned tables and indexes, the compression option can be configured for each partition.

237. What are the Limitations and Restrictions of Data Compression?

Ans:

➢ System tables cannot be enabled for compression.

- If the table is a heap, the rebuild operation for ONLINE mode will be single threaded. Use OFFLINE mode for a multi-threaded heap rebuild operation.
- You cannot change the compression setting of a single partition if the table has nonaligned indexes.

238. Why Table variables or Derived tables or bad for huge amounts of data?

Ans:

- We cannot create explicit indexes on both Table Variables and Derived tables where Table Variables can have implicit indexes (PrimaryKey, Unique).
- Statistics are not maintained for both kind of tables which in turns a bad optimization plan

239. What is connection pooling in SQL Server?

Ans:

- Process of establishing a connection to a database typically having a list of phases. To minimize the cost of opening connections, ADO.NET uses an optimization technique called connection pooling. When a new call initiated to a database a connection pool is being created.
- Once the connection is closed instead of closing the connection the connection returns to the pool and when the next call initiated with the same connection string, that call can be served with the existing connection pool.
- Only connections with the same configuration can be polled. Different pools will be created for different configurations. Even the order of parameters should be same to use the same pool.
- If number of pools reached maximum configured value and all pools are busy to serve a newly initiated call then the new call will be queued. It waits for next 15 seconds and then thrown a timeout error.

240. You are assigned to look into a performance issue on SQL Server 2008 production environment. You were failed to reproduce the same issue on Dev/QA/Stag. Now your team decided to run the profiler trace and capture the trace details and then you can find out the bottleneck. Note that production DBA team confirmed it should be from database/code only as they verified from all other aspects and no issue from server side. Now how you suggest proceeding ahead?

Ans:

Yes in these kind of cases we have to run the profiler trace but remember the below points.

- Always run Server Side Trace, running client side profiler UI can easily kill your application.
- Choose necessary events only.
- Keep trace file location in a disk where enough space available and with low traffic
- Limit server-side trace file size and manage space usage
- Avoid redundant data (e.g. SQL:BatchStarting and SQL:BatchCompleted)

241. How to get the script to run on server side?

Ans:

Open SQL Profiler and once you complete choosing all required events, classes and filters, there is an option available to script/export. Once you get that you can change the trace file location over there before running the trace.

242. How to stop and delete Server Side Trace?

Ans:

```
sp_trace_setstatus traceid,0
sp_trace_setstatus traceid, 2
```

243. How to get details from trace file?

Ans:

```
--Insert into a SQL table from trace file
SELECT * INTO sqlTableToLoad
FROM ::fn_trace_gettable('traceFileName', DEFAULT)
--to directly get data from trace file:
SELECT *
FROM fn_trace_gettable('c:\inside_sql.trc', 1)
```

244. Any idea about Ghost cleanup?

Ans:

It's a background process that cleans up ghost records. A ghost record is one that's just been deleted in an index on a table. Such a delete operation never physically removes records from pages and it only marks them as having been deleted, or ghosted. This is a performance optimization that allows delete operations to complete more quickly. It also allows delete operations to rollback more quickly. The deleted record will be physically removed (its slot will be removed – the record data is not actually overwritten) later by the background ghost cleanup task.

When a record deleted from a page, page header is marked as the page is having ghost records. Ghost Cleanup runs in background for every 5 seconds and scan pages and find if there are any ghost records it cleanup those slots. Also in every scan it limits the page count to 10, so it doesn't need to swap the system. It checks all databases one by one.

245. How to avoid bookmark lookups/key lookups/RID lookups?

Ans:

SQL Server optimizer will try to use a non-clustered index on the column or columns contained in the WHERE clause to retrieve the data requested by the query. If the query requests data from columns not present in the non-clustered index, SQL Server must go back to the data pages to get the data in those columns. Even if the table has a clustered index or not, the query will still have to return to the table or clustered index to retrieve the data.

If table has clustered index, it is called **bookmark lookup** (or key lookup from 2005 sp1); if the table does not have clustered index, but a non-clustered index, it is called **RID lookup**. This operation is very expensive.

To remove the key lookup/rid lookup, we have to create a non-clustered covering index or create a non-clustered index with include columns.

246. How to view statistics of a table/index?

Ans:

Below are the ways to check the statistics for any given table or index.

- USE AdventureWorks2012;

  GO

  DBCC SHOW_STATISTICS ("Person.Address," AK_Address_rowguid);

  Or

- Use the below query
- USE AdventureWorks2012;

  GO

  SELECT name AS index_name,

  STATS_DATE (OBJECT_ID, index_id) AS StatsUpdated

  FROM sys.indexes

  WHERE OBJECT_ID = OBJECT_ID ('Person.Address')

  GO

- To update the statistics use the below statement.
- UPDATE STATISTICS Person.Address WITH FULLSCAN

Note: FULL SCAN option is specified to scan entire table and update statistics.

247. What is a SPARSE column in SQL Server?

Ans:

The SPARSE column property is a special, NULL-friendly column option introduced with SQL Server 2008. Sparse column data storage is extremely efficient for NULL values. However, the storage requirement for a non-NULL value is increased by up to 4 bytes when the SPARSE column property is used. In the SPARSE column when the column value is NULL for any row in the table, the values require no storage.

Microsoft recommends not using sparse columns unless the percentage of NULL values in a column is high enough that a 20 percent to 40 percent storage savings gain would result. Also this ratio of null values is different for different datatypes. For example for DATETIME data type, 52% of the values must be NULL in order to save 40% in storage, but for the bit data type, 98% must be NULL to save 40% in storage.

248. What are the limitations of a SPARSE column?

Ans:

- Sparse columns cannot have default values, and must accept NULL values
- A computed column cannot be SPARSE
- Sparse columns do not support data compression
- A sparse column cannot be a primary key

249. What are Sparse Column Sets?

Ans:

There is an enhancement for Sparse Columns in 2012 is called Sparse Column Set. A sparse column set gathers all sparse columns into a new column that is similar to a derived or computed column, but with additional functionality; its data can be updated and selected from directly. A column set is calculated based on the sparse columns in a table, and it generates an un-typed XML representation of all sparse columns and values.

250. When we call a database is VLDB (Very Large Data Base)?

Ans:

Usually in an enterprise environment we do call a database as VLDB when it's size > 2 TB.

251. What are the administrative challenges that we need to face when dealing with VLDB?

Ans:

As a DBA we should be very careful in dealing with VLDB and we may need to handle administration activities differently than normal process. Below are the areas where we may need to concentrate in administrating VLDB:

- Index maintenance
- Backups
- Integrity checks
- Archiving/purging data
- Partitioning management
- Disk/disk space management
- Disk performance

252. What are your suggestions in implementing the optimized backup strategy on a VLDB?

Ans:

- Use fast disks to maximize write speed
- Use dedicated drives to avoid I/O contention with user databases or other processes
- Split the backup into different drives which can maximize the storage throughput.

- Use differential backups to reduce the frequency that you run full backups
- Perform partial backups to spread out the backup load
- Back up read-only file groups infrequently and read-write file groups frequently
- Use backup compression to reduce the amount of I/O that has to be written to disk
- When releasing scripts to production, take a snapshot instead of backup

253. What are your suggestions in implementing the optimized index maintenance strategy on a VLDB?

Ans:

- Do not reorganize/rebuild all indexes in database. Do analyse and identify the indexes which needs be maintained on frequent basis.
- Once the frequently fragmented indexes identified remove the fragmentation check and directly implement the rebuild/reorganize operation as fragmentation check itself may take lot of time on VLDB.
- Define the rule for reorganization and rebuild based on fragmentation levels.
- When rebuilding select the suitable process Offline/online
- When reorganizing do not forget to update statistics
- Do maintain indexes at partition level if the table is partitioned.
- Get the benefit from the column-store index
- Never ever allow duplicate or unnecessary indexes

254. We need to perform a DELETE operation on various tables on a VLDB. What are your suggestions to optimize the delete process on huge tables?

Ans:

Delete in chunks: Write your code to delete the required data in chunks which can reduce the pressure on log file and other system resources

Soft Delete: Design your table to make it possible for marking deleted records. So that we can mark all required records as deleted and we can move these deleted records to archive in off-peak hours.

Targeted Deletes: Identify the primary key values for the records to be deleted, store them on a temporary table and then issue the DELETE operation by applying the filter on primary key values. This process can reduce the number of locks issued for delete operation.

Log File Management: Manage the log file by issues the frequent log backups or if it is in simple recovery model issue frequent checkpoints.

Index and Statistics: Always check the fragmentation after deleting the huge records and apply rebuild/reorganize based on fragmentation levels. Also take care of statistics

CHAPTER 12

SQL Server DBA General

Interview Questions and Answers

Introduction: This chapter takes you through the SQL Server DBA general interview questions and answers. These questions are helpful for range of database administrators staring from a junior to an expert level DBA while preparing for a technical interview. These questions and answers are deals with the below topics:

- DBCC
- General
- Snapshots
- Transaction Log
- Shrink
- Boot Page
- XML
- Triggers
- Identity
- DBA Responsibilities
- Database Design

DBCC

1. What are DBCC commands in SQL Server?

Ans:

Microsoft provides a set of SQL Server DBCC Commands originally that stood for Database Consistency Check commands. The DBCC commands are divided into four main categories:

- Status
- Validation
- Maintenance
- Miscellaneous

2. Can you be able to list our one or two commands under each category listed above?

Ans:

Status Commands:

The status commands are the ones you normally run first. With these commands, you can gain an insight into what you're server is doing.

- DBCC Showcontig
- DBCC Show_statistics
- DBCC Opentran
- DBCC Inputbuffer
- DBCC Outputbuffer
- DBCC Proccache
- DBCC Sqlperf
- DBCC Tracestatus
- DBCC Useroptions

Validation Commands:

These are useful when you see problems with the database due to page corruptions, fragmentation etc.

- DBCC Checkdb
- DBCC CheckTable
- DBCC CheckCATALOG
- DBCC CheckConstraints
- DBCC CheckFILEGROUP
- DBCC CheckIdent

Maintenance Commands:

The maintenance commands are the final steps you normally run on a database when you're optimizing the database or fixing a problem.

- DBCC DBreindex
- DBCC Indexdefrag
- DBCC Shrinkdatabase
- DBCC Shrinkfile
- DBCC Updateusage

Miscellaneous Commands:

- DBCC Dllname
- DBCC Help
- DBCC Pintable

- DBCC Traceon
- DBCC ERRORLOG
- DBCC DROPCLEANBUFFERS
- DBCC FLUSHPROCINDB
- DBCC MEMORYSTATUS

3. Can you explain how to use DBCC CHECKDB?

Ans:

Let's take a look at a couple of the more common options to know how to use DBCC CHECKDB in SQL Server. Steps to execute the DBCC CHECKDB:

Step 1:

```
USE MASTER;
GO
DBCC CHECKDB ('TestDB', NOINDEX) WITH NO_INFOMSGS;
```

The command above checks the "TestDB" database but not its indexes. This won't take long at all. The output returned will tell you if there are problems with the database. If so, check to make sure your backup is handy and then you can run the next level of this command. If find any errors in step 1 execution, execute the next level of DBCC command as below.

Step 2:

```
USE MASTER;
GO
ALTER DATABASE TestDB SET SINGLE_USER WITH ROLLBACK IMMEDIATE;
GO
DBCC CHECKDB ('TestDB', REPAIR_FAST) WITH NO_INFOMSGS;
GO
ALTER DATABASE TestDB SET MULTI_USER;
```

This command will attempt to fix errors, but won't allow any data to be lost. If that doesn't work, the next level of the command is in step 3. From 2014/2016 this option is only for backward compatibility. It actually doesn't repair anything.

Step 3:

```
USE MASTER;
GO
ALTER DATABASE TestDB SET SINGLE_USER WITH ROLLBACK IMMEDIATE;
GO
DBCC CHECKDB ('TestDB', REPAIR_REBUILD) WITH NO_INFOMSGS;
GO
```

```
ALTER DATABASE TestDB SET MULTI_USER;
GO
```

It performs repairs that have no possibility of data loss. This can include quick repairs, such as repairing missing rows in non-clustered indexes, and more time-consuming repairs, such as rebuilding an index. The next level of this command will potentially lose data. Now execute the below DBCC command as a last and final repair trail.

Step 4:

```
USE MASTER;
GO
ALTER DATABASE TestDB SET SINGLE_USER WITH ROLLBACK IMMEDIATE;
GO
DBCC CHECKDB ('TestDB', REPAIR_ALLOW_DATA_LOSS) WITH NO_
INFOMSGS;
GO
ALTER DATABASE TestDB SET MULTI_USER;
```

As you can probably guess, this command could potentially lose data or make your applications unusable.

Info:

Use the REPAIR options only as a last resort. To repair errors, we recommend restoring from a backup. If you must use REPAIR, run DBCC CHECKDB without a repair option to find the repair level to use. If you use the REPAIR_ALLOW_DATA_LOSS level, we recommend that you back up the database before you run DBCC CHECKDB with this option.

Note: If we want to repair the database the database should be in single user mode.

4. How to know the estimated TEMPDB space required for running CHECKDB command?

Ans:

Below command calculates the amount of space in "TEMPDB" required to run DBCC CHECKDB statement. However, the actual statement isn't executed.

```
DBCC CHECKDB ('TestDB') WITH NO_INFOMSGS, ESTIMATEONLY
```

Sample Output:

```
Estimated TEMPDB space (in KB) needed for CHECKDB on database TestDB = 6291456.
```

5. How to fast up the DBCC CHECKDB execution process?

Ans:

The below command forces to obtain an exclusive lock on database which makes bit faster the process.

```
DBCC CHECKDB ('TestDB') WITH NO_INFOMSGS, TABLOCK
```

6. What is PHYSICAL_ONLY option in DBCC CHECKDB?

Ans:

This command limits the checking to the integrity of the physical structure of the page and record headers, but it can also detect torn pages, checksum failures, and common hardware failures. Using the PHYSICAL_ONLY option may cause a much shorter run-time for DBCC CHECKDB on large databases and is recommended for frequent use on production systems. Specifying PHYSICAL_ONLY causes DBCC CHECKDB to skip all checks of FILESTREAM data.

```
DBCC CHECKDB ('TestDB') WITH NO_INFOMSGS, PHYSICAL_ONLY
```

7. How to check data purity using DBCC CHECKDB?

Ans:

Below command causes DBCC CHECKDB to check the database for column values that are not valid or out-of-range. For example, DBCC CHECKDB detects columns with date and time values that are larger than or less than the acceptable range for the DATETIME data type; limits the checking to the integrity of the physical structure of the page and record

```
DBCC CHECKDB ('TestDB') WITH NO_INFOMSGS, DATA_PURITY
```

8. Have you ever used the option "EXTENDED_LOGICAL_CHECKS" in DBCC CHECKDB?

Ans:

Yes! When we mention the (EXTENDED_LOGICAL_CHECKS) option in DBCC CHECKDB If the compatibility level is 100 (SQL Server 2008) or higher, performs logical consistency checks on an indexed view, XML indexes, and spatial indexes, where present.

9. I am writing a stored procedure which we are going to schedule for database maintenance for one of the premium database. We have included DBCC CHECKDB also we have two major transactional tables for which we wanted to perform DBCC CHECKTABLE from the same procedure. Can we run both DBCC statements?

Ans:

No! Not required. Let me explain what DBCC CHECKDB validates on a database:

- Running DBCC CHECKDB internally runs DBCC CHECKALLOC + DBCC CHECKTABLE + DBCC CHECKCATALOG on the database
- Validates the contents of every indexed view in the database
- Validates link-level consistency between table metadata and file system directories and files when storing VARBINARY(max) data in the file system using FILESTREAM
- Validates the Service Broker data in the database

10. We are using In-Memory feature for one of our production database. The database contains memory-optimized tables. Can we run DBCC CHECKDB on this database? Does it support?

Ans:

Yes!

- DBCC CHECKDB is supported on databases that contain memory-optimized tables but validation only occurs on disk-based tables.
- However, as part of database backup and recovery, a CHECKSUM validation is done for files in memory-optimized FILEGROUPS.
- Since DBCC repair options are not available for memory-optimized tables, you must back up your databases regularly and test the backups.

11. What are the most commonly used DBCC commands?

Ans:

People who started working on SQL Server from 2000/2005 can know the value of DBCC commands. Starting from 2008/2012/2014/2016 there are lot of changes happened and SQL Server team introduced alternatives for DBCC commands. For example for INDEX related operations now we can use ALTER INDEX statements. However still we get benefit from DBCC commands for the quick results. Here is the list of most commonly used DBCC commands.

DBCC SHOWCONTIG:

DBCC SHOWCONTIG shows how fragmented a table, view or index is. Fragmentation is the non-contiguous placement of data. Just like a hard drive, it's often the cause of the slowness of a system.

Syntax: DBCC SHOWCONTIG (table/View/Index Name)

Example: DBCC SHOWCONTIG (Test)

Output:

DBCC SHOWCONTIG scanning 'Test' table…

Table: 'Test' (1474104292); index ID: 1, database ID: 17

TABLE level scan performed.

– Pages Scanned…………………………..: 126

– Extents Scanned…………………………: 29

– Extent Switches…………………………: 66

– Avg. Pages per Extent……………………: 4.3

– Scan Density [Best Count:Actual Count]…….: 23.88% [16:67]

– Logical Scan Fragmentation ………………: 62.70%

– Extent Scan Fragmentation ……………….: 89.66%

– Avg. Bytes Free per Page…………………: 1673.2

– Avg. Page Density (full)…………………: 79.33%

DBCC execution completed. If DBCC printed error messages, contact your system administrator.

Observation: The most telling piece of information is the "Scan Density." The closer this number is to 100, the more contiguous the data.

DBCC OPENTRAN:

It displays information about the oldest active transaction and the oldest distributed and non-distributed replicated transactions, if any, within the specified database.

Syntax: DBCC OPENTRAN (Database Name)

Example: DBCC OPENTRAN (TestDB) WITHNO_INFOMSGS

Observation: We can get the transaction opened time and id so that we can capture as much as information required using DMV's or other DBCC commands and we can take the action.

DBCC INPUTBUFFER:

It displays the last statement sent from a client to an instance of Microsoft SQL Server.

Syntax: DBCC INPUTBUFFER (SessionID/RequestID)

Example: DBCC INPUTBUFFER (97) WITHNO_INFOMSGS

Observation: It returns the latest statement executed from the session 97. But there is a limitation for the text return by this command. It returns only the first 4000 characters. But people who started their career after SQL Server 2008 may habituate to use DMV's to get input-buffer query.

DBCC SQLPERF:

It provides transaction log space usage statistics for all databases. It can also be used to reset wait and latch statistics.

Syntax: DBCC SQLPERF

([LOGSPACE]/["sys.dm_os_latch_stats", CLEAR]/["sys.dm_os_wait_stats", CLEAR])

[WITH NO_INFOMSGS]

Example: DBCC SQLPERF (LOGSPACE) WITHNO_INFOMSGS

Observation: The following example displays LOGSPACE information for all databases from the current SQL Server instance.

DBCC USEROPTIONS:

It returns the active SET options (Ex: SET NOCOUNT ON) for the current connection. Along with that it also displays "Date Format," "Isolation Level" etc.

Syntax: DBCC USEROPTIONS

Example: DBCC USEROPTIONS

Info: We can see the all set options for the current connection.

DBCC CHECKDB:

It's one of the most widely used DBCC commands. This command has two purposes: To check a database consistency, and to correct it.

Syntax: DBCC CHECKDB ('<DBName>',

[NOINDEX |

REPAIR_FAST |

REPAIR_REBUILD |

REPAIR_ALLOW_DATA_LOSS]) WITHNO_INFOMSGS

NOINDEX: Checks only database and no impact on indexes

REPAIR_FAST: It tries to repair errors without any data loss. But in 2014 and 2016 it is deprecated

REPAIR_REBUILD: Performs repairs that have no possibility of data loss. This can include quick repairs, such as repairing missing rows in non-clustered indexes, and more time-consuming repairs, such as rebuilding an index.

REPAIR_ALLOW_DATA_LOSS: It tries to repair all possible errors but it can cause data loss.

DBCC CHECKIDENT:

Checks the current identity value for the specified table and, if it is needed, changes the identity value. You can also use DBCC CHECKIDENT to manually set a new current identity value for the identity column. We usually use this command when TRUNACTE table and need to reset the identity column back to its initial value.

Syntax: DBCC CHECKIDENT (<table_name>, NORESEED/RESEED, new_reseed_value)

WITH NO_INFOMSGS

Example:

DBCC CHECKIDENT (TestTab) – Checks current identity value

DBCC CHECKIDENT (TestTab, NORESEED) – Identity value shouldn't be changed

DBCC CHECKIDENT (TestTab, RESEED, 0) – Identity value reset to 0

Observation: The specific corrections made to the current identity value depend on the parameter specifications. We have two more functions which help us to find the seed and incremental values for a table or a view:

SELECT IDENT_SEED('MemberDetails')

SELECT IDENT_INCR('MemberDetails')

General

12. What are the ports used in SQL Server?

Ans:

SQL Server Default Instance: TCP 1433

Dedicated Admin Connection: TCP 1434

SQL Server Browser Service: UDP 1434

SQL Server instance running over an HTTP endpoint: TCP: 80

SQL Server instance running over an HTTPS endpoint: TCP: 443

Service Broker: TCP 4022

Transact-SQL debugger: TCP: 135

Analysis Services Default Instance: TCP 2283

Analysis Services Configured for HTTP: TCP 80

Analysis Services Configured for HTTPS: TCP 443

Reporting Services Configured for HTTP: TCP 80

Reporting Services Configured for HTTPS: TCP 443

Integration Services Runtime Uses MS RPC: TCP 135

Microsoft Distributed Transaction Coordinator: TCP 135

IPsec traffic: UDP: 500 and UDP: 4500

13. What are the most common issues a SQL DBA should deal with as a part of DBA daily job?

Ans:

- Backup Failure
- Restore Failure
- Log Full Issues
- Blocking Alerts
- Deadlocks Alerts
- TEMPDB full issues
- Disk Full Issues
- SQL Connectivity Issues
- Access issues
- Installation and Upgrade Failures
- SQL Agent Job failures
- Performance Issues
- Resource (Memory/IO/CPU etc.) Utilization Alerts
- High-Availability and Disaster Recovery related issues

14. How to recover a database that is in suspect stage?

Ans:

- ALTER DATABASE test_db SET EMERGENCY
- After you execute this statement SQL Server will shut-down the database and restart it without recovering it. This will allow you to view/query database objects, but the database will be in read-only mode. Any attempt to modify data will result in an error similar to the following:

  Msg 3908, Level 16, State 1, Line 1 Could not run BEGIN TRANSACTION in database 'test' .....Etc.
- Now set the database in single user mode

  ALTER DATABASE test SET SINGLE_USER

  GO
- Execute DBCC CHECKDB

  DBCC CHECKDB ('test', REPAIR_ALLOW_DATA_LOSS) GO

If DBCC CHECKDB statement above succeeds the database is brought back online (but you'll have to place it in multi-user mode before your users can connect to it). Before you turn the database over to your users you should run other statements to ensure its transactional consistency. If DBCC CHECKDB fails then there is no way to repair the database - you must restore it from a backup.

15. What is your approach in AUTO_GROWTH option while creating a new database?

Ans:

Auto Growth setting plays a vital role from the database performance prospective. There are two things we should handle.

File Growth (In Percent/In MB)

Maximum File Size (Restricted/Unrestricted)

Remember below points while setting Auto Growth option:

- Auto grow (Additional space will be allocated to database) happens when database is out of space. Most likely this new space will not be physically right next to the existing space, means it allocates space on somewhere on available disk which leads to a physical fragmentation.
- Pre-Size your database and establish appropriate auto-growth settings for your databases based on their growth profile.
- Minimize future auto-growth events by monitoring the growth of your databases, and re-establishing auto-growth settings when a database growth profile changes.
- Monitor auto-growth events so you can be alerted when your databases grow.
- Consider defragmenting your database file system if you have let your auto-growth run wild.

16. "model" system DB is down and we are trying to create a new database. Is it possible to create a new database when model DB is down?

Ans:

We can't create a new database when model database is down

SQL Server restart will be unsuccessful when model database is down as TEMPDB creation failed. TEMPDB is created based on model DB configurations, since model DB is down TEMPDB will not be created.

17. Which operation is faster COMMIT or ROLLBACK? Why?

Ans:

It's obviously COMMIT is faster than ROLLBACK. Let me explain with an example:

Let's say we opened a transaction and updated 8000 records:

Commit: It's completed quickly as the operation is already completed and it just marks those dirty pages as committed and when checkpoint happens all those dirty pages will be written to disk.

Rollback: The operation is already updated 8000 records if we need to rollback then again all these updates has to be rolled back which means there are another 8000 log records will be written to LDF which will take time when compared to commit.

18. What are the different ways to know when your SQL Server Last restarted?

Ans:

- Using T-SQL Script:
  - ✓ SELECT sqlserver_start_time FROM sys.dm_os_sys_info;
  - ✓ SELECT login_time FROM sys.dm_exec_sessions WHERE session_id = 1;
  - ✓ SELECT start_time FROM sys.traces where is_default = 1
  - ✓ SELECT crdate FROM sysdatabases WHERE name='TEMPDB'
  - ✓ SELECT create_date FROM sys.databases WHERE name = 'TEMPDB'
- From SQL Server ERRORLOG
- SQL Server Instance Reports à Server Reports à Server Dashboard
- From Windows Event Viewer

19. You got an alert by saying that a SQL Agent job has been failed on one of the server. You need to find the root cause. What is approach?

Ans:

There are certain things we need to quickly check when a job failed:

- Job History
- SQL Server Error Log
- Log file – If you configure any log file at Job Step advanced properties
- Window Event Log
- Job Execution Time Delta – Time Difference between the current and last execution

The above checklist will give you maximum information that causes the job failure. To do further RCA, note down the job execution time and capture below details in that particular time period:

- CPU usage
- Memory usage
- I/O usage
- Blocking and Deadlocks if any
- Any dump file created
- Log full issues if any
- Any other suspecting errors

20. We have a SQL Server 2014 default instance is available on Windows Server 2012 R2. We used to access this by using IP address and the port 1433. Now as client required

we have installed a named instance on the same host. Do we need to enable SQL Browser Service? Is it mandatory to access named instance?

Ans:

Not exactly! Browser service is actually to redirect the client request to the correct named instance when our named instance is using dynamic port. If you configure your named instance to use a static port then the redirection is automatically taken care and no SQL Browser service needs to be enabled.

21. What is the quickest way to get SQL Server memory usage?

Ans:

DBCC MEMORY STATUS

22. Can you be able to explain how to analyse the result from DBCC MEMORYSTATUS?

Ans:

It gives as much as memory usage information based on object wise/component wise. First table gives us the complete details of server and process memory usage details and memory alert indicators. We can also get memory usage by buffer cache, Service Broker, Temp tables, Procedure Cache, Full Text, XML, Memory Pool Manager Etc.

23. How can we check whether the port number is connecting or not on a Server?

Ans:

TELNET <HOSTNAME> PORTNUMBER

TELNET TESTPRODSERVER 1433

TELNET TESTPRODSERVER 443

24. Start SQL Server in different modes?

Ans:

Single User Mode (-m): sqlcmd –m –d master –S PAXT3DEVSQL11 –c –U sa –P *******

DAC (-A): sqlcmd –A –d master –S PAXT3DEVSQL11 –c –U sa –P *******

Emergency: ALTER DATABASE test_db SET EMERGENCY

25. SQL Server is not responding. What is action plan?

Ans:

Connect using DAC via CMD or SSMS

Connect via CMD:

SQLCMD -A –U myadminlogin –P mypassword -SMyServer –dmaster

Once you connect to the master database run the diagnostic quires to find the problem

Correct the issue and restart the server

Find the errors from SQL log using:

SQLCMD –A –SmyServer –q"Exec XP_READERRORLOG" –o"C:\logout.txt"

A long running query blocking all processes and not allowing new connections:

Write a query and put the script file on hard disk Ex: D:\Scripts\BlockingQuery.sql

```
use master;
select p.spid, t.text
from sysprocesses p
CROSS APPLY sys.dm_exec_sql_text (sql_handle) t
where p.blocked = 0
and p.spid in
( select p1.blocked
from sysprocesses p1
where p1.blocked > 0
and p1.waittime > 50 )
```

From command prompt run the script on SQL Server and get the result to a text file

SQLCMD -A - SMyServer -i"C:\SQLScripts\GetBlockers.sql" o"C:\SQLScripts\blockers.txt"

Recently added some data files to temp DB and after that SQL Server is not responding:

This can occur when you specify new files in a directory to which the SQL Server service account does not have access.

Start the SQL Server in minimal configuration mode using the STARTUP parameter "–f." When we specify –f the SQL Server creates new TEMPDB files at default file locations and ignore the current TEMPDB data files configuration. Take care when using –f as it keep the server in single user mode.

Once the server is started change the TEMPDB configuration settings and restart the server in full mode by removing the flag -f

A database stays in a SUSPECT or RECOVERY_PENDING State:

Try to resolve this using CHECKDB and any other DBCC commands if you can.

Last and final option is put the DB in emergency mode and run CHECKDB with repair_allow_data_loss

(Note: Try to avoid this unless you don't have any option as you may lose large amounts of data)

26. What are the different log files and how to access it?

Ans:

- *SQL Server Error Log:* The Error Log, the most important log file, is used to troubleshoot system problems. SQL Server retains backups of the previous six logs, naming each archived log file sequentially. The current error log file is named ERRORLOG. To view the error log, which is located in the %Program-Files%\Microsoft SQL Server\MSSQL.1\MSSQL\LOG\ERRORLOG directory, open SSMS, expand a server node, expand Management, and click SQL Server Logs

- *SQL Server Agent Log:* SQL Server's job scheduling subsystem, SQL Server Agent, maintains a set of log files with warning and error messages about the jobs it has run, written to the %ProgramFiles%\Microsoft SQL Server\MSSQL.1\MSSQL\LOG directory. SQL Server will maintain up to nine SQL Server Agent error log files. The current log file is named SQLAGENT.OUT, whereas archived files are numbered sequentially. You can view SQL Server Agent logs by using SQL Server Management Studio (SSMS). Expand a server node, expand Management, click SQL Server Logs, and select the check box for SQL Server Agent.
- *Windows Event Log:* An important source of information for troubleshooting SQL Server errors, the Windows Event log contains three useful logs. The application log records events in SQL Server and SQL Server Agent and can be used by SQL Server Integration Services (SSIS) packages. The security log records authentication information, and the system log records service STARTUP and shutdown information. To view the Windows Event log, go to Administrative Tools, Event Viewer.
- *SQL Server Setup Log:* You might already be familiar with the SQL Server Setup log, which is located at %ProgramFiles%\Microsoft SQL Server\90\Setup Bootstrap\LOG\Summary.txt. If the summary.txt log file shows a component failure, you can investigate the root cause by looking at the component's log, which you'll find in the %Program-Files%\Microsoft SQL Server\90\Setup Bootstrap\LOG\Files directory.
- *SQL Server Profiler Log:* SQL Server Profiler, the primary application-tracing tool in SQL Server, captures the system's current database activity and writes it to a file for later analysis. You can find the Profiler logs in the log .trc file in the %ProgramFiles%\Microsoft SQL Server\MSSQL.1\MSSQL\LOG directory.

27. Explain XP_READERRORLOG or SP_READERRORLOG

Ans:

XP_READERRORLOG or sp_readERRORLOG has 7 parameters.

XP_READERRORLOG <Log_FileNo>,<Log_Type>,<Keyword-1>,<Keyword-2>, <Date1>,<Date2>,<'Asc'/'Desc'>

Log_FileNo: -1: All logs

0: Current log file

1: No1 archived log file etc.

Log_Type: 1: SQL Server

2: SQL Agent

KeyWord-1: Search for the keyword

KeyWord-2: Search for combination of Keyword 1 and Keyword 2

Date1 and Date2: Retrieves data between these two dates

'Asc'/'Desc': Order the data

Examples:

EXEC XP_READERRORLOG 0 -- Current SQL Server log

EXEC XP_READERRORLOG 0, 1 -- Current SQL Server log

EXEC XP_READERRORLOG 0, 2 -- Current SQL Agent log

EXEC XP_READERRORLOG -1 -- Entire log file

EXEC XP_READERRORLOG 0, 1, 'dbcc' -- Current SQL Server log with dbcc in the string

EXEC XP_READERRORLOG 1, 1, 'dbcc', 'error' -- Archived 1 SQL Server log with DBCC and error in the string

EXEC XP_READERRORLOG -1, 1, 'dbcc', 'error', '2012-02-21', '2012-02-22','desc'

--Search entire SQL Server log file for string 'dbcc' and 'Error' within the given dates and retrieves in descending order.

28. What is the common trace flags used with SQL Server?

Ans:

Deadlock Information:	1204, 1205, 1222
Network Database files:	1807
Log Record for Connections:	4013
Skip STARTUP Stored Procedures:	4022
Disable Locking Hints:	8755
Forces uniform extent allocations instead of mixed page allocations	1118
(SQL 2005 and 2008) To reduces TEMPDB contention.	
To disable Lock escalation	1211
To disable lock escalation only when no memory pressure	1224

29. Do you know about Resource Database?

Ans:

All sys objects are physically stored in resource database and logically available on every database. Resource database can faster the service packs or upgrades

30. Really does resource faster the upgrades? Can you justify?

Ans:

- Yes, in earlier versions upgrades requires dropping and recreating system objects now an upgrade requires a copy of the resource file.
- We are also capable of rollback the process, because it just needs to overwrite the existing with the older version resource copy.

31. Any idea what is the Resource DB MDF and LDF file names?

Ans:

- mssqlsystemresource.MDF and
- mssqlsystemresource.LDF

32. How many data files I can put in TEMPDB? What is the effect of adding multiple data files?

Ans:

By far, the most effective configuration is to set TEMPDB on its own separate fast drive away from the user databases. I would set the number of files based on # of cpu's divided by 2. So, if you have 8 cpu's, then set 4 TEMPDB files. Set the TEMPDB large enough with 10% data growth. I would start at a general size of 10 GB for each size. I also would not create more than 4 files for each MDF/LDF even if there were more than 8 CPU. You can always add more lately.

Remember all files should be of the same size as database engine follows round robin algorithm to allocate space for a new object in TEMPDB. It finds the file based on the space occupied and chooses the least occupied.

33. Have you ever used COUNT_BIG (*)?

Ans:

Count (*) returns INT whereas COUNT_BIG (*) returns BIGINT

34. What is throw option in exception handling?

Ans:

- THROW is simple to use than RAISEERROR.
- When using THROW once error THROWN next statements will not be executed where as in RAISEERROR next statements will be executed.
- With THROW we can get the correct error number and line number
- We can simply THROW user defined error messages using THROW where as to use user defined message in RASIEERROR first that message has to be added to sys.messages using SP_ADDMESSAGE

35. What is NVARCHAR data type?

Ans:

We use NVARCHAR to store data for UNICODE characters (Korean, Japanese, Arabic etc.)

36. Can you be able to create a partition on Heap?

Ans:

Yes we can create partition on a Heap.

37. What are the different ways available to insert data from a file into SQL Server database table?

Ans:

These are the different ways:

- BCP
- BULKINSERT
- OPENROWSET
- OPENDATASOURCE
- OPENQUERY
- LINKED SERVER
- IMPORT/EXPORT WIZARD
- SSIS

Now let me explain each in detail:

BCP:

- BCP Stands for Bulk copy
- Mostly used for import/export text files
- Can be used from Windows Command Prompt or in SSMS using XP_CMDSHELL
- It can also be useful for generating the file format in XML format
- Ex: Import data from C:\Temp\emp.txt into a table dbo.emp
- C:\>bcp dbo.emp in 'C:\Temp\emp.txt ' -T –S serverName\instanceName

BULK INSERT:

- A T-SQL statement that imports data directly from a data file into a database table or non-partitioned view.
- This can only import the data from files to SQL Server
- It doesn't support data export from SQL Server to a file
- We can provide the file format along with the data file so it can handle the data conversion part
- Ex: BULK INSERT dbo.emp FROM 'C:\Temp\emp.txt'
- WITH (FIELDTERMINATOR =',', FIRSTROW = 2)

OPENROWSET:

- T-SQL command that allows you to query data from other data sources directly from within SQL Server.
- This can only import the data from other data sources ex: Excel File
- OPENROWSET function can also be referenced as the target table of an INSERT, UPDATE, or DELETE statement,

- We can provide the file format along with the data file so it can handle the data conversion part
- We can use SQL statements for pulling data thereof there is more flexibility in applying filters and selecting the required data.
- Ex: INSERT INTO dbo.Emp

  SELECT * FROM OPENROWSET ('Microsoft.Jet.OLEDB.4.0',

  'Excel 8.0;Database= C:\Temp\emp.xls', 'SELECT * FROM [Sheet2$]')

OPENDATASOURCE

T-SQL command that allows you to query data from other data sources directly from within SQL Server.

This is similar to the OPENROWSET command.

Ad Hoc Distributed Queries advanced configuration option should be enabled.

We can use in SELECT, INSERT, UPDATE AND DELETE statements

We can execute a remote stored procedure using OPENDATASOURCE

Ex: We can directly query a table "Employee" from other SQL Server instance "SQL2012EP"

SELECT * FROM OPENDATASOURCE('SQLNCLI',

'Data Source=SQL2012EP;Integrated Security=SSPI')

.AdventureWorks2012.HumanResources.Employee

OPENQUERY:

- OPENQUERY can be referenced in the FROM clause of a query as if it were a table name. OPENQUERY can also be referenced as the target table of an INSERT, UPDATE, or DELETE statement.
- OPENROWSET requires a linked server to be created to the target data source.
- Ex: Linked Server "OracleSvr" is created to an Oracle instance to insert data into a table in Oracle from SQL Server

  INSERT OPENQUERY (OracleSvr, 'SELECT name FROM joe.titles') VALUES ('Sr Engineer);

  Update a table in Oracle using OPENROWSET

  UPDATE OPENQUERY (OracleSvr, 'SELECT name FROM joe.titles WHERE id = 101') SET name = 'Sr.Engineer';

LINKED SERVER:

- Link with the other datasource and directly refer the remote objects in local queries.
- We can directly use the remote objects by referring the four part name
- "LinkedServer.Database.Schema.Object"
- We can create a linked server to ODBC Data source, MS Excel, MS Access, File System, OLEDB Data Source, Other SQL Server, Oracle 8.0 and above, IBM DB2, Azure SQL Database.

```
Ex: EXEC sp_addlinkedserver 'EmpExcel',
'Jet 4.0', 'Microsoft.Jet.OLEDB.4.0',
'C:\Temp\Emp.xls',
NULL,
'Excel 8.0'
GO
INSERT INTO dbo.Emp SELECT * FROM EmpExcel...Sheet2$
```

IMPORT/EXPORT WIZARD: Native tool for data imports/exports.

SSIS PACKAGE: We can build an ETL package for data transformation between data sources using SQL Server Integration Services.

38. Have you ever faced any issues with Date functions? Can you tell me a recent one?

Ans:

Yes! We had a requirement that we need to capture a time in mille seconds and need to add to the given date. When we tried it with DATEADD:

```
DATEADD (MS,(Time_In_ms),@Date);
```

It was failing with the error "Arithmetic overflow error converting expression to data type int."

When investigated the problem is with DATEADD function it accepts "Increment" value in INT where as in our procedure it's Bigint.

Then we have converted it into Hours and the problem got resolved.

39. What are the limitations in view?

Ans:

Order by doesn't work:

Msg 1033, Level 15, State 1, Procedure vw_ViewLimit1, Line 5

The ORDER BY clause is invalid in views, inline functions, derived tables, subqueries, and common table expressions, unless TOP or FOR XML is specified.

Index cannot be created on view when it contains "Union":

Msg 10116, Level 16, State 1, Line 1

Cannot create index on view 'TEMPDB.dbo.SampleView' because it contains one or more UNION, INTERSECT, or EXCEPT operators. Consider creating a separate indexed view for each query that is an input to the UNION, INTERSECT, or EXCEPT operators of the original view.

SELECT * and Adding Column Issue in View:

Sometimes the column may not reflect in view. For this we have to run "sp_refreshview" explicitly

40. What is the difference between Deterministic and non- Deterministic functions?

Ans:

Deterministic functions: always returns the same output result all the time it is executed for same input values. I.e. ABS, DATEDIFF, ISNULL etc.

Nondeterministic functions: may return different results each time they are executed. i.e. NEWID, RAND, @@CPU_BUSY etc. Functions that call extended stored procedures are nondeterministic.

41. Can you tell me few T-SQL commands with SQL Server that you have used in SQL Server 2008 and above and what value do they offer?

Ans:

- *ROW_NUMBER ()* - Means to page through a result set and only return the needed portion of the result set
- *EXCEPT* - The final result set where data exists in the first dataset and not in the second dataset
- *INTERSECT* - The final result set where values in both of the tables match
- *PIVOT\UNPIVOT* - Expression to flip rows to columns or vice versa to provide the cross tab result sets.
- *Synonyms* - Alias to an object (table, stored procedure, function, view) to maintain the original object and refer to the new object as well
- *TOP (@n)* – We do not have the top n clause in 2000. If we have to do this we had to where as in 2005 we can directly specify like

  SELECT TOP(@n) FROM <TableName>
- *Cross/Outer Apply* – UDF's can be used in sub quires
- *RANK ()* – Rank function is similar to the ROW Number function, the key difference between them been that, rows with tied value will receive the same Rank Value.
- *DENSE_RANK ()* - the difference between RANK and DENSE_RANK been that it returns results without gaps in the rank values.
- *NTILE ()* - NTILE divides the result set into a specified number of groups based on the ordering and optional partition.
- *Output Clause* - The Output Clause returns information about each row affected by an INSERT, UPDATE, or DELETE statement. The results can be used for audit purpose by inserting the data into a table.
- *Error Handling (Try – Catch- Throw)* – Error handling has been improved we can use try catch block and Throw to handle errors instead of @@Error.
- *TABLESAMPLE Clause* - Limits the number of rows returned from a table in the FROM clause to a Sample number or percent of rows. TABLESAMPLE clause can be beneficial in situations where only a sampling of rows is necessary for the application instead of full result set.

42. What is an Output clause?

Ans:

An awesome feature added to T-SQL. We can trace the output of an operation (Just like magic tables work in triggers).

Using this clause we can trace the values before Insert/Update/Delete and after insert/Delete/ Update operation.

Example:

UPDATE:

```
UPDATE TOP (10) HumanResources.Employee
SET VacationHours = VacationHours * 1.25, ModifiedDate = GETDATE()
OUTPUT inserted.BusinessEntityID,
deleted.VacationHours,
        inserted.VacationHours,
        inserted.ModifiedDate
INTO @MyTableVar;
```

DELETE:

```
DELETE Sales.ShoppingCartItem
OUTPUT DELETED.*
WHERE ShoppingCartID = 20621;
```

INSERT:

```
INSERT Production.ScrapReason
OUTPUT INSERTED.ScrapReasonID, INSERTED.Name, INSERTED.ModifiedDate
INTO @MyTableVar
VALUES (N'Operator error', GETDATE());
```

43. How can we avoid cursors?

Ans:

- Temporary tables with Identity Column
- Temporary tables without identity column

In some cases we may not be able to create an identity column in temp table. Populate temp table with the data and create an index on the table with fill factor 100%. Use top clause to row by row processing and delete each row after performing the operation (Condition: @@ rowcount>0)

44. How change data capture works?

Ans:

- Log serves as a source for capturing the change data.
- First the CDC should be enabled to the database – sys.cdc_enable_db
- We need to enable the CDC for required table – sys.cdc_enable_table
- All CDC enabled tables/indexes details can be retrieve - sys.sp_cdc_help_change_data_ capture.

- All CDC objects are stored in the database once you enable the CDC. Objects are stored under the change data capture schema.
- All change data is retrieved and stored in change table. Each table that enabled CDC is having a corresponding change table
- From the change table we can find the change data using columns like _$start_lsn indicates the starting of a transaction and _$seqval (Order of the operations) and _$Operation (1=Delete,2=Insert,3=Update Before image 4= Update after image).
- Two jobs are created when you enable CDC to a database.
  - ✓ *CDC-Capture job:* When the first table enabled in the database and not Transactional replication is enabled and running for that database. If TRAN repl is enabled then replication log reader agent will take care of populating the change table. The job simply called the sp_replcmds to populate the change table and continuously running (Can scan 1000 transaction per 5 seconds) as transactional replication.
  - ✓ *CDC-Cleanup job:* When the database is enabled for CDC. This job runs daily at 2 A.M. It retains change table entries for 4320 minutes or 3 days, removing a maximum of 5000 entries with a single delete statement.

45. What is the difference between Temp tables and Derived tables?

Ans:

- In Temp tables, Explicit Indexing and Constraints are allowed. there is no need to create or declare, we can use the INTO clause to create this object and it is Recommended when the data is huge & if there is any manipulation on the result
- In Derived tables, Explicit Indexing and Constraints are not Applicable and this can be used only on the current query and it is recommended for inline quires. We cannot update derived table in SQL 2000 where as it can be done from 2005 and above versions.

46. What is the difference between Table variables and temporary tables?

Ans:

- Temporary Tables are real tables so you can do things like CREATE Indexes, etc. If you have large amounts of data for which accessing by index will be faster than temporary tables are a good option.
- Table variables can have indexes by using PRIMARY KEY or UNIQUE constraints. (If you want a non-unique index just include the primary key column as the last column in the unique constraint. If you don't have a unique column, you can use an identity column.). Remember we can create indexes on table variables but there is no use as statistics can't be considered by optimizer while building the execution plan.
- Table variables don't participate in transactions, logging or locking. This means they're faster as they don't require the overhead, but conversely you don't get those features. So for instance if you want to ROLLBACK midway through a procedure then table variables populated during that transaction will still be populated!

- Table variables and temp tables both use TEMPDB. When we have a very small number of rows then the table variable will almost always be faster. If your result set is very large, then you probably want to use a temp table.
- We cannot use Tables Variables in dynamic quires as validation failed in compilation phase.

47. What is the scope of different temp objects?

Ans:

Local Temp Table: "CREATE TABLE #TempTable"

Local temporary tables are visible only in the current session, and can be shared between nested stored procedure calls

Table Variable: "DECLARE TABLE @TempTable"

The scope of a local variable is the batch, stored procedure, or statement block in which it is declared. They can be passed as parameters between procedures. They are not subject to transactions and will retain all rows following a rollback.

Derived Table: "SELECT * FROM (SELECT * FROM Customers) AS TempTable"

is visible to the current query only

Global Temp Table: "CREATE TABLE ##TempTable"

This differs from a #temp table in that it is visible to all processes. When the creating process ends, the table is removed (but will wait until any current activity from other processes is done).

CTE: Common Table Expression

```
Example CTE:
;WITH YourBigCTE AS
(
big query here
)
SELECT * FROM YourTable1 WHERE ID IN (SELECT ID FROM YourBigCTE)
UNION
SELECT * FROM YourTable2 WHERE ID IN (SELECT ID FROM YourBigCTE)
```

Scope is next immediate select command. Can be used multiple times within the same CTE command, even recursively, and will last for the duration of the CTE command.

48. Can you give me an example of CTE?

Ans:

```
USE AdventureWorks2008R2;
GO
-- Define the CTE expression name and column list.
;WITH Sales_CTE (SalesPersonID, SalesOrderID, SalesYear)
AS
```

```
-- Define the CTE query.
(
SELECT SalesPersonID, SalesOrderID, YEAR (OrderDate) AS SalesYear
FROM Sales.SalesOrderHeader
WHERE SalesPersonID IS NOT NULL
)
-- Define the outer query referencing the CTE name.
SELECT SalesPersonID, COUNT (SalesOrderID) AS TotalSales, SalesYear
FROM Sales_CTE
GROUP BY SalesYear, SalesPersonID
ORDER BY SalesPersonID, SalesYear;
GO
```

49. Please explain MERGER clause in T-SQL?

Ans:

Here is the scenario

- Delete the records whose marks are more than 250.
- Update marks and add 25 to each as internals if records exist.
- Insert the records if record does not exist.

```
MERGE StudentTotalMarks AS stm
USING (SELECT StudentID,StudentName FROM StudentDetails) AS sd
ON stm.StudentID = sd.StudentID
WHEN MATCHED AND stm.StudentMarks > 250 THEN DELETE
WHEN MATCHED THEN UPDATE SET stm.StudentMarks = stm.StudentMarks + 25
WHEN NOT MATCHED THEN
INSERT(StudentID,StudentMarks) VALUES(sd.StudentID,25);
GO
```

There are two very important points to remember while using MERGE statement.

- Semicolon is mandatory after the merge statement.
- When there is a MATCH clause used along with some condition, it has to be specified first amongst all other WHEN MATCH clause.

50. What are the different types of UDF's?

Ans:

There are three types:

Scalar UDF: Scalar UDFs return a single value. They are similar to built-in functions such as DB_NAME ()

Table Valued UDF:

- ***Inline Table Valued UDF:*** In-line UDFs return a single row or multiple rows and can contain a single SELECT statement
- ***Multi Table Valued UDF:*** Finally, the multi-statement UDFs can contain any number of statements that populate the table variable to be returned. Notice that although you can use INSERT, UPDATE, and DELETE statements against the table variable being returned, a function cannot modify data in permanent tables. Multi-statement UDFs come in handy when you need to return a set of rows

51. How to change the collation of a server and then database?

Ans:

To change the running/production server collation:

- Export data from existing databases.
- Drop all user databases
- Rebuild the master database specifying the new collation in the SQLCOLLATION property of the **setup** command. For example:

  Setup/QUIET/ACTION=REBUILDDATABASE/
  INSTANCENAME=InstanceName/SQLSYSADMINACCOUNTS=accounts/[
  SAPWD= StrongPassword]/SQLCOLLATION=CollationName

We can choose the collation configuration while installing SQL Server:

- We can view the current collation setting using
- SELECT collation_name FROM sys.databases

52. How to pass Table as a parameter to a stored procedure?

Ans:

We need User Defined TABLE type.

```
CREATE TYPE ItemInfo AS TABLE
(ItemNumber VARCHAR (50), Qty INT)
CREATE PROCEDURE TableParamDemo
( @Items ItemInfo READONLY)
AS
SELECT * FROM @Items
```

53. What is COMPUTE and WITH TIES clause in SQL?

Ans:

The COMPUTE clause is placed at the end of a query to place the result of an aggregate function at the end of a listing.

e.g.: COMPUTE SUM (TOTAL)

The SELECT TOP N query always return exactly N records, and arbitrarily drops any record that have the same value as the last record in the group. The WITH TIES clause can do away with this. It returns the records that have the same value even if the number declared after the TOP has been exceeded.

54. Can you update system tables in SQL Server, and if so, how?

Ans:

Before SQL Server 2005: Yes - to allow updates to the system CATALOG, update the 'allow updates' system configuration option to a value of 1 and reconfigure the server. This will allow you to make direct updates to the system CATALOG.

SQL Server 2005 Onwards: No - updates to the system CATALOG are explicitly prohibited. The 'allow updates' system configuration option still exists, however it is completely ignored.

55. Can you tell me what kind of cursors we have and syntax of a cursor?

Ans:

If we want to do row by row processing from database cursors can help us. We have to consider the cursors as a final option after all the existing once like "While," "Temporary Tables," "Table Variables," "Sub Quires" etc.

Types:

- **LOCAL**: Is available only to a batch, SP or to a trigger
- **GLOBAL**: Is available to the entire connection itself
- **READ_ONLY**: We can't update the cursor values
- **FORWARD_ONLY**: We can only trace the cursor in forward direction
- **SCROLL**: We can move either way of the cursor.
- **STATIC**: Snapshot of the row set is created and changes made to base tables are not effected
- **DYNAMIC**: Changes made to base table reflects in Cursor
- **FAST_FORWARD**: Combination of FORWARD_ONLY and READ_ONLY

Example:

```
Declare CurVar CURSOR
READONLY/FORWARD_ONLY/SCROLL/FAST_FORWARD/
STATIC/DYNAMIC
FOR SELECT QUERY
OPEN CurVar
FETCH NEXT/PRIOR/FIRST/LAST
FROM @CurVar INTO <@Defined Variable>
CLOSE CurVar
DEALLOCATE CurVar
```

56. What are the wild characters in SQL SERVER?

Ans:

%	Characters to Match
_	Single Character to Match
^	Characters to Not Match

57. What are constraints? Explain different types of constraints.

Ans:

Constraints enable the RDBMS enforce the integrity of the database automatically, without needing you to create triggers, rule or defaults. Types of constraints: NOT NULL, CHECK, UNIQUE, PRIMARY KEY, FOREIGN KEY.

58. Define candidate key, alternate key and COMPOSITE key.

Ans:

A candidate key is one that can identify each row of a table uniquely. Generally a candidate key becomes the primary key of the table. If the table has more than one candidate key, one of them will become the primary key, and the rest are called alternate keys. A key formed by combining at least two or more columns is called composite key.

59. What is user defined data types and when you should go for them?

Ans:

User defined data types let you extend the base SQL Server data types by providing a descriptive name, and format to the database. Take for example, in your database, there is a column called Flight_Num which appears in many tables. In all these tables it should be VARCHAR (8). In this case you could create a user defined data type called Flight_num_type of VARCHAR (8) and use it across all your tables. See sp_addtype, sp_droptype

60. What is an extended stored procedure? Can you instantiate a COM object by using T-SQL?

Ans:

An extended stored procedure is a function within a DLL (written in a programming language like C, C++ using Open Data Services (ODS) API) that can be called from T-SQL, just the way we call normal stored procedures using the EXEC statement.

Yes, you can instantiate a COM (written in languages like VB, VC++) object from T-SQL by using sp_OACreate stored procedure.

61. Can you give some examples for One to One, One to Many and Many to Many relationships?

Ans:

One to One: Citizen - UID

A citizen can have only one UID - A UID can represent only one citizen

One to Many: Customer - Products

A customer can sale number of products - A product can be brought by only one customer

Many to Many: Book - Author

A book can be written by more than one author - An author can write more than one book

62. Recently we have got a situation where we had to change one of a key column data type to BIGINT as it's already reached INTEGER range. My manager raised a question "Now we are changing its datatype to BIGINT; Are you sure BIGINT never been out of scope?

Ans:

We really didn't think about it, but yah we answered him on the next day. I actually didn't remember the original author blog. One of the blogger has given this beautiful analysis.

Let's take few examples and see how many years will it take for BIGINT to reach its upper limit in a table:

(A) Considering only positive numbers, Max limit of BIGINT = 9,223,372,036,854,775,807

(B) Number of Seconds in a year = 31,536,000

Assume there are 50,000 records inserted per second into the table. Then the number of years it would take to reach the BIGINT max limit is:

9,223,372,036,854,775,807/31,536,000/50,000 = 5,849,424 years

Similarly,

If we inserted 1 lakh records per second into the table then it would take 2,924,712 yrs.

If we inserted 1 million (1000000) records per second into the table then it would take 292,471 yrs.

If we inserted 10 million (10000000) records per second into the table then it would take 29,247 yrs.

If we inserted 100 million records per second into the table then it would take 2,925 yrs.

If we inserted 1000 million records per second into the table then it would take 292 yrs.

By this we would have understood that it would take extremely lots of years to reach the max limit of BIGINT.

63. What is stuff function? Difference between stuff and replace?

Ans:

- Stuff function works like replace function but the difference is replace function replaces all occurrences of a specified string with the last string provided.

  SELECT REPLACE ('Abcabcabc', 'bc', 'xy') --> Axyaxyaxy

- But the stuff function will replace the specified string with the given string as it accepts the start and end positions.

  SELECT STUFF ('Abcabcabc', 2, 3, 'xyz') --> Axyzbcabc

64. What is the difference between CROSS/OUTER APPLY AND JOINS in T-SQL?

Ans:

CROSS APPLY works like Inner Join and OUTER APPLY works like LEFT OUTER JOIN. But the difference comes when we need to join with a Table Valued Expression on the right side. We can't accomplish with the joins when we need to join a resultset from a function. Moreover there are cases where we see performance improved with CROSS APPLY. Also CROSS APPLY works well with XML.

When we are in Canon, we have seen a strange issue. We have a table which is holding different campaigns (Adds, banner ads advt etc.) time data. Data is being populated for every minute on 24*7 for 365 days. Now we have a simple query to get the add details which are having start and end time more than 3 min between the times 9:00 AM and 3:00 PM. The query is returning 230 rows but it was taking 6 min of time we have modified it with CROSS APPLY with only selected campaign data as a sub query.

65. When to use CROSS APPLY over Join?

Ans:

- When there are range operations (Between or <= >= etc.) on large datasets.
- When there are too many conditions on join clause.
- When we need join a result set returning from a user defined function

66. How to update text, VARCHAR (max), NVARCHAR (max) columns?

Ans:

You can use REPLACE to create expressions in UPDATE statements that modify char, NCHAR, V A RCHAR, and NVARCHAR values. However, you cannot use REPLACE for TEXT, NTEXT, or image data. In previous versions of SQL Server, you needed to use UPDATETEXT, and that is still supported but is deprecated. However, if you are using the new VARCHAR (max), NVARCHAR (max), or BINARY (max) data types, you can use the .WRITE clause in an UPDATE statement.

67. What is XACT_ABORT option?

Ans:

When SET XACT_ABORT is ON, if a Transact-SQL statement raises a run-time error, the entire transaction is terminated and rolled back.

When SET XACT_ABORT is OFF, in some cases only the Transact-SQL statement that raised the error is rolled back and the transaction continues processing. Depending upon the severity of the error, the entire transaction may be rolled back even when SET XACT_ABORT is OFF. OFF is the default setting.

Compile errors, such as syntax errors, are not affected by SET XACT_ABORT.

68. What is the Lock Escalation improvement in SQL Server 2008?

Ans:

In previous versions of SQL Server, lock escalation use to happen from ROW to TABLE. In SQL Server 2008, you can benefit from partition level locking if the table is partitioned. However,

TABLE level locking is still the default. If you want to use partition level-locking as the default, you need to set that.

69. What happens if we specify NOLOCK hint in select query?

Ans:

- NOLOCK hint indicates "READ UNCOMMITTED" isolation level.
- When we wanted to implement this isolation level selectively, means just for a selected list of statements we have a choice of using with (NOLOCK) query hint. If we want to use it throughout the application, configure the isolation level at database level.
- Remember we are not supposed to use this query hint for OLTP as it leads to below anomalies
  - ✓ Dirty Reads
  - ✓ Non Repeatable Reads
  - ✓ Phantom Reads

Note: NOLOCK hint doesn't work when a schema change happens inside a transaction.

70. Can we use two CTE's in a same select query?

Ans:

Yes we can. It looks like below

```
;WITH CTE1 AS (SELECT 1 AS Col1),
CTE2 AS (SELECT COL1+1 AS Col2 FROM CTE1)
SELECT CTE1.Col1,CTE2.Col2
FROM CTE1
CROSS JOIN CTE2
GO
```

71. Have you ever used recursive CTE? If yes how can you handle infinite recursive conditions?

Ans:

Yes I have used recursive CTE's in T-SQL. We can handle infinite situations by using the **"OPTION MAXRECURSION"** as below.

```
USE AdventureWorks
GO
WITH Emp_CTE AS (
SELECT EmployeeID, ContactID, LoginID, ManagerID, Title, BirthDate
FROM HumanResources.Employee
WHERE ManagerID IS NULL
UNION ALL
```

```
SELECT e.EmployeeID, e.ContactID, e.LoginID, e.ManagerID, e.Title, e.BirthDate
FROM HumanResources.Employee e
INNER JOIN Emp_CTE ecte ON ecte.EmployeeID = e.ManagerID
)
SELECT *
FROM Emp_CTE OPTION (MAXRECURSION 5)
GO
```

72. What is a FORCESEEK and FORCESCAN table hints in SQL Server?

Ans:

These table hints are introduced in SQL Server 2008. By specifying these hints means explicitly we force optimizer to use the specified index seek operation.

```
SELECT * FROM test WITH (FORCESEEK)
WHERE column_1 = 1 or Column_1 = 100
```

I never prefer using these hints as optimizer has more intelligence than us in choosing the proper index as long as all statistics are up-to-date.

73. Can we use a table variable inside a nested stored procedure if the table variable created in parent stored procedure? If the answer is no can you explain why?

Ans:

No, we can't directly use a variable/table variable (created in parent procedure) inside a nested stored procedure directly. We can use them by passing as procedure parameters because the scope of a variable is the current execution batch. Let's have a look when a new batch created in SQL.

- GO Statement
- Each normal set of statements execution
- A procedure has a different scope even if it calling from a batch
- Each execution of a external program is a separate batch

74. Do you know the limitations of the option "SET ROWCOUNT"?

Ans:

"SET ROWCOUNT" is not applicable while accessing/querying remote tables, local and remote partitioned views. This option is overwrite the "TOP" clause if the ROWCOUNT is set to be small value then "TOP" clause value. This option is executed at RUN TIME not at PARSE time.

75. What is the difference between table variable and temporary table?

Ans:

Temp Tables:

- Can participate in transactions
- Operations write to log file

- It can qualify for Parallelism
- Statistics can be created
- It is effected when recompile
- Allows Non-Clustered Indexes
- Allows Clustered Indexes
- Supports SELECT INTO
- Can be accessed from nested stored procedures
- Can be defined globally
- Can't be used in user defined functions
- Data can be inserted from EXEC
- Allows TRUNCATE
- Allows ALTER TABLE

Table Variable:

- Can't be participated in transactions
- It doesn't touch log file
- It can't qualify for Parallelism
- Statistics can't be created
- It doesn't get effected when recompile
- We can't create explicit Non-Clustered Indexes
- We can't create explicit Clustered Indexes
- Doesn't support SELECT INTO
- Can't be accessed from nested stored procedures
- Can't be defined globally
- Can be used in user defined functions
- Data can be inserted from EXEC
- Doesn't allows TRUNCATE
- Doesn't allows ALTER TABLE

76. What's the difference between DELETE TABLE and TRUNCATE TABLE commands?

Ans:

Truncate:

- De-allocates the data pages in a table and only this deallocation is stored in transaction log.
- It acquires only table and page locks for the whole table. Since no row locks are used less memory is required.
- Resets identity column if available

- Removes all pages. NO empty pages are left behind in a table
- Fast(er)
- Doesn't fire delete triggers

Delete:

- Removes one row at the time and every deleted row is stored in the transaction log
- It acquires table and/or page and row locks for the whole table
- Leaves identity column alone
- Can leave empty pages in a table since empty page removal requires a table lock which doesn't necessarily happen
- Slow(er)
- Fires delete triggers.

77. Does TRUNCATE is a DDL or DML and why?

Ans:

TRUNCATE is a DDL command as it directly works with table schema instead of row level.

This we can observe by using "sys.dm_tran_locks" while executing the "TRUNCATE" command on a table. It issues a schema lock (sch-M) where as "DELETE" issues exclusive lock. Schema lock issued as it requires resetting the identity value.

78. See I have written a recursive CTE, it's been running infinitely and failed with an error. The requirement is that the recursion required for 45000 times. How could you be able to handle the situation?

Ans:

There is a hint called "MAXRECURSION." In select query after CTE, we can use this hint by specifying a number which indicates number of recursions the CTS can be called recursively. Unfortunately max value is 32767. Now in our case there is 45 k rounds required, only solution is simply remove the CTE and replace it with a table variable or temp table.

79. Can we issue "TRUNCATE" command on a table when it is referenced in child tables using foreign key? Can you explain why?

Ans:

No!

Truncate command is works with pages not with individual rows. It doesn't see data in pages rather it just de-allocate pages. Therefore it can't validate if the same row is referenced in any other child tables. That is the reason to not allowing TRUNCATE command on tables which are referenced using foreign keys.

Also that's again the reason TRUNCATE TABLE doesn't fire triggers as it works with pages not with data/rows in those pages.

80. What is the difference between CHARINDEX and PATINDEX?

Ans:

Both are the string functions and return the location of the first occurrence of the given string.

But PATINDEX allow us to use wildcard whereas CHARINDEX doesn't allow.

Here are the wildcard:

"_": One character

"%": 0 or more characters

"^": Matching the character but not matching the specified set

"[]": To matches the range of characters.

"DECLARE @Str VARCHAR (150)

SET @Str = 'SQL Server 2016 CTP 3.3 has been recently released with more options on cloud for the first time' + 'PATINDEX matches the pattern'

SELECT PATINDEX('%r_2%', @str) AS 'r 2',

PATINDEX('%re%', @str) AS 'recently',

PATINDEX('%pat[^i]%', @str) AS 'pattern',

PATINDEX('%f[a-i]r%', @str) AS 'first' "

"r 2" - 10: Serve"r 2"016

"recently" - 34: "recently" released

"pattern" - 118: This matches two words PATINDEX and PATTERN, but here ^I indicates no "I" so it's pattern.

"first" - 87: Two words matching; FOR and FIRST but here letters between F&I should be in between "a-I" then it's "First" not "For"

81. Can we use CASE in PRINT statement?

Ans:

Yes! We can.

PRINT CASE WHEN 1=0 THEN 'FALSE' WHEN 2=2 THEN 'TRUE' ELSE 'ZERO' END;

82. We know we cannot use Order by inside a view. Can you tell me why?

Ans:

Even I did a lot of research on the question "WHY?" but I could not find any specific answer from MSDN blogs. But one of the Authors answered this question which is more conveying.

"A view is just like a Table. As per the RDBMS rules we have to use table data and produce a result set, we can apply as many as transformations while producing the result set but not at the source (in Table/View).

Let's say we have a facility to use Order By clause inside a view.

In most of the scenarios we do join view data with other dataset (A View or Table) which produces a new result set. In this case we have done extra processing in sorting data at initial level.

If we need view data needs to be in a sorted order we can simply apply Order by on view but not from inside view.

83. What is the output for the query "SELECT SUM (SAL) FROM EMPLOYEE WHERE 1=2"?

Ans:

NULL!

SUM () or any aggregate will return NULL in 2 cases:

- When all returned rows are null
- When no rows returned

I have seen most of the people concerned about returning NULL when no rows matching criteria.

Let's consider an example:

You are asked "What is the current balance in your CITI bank account?"

If you say "0" means your account is empty. But let's say you don't have a CITI bank account would you still say "0":)

You would say no account means no rows returned:)

Now in this situation we can handle the situation using ISNULL (SUM (<COLUMN>),0)....

84. What is optimistic and pessimistic locking and differences?

Ans:

Optimistic and pessimistic locking are two ways that the data access controlled in database. Consider the below example.

User A reads the row from employee table for emp_id 1001

User B reads the row from employee table for emp_id 1001

User B updates the row for emp_id 1001

User A updates the row for emp_id 1001

Pessimistic: The pessimistic concurrency control approach is to have the database server lock the row on User A's behalf, so User B has to wait until User A has finished its work before proceeded. We effectively solve the problem by not allowing two users to work on the same piece of data at the same time. Ex: Read Committed

Optimistic: The optimistic concurrency control approach doesn't actually lock anything - instead, it asks User A to remember what the row looked like when he first saw it, and when it's time to update it, the user asks the database to go ahead only if the row still looks like he remembers it. It doesn't prevent a possible conflict, but it can detect it before any damage is done and fail safely that means user "A" update will fail as "B" is already updated the data.

85. What is the difference between sub query and co-related sub query?

Ans:

Sub Query: A nested query

Co-Related Sub Query: Nested query using the values from main query

- *Looping:* Co-related sub-query loop under main-query; whereas nested not; therefore co-related sub-query executes on each iteration of main query. Whereas in case of Nested-query; subquery executes first then outer query executes next. Hence, the maximum no. of executes are NXM for correlated subquery and N+M for subquery.
- *Dependency (Inner to Outer vs Outer to Inner):* In the case of co-related subquery, inner query depends on outer query for processing whereas in normal sub-query, Outer query depends on inner query.
- *Performance:* Using Co-related sub-query performance decreases, since, it performs NXM iterations instead of N+M iterations. ¨ Co-related Sub-query Execution.

86. How to debug a stored procedure in SQL Server?

Ans:

There are two ways to debug a stored procedure:

SSMS:

- Open the procedure and start debugging by clicking on the debug button (Green Play Button next to Execute) and give the required inputs and that's it.

Visual Studio:

- From server explorer create a connection to the required database
- Expand the stored procedures and open the required stored procedure
- Right click on the stored procedure name and click on "Step Into Stored Procedure."
- Run procedure appears, give all required inputs.

Limitations:

- While running from SSMS, the SSMS service should be running on a service (SQL/ Windows) which is a member of SYSADMIN role.
- We can only use SSMS "Debug" feature only from SQL Server 2008. We can't run debug on 2005 connection even though the connection made from 2008 SSMS.
- Make sure the member who needs to execute "Step into Stored Procedure" from VS should be member of admin group on that machine.

87. What is the difference between memory and disk storage?

Ans:

Memory and disk storage both refer to internal storage space in a computer. The term "memory" usually means RAM (Random Access Memory). The terms "disk space" and "storage" usually refer to hard drive storage.

88. What are the dynamic management objects?

Ans:

Dynamic Management Objects are Dynamic Management Views and Functions. These are first introduced in SQL Server 2005 and after that in each version DMV's are improved by adding more columns and new DMV's. A DMV gives the current state of the SQL Server machine. These results will help the administrator to diagnose problems and tune the server for optimal performance. This is the quickest way to know about the current server state. There are two types of DMV:

- Server Scoped
- Database Scoped

89. What is the permission required to use DMV?

Ans:

To query a server scoped DMV, the login must have SELECT privilege on VIEW SERVER STATE and for database scoped DMV, the user must have SELECT privilege on VIEW DATABASE STATE.

```
GRANT VIEW SERVER STATE to <Login>
GRANT VIEW DATABASE STATE to <User>
```

To deny the permission:

```
DENY VIEW SERVER STATE to <Login>
DENY VIEW DATABASE STATE to <User>
```

90. I have a doubt here, can we believe foreign key constraints, I mean when there is a foreign key defined on a child column, and does it be strong enough to say that the child contains data from parent only.

Example:

Dept (DeptId, Name) – Id Primary Key

Emp (Id, Sal, DeptId) – DeptID Foreign Key Dept (DeptId).

My question is are we sure that all Emp.DeptId is available in Dept.DeptID?

Ans:

No! We can't guarantee on that, because there is a chance that the foreign key constraint might be disabled and inserted data which is not in parent (Dept.DeptId). Let's say we have only 5 DeptID on Dept table but there is a chance to insert 6 on Emp.DeptID by disabling the foreign key.

SQL Server identifies this integrity violation we too can know whether the FOREIGNKEY relationship can be trusted or not using the query:

"SELECT * FROM sys.foreign_keys WHERE IS_NOT_TRUSTED = 1."

91. We have a scenario, I have a customer table. You are using a stored procedure to update the table. When a customer updates his/her information this update stored procedure is called from the front end application by passing the updated column information. Now my requirement is we have to capture the old phone number when customer updates it with the new number. We don't bother about other columns but our business requires phone column to be archived for the audit purpose. Now tell

me what is your approach? By the way as per our environment policy we don't use triggers.

Ans:

Since we are already using a stored procedure we implement this by using:

Traditional Way: Select the old data for the given customer before the update and insert these details into archive table.

OUTPUT Clause: This can be actually easier our job.

```
Ex:
DECLARE @TC_AUDIT TABLE
(ID INT,
OLD_PHONE VARCHAR (12),
NEW_PHONE VARCHAR (12));
UPDATE T_Customer SET PHONE = '9898767689'
OUTPUT
INSERTED.ID,
DELETED.PHONE,
INSERTED.PHONE INTO @TC_AUDIT (ID,OLD_PHONE,NEW_PHONE)
WHERE ID = 62333;
SELECT * FROM @TC_AUDIT;
```

This is just an example this way we can implement using the procedure arguments

92. In your environment how do you handle the old history and backups?

Ans:

For the current client we designed maintenance plans to take care of History and Maintenance cleanup. We use tasks History Cleanup and Maintenance Cleanup tasks from maintenance plans.

Maintenance Plan log files: Delete all files older than 4 weeks

History Cleanup: Delete all history for Backup & Restore, Agent Job & Maintenance Plan older than 4 weeks.

Database Full backups (Weekly): Delete full backups older than 2 weeks

Database Diff and Log (Daily/Hourly): Delete all backups older than 2 weeks

Note: For backups even though we delete from the disk those files will be maintained on archive for 6 months

93. Have you ever faced any issues with SQL Server Error Log? How do you manage SQL Server Error log

Ans:

Yes! We should have to maintain the SQL Server ERRORLOG based on its growth and requirement. We might be in trouble if SQL Server error log becomes as a huge file as it needs to be loaded into memory when we switch on the ERRORLOG GUI. In most of the environments I have seen SQL Server keeps up to 6 log files (1 Active + 6 Archive) and we can change this default value from SQL Server ERRORLOG properties. SQL Server creates a new log file in two cases when SQL Server restarts or when we execute SP_CYCLE_ERRORLOG system stored procedure.

We usually create a user table and archive ERRORLOG periodically thereof it can be available for root cause analysis.

94. What is SQL DUMP? Have you ever dealt with this?

Ans:

When SQL Server is crashed or in hung state due to a Memory/Disk/CPU problems it creates a SQL DUMP file. A DUMP files is a file containing a snapshot of the running process (in this case SQL Server) that includes all of the memory space of that process and the call stack of every thread the process has created. There are two major types of DUMP files:

Full DUMP: It contains entire process space and takes lot of time and space

Mini DUMP: It's a smaller file contains the memory for the call stack of all threads, the CPU registers and information about which modules are loaded.

95. How do you understand/analyse SQL DUMP files?

Ans:

Using a debugger, such as WinDbg, you can analyze a dump file.

We can analyze SQL DUMP files using a debugger like "WinDbg." But usually when SQL DUMPS created we can identify the root cause by analyzing SQL Server and Windows error logs but in-case of premier servers we need to give complete end to end report by specifying why DUMP files created. In those situations we do raise a case with Microsoft team and MS support engineer analyze these DUMP files and gives us the report.

96. Can you quickly explain the difference between Clustered and Non-Clustered index?

Ans:

Clustered Index:

- Clustered Index determines the physical order of table rows on disk. That's the reason a table can have only one clustered index.
- The leaf node of a Clustered Index contains data pages of the table on which it is created.
- If the table does not have Clustered Index it is referred to as a "Heap" if clustered index defined on it then the table is referred as clustered table.
- A Primary Key constraint creates a Clustered Index by default but we can always specify the clustered or Non-Clustered index while creating the primary key.

Non-Clustered Index:

A Non-Clustered Index defines a logical order that need not match the physical order on disk. That's the reason a table can have more than one non-clustered index.

The leaf nodes of a Non-Clustered Index consists of Index pages which contain Clustering Key (If table is having clustered index) or RID (if table is a HEAP) to locate Data Row

A Unique Key constraint created a Non-Clustered Index by default but we can always specify the clustered or Non-Clustered index while creating the Unique key

97. On a production server TEMPDB is getting full and how do you fix it?

Ans:

We usually don't try to fix issues on production TEMPDB without a maintenance window. When we see TEMPDB is getting full we identify the active queries and from those active queries we'll identify queries/SPID causing the TEMPDB full and then kill that SPID. When we need to give a permanent fix on TEMPDB we take a maintenance window and then apply the required fix that may include increasing the TEMPDB data file size, creating a new data file with the same size, creating filter indexes based on problematic queries to reduce load on Temdb etc.

98. We are not able to connect to SQL Server. Can you list out what are all the possible issues and resolutions?

Ans:

This is one of the most common problems every DBA should be able to handle with. Here are the list of possible problems and resolutions. All the problems can be categorized into:

- Service Down/Issue
- Network Access/Firewall Issue
- Authentication and Login issue
- SQL Server configuration Issue
- Application Driver or Connection String Issue

Possible Problems:

- Using a wrong instance name/IP or port
- Using a wrong user name or password
- User access might be revoked
- Trying to access from outside organization VPN
- SQL Server is down
- SQL Server is not responding due to high CPU/Memory/Disk I/O
- Might be a disk full issue
- Master database might be corrupted
- User default database may not be online
- SQL Server port might be blocked
- We are using named instance name and SQL Browser service is down
- Using the wrong network protocol
- Remote connections may not be enabled
- Network issue with the host windows server
- Using a wrong client driver (32 bit – 64 bit issues or Old driver using for new version)

- Version Specific issues, for example an application cannot connect to a contained database when connection pooling is enabled. This issue got fixed in SQL Server 2014 CU1

Resolutions:

The error message itself can tell you how to proceed ahead with the resolution:

- If possible first thing should be done is, check SQL Server and Windows error log as it can tell us the exact problem and based on that we can determine the possible best resolution.
- Please cross check connection string information before complaining
- Cross check hosted windows server and SQL Server are up and running
- Make sure the SQL login default database is online and accessible
- Make sure the user access is not revoked
- Make sure all system databases are up and running
- Cross check all resource usage that includes Memory, CPU, Disk I/O, Disk Space etc.
- Try to use IP address and port number instead of instance name, also try with FQDN
- Try to connect from different possible places/systems to make sure the source system has no issues
- Check windows server is reachable from remote location using PING
- Check SQL Server listening on the given port using TELNET <IP> <Port>. Try both from local and remote
- If the port is blocked add this port to exception list in windows firewall INBOUND rules
- Make sure SQL Server is configured to allow remote connections
- If you are also not able to connect then try to connect using DAC and fix the issue by running DBCC commands
- Try if you can connect using SQLCMD
- Cross check if there is any recent changes happened in Active Directory security policy
- Make sure you are using the correct driver to connect to application
- Cross check if there is any blocking on system process

99. One of the disk drive is 95% full within a very less time. Now you started getting disk full alerts and you need to free up the space. What are the different options you try to clear the space? And what are the possible reasons that cause the sudden disk full issues?

Ans:

This is also a very common alert/issue in DBA's life. Let me explain the different options we'll try to handle the disk space issues. From my experience here are the possible reasons:

Possible Reasons:

- Huge data load happens and it increased the data file size as auto growth is enabled
- An open transaction causes to increase a database log file increased when it's auto grow option is on

- A big transaction log/differential backup generated
- TEMPDB might filled the disk due to a huge query sorting and maintenance
- Huge number of SQL Mini DUMP files created on log folder
- It's may not always SQL Server causes the DISK FULL issue, check the huge files on disk manually and find if any other application or OS causing the issue.
- Disk size was gradually increased as per the process but the alert was disabled and just it got enabled and it started sending alert messages

Resolutions:

- We quickly identify if there are any files that can be moved to other drive
- Remove if you find any old/unnecessary backups, SQL Server logs or crashed logs
- If it is log file full issues handle it properly and shrink the log file
- If you find any low risk or small databases located on that drive then try to move those database files to other drive using detach and attach method
- If you identify any open transaction which is causing the disk full then collect all possible details of that transaction and kill it.
- Talk to the server owner and ask for more space on that drive or request for a new drive, take a maintenance window and increase the drive space or attach a new drive.

100. What are the different phases in database testing?

Ans:

UNIT TESTING: Test all parts of your object working fine

FUNCTIONAL TESTING: Test the code to make sure it is processing data as per the (domain acceptance) requirement document.

INTIGRITY TESING: Test data insertions/updates/Deletions are all following Domain, Referential and Entity Integrity.

UI TESTING: Check data values are matching between source and destination using UI/Application

LOAD/STRESS TESING: Test your code can handle huge data loads and concurrent access

PERFORMANCE TESTING: Test performance is not downgraded

SECURITY TESTING: check code should be compatible with the standard security policies

101. We have configured Database Mail and tested by sending an email and all working fine. We setup an operator and assign the operator to a SQL Agent job to send a notification email when the job completes. Job executed successfully but we are not getting emails. We are getting emails when we send test mail from Management à Database Mail and also from T-SQL using SP_SEND_DBMAIL but the mail is not working as excepted from jobs. Do you have any idea on this? BTW we have also verified database mail log but nothing logged over there.

Ans:

Yes! This is a common mistake DBA do when configured DB Mail in SQL Server. Once we configure the database mail to enable mail support for agent jobs we have to manually setup SQL Server Agent properties à Alert System à Select the Mail system as Database Mail and Mail Profile name as you configured. That's it then the jobs start sending emails to the intended operators as configured.

102. Let's say we are not receiving emails from last 4 hours as there is a problem with database mail. Now we would like to restart the database mail. Have you ever faced this issue? If yes how do you restart the database mail?

Ans:

Yes! We have seen these issues.

The most important point is we should check the external queue before restarting the database mail. If we restart the database mail without checking the unsent items it might trigger all unsent items in one go which might create confusion in team and you may need to answer lot many questions.

From MSDB check SYSMAIL_UNSENTITEMS, EXTERNALMAILQUEUE and clear the queue. We have a pre written script to clear the queue thereof we will just execute the script to clear the pending queue and then we start the database mail using "EXEC SYSMAIL_START_SP"

103. Is it possible to configure Database Mirroring/Log Shipping when servers are having different drive structure?

Ans:

Yes! It is absolutely possible. But Microsoft strongly suggests that never configure any topology when primary and secondary is having different drive structure. There are some issues/manual interruption required if you configure mirroring with principal and mirror are having different drive structure. When we are adding/restoring backup from Principal/Primary to Mirror/Secondary we should use WITH MOVE option. Once mirroring/log shipping is configured successfully and later in sometime if we need to add a file (.NDF) on principal/primary then we need to follow a specific process to make the topology functioning.

Snapshots

104. What is a database snapshot?

Ans:

- A database snapshot is a read-only, static view of a SQL Server database
- Taking a snapshot is nothing taking a photograph of the database image at the given point of time
- Database snapshot always exists on the Source database server
- Database snapshot works on data pages
- We can consider this feature as a real time option for point in time restores

- Snapshot takes very little disk space when compared to the original database. The space occupied by the snapshot is nothing but the changed data pages. For unchanged pages, it still fetches the data from the actual database.

105. Can you explain how database snapshots works?

Ans:

Let me explain what happens when we create a database snapshot

- It creates an empty file known as sparse file for each source database data file
- Uncommitted transactions are rolled back, thus having a consistent copy of the database
- All dirty pages will be returned to the disk
- The user can query the database snapshot
- Initially the sparse file contains an empty copy of source database data file
- Snapshot data points to the pages from source database datafile
- When any modification occurred (INSERT/DELETE/UPDATE) on source database, all modified pages are copied to the sparse file before the actual modification. That means the sparse file contains the old/point in time data (when the time the snapshot taken).
- Now if you query the snapshot all modified pages are read from sparse file and remaining all unchanged pages are read from the original (source database) data file.

106. Can you explain if I query a table from database snapshot from where the read operation happens? Is that the sparse file or from the original source database data file?

Ans:

If a page is modified, read operation occurs on sparse File

If the page is not modified it still points to the source database page

107. Where are the real time situations where we can use database snapshots?

Ans:

Reporting: Report users can be redirected to database snapshot which reduces the pressure on source database

Statistical Analysis: Periodical data analysis for a particular product

Quick Point in time restores: In enterprise environments we do use snapshots at the time of production script releases, especially when database is VLDB. We can use Backup and Restore but it requires considerable system resources and time. Snapshots are really useful for quick rollbacks

High Availability: In log shipping and mirroring we use database snapshots to make database available for reporting users.

108. What are the various limitations of database snapshots?

Ans:

- A database snapshot can be created onto the source server only. It cannot be moved to another server

- We can't drop an Original Source Database as long as a referring snapshot exists in that database
- It cannot be Backed up and also detach\attach doesn't work with database snapshots
- You cannot create database snapshots on FAT32 file system or RAW partitions. The sparse files used by database snapshots are provided by the NTFS file system.
- Snapshots are read-only. Since they are read only, they cannot be upgraded.
- Snapshots can be created for only user databases, not for the master, model and MSDB
- If we revert to a snapshot log Chain will get broken, thus we have to take a full or differential backup to bridge the log chain sequence
- FILESTREAM FILEGROUPS are not supported by database snapshots.
- If a source database becomes RECOVERY_PENDING, its database snapshots may become inaccessible.
- Both the source DB and the snapshot will be unavailable when the actual reversion process is in progress
- If the source database is unavailable or corrupted we cannot use the database snapshot to revert it to the original state
- We cannot add new users for database since it is a read-only copy
- There is no graphical user interface for creating and reverting back the snapshot, this need to be done from query only
- There is some overhead for every DML operation as before operation page needs to be moved out
- If the drive in which snapshot exists is out of space which causes any DML to fail the snapshot will be in suspect mode and non-recoverable
- The full-text index is not available with a snapshot
- It is available with enterprise edition only
- Database files that were online during snapshot creation should be online during the snapshot revert also
- When a page getting updated on the source database is pushed to a snapshot, if the snapshot runs out of disk space or encounters some other error, the snapshot becomes suspect and must be deleted.
- A database snapshot cannot be configured as a scalable shared database.

109. A database is in Bulk-Logged recovery model. Can we create a snapshot for this database?

Ans:

Yes! There is no dependency for the recovery model as it works with full, bulk-logged and simple also.

110. Can we create more than one snapshot for the same database?

Ans:

Yes! We can create multiple database snapshots which maintains a separate sparse file for each individual snapshot.

Transaction Log

111. You got an alert that says a user database log file is growing and it reached 85%. How do you handle the situation?

Ans:

I'll first check if there are any open transactions using DBCC OPENTRAN. Then I'll check why SQL Server is unable to reuse the space inside the LDF using below query:

```
SELECT NAME, LOG_REUSE_WAIT_DESC FROM SYS.DATABASES
```

Most of the times we could see either of "Nothing" or "Log Backup" then I'll take the action to reduce the LDF file size

When database is in SIMPLE recovery model:

- Issue the CHECKPOINT manually
- SHRINK the log file
- Repeat the above two steps again and again till the log file get reduced

When database is in FULL or BULK LOGGED recovery model:

- Backup the database log file
- Perform the shrink operation on log file
- Repeat the above two steps again and again till the log file get reduced

If the log file is waiting on an open transaction:

- Try to increase the log file size to accommodate the longest transaction on that database
- Check if it is possible to kill the transaction based on its criticality.
- If no space available on the drive but the transaction is still running and that transaction should not be killed then create an extra log file on other drive. Remember this is just a temporary solution as SQL Server can utilize only one log file but for DATAFILES it can utilize multiple DATAFILES in parallel.

112. My database is in full recovery mode and log file is reaching 95%. Recently huge log backups generated due to a bulk data import followed by an index maintenance. Now the problem is we don't have space available to either to increase the log size or to take the next log backup. What we can do to reduce the log size to normal?

Ans:

I have faced some situations like this. When we don't have any option available to handle a log file growth then there is only way to change the database recovery model to SIMPLE.

- SET Recovery model to simple – It break the log chain
- Perform SHRINK operation and CHECKPOINT
- Once log file size reduced then make database recovery mode to FULL
- Immediately perform a full backup
- Then we can delete the old huge transaction log files to get some more free space
- As per the schedule log backups should starts

113. One of our databases is in simple recovery mode but still the log file is growing and it's not getting reduced after CHECKPOINT and SHRINK. Why it's log file is not getting reduced when the database is in simple recovery mode?

Ans:

There might be an explicit or implicit transaction is running that holds the log file (VLF's). For example deleting a huge number of rows from a table might easily fill the transaction log but these records will not be cleared until the entire transaction is done. That's the reason it's not responding for CHECKPOINT and SHRINK operations. When dealing with huge number of rows to avoid these situations we should always consider the batch processing instead of performing in one single go.

114. How to size the LDF file?

Ans:

There is no specific formula to size a log file. We can do that based on log file usage:

Simple Recovery:

We usually keep LDF file size as 10 to 15 percent of its MDF file size. But still monitor the file usage and make sure the file is properly sized to handle the longest transaction.

Full Recovery:

We usually size LDF file size as 80 to 90 percent of its MDF file size. It essentially depends on three factors. 1. MDF file size; 2. Log backup interval and 3.Largest Transaction.

115. SQL Server database log file (.LDF) contains modified pages correct?

Ans:

No! Log file is not about data it stores the operations applied on DATA. I'll try to explain with simple example "UPDATING 1000 ROWS IN A TABLE":

- First it captures all those rows related table pages from DISK (MDF) to Memory
- It applies update operation one by one on pages available in memory
- These operations are logged in LDF file. These UPDATE statements are logged into LDF. As per the given example total 1000 update statements are logged into LDF
- Once transaction is committed then first it marks the transaction status as committed in LDF file
- When next checkpoint happen all pages related to committed transaction will be written back to DISK (MDF).

- The same CHECKPOINT can clear these 1000 update statements from LDF file if database is in simple recovery mode. If it is in FULL recovery then it will wait till log backup happens.

116. What is a VLF in SQL Server?

Ans:

VLF stands for Virtual Log File. While performing DDL, DML operations on a SQL Server database, all these operations are sequentially logged into transaction log file. SQL Server transaction log file internally divided into smaller chunks called Virtual Log Files (VLF).

- The number of virtual log files is not limited or fixed per transaction log file.
- There is no fixed size of virtual log file
- SQL Server determinates the size of a virtual log file dynamically when the transaction log file is created or extended

117. How Many VLFs should we have for our database?

Ans:

There is no direct answer for this question. It always depends on data growth and log file auto growth settings. But for SQL Server it is easier to deal with smaller number of VLF's. We cannot control this especially when we are dealing with large databases.

118. Is there any impact if log file having more VLF's?

Ans:

Yes! We might see some performance impact on below:

- Slowdown the transaction log backup
- Slowdown the database recovery
- Impact performance of INSERT/UPDATE/DELETE operations

119. Can you explain what happens to VLF's when we see the error "Log File is full"?

Ans:

- SQL Server starts writing records into transaction log file. Initially it starts writing into the first available VLF.
- It moves to the next VLF when the first VLF is full. It continues writing transactions till the last VLF in the physical transaction log file.
- Once it reaches the last VLF then the control comes to the first VLF and sees if any VLF can be reused.
- If no VLF can be reused and Auto-Growth is enabled it tries to acquire the space and create new VLF's.
- If Auto-Growth is not enabled or there is no physical space available to grow the log file it in turns to an error "Log file is full" which holds your transactions and make your database read only.

120. Do you have any idea on VLF creation algorithm? If yes can you explain with an example?

Ans:

Yes! There is a big change happened in VLF creation algorithm from SQL Server 2014. Thanks to "Paul S. Randal" for the wonderful explanation

Before SQL Server 2014:

- Up to 64 MB: 4 new VLFs, each roughly 1/4 the size of the growth
- 64 MB to 1 GB: 8 new VLFs, each roughly 1/8 the size of the growth
- More than 1 GB: 16 new VLFs, each roughly 1/16 the size of the growth

From SQL Server 2014:

- Is the growth size less than 1/8 the size of the current log size?
- Yes: create 1 new VLF equal to the growth size
- No: use the formula above

Let me take an example how the VLF creation works in (SQL Server 2012/2008 R2 and before) and SQL Server 2014 and 2016. Now we'll calculate the total number of VLF's created as per the log file configurations. Clearly observe the difference in calculating number of VLF's created in each Auto-Growth:

Log File Configurations:

Initial Log file Size = 1 GB

Auto Grow: 512 MB

File Size Reached: 300 GB

Before SQL Server 2014:

Formula: Initial VLF's + (Total Number of Auto-Growth's X VLF's created in Each Auto Grow)

Initial 1 GB: 8 VLF

Total Number of Auto Growths: (300 – 1) GB/(0.5 GB or 512 MB) = 299/0.5 = 598

VLF's created in Each Auto – Growth:

8 VLF: If Auto Grow < 1 GB

16 VLF: if Auto Grow is > 1 GB

In this case it is 512 MB – 8 VLF's created for each auto grow

Total Number of VLF's created:

Total Number of Auto Growths X VLF's created at each Auto-Grow

598 X 8

4784

From SQL Server 2014/2016:

Formula:

Initial VLF + (Total Auto Growths when Auto Growth Size > 1/8 of Log file Size X 8) + (Total Auto Growths when Auto Growth Size < 1/8 of Log file Size X 1)

Initial 1 GB: 8 VLF

Total Number of Auto Growths: (300 – 1) GB/(0.5 GB or 512 MB) = 299/0.5 = 598

VLF's created in Each Auto – Growth:

8 VLF: If Auto Grow Size > 1/8 of Total Log File Size

1 VLF: If Auto Grow Size < 1/8 of Total Log File Size

Total Number of VLF's created:

Total Number of Auto Growths X VLF's created at each Auto-Grow

8 VLF + (

1.5 GB – Auto Growth 512 MB > 1/8 of 1.5 GB - 8 VLF +

2 GB – Auto Growth 512 MB > 1/8 of 1.5 GB - 8 VLF +

2.5 GB – Auto Growth 512 MB > 1/8 of 2 GB - 8 VLF +

3 GB – Auto Growth 512 MB > 1/8 of 2.5 GB - 8 VLF +

3.5 GB – Auto Growth 512 MB > 1/8 of 3 GB - 8 VLF +

4 GB – Auto Growth 512 MB > 1/8 of 3.5 GB - 8 VLF +

4.5 GB – Auto Growth 512 MB > 1/8 of 4 GB - 8 VLF) +

(

5 GB – Auto Growth 512 MB < 1/8 of 4.5 GB - 1 VLF

Starting from 5 GB to 300 GB it creates only one VLF for each Auto-Growth);

Initial VLF + (Total Auto Growths when Auto Growth Size > 1/8 of Log file Size X 8) + (Total Auto Growths when Auto Growth Size < 1/8 of Log file Size X 1)

8 + (7X8) +

((598 – 7) X 1)

= 655

Results:

No of VLF Created – Before SQL Server 2014: 4784

No of VLF Created – In SQL Server 2014/2016: 655

"655"VLF's is a decent number of VLF's when compared to "4784." We can see a lot of positive impact on performance.

121. How to know the number of VLF created on a given database log file?

Ans:

Run DBCC LOGINFO; Number of rows returned = Total number of VLF. If it is more than 50 means we need to control the Auto-growth rate. Number of times Auto Grow happens means it increases the number of VLF's.

122. What are the cases when log file is truncated automatically?

Ans:

- Under the simple recovery model, after a checkpoint.
- Under the full recovery model or bulk-logged recovery model, after a log backup, if a checkpoint has occurred since the previous backup.

123. What are the various factors that delays log truncation?

Ans:

Query sys.databases to identify delays in log truncation, log_reuse_wait and log_reuse_wait_desc columns can tell us the maximum information which is holding the transaction log:

Log_Reuse_Wait_Desc – NOTHING: Currently there are one or more reusable virtual log files

Log_Reuse_Wait_Desc – CHECKPOINT: No checkpoint has occurred since the last log truncation, or the head of the log has not yet moved beyond a virtual log file in all recovery models

Log_Reuse_Wait_Desc – LOG-BACKUP: A log backup is required to move the head of the log forward in both full and bulk-logged recovery models.

Log_Reuse_Wait_Desc – ACTIVE_BACKUP_OR_RESTORE: A data backup or a restore is in progress. A data backup works like an active transaction, and, when running, the backup prevents truncation

Log_Reuse_Wait_Desc – ACTIVE_TRANSACTION: An active transaction blocking the log truncation

Log_Reuse_Wait_Desc – REPLICATION: During transactional replications, transactions relevant to the publications are still undelivered to the distribution database

Log_Reuse_Wait_Desc – DATABASE_SNAPSHOT_CREATION: A database snapshot is being created

Log_Reuse_Wait_Desc – LOG_SCAN: A log scan is occurring

124. How do you troubleshoot transaction log full issue?

Ans:

Columns **log_reuse_wait** and **log_reuse_wait_desc** of the sys.databases CATALOG view describes what is the actual problem that causes log full/delay truncation.

- Backing up the log.
- Freeing disk space so that the log can automatically grow.
- Moving the log file to a disk drive with sufficient space.
- Increasing the size of a log file.
- Adding a log file on a different disk.
- Completing or killing a long-running transaction.

125. Can you describe factors that causes the logfile grow?

Ans:

- CHECKPOINT has not occurred since last log truncation

- No log backup happens since last full backup when database is in full recovery
- An active BACKUP or RESTORE operation is running from long back
- Long running active transactions
- Database mirroring is paused or mode is in high performance
- In replication publisher transactions are not yet delivered to distributer
- Huge number of database snapshots is being created

SHRINK

126. What happens when issued SHRINK on Data File?

Ans:

- A data file shrink operation works on a single file at a time
- It uses the GAM bitmaps to find the highest page allocated in the file.
- It then moves the page as far towards the front of the file as it can.
- The same process continues for all the pages based on page occupancy.
- This entire process completely reversed the order of the clustered index, taking it from perfectly defragmented to perfectly fragmented.
- DBCC commands SHRINKDATABASE, SHRINKFILE and Auto shrink option, these all are equally bad.

127. Do you prefer performing SHRINK on DataFile? Justify

Ans:

- No! Never Ever prefer performing SHRINK on a DataFile.
- Results in massive index fragmentation
- Results in File System Fragmentation
- Generates lots of I/O and causes the high CPU
- Generates lots of transaction log as everything is fully logged
- After the SHRINK again datafile has to be grow when new data coming in. Growing a DATAFILE size is an expensive operation.
- Repeated SHRINK operation may produce a lot of transaction log and causes many virtual log files which leads to a longer start up time for the database.

128. If SHRINK DATAFILE is having the bad impact why it's still available in SQL Server?

Ans:

There are certain scenarios where we may not have a choice:

- Large portion of your database is deleted and there is less space to grow the datafile.
- To maintain the compatibility for the older versions

129. When to perform Database Shrink in SQL Server?

Ans:

Usually we don't suggest Database Shrink operation but there are certain scenarios where we can get benefit from shrink operation. There are:

- After dropping large number of tables
- After substantial changes in a table's data types
- After huge data archival job execution

130. What are the limitations of shrink operations?

Ans:

- It is not possible to perform SQL Server database shrinking while a database backup process is running, and vice-versa.
- A database cannot be shrunk indefinitely. When the database was initially created, the minimum size of database has been specified and shrinking a database can't make it smaller than this value.

131. What are the disadvantages of Database Shrink operation?

Ans:

- Shrinking a SQL Server database completely ignores logical index fragmenting, and results in massive fragmentation of all indexes. This can have a negative impact on query performance
- Shrunken files will inevitably grow again. This means that the database file will be increasing in size, and this process takes times.
- Performing shrinking of multiple databases on multiple occasions may result in disk fragmentation (file system fragmentation) which can cause performance issues
- The process of page allocation will be written as an activity in the transaction log file, which can result in massive transaction log file growth, especially on databases in the full recovery model
- Subsequent shrinking and transaction log files growth will slow down database start-up, restore and replication time

132. We have a situation where we need to perform delete on large portion of a database sized 4.3 TB. How to avoid shrink operation?

Ans:

Paul S. Randal suggested a best way to avoid shrink operation:

- Create a new FILEGROUP
- Move all affected tables and indexes into the new FILEGROUP using the CREATE INDEX ... WITH (DROP_EXISTING = ON) ON syntax, to move the tables and remove fragmentation from them at the same time
- Drop the old FILEGROUP that you were going to shrink anyway (or shrink it way down if it's the primary FILEGROUP)

133. What happens when issued SHRINK on a log file?

Ans:

Transaction log file contains unused space which can be reclaimed by reducing the size of the transaction log. This process is known as shrinking the log file. Shrinking can occur only while the database is online and, also, while at least one virtual log file is free.

Log Truncation occurs automatically when:

- Database is in simple recovery mode and when checkpoint occurs
- Database is in full recovery mode and when performed the log backup

Shrinking transaction log:

- Reduces the log file physical size by removing one or more inactive virtual log files
- A shrink-file operation can remove only inactive virtual log files
- If no target size is specified, a shrink-file operation removes only the inactive virtual log files beyond the last active virtual log file in the file.
- If a target size is specified, a given shrink-file operation removes only enough inactive virtual log files to approach but not exceed the target size.
- When a transaction log file is shrunk, enough virtual log files from the end of the log file are freed

Boot Page

134. Any idea about boot page?

Ans:

In every database there is a page available which stores about the most critical information about that database.

This page is called boot page. Boot Page is page 9 in first file on primary file group.

We can examine the BOOTPAGE using DBCC PAGE or DBCC DBINFO

135. What kind of information we can get from BOOTPAGE?

Ans:

- Database Current version and the actual version number when it was created.
- dbi_RebuildLogs: Number of times the transactional log rebuild for this database. This can help us if incase database corruption is due to huge number of log rebuilds.
- dbi_dbccLastKnownGood: When last time dbcc executed successfully
- dbi_LastLogBackupTime: When last time Log backup happened successfully
- dbi_differentialBaseGuid: This is the GUID of last full backup. If you want to restore any differential backup those GUID should match with this GUID.

136. Let's say our database BOOTPAGE is corrupted. How do you recover the DB?

Ans

When BOOTPAGE corrupted:

- We cannot run DBCC
- We cannot run repair
- We cannot put database in EMERGENCY mode
- There is no way that we can get recover data except restoring available backups

XML

137. What is an XQuery expression?

Ans:

An XQuery expression identifies the XML components to be retrieved or modified, and any actions to be taken on those components. XQuery is a scripting language used specifically to access XML data, contains the elements necessary to create complex expressions that can include functions, operators, variables, and values.

138. What are the different XML methods available to work with XML datatype in SQL Server?

Ans:

There are 5 XML methods available in SQL Server:

- query()
- value()
- exists()
- nodes()
- modify()

Query ():

- The query () method retrieves a subset of un-typed XML from the target XML instance.
- It returns a XML data type
- We need to specify XPATH expression in the XQUERY parameter

  Ex 1: Retrieves XML between tags Name under Employee 1 in Dept 1 SELECT EmpDetails.query(/Org/Dept[1]/Employee[1]/Name) FROM Survey WHERE OrgID = 4

  Ex 2: Retrieves a single string which is a value for employee 1 name in Dept 1 SELECT EmpDetails.query(/Org/Dept[1]/Employee[1]/Name/text()) FROM Survey WHERE OrgID = 4

Value ():

- The value() method returns a scalar value from the targeted XML document.
- It returns a single or a list of values from XML
- It easier job for converting from XML to a relational
- It also enables us to apply a datatype conversion

  Ex: Retrieve Employee 1 Name from Dept 1 and convert the name to NVARCHAR(50)

  SELECT EmpDetails.value((/Org/Dept[1]/Employee)[1], 'NVARCHAR(50)') FROM Survey WHERE OrgID = 4

Exists ():

- The exist () method lets you test for the existence of an element or one of its values.
- It returns 0 or 1 or NULL based on element existence in XML

  Ex: It checks the existence of Department ID 109 for organization id 4

  SELECT EmpDetails.exist((/Org/Dept [@DeptID = 109] ') FROM Survey WHERE OrgID = 4

Nodes ():

- nodes() method is a great way to manipulate XML data both when it comes into the server for persisting as a relation rowset.
- The method works like a table valued function that accepts a single parameter, which is an XQuery statement which will result in a set of nodes.
- nodes() method get the maximum benefit from XML indexes.
- It gives us more flexibility in traversing the XML document
- We can also apply filters on data retrieval from XML to rowset
- It is more useful in situations; from employee details XML I want to get ID of all employees in one go, at the same time need to all employees Name etc.

  Ex: I have an XML column Survey.EmpDetails. Now XML for OrgID = 4 is having 28000 employees details. Get all 28000 employees name and age in single go

```
SELECT
Dept.emp.value('(Name/text())[1]', 'NVARCHAR(50)') as [name],
Dept.emp.value('@age', 'smallint') as [age]
FROM Survey S
CROSS APPLY S.EmpDetails.nodes('/Org/Dept/Employee') Dept(Emp)
WHERE OrgID = 4;
```

Modify ():

- It allows us to update XML data using T-SQL
- We can add, update and delete components to XML

  Ex 1: Update Emp 1 name from Dept 1 to "John"

UPDATE Survey SET EmpDetails.modify ('replace value of (/Org/Dept[1]/Employee[1]/Name/text()) [1] WITH "John"') FROM Survey WHERE OrgID = 4

Ex 2: Insert comments tag after Department

UPDATE Survey SET EmpDetails.modify ('insert(<Comments>EP Survey 2016</Comments>) after(/Org/Dept)[1]') WHERE OrgID = 4

Ex 3: Delete comments tag which we inserted above

UPDATE Survey SET EmpDetails.modify (delete(/Org/Comments)[1]') WHERE OrgID = 4

139. What is OPENXML?

Ans:

OPENXML helps in transforming a XML document into a row set. But OPENXML we used to use before SQL Server 2005. From 2005 till todays 2016 we can use the native XML support method node () for row transformations.

Let me explain how OPENXML works:

- Prepare the XML document by calling the stored procedure sp_xml_preparedocument which returns an integer that identifies the prepared XML.
- OPENXML is a rowset provider which means you can use it the same as if it were a table. Extract the required data from XML to rowset.
- The final step in using OPENXML is to "free" the prepared XML document by calling the stored procedure sp_xml_removedocument.
- The above xml stored procedures utilize the common MSXML parser component.
- OPENXML – SP_XML_PREPAREDOCUMENT and then we have to use DocHandle to get rows using OpenXML.

Note: Prepared XML document stores in SQL Server internal cache and we should make sure the document got cleared at the end of the execution.

140. What are the limitations of XML data type?

Ans:

- The stored representation of xml data type instances cannot exceed 2 GB.
- This means an xml data type cannot be used in a GROUP BY/ORDER BY statements.
- It does not support casting or converting to either text or ntext. Use VARCHAR(max) or NVARCHAR (max) instead.
- It cannot be used as a key column in an index. However, it can be included as data in a clustered index or explicitly added to a nonclustered index using INCLUDE
- It cannot be used as a parameter to any scalar, built-in functions other than ISNULL, COALESCE, and DATALENGTH.

141. Let's say XML data type is not available in SQL Server. Can we be able to store XML files in SQL Server?

Ans:

Yes! We can use VARCHAR (MAX) or NVARCHAR (MAX)

142. In that case why XML data type is required? Can't we manage XML data on LOB data types?

Ans:

- Structure of your data may change significantly in the future.
- Your data represents containment hierarchy, instead of references among entities, and may be recursive
- You need to query into the data or update data elements based on its structure.
- Your application required interoperability between relational and XML data
- Your business required query and data modification for cross-domain applications
- You want to validate your XML data based on defined XML schema
- You need the admin functionality for XML data type that includes indexing, backup, recovery, and replication.

If none of these conditions is satisfied with your business requirement, it may be better to store your data as a non-XML, large object type, such as [n]VARCHAR(max) or VARBINARY(max).

Triggers

143. What are the types of Triggers?

Ans:

- DML
  - ✓ INSTEAD OF: Override INSERT/DELETE/UPDATE operation. It is mainly used for security purpose and to implement specific business constraint.
  - ✓ AFTER: Action performed after INSERT/DELETE/UPDATE. Performs an Audit/ Logging
- DDL
- CLR
- LOGON

144. Can we create a Trigger on views?

Ans:

Yes! Only INSTEADOF Trigger can be created.

145. How many Triggers can be created on a table?

Ans:

One INSTEADOF Trigger and any number of AFTER Triggers

146. Can we use transactions inside a Trigger?

Ans:

Yes! We can use transactions inside a Trigger. COMMIT/ROLLBACK acts same like with nested procedures. When you commit a transaction inside a Trigger, it commits the nested transaction that opened inside the trigger. If issued "Rollback" inside a Trigger, it rollback all actions from the parent batch from which the Trigger got fired.

147. Can we be able to control the order of execution when a table is more after triggers defined on it?

Ans:

Yes! We can control using SP_SETTRIGGERORDER procedure

148. Can we call a stored procedure from a Trigger?

Ans:

Yes! We can call a stored procedure from a trigger.

149. Can we call a function from a Trigger?

Ans:

Yes! We can call a function (Ex: rownumber ()) inside a trigger. But remember a function will return a value/table which needs to be hold on a temp table and needs to be processed using a while loop or cursor.

150. Do you see any alternatives for Triggers?

Ans:

Yes! For some of the scenarios we can implement the same constraints using alternative methods as below:

- OUTPUT clause
- Cascading Update/Delete
- Stored Procedure

151. What are the pseudo tables?

Ans:

These are also known as Magic Tables. These are INSERTED/DELETED.

INSERTED: Table holds new data.

DELETED: Table holds old data.

152. Is there any magic table called "UPDATED"?

Ans:

No! For update operation also the old and new data available on INSERTED and DELETED tables.

153. Inside a trigger I want to alter the table INSERTED. Is it possible?

Ans:

No! DDL is not allowed on magic tables.

154. You are saying that Magic Tables are generated for both INSTEADOF and AFTER triggers. Any idea where this data is stored/available?

Ans:

On TEMPDB INSTEADOF triggers stores data under "INTERNAL OBJECTS" and AFTER Triggers stores data under "VERSION STORE" category.

155. What are the top reasons where we use Triggers?

Ans:

- Compare before and after modification data to implement a business constraint
- Rollback the operation
- Read/update data from other/remote databases based on current operation
- Execute local and remote stored procedure based on a logic

156. I have a table called "Employee." A foreign key defined on a column "DeptID" and there is an after trigger defined on the same column. This trigger will update other column based on the incoming data. If I try to insert a row which fails in validating referential integrity (foreign key) does the trigger fires?

Ans:

No! On a given column if any constraint fails then the next actions will be aborted. Since we are using After Triggers, these are fired after the actual operation which is failed in this case.

157. How to handle nested Triggers?

Ans:

We can configure "Nested Triggers" at server level using SP_CONFIGURE.

IDENTITY

158. What are the various ways to get the latest IDENTITY value from a table and what are the differences?

Ans:

There are three ways "@@IDENTITY," SCOPE_INDENTITY ()," "IDENT_CURRENT ()."

@@IDENTITY: Returns last IDENTITY value inserted into a table in the current session.

Ex: Let's take a transaction

- A row inserted on a table A, an IDENTITY value (77) generated.
- Since a Trigger is defined on that table it was fired and inserted a record on other table B and an IDENTITY generated 12001.
- Now if we query SELECT @@IDENTITY, it returns the last IDENTITY value inserted in your session which is 12001.

SCOPE_IDENTITY (): Returns the IDENTITY value inserted into a table in the current scope. It gets the IDENTITY value that is generated directly from the latest insert statement in your batch. It ignores IDENTITY generated by Triggers or User defined Functions etc.

Ex: From above example if we query using SCOPE_IDENTITY() it returns the value 77.

IDENT_CURRENT (<Table Name>): It returns the latest IDENTITY inserted on the given table.

Ex: From above example if we query using IDENT_CURRENT (A) it might return the value 77. Remember it is not related to any specific scope rather it relates to the Table thereof it gets the latest IDENTITY inserted on that table the value might be inserted from our transaction or from other transaction.

159. How to reset the IDENTITY column in SQL Server?

Ans:

DBCC CHECKIDENT (<Table_Name>, RESEED, <New_Reseed_Value>)

160. Did you face any issues with IDENTITY column?

Ans:

Yes, on 2012 we have recently got an issue with an IDENTITY column. Problem is "IDENTITY" value is skipping 1000 values for INT and 10000 values for BIGINT datatype. This skip happens when the SQL Server database engine restarts.

Solution:

- Use sequences
- Register trace flag 272 in SQL Server STARTUP parameter

Apart from this we know that removing IDENTITY property from a column is a tough task.

161. How to remove Identity property from a column?

Ans:

This can be done by changing the column properties by setting IS_Identity to "No." But remember it's a painful operation when the table is having millions of records. Below are the steps performed by database engine to remove an Identity property.

- Create a similar table with no identity.
- Move data from main table to the newly created table.
- Drop the original table.
- Rename the similar table name to the original table.

It really hurts the performance and there will be problems with logs, space etc.

Note: This is the process performed internally when we enable or disable an IDENTITY property.

There is another easy way:

- Create an extra column
- Fill the column with the required data from the original column
- Drop the original column (Also need to drop if there are any constraints defined)
- Rename the extra column as original column
- Recreate all required indexes and constraints

162. How to manually insert data in identity column when IDENTITY property is ON for a column?

Ans:

We can do this using SET IDENTITY_INSERT ON

163. Can we have more than one identity column in a table?

Ans:

No! We can't have more than one IDENTITY column in a table. Usually in any business scenario we do not see scenarios where two identity columns required. If in case that is required we can use sequences from 2012 or use a Trigger to populate the secondary identity column based a custom logic.

DBA Responsibilities

164. What are the key responsibilities of a SQL DBA?

Ans:

We can categorize DBA responsibilities into 7 types. Remember Monitoring and troubleshooting is common for all categories.

- *Capacity Management:* Analyze the past, present and predict the future data growth and usage. Ex: Suggesting and troubleshooting Memory, CPU, and Storage etc.
- *Security Management:* Understand the organization security policy and implement the enterprise level database security policies and Audit practices to prevent the security breaches.
- *HA & DR Management:* Managing High Availability and Disaster Recovery solutions that includes backup & recovery, replication, log shipping, database mirroring, failover clustering and ALWAYSON availability groups.
- *Performance Tuning:* Making sure that database systems are optimized by taking care of server and database level configurations. Identifying and optimizing queries and procedures.
- *Process Management & Improvements:* Following the process (ITIL/Environment Basis) and managing based on the rules and regulations. Designing and implementing process improvements Ex. Automated health checks for database servers.
- **Daily, Weekly and Monthly maintenance**
- **Architecture & Team Management**

165. In a given day what are activities a SQL DBA may need to involve?

Ans:

On daily basis a typical DBA should monitor and handle below:

- Backups
- Disk space
- Jobs/Maintenance Plans
- Servers/Databases

- Logs
- Security
- High Availability
- Request Handling & Process Management

Backups:

- Confirm that backups have been made and successfully saved to a secure location
- Check the backup failure alerts, correct the errors and rerun the backups
- Review the average duration of backup, any significant changes occurred investigates on this. Most of the time it happens due to networking low bandwidth
- Validate the backup files using restore verify only. We can create jobs to take care of the task and to send a notification if it fails to verify any backup.
- Monitor all backup and log history is cleaning if it is designed.
- Find out the newly added databases and define the backup plan

Disk Space:

- Verify the free space on each drive on all servers. If there is significant variance in free space from the day before, research the cause of the free space fluctuation and resolve if necessary. Often times, log files will grow because of monthly jobs.
- Automate through a job. The job runs for every one hour and reports any drive which is having less than 15 % of free space. We can design a SSRS report to showcase and review the delta values.

Jobs/Maintenance plans:

- Check for the failed jobs, investigate the route cause and resolve the issue. Native SQL notification alert sends a mail to DBA team and also we can design a customized SSRS report which reports all failed/success job details with delta value.
- Check for the job execution duration and if any significant changes find the root cause and resolve the issue.
- Make sure that all process related jobs/maintenance plans completed. That includes data pulling jobs, data update jobs etc.
- All cleanup jobs are running fine, temp tables, logs, history, backup files etc.

Servers/Databases:

- Confirm all servers/databases are up and running fine.
- Usually in an Enterprise Database Environment Third Party Tools are used to monitor Servers (Ex: "SCOM," "M360," "What's Up" etc.)
- For database monitoring we can design a native SQL Server solution using T-SQL code and a maintenance plan, it run min by min and send an email to DBA team if it is not able to connect to any of the database in the instance.

Performance:

- Regularly monitor and identify blocking issues. We can design a procedure that continuously run on all PROD servers and notifies DBA team if any blockings, long running quires/ transactions.
- Check Performance counters on all production servers and verify that all counters are within the normal range. We can design a SSRS metrics report to review the counters for every one hour.
- Throughout the day, periodically monitor performance using both System Monitor and DMV.
- Check the fragmentation and rebuild/reorganize the indexes. We can use a native procedure which takes care of the task.
- Make sure all Stats Update/nightly_checkalloc/Index_Rebuild jobs are completed without any issue.

Logs:

- Have a look at both SQL Server logs and Windows logs. If you find any strange issues notify the network or storage teams. Most of the times we find Network related or I/O related issues.
- Check the centralized error logs if any.

Security:

- Check the error logs for failed logins and notify the audit team if necessary
- Security Logs - Review the security logs from a third party solution or from the SQL Server Error Logs to determine if you had a breach or a violation in one of your policies.
- Granting/denying access to users based on requirement.

High-Availability:

- High Availability or Disaster Recovery Logs - Check your high availability and/or disaster recovery process logs. Depending on the solution (Log Shipping, Clustering, Replication, Database Mirroring, ALWAYSON AG, etc.) that you are using dictates what needs to be checked.
- We can design native scripts using T-SQL and we can automate the monitoring process.
- In most of the environments we see third party tools in monitoring Clusters or we can design our own native scripts using Windows Batch Programming, Powershell and T-SQL.

Request Handling & Process Management:

- Check the escalated issues and high priority requests first
- Check the current queue for requests and identify requests to be processed and work on the issue.
- We usually process the requests based on the SLA (Service Level Agreement)
- Apart from the customer requests DBA should be taken care of failure notifications coming from SQL Server or a third party tool

166. In an enterprise environment what the DBA weekly/monthly checklist contains?

Ans:

- Backup Verification (Comprehensive)- Verify your backups and test on a regular basis to ensure the overall process works as expected. Contact your off site tape vendor and validate the type does not have any restore errors
- Check the logins, service accounts for expire dates
- Backup Verification - Verify your backups on a regular basis. Randomly choose one or two backups and try to restore verify.
- Windows, SQL Server or Application Updates - Check for service packs/patches that need to be installed on your SQL Server from either a hardware, OS, DBMS or application perspective
- Capacity Planning - Perform capacity planning to ensure you will have sufficient storage for a specific period of time such as for 3, 6, 12 or 18 months.
- Fragmentation - Review the fragmentation for your databases to determine if you particular indexes must be rebuilt based on analysis from a backup SQL Server.
- Maintenance - Schedule an official maintenance, do all required health checks on all premium databases and servers.
- Security - Remove unneeded logins and users for individuals that have left the organization, had a change in position, etc.
- Moving data from production to archive: If your environment requires any specific DBA related data for a long time, plan for an archival procedure. We can achieve data from actual OLTP system to other dedicated DBA Server/Database

167. Typically in any enterprise environment DBA should involve with the other teams right? Can you tell me what the other teams that you interacted with?

Ans:

- We need to work with the other teams to make sure that all servers are at health condition and to balance the infrastructure.
- Usually we approach other teams for below
  - ✓ Found I/O errors
  - ✓ Networking issues
  - ✓ F/R – Flatten and Rebuild
  - ✓ Adding space/drives
  - ✓ Starting a Server – When a manual interaction needed
  - ✓ Backup Tapes – Archived backups
  - ✓ Security Team – When we require a port needs to be opened etc.
  - ✓ Application Owners – For giving notifications and for taking maintenance approvals
  - ✓ Third Party tool Teams
  - ✓ Product Owners – Ex: Opening a case with Microsoft when we are seeing frequent memory dumps.

168. Documentation is part of a DBA responsibility. Can you describe what all the things a DBA should document?

Ans:

- Document all changes you make to the environment that includes:
  - ✓ Installations/Upgrades
  - ✓ Service packs/HotFixes applied
  - ✓ New databases added
  - ✓ Logins\Roles added/removed
  - ✓ Check lists
  - ✓ Infrastructure changes
  - ✓ Process improvements
- Maintain a centralized inventory with all details for below items
  - ✓ Database Servers
  - ✓ Application Servers
  - ✓ Web Servers
  - ✓ Logins (Both SQL Server and Windows)
  - ✓ Database Instances
  - ✓ Databases (Dev/Stag/QA/PROD)

Note: Document as much as information. It really helps in critical situations, reduces the dependency and increases the productivity. Try to add owner at each level, for example application owners, server owners etc. We can easily reach them in-case of any emergencies/Maintenance.

169. What do you mean by Architecture & Team Management in DBA responsibilities?

Ans:

For the senior roles like LEAD DBA, Principal DBA, SME, Database Architect etc. there are more responsibilities added in their queue apart from the above basic routine.

- *Suggesting enterprise best practices:* Based on your environment and business requirement suggest and implement enterprise database best practices
- *Analyzing the problems and suggesting a solution* Ex: A task has been consuming a lot of time, manual interaction and failing in some cases. You should be able to suggest a better solution to get it done as per the business requirement.
- *Analyzing the requirement and designing the solution*. For example you get a new database requirement from the client to configure a Disaster Recovery solution for one of the newly lunching databases. You should be able to understand the requirement, analyze the existing environment and suggest and design the suitable Disaster Recovery Solution
- *Managing the team:* Usually in a 24X7 enterprise environment DBA LEAD handles the high priority and escalated issues, also Leads will be taken care of resource shift alignments.

Requirement gathering and onsite – offshore communication. Apart from these leads should carry other LEAD responsibilities based on organization.

- *Understanding Internals:* Ex: SME (Subject Mater Expert) should be able to understand the internals of both technology and business.

170. What is L1, L2, L3, L4 support levels in IT Operations Management?

Ans:

L1, L2, L3 and L4 line support is designed based on responsibilities and capabilities.

L1 – First Line Support:

This support level receives inbound requests through channels like Ticketing tool, phone, Web forms, email, chat, or other means based on the documented agreement with the Client. L1 support typically includes individuals that have very limited technical expertise. L1 support logs, categorizes, prioritizes, tracks, and routes to the correct team. L1 resources acknowledge the notifications and requests. L1 is intended to be the first to acknowledge an incident. L1 support tracks tickets until successfully resolved. L1 engineers can implement basic, documented break-fix tasks.L1 personnel will typically escalate to an L2 resource and follow documented escalation procedures, L1 technicians will have from 0 to 4 years of prior relevant experience.

L2 – Second Line Support:

These technicians have more experience than L1 support technicians and manage incidents raised by the L1s or as agreed in documented SLA (Service Level Agreement) timelines. L2 technicians follow documented processes and workflows provided by Clients or higher level support representatives, vendors, product management, etc. L2s usually have and maintain a Run-Book which they can use for immediate resolutions. L2 engineers will typically escalate to an L3 resource and follow documented escalation procedures. L2 technicians will have from 4 to 8 years of prior relevant experience.

L3 – Third Line Support:

L3 technical experts resolve issues that are typically difficult or subtle. L3 engineers participate in management, prioritization, minor enhancements, break fix activities, problem management, stability analysis, etc. These support leaders have specific, deep understanding and expertise in one or two technology platforms. L3 engineers are proactive in nature, identifying problems in advance and looking for continuous service improvement opportunities. If a fix involves a major enhancement or a development, then the problem is transferred to engineering or development teams, Level 4. L3 engineers may have root or administrator access to basic systems. L3 technicians will have from 6 plus years of prior relevant experience.

L4 – Product and Vendor Support:

L4 support refers to product or vendor support and often involves vendor product architects, engineers, software developers, hardware designers and the like. When all other levels of support cannot solve a problem, a request is made to this level of support. These escalations can often involve product bugs, detailed configuration requirements, or other expert level guidance. L4 technicians will have 8 + years of prior relevant experience.

171. What is SLA?

Ans:

SLA means Service Level Agreement. SLAs are agreements between you and your customers. If you're a DBA, then your customer is typically the company for whom you work.

As a DBA, your job is to provide database systems that are reliable, secure and available when required. In order to achieve these goals, you must understand your customer's service requirements, usually conveyed through Service Level Agreements.

SLA's are designed differently for different customers based on customer requirement but most of the SLA falls into below categories:

System Availability: Ex. The database servers must be online 7 days a week, from 5am to midnight

Acceptable Data Loss: Ex: No more than 15 minutes of data entry can be lost in-case of any disaster

Recovery Time: Ex: In the event of a disaster, the systems should be back online and running within one hour.

Performance: Ex: Transaction response time should not exceed 3 seconds.

Communication & Service: Ex: Alerts from premium servers should be acknowledged within 3 min and should provide the primary analysis within an hour etc.

172. What is a service request?

Ans:

A request from a User for information, or advice, or for a Standard Change or for access to an IT service is known as Service Request. For example to reset a password, or to provide standard IT Services for a new User. Service Requests are usually handled by a Service Desk.

173. What is a change request?

Ans:

The addition, modification or removal of anything that could have an effect on IT Services is known as a Change Request. The Scope should include all IT Services, Configuration Items, Processes, documentation etc. Changes can include replacing or upgrading the capacity of hardware, upgrading to a new version or rolling back to an old version of software, or switching to new vendors of IaaS and PaaS solution. Changes can both be a response to problems and incidents as well as causes of them.

174. What is an incident?

Ans:

- Incident is an unplanned interruption to an IT Service or a reduction in the Quality of an IT Service. Failure of a Configuration Item that has not yet impacted one or more Services is also an Incident. For example: Failure of one disk from a mirror set, timeout error coming in one of the application page.
- The objective of the Incident Management Lifecycle is to restore the service as quickly as possible to meet Service Level Agreements.

- An incident needs to be fixed within a stipulated timeline.
- The process is primarily aimed at the user level.

175. What is a problem request?

Ans:

- A Problem is a condition from a number of incidents that are related or have common issues. This means that it is more serious than an Incident and needs separate follow up at a deeper level to avoid future Incidents.
- However problems are not incidents. An incident can raise a problem, in cases where there is a high possibility that the incident might happen again.
- Managing a Problem means finding the underlying root causes so that the Incidents do not reoccur.
- Problem Management deals with solving the underlying cause of one or more incidents.
- Problem Management is to resolve the root cause of errors and to find permanent solutions.
- This process deals at the enterprise level.
- **For Example:** Timeout error coming in an application page may cause an incident, Dba opened and incident and found it was due to blocking and closing the blocker session resolved the issue. If the same incident triggered again this time we'll raise a problem request for a Root Cause Analysis and a permanent solution.

176. How do you define High Availability, Disaster Recovery and Load Balancing?

Ans:

High Availability (HA): This is a technology solution to make sure server/databases are available 24X7 and 365 days. The principal goal of a high availability solution is to minimize or mitigate the impact of downtime. Ex: ALWAYSON AG, Failover Clustering, Database Mirroring, Log Shipping etc.

Disaster Recovery (DR): A disaster can be numerous that includes power failure, hardware failure, virus attack, natural disaster, human error, etc. A SQL Server disaster recovery plan (DRP) is a process to have SQL Server up and running, and to overcome data loss after a disaster. It refers to restoring your systems and data to a previous acceptable state in the event of partial or complete failure of computers due to natural or technical causes. Ex: Backup & Restore, Replication, Failover Clustering, ALWAYSON AG, Database Mirroring, Log Shipping etc.

Load Balancing (LB): Load balancing is distributing the load across multiple SQL Server instances using the available technology solutions is known as Load Balancing. Ex: Peer to Peer Replication, Log Shipping, Failover Clustering with Active-Active, ALWAYSON AG with Read-only Replicas etc.

177. Have you ever heard the words "RTO," "RPO" and "RLO"?

Ans:

Yes! We use these parameters when we are designing a high availability/disaster recovery solution for a customer requirement.

RTO (Recovery Time Objective): It determines the potential recovery time in seconds/minutes. In other way RTO means the duration of acceptable application downtime whether from unplanned outage or from scheduled maintenance/upgrades. The primary goal is to restore full service to the point that new transactions can take place.

RPO (Recovery Point Objective): It determines the potential data loss in seconds/minutes. The ability to accept potential data loss from an outage is called RPO. It is the time gap or latency between the last committed data transaction before the failure and the most recent data recovered after the failure. The actual data loss can vary depending upon the workload on the system at the time of the failure, the type of failure, and the type of high availability solution used.

RLO (Recovery Level Objective): This objective defines the granularity with which you must be able to recover data, whether you must be able to recover the whole instance, database or set of databases, or specific tables.

178. Since you worked with various HA/DR SQL Server solutions, can you explain RPO, RTO and automatic failover capabilities of any few HA/DR solutions?

Ans:

ALWAYSON Availability Group – Synchronous Commit:

- RPO (Data Loss): Zero
- RTO (Down Time): Seconds
- Automatic Failover: Yes

ALWAYSON Availability Group – Asynchronous Commit:

- RPO (Data Loss): Seconds
- RTO (Down Time): Minutes
- Automatic Failover: No

ALWAYSON Failover Cluster Instance:

- RPO (Data Loss): NA
- RTO (Down Time): Minutes
- Automatic Failover: Yes

Database Mirroring – High-Safety (Synchronous + Witness):

- RPO (Data Loss): Zero
- RTO (Down Time): Seconds
- Automatic Failover: Yes

Database Mirroring – High-Performance (Asynchronous):

- RPO (Data Loss): Seconds
- RTO (Down Time): Minutes
- Automatic Failover: No

Log Shipping:

- RPO (Data Loss): Minutes
- RTO (Down Time): Minutes to Hours
- Automatic Failover: No

Backup & Restore:

- RPO (Data Loss): Hours
- RTO (Down Time): Hours to Days
- Automatic Failover: No

179. In HA & DR solutions which servers you select for configuration which means you select servers from same data center or from the different datacentres?

Ans:

It always depends on business requirement and data criticality.

- Choose servers from the same datacenter which can save us from server/disk failure.
- Choose different data centers from the same region - So data moment will be faster and can save us from datacenter failure
- Choose different data centers from different regions - For a highly critical databases and can save us from area/region failures due to natural disasters, but we need to have dedicated network lines.
- Choose a Multi Configuration: Choose servers from the same datacenter configure ALWAYSON failover clustering and implement log shipping to remote datacenter.

Database Design

This is one of the most common areas where you should have some knowledge up to some extent. But it becomes as a primary area when you are working as a database modeler/designer/architect. Even if you are a DBA and applying for a mid-level services company or to a product based company they would expect you to understand the database design concepts and you might be asked these questions.

180. How to design a database? What are the various phases involved in designing a new database?

Ans:

These are phases involved in designing a new database.

- Requirement Specification and Analysis
- Conceptual\Semantic Database Design
- Implementation\Logical Schema Design
- Physical Schema Design
- Optimization\Administration

Requirement Specification and Analysis:

- In this phase a detailed analysis of the requirement is done. The objective of this phase is to get a clear understanding of the requirements.
- The database designer's first step is to draw up a data requirements document. The requirements document contains a concise and non-technical summary of what data items will be stored in the database, and how the various data items relate to one another.
- Taking the 'data requirements document', further analysis is done to give meaning to the data items, e.g. define the more detailed attributes of the data and define constraints if needed. The result of this analysis is a 'preliminary specifications' document.
- Some of the information gathering methods are:
  - ✓ Interview
  - ✓ Analyzing documents and existing system or data
  - ✓ Survey
  - ✓ Site visit
  - ✓ Joint Applications Design (JAD) and Joint Requirements Analysis (JRA)
  - ✓ Prototyping
  - ✓ Discussions/Meetings
  - ✓ Observing the enterprise in operation
  - ✓ Research
  - ✓ Questionnaire
- From all these methods we need to:
  - ✓ Identify essential "real world" information
  - ✓ Remove redundant, unimportant details
  - ✓ Clarify unclear natural language statements
  - ✓ Fill remaining gaps in discussions
  - ✓ Distinguish data and operations
- Go to the next phase to give the model for the existing data.

Conceptual Database Design:

The requirement analysis is modeled in this conceptual design. Conceptual database design involves modeling the collected information at a high-level of abstraction. The ER diagram is used to represent this conceptual design. ER diagram consists of Entities, Attributes and Relationships.

- Why conceptual design:
  - ✓ Allow easy communication between end-users and developers.
  - ✓ Has a clear method to convert from high-level model to relational model.
  - ✓ Conceptual schema is a permanent description of the database requirements

- What should be the outcome from this phase:
    - ✓ Entities and relationships in the enterprise
    - ✓ Information about these entities and relationships that we need to store in the database
    - ✓ Integrity constraints or business rules that hold
    - ✓ Type of relationship or Cardinality (1:1, 1:N, N:M) should be defined
- At the end of this phase the database `schema' in the ER Model can be represented pictorially (ER diagrams).

Logical Schema Design:

Once the relationships and dependencies are identified the data can be arranged into logical structures and is mapped into database management system tables. Normalization is performed to make the relations in appropriate normal forms.

- Map all entities, attributes and relationships from ER diagrams to relational database objects
    - ✓ Map regular entities
    - ✓ Map weak entities
    - ✓ Map binary relationships
    - ✓ Map associative entities
    - ✓ Map unary relationships
    - ✓ Map ternary relationships
    - ✓ Map super-type/subtype relationships
- Find out the anomalies
    - ✓ Insertion: Data about an attribute inserted at more than one place
    - ✓ Deletion: Removing data of an attribute required delete operation at more than one place
    - ✓ Update: Updating data of an attribute required Update operation at more than one place
- Identify the candidate\primary keys
- Normalize all the relations in database be following the normal forms
    - ✓ First normal form (No Multivalued Dependency)
    - ✓ Second normal form (No Partial Dependency)
    - ✓ Third normal form (No Transitive Dependency)
    - ✓ Boyce-Codd normal form
    - ✓ Fourth Normal form
    - ✓ Fifth Normal form

- Apply all constraints from ER diagrams to make sure that the database is integrated
  - ✓ Domain integrity – Allowable values to an attribute in the domain
  - ✓ Entity integrity – No primary key attribute may be null
  - ✓ Referential integrity – Data must be consistent (Primary foreign key matching) and Enforcement on Delete (Cascade)

Physical Schema Design:

It deals with the physical implementation of the database in a database management system. It includes the specification of data elements, data types, indexing etc. All these information is stored in the data dictionary.

- Information needed for physical file and database design includes:
  - ✓ Normalized relations plus size estimates for them
  - ✓ Definitions of each attribute
  - ✓ Descriptions of where and when data are used (entered, retrieved, deleted, updated, and how often)
  - ✓ Expectations and requirements for response time, and data security, backup, recovery, retention and integrity
  - ✓ Descriptions of the technologies used to implement the database

Things that should be considered in the physical schema design:

- Usage Type: OLTP, OLAP, Production, Dev, Test, etc.
- Data Storage: Choose the appropriate data type. Main Memory and Secondary Memory
- Database Size (Data File and Log File growth expecting): Size of Relations -> tuples
- Processing Time: Processors using and speed according to the expected growth
- Operating System: OS capacity
- Access Methods (Physical Sequential, Indexed Sequential, Indexed Random, Inverted, Direct, Hashed)
- CRUD Matrix (Database Usage – Create, Retrieve, Update and Delete)
- Security – Security considerations while storing data files
- HA & DR – High availability & Disaster Recovery planning according to the business
- Indexing: Index primary, foreign keys, attributes that uses in filters and in sorts. Do not index attribute that are having few values.
- Cashing
- De-normalizing

Optimization\Administration:

- Define the benchmarks for performance parameters. Ex: Response time, Throughput, Maximum Execution time etc.

- Prepare the best practices checklist and implement it.
- Design administration jobs and maintenance plans to take care of database backups, auditing, index maintenance, statistics update, history cleanup, health checks etc.

181. What is normalization and different types of normal forms?

Ans:

Normalization is a method of arranging the data elements in an organized format to optimize the data access. Normalization Avoids:

- Duplication of Data
- Insert Anomaly
- Delete Anomaly
- Update Anomaly

Normal Forms:

There are 5+ normalization rules (5 Normal Forms and Boyce-Codd), but most day-to-day database creation focuses on the first three. These rules are used to help create flexible, adaptable tables that have no redundancy and are easy to query. Before normalizing begin with a list of all of the fields that must appear in the database. Think of this as one big table.

First Normal Form:

- Remove repeating groups by moving those groups into new tables.
- Example1: Divide Name column into "First_Name" and "Last_Name"
- Example2: One field called "Month" instead of 12 columns called "Jan," "Feb" etc.

Second Normal Form:

- Remove Partial Dependencies.
- *Partial Dependency* A type of functional dependency where an attribute is functionally dependent on only part of the primary key (primary key must be a composite key). A column in a table is partially dependent on a primary key.
- Ex: Below table is having a composite primary key on (StudentID and CourseID) and it is not in second normal form because the column StudentName is partially dependent on Primary Key (Only on StudentID)

  StudentID, CourseID, StudentName, Grade

  Remove partial dependency by dividing into two different tables.

  StudentID, CourseID, Grade

  and

  StudentID, StudentName

  Now above tables are in 2nd normal form.

Third Normal Form:

- Remove transitive dependencies. (C → B → A. Indirectly C → A not directly)

- *Transitive Dependency* is a type of functional dependency where an attribute is functionally dependent on an attribute other than the primary key. Thus its value is only indirectly determined by the primary key.
- Ex: In below table CourseID is primary key. But the column FacultyOffice is not directly depends on primary key and it depends on a non-primary key column "FacultyID."

  FacultyOffice à FacultyID à CourseID

  CourseID, Section, FacultyID, FacultyOffice

  Hence divide the table to remove the transitive dependency.

182. What are the types of relationships in RDBMS?

Ans:

There are three types of table relationships. Each has its own unique purpose in helping to organize the data within the database. These relationships can be used to determine joins in queries as well.

One-to-One Relationships: one record in a table is related to one record in a related table; creates equally dependent tables

Ex. one student has only one PSU ID

***NOTE:** This type of relationship is rarely used.

One-to-Many Relationships: one record in a primary table is related to many records in a related table; however, a record in the related table has only one related record in the primary table

Ex. a student can live in one residence hall at a given time, but many students can live in a residence hall at a given time

***NOTE:** This is the most common type of relationship.

Many-to-Many Relationships: several records in the primary table are related to several records in a related table

Ex. one student can be enrolled in many subjects and each subject can have many students enrolled

183. What are the signs of Good Database Design?

Ans:

- Thoughtfully planned
- Works for the intended situation and purpose
- Streamlines a process
- Shows consistency among data (Fall 16 vs. fall 2016)
- Eliminates redundancy as much as possible, i.e. tables are normalized
- Provides users with an easy way to enter, store, and retrieve data
- Does NOT promote deleting data, but rather making designations or archiving it
- Provides unique identifiers (primary keys) for records
- Grows, changes, and improves as needed
- Automatic policies implemented to prevent the unauthorized access and changes

184. What is data integrity?

Ans:

Enforcing data integrity ensures the quality of the data in the database. For example, if an employee is entered with an employee_id value of 123, the database should not allow another employee to have an ID with the same value. Data integrity falls into these categories:

- Entity integrity
- Domain integrity
- Referential integrity
- User-defined integrity

Entity Integrity:

The intention of entity integrity is to uniquely identify all the rows in a table. For this we need to add primary key to a column.

Domain Integrity:

A domain defines the possible values of an attribute. Domain Integrity rules govern these values. In a database system, the domain integrity is defined by:

- The data type and the length
- The NULL value acceptance
- The allowable values, through techniques like constraints or rules
- The default value We can use the check constraint to restrict the column values

Referential Integrity:

Referential integrity is a database concept that ensures that relationships between tables remain consistent. When one table has a foreign key to another table, the concept of referential integrity states that you may not add a record to the table that contains the foreign key unless there is a corresponding record in the linked table. It also includes the techniques known as cascading update and cascading delete, which ensure that changes made to the linked table are reflected in the primary table. We can implement this by using foreign key constraints.

User-Defined:

Integrity User-defined integrity allows you to define specific business rules that do not fall into one of the other integrity categories. All of the integrity categories support user-defined integrity (all column- and table-level constraints in CREATE TABLE, stored procedures, and triggers).

185. When might we need to de-normalize database tables?

Ans:

De-Normalization is typically done for performance reasons, to reduce the number of table joins. This is not suggested in a transactional environment as there are inherent data integrity risks or performance risks due to excessive locking to maintain data integrity.

CHAPTER 13

SQL SERVER DBA ARTICLES

This chapter takes you through few articles which may helpful for your interview preparation. Below are the articles:

SQL DBA – Interview Preparation

An interview Experience with Microsoft R&D

Stored Procedure Code Review checklist

Database Career Paths

How to Become an Expert in your Career

SQL DBA – Interview Preparation

If you are reading this article which means you must be a Microsoft SQL Server Database Administrator/professional☺. In today's corporate world attending or taking a technical interview is mandatory whether it's for a new role in current organization, new customer/client or for a new organization. Getting ready for an interview is always a challenge. We have randomly chosen SQL Server database professionals from three different experience levels and had a deep discussion on "How to prepare for a technical interview."

- **Fresher/Junior** – Should know the basics of process and technology
- **Mid-Level** – Should be able to expertise in one or two areas and know the process
- **Senior Level** - Should be expertise in technology and able to drive the process

If you are working on SQL Server, you already chosen one of the best RDBMS and you have plenty of opportunities in IT. There are few points that can help you to get succeed in an interview.

- Profile
- Preparation
- Communication
- Interview Process
- Preparing a Topic

Profile

This is the first piece of information that tells about you so please be careful in preparing your profile:

- Don't add the generic skillset: Include only the topics that you are experienced or learned.

- ➢ Add your professional experience, key skills, education details, your achievements, certifications, trainings and projects.
- ➢ Number of pages should be restricted to 3 or 4.
- ➢ Maintain a profile on professional network like LinkedIn and add a link to your profile (I have seen a lot of opportunities are hitting through professional networks)
- ➢ Remember you should know/learn/prepare/experience each and everything you mentioned in your profile as the interview questions are always depends on summary points that you showcase in your profile.

Preparation

When you are not prepared for an interview you will not be going to make a WIN. Preparation makes you to feel more confident and plays the main role in your success. Prepare a self-reference guide with all your experiences, your tough times, difficult technical issues you faced, complex requirements and resolutions and your own interview experiences. Now we'll see WHAT should be in our preparation list:

Top Questions:

Prepare top 10 questions in each category, let's say you mentioned you are experienced in Performance Tuning, DBA daily activities, Replication and Clustering. You must be ready to answer top 10 questions from these categories. TOP 10 is different from person to person let's say you are mostly handles SQL Server AlwaysOn Failover Cluster installations, person B might be expert in troubleshooting clustering issues and Person C mostly experienced in RCA and Performance Tuning in clusters. Based on your experience prepare your own list and see this is just a onetime activity and you can use the reference guide throughout your career.

Environment:

This is the most critical area where 80% failures in answering the questions. This is the primary area to test your experience, so prepare well. Environment includes different things that one can learn only through experience. We'll see the common questions on environment:

Versions:

Remember the versions you worked on:

- ➢ Prepare at least few new features added in the latest version you worked in (Ex: 2012 when compared to 2008 R2).
- ➢ Have a look at new features added in latest SQL Server version. Ex: 2016
- ➢ You might be asked SQL Server components, try to remember few major components

Servers/Instances/Databases:

If you are experienced you must be confident in answering the question "How many total windows/SQL servers/Instances and Databases available in your previous work environment?" Below we are giving an average values that we got from various professionals working in different organizations. It always depends on business Application requirement

Number of SQL Servers/Instances:

- Enterprise Big Environment: 100 to 800
- Mid-Level: 50 to 100
- Small: 10 to 60

Number of databases:

We always have an average figure as an answer for this question, because we can't know the exact count as we maintain databases for different environments. For example an application can require 4 databases, then the same number of databases may require for DEVELOPMENT, TESTING, STAGING and in PRODUCTION. If any DR/HA is configured then those replicas should also be considered. Thereof we usually do not count the number of databases but yes we can see inventories for database details. Here are the average counts:

- Big Environments: 1000 to 4000
- Mid-Level Environments: 500 to 1000
- Small Environments: 100 to 500

Database Size:

- **Big Enterprise:**
  - ✓ OLTP: 50 GB – 2 TB
  - ✓ OLAP: 600 GB – 12 TB
- **Mid-Level Enterprise:**
  - ✓ OLTP: 10 GB – 2 TB
  - ✓ OLAP: 100 GB – 5 TB
- **Small Environment:**
  - ✓ OLTP: 1 GB – 200 GB
  - ✓ OLAP: 50 GB – 1 TB

Team Size:

- **Enterprise Environments:** 50 to 100
- **Mid-Level:** 5 to 20
- **Low Level:** 1 to 5

Hardware specs (CPU, Memory, and Storage):

CPU: Processors: Most of the servers use processor from AMD, DELL or Intel X series

Cores: It's the most important thing as SQL Server licenses based on the number of cores. It's starting from 4 and 16, 64 etc.

Memory:

Minimum: 4 GB (We still see in some small instances in DEV and QA)

Medium: 64 to 128 GB

Maximum: 512 GB+ (For a premium prod server)

Storage: SAN, SMB, NFS, iSCSI, EBS – if it's AWS, Virtual Volumes – If it's VMware etc.

Software & Tools:

- Make a note on third party tools you used in your environment ex: LITESPEED, REDGATE etc.
- Also make a note on how licensing happening for SQL Server in your environment
- Make a note on version number of names for ticketing and monitoring tools Ex: SCOM, TFS, and SVN etc.

Processes:

This is one of the most important key points. Processes related questions can be from:

- How request handling happening in your environment if you are working on ITIL
- Timeframe and other details on SPRINT/SCRUM if you are into agile
- Documenting process
- Inventory management
- Onsite Offshore communication
- How frequently you communicate with your client
- How an incident is handled
- What is bridge call?
- Escalation Matrix: How escalation happens in your environment etc.
- SLA: What is the Service Level Agreement for acknowledging the critical alerts?
- Policies: What are the Backup policies for PROD, QA and DEV environments?
- Experiences: Make a quick notes on strange/bad/good experiences from your daily routine
- Projects: Know something about your projects/actual business

Responsibilities:

- Be prepared to answer the question "what are your current job responsibilities?"
- Prepare the details on Daily/Weekly/Monthly/Quarterly maintenance tasks

Behavioural Questions:

When you are targeting a critical role with a "Big IT Giant," you should be prepared the answers for these questions as well:

- Your next 5 years plan?
- Most difficult situation you handled?
- The situation you failed in?
- Why you are leaving the current role?
- Any innovative idea you initiated?
- How do you define the success?

- Best/Worst day in your life?
- What are your top 3 wishes if god gives you a chance?
- Most difficult person you faced in your work place?
- Your manager is submitting a wrong bill to company, how do you react?
- You got 3 offers: 1. Dream Company, 2. Dream location, 3. Dream Salary. Which one you choose and why?
- Your strength and weakness
- Who is your role model and Why?
- When the last time you made a controversy in working place?
- You have an emergency in your office and family what's your priority and why?
- Why this company?
- Why we should hire you?
- Etc.

Communication

I have seen people blaming themselves "I am not great in English" yes that's true you can't be great in English unless English is your mother tongue. But you can be good in any language with some practice. So again practice well, let's practice answering the first question "Tell me about yourself?" and also practice answering the top 10 questions on your most interested area. Take some breath time and answer the questions. Remember communication plays 60% role in your success.

Preparing a Topic

Here we'll see how to prepare a specific topic. Let's say you have added "Replication, Clustering, Performance Tuning are your strong points." Now we'll see what questions we might expect from Replication:

Replication Components: Replication Agents, Methodology, advantages etc.

Types and Differences: Types of replication topologies and differences between them

Common Issues/Scenarios & Resolutions: Found duplicate records in subscriber, No-records found at subscriber, Log is getting full at Publisher, adding a new article without generating new snapshot etc.

New Features: Try to remember at least one new feature added in replication on the latest version in your experience Example: 2012/2014/2016.

Monitoring: A very common question is "How to monitor replication health?" Replication Monitor, Tracer Tokens, DMV etc.

Top 5 Questions: You should be prepared the top 5 common questions on topic replication. For example Different types of replications, implementations (Advantages) of Transactional and Merge, Can we issue TRUNCATE command on publisher, How to monitor replication, Replication Agents etc.

Interview Process

If you are in crisis or targeting a role in your dream company then take it seriously and follow these tips:

- Be on time at interview venue
- I don't see people coming in formal dresses in today's interviews, that's not an issue but try to be a professional.
- For the first question "Introduce Yourself," give your experience details, your achievements and then education if still you have time and they are listening then continue with other details
- If you guessed the answer then you can tell that are guessing "This is just a guess from my analysis"
- Drive the interview process. If you want to drive the process you should be prepared well which means if you say "I am good in Performance Tuning" please do not expect a question like "What is an index" rather you can expect "Why indexed view when filter index is there?."
- Remember that in most of the cases your next question is based on the current question answer isn't it? Let's say if you are asked "What are the common issues with TEMPDB?," if you answer something like, TEMPDB full, Space issue, Version store full, forced to shrink, Latch Contention etc. Then the next question will be on one of these 5 reasons. You might be asked "What is Latch Contention?" and then "How do you troubleshoot it?" etc.
- Be focused and here the question completely, try to give the straight answer unless you are asked to explain in detail.
- Ask the right questions for which we need to do some research required on that organization, role.
- We can ask for the answer if you can't answer any question.
- Don't be dumb when you don't aware of something. See I have seen people kept silent or try to cover with the false answers. If you are asked a scenario based question in replication, but you don't know the answer then you can accept that by saying "I am really not getting but I have seen similar kind of issue when duplicates are inserted in subscribers and that time we did give XXXX resolution."
- If you are asked something really strange that you don't know then you should admit that you didn't get a chance to work on that. If you try to skip then immediate question also be from the same area.
- Remember no one knows everything, you are asked scenario based questions to check how you are reacting and using your analysis to get the answer.
- Never ever blame your previous/current work place or colleagues
- Do not reveal previous clients information, database/server names etc. Ex: You can say I worked with world's largest bank instead of XXXXX Bank.
- Do the proper follow up post the interview

Final note:

Interview process is not just to test your technical knowledge instead your analytical skills, how you handle stress, management skills, problem solving skills, way of thinking, experience and of course your technical knowledge. Prepare well, be confident and get the success in your next interview.

An Interview Experience with Microsoft R&D

For the people who work on Microsoft technologies will be having a common dream place to work is "Microsoft R&D." Here with sharing an interview experience with Microsoft R&D. This interview is conducted for a profile Sr.DBA. This profile should know all areas of SQL Server (Administration, Development, and MSBI) and should be expert in performance tuning.

I have got a call from Microsoft division and told me that they have got my profile from a job portal and wanted to check with me if I am looking for job change. I was actually not looking for any job change but its exception for Microsoft. I said yes to proceed ahead. 3 days later I got a call from MS staff and said I need to go through a general discussion. A telephonic interview scheduled for the very next day and it went on for 45 Min. Discussed about my experience, projects, technology, current role etc. Later 2 days I was informed that my profile got shortlisted and scheduled a face to face interview.

Day I

It's Saturday, I have reached MS OFFICE ☺ on time at 9:00 AM, given my profile, got Microsoft visitor Badge and was being waiting for the interview call.

Someone from staffing team came to me and took me to the **Interviewer** cabin. He introduced to me to the **Interviewer**.

Technical Interview - I

Interviewer: This is XXXXX, how are you doing?

Me: I am very fine and actually excited as this is the first time I am giving my interview at Microsoft

Interviewer: That's ok, you just relax we'll start with a general discussion. Can you tell me about your experience?

Me: Have explained how I have been handling projects, how good I am in Database Administration, SQL coding, database designing, troubleshooting and given brief details about my current role and previous experience.

"He didn't interrupt me till I finish this."

Interviewer: What are you more interested in? Coding, designing or troubleshooting? You can choose anything where you feel more comfortable......

Me: Well, I am good in database administration and development and performance tuning

Interviewer: Have you ever tried to know the SQL Server architecture?

Me: Yes! I have an idea on component level architecture.

Interviewer: Ohh that's good to know, can you tell me why a SQL developer or any DBA should know the architecture? Means what is the use in getting into architecture details?

Me: I have given the answer why a SQL developer or SQL DBA should know architecture and taken an example. "A simple requirement comes and a SQL Developer needs to write a stored procedure," I have explained how a person who understand architecture deals the requirement. A DBA needs to do a Root Cause Analysis and should give a permanent solution then how a DBA deal with that when he/she knows architecture.

Interviewer: What is a Latch?

Me: Explained the Latches and Latch Waits (You can get these from Chapter 10)

Interviewer: How do differentiate Latches from Locks?

Me: Answered! (You can get these from Chapter 10)

Interviewer: What is column store index? Have you ever used it?

Me: Explained! How column store index works and improves the performance in OLAP environments

Interviewer: What is the difference between Delete and Truncate commands?

Me: I have given basic differences

Interviewer: Is Delete and Truncate are DDL or DML?

Me: Delete is DML and TRUNCATE is DDL

Interviewer: Why TRUNCATE DDL?

Me: Given the answer: Because it deals with schema instead of just data.

Interviewer: Ok we have a requirement as one of the integration users should have access on our database and should be able to TRUNCATE a single table and shouldn't have TRUNCATE permission on any other table. Can you tell me how do you implement this?

Me: Explained 2 cases Ex: Will create a procedure to truncate the given table WITH EXECUTE AS OWNER and gives user execute permission only on that procedure. (Can find answers in Chapter 3 Security)

Interviewer: In application one of the pages is giving timeout error, what is your approach to resolve this?

Me: I answered by giving detailed information on how to find the actual problem, have to quickly check and confirm with which layer the problem is with: Application, Web service, Database services and we can provide resolution based on the problem.

Interviewer: Ok, you confirmed that Application and web service are fine and the problem is with database server. Now what is your approach?

Me: Quickly check few primary parameters "Services," "Memory," "CPU," "Disk Space," "Network," "I/O," "Long Running Queries," "MAXDOP" and other configurations using DMV's, Performance monitor, performance counters, extended events, profiler trace or if you are using any third party tools.

Interviewer: Ok, all parameters are fine except there is a procedure which is causing this problem. This procedure was running fine till last day but it suddenly dropping the elapsed time. What are the possible reasons?

Me: A data feed might happen which causes a huge fragmentation, or nightly index maintenance might failed, statistics might be outdated, other process might be blocking

Interviewer: Ok, all these parameters are fine, no data feed happened, no maintenance failed, no blocking and statistics are also fine. What else might be the reason?

Me: May be due to a bad parameter sniffing

Interviewer: What is bad parameter sniffing?

Me: Explained what the bad parameter sniffing is and how it impact the performance badly

Interviewer: What is your approach in case of bad parameter sniffing?

Me: Answered the question (Check Chapter 11)

Interviewer: Ok, it's not because of parameter sniffing, what else might be causing the slow running?

Me: Explained scenarios from my past experience. There are few "SET" options also might cause the sudden slow down issues.

Interviewer: All required SET options are already there, are there any other reasons you see?

Me: I had a bad experience with recursive calling of a SQL procedure from application code. When we find that the execution time for that procedure is <= 1 second but when the same procedure is recursively called from front end it may create issues.

Interviewer: Ok, that might be the reason but in our case we checked and not found any such kind of recursive calling. What else we can check?

Me: Ok, we'll try to quickly identify tables which are being used in that page and check if any page level errors using DBCC commands?

Interviewer: Hmm...May be sometimes page level errors might impact performance, but mostly page level corruptions can cause an error. But ok we checked it using DBCC commands and all tables are working perfectly. What else we can check?

Me: Hmm......!!! I am sorry not getting any other clue ☹

Interviewer: That's ok no problem

Interviewer: Can you draw SQL Server Architecture?

Me: Have drawn a diagram and explained each component

Interviewer: Ok, now I am giving a simple SELECT and UPDATE queries. Can you explain how each component works in dealing with these "SELECT" and "UPDATE" commands?

Me: Explained the end to end process starting from initializing a database request from end-client to how each component works to accomplish the given task. (Check Chapter -1 for answers)

Interviewer: You joined a new team. There are a lot of deadlocks in that application and you are asked to provide a resolution. What is your approach?

Me: Have explained 3 things, what is deadlock, how to identify the deadlock information and how to prevent from deadlocks and how to resolve deadlock situations, deadlock related traces, deadlock priority etc.

Interviewer: Ok, you found that there is an INDEXID that is causing the frequent deadlocks. Can you be able to find what type of index from ID?

Me: I have explained how to identify type of index from index id 0, 1, 255

Interviewer: Have you seen any lock type information in deadlock log?

Me: Yes I have! And explained about SH_, UP and PR_ etc.

Interviewer: Any idea about Lazywriter?

Me: Explained about Lazywriter process and how it initiated when there is a memory pressure.

Interviewer: How checkpoint is differentiated from Lazywriter?

Me: There are multiple points I have explained but the major difference is CHECKPOINT occurs periodically based on server/database setting but the lazywriter occurs when only there is a memory pressure on SQL Server buffer cache. Explained all other points as well!

Interviewer: Any idea about Ghost cleanup?

Me: Yes! Explained and how it clears the deleted records offline.

Interviewer: Why to use a VIEW?

Me: Explained "Security," "Simplify Querying" etc.

Interviewer: Order By is not works in a view right, can you explain why?

Me: I know it does not work but not sure why it's does not work properly

Interviewer: Have you ever worked on Indexed views?

Me: Yes!

Interviewer: Can you tell me any two limitations of an Indexed view?

Me: Given limitations: Self Join, Union, Aggregate functions etc.

Interviewer: Have you ever used Triggers?

Me: Yes!

Interviewer: Can you explain the scenario's when you used Triggers and Why Triggers used?

Me: Explained in detail

Interviewer: What are the alternatives for a Trigger?

Me: Given some scenarios ex: Using Output clause, implementing through procedures etc.

Interviewer: What are the top 2 reasons to use a Trigger and not to use a Trigger?

Me: Explained scenario's where there is no alternative better than Triggers and also explained cases where performance impacted when using a Trigger.

Interviewer: You are asked to tune a SSIS package, what is your approach?

Me: Have explained all possible options and parameters we need to check and improve starting from connection managers, control flows, data flow, fast loads, transformations and other parameters.

Interviewer: Your manager asked you design and implement an ETL process to load a data feed to data warehouse on daily basis. What is your approach?

Me: Explained how I design a new process and implementation steps

Interviewer: Have you ever used stored procedures in source in any data flow?

Me: Yes I have used

Interviewer: Ok you need to execute a stored procedure and use the result set as source. What is your approach?

Me: Explained in detail on paper

Interviewer: Can you explain the basic reasons that results into incorrect Meta data from stored procedure?

Me: Have explained various cases. Ex: When using dynamic queries, when SET NOCOUNT OFF etc.

Interviewer: Ok, how do you deal/map column names when your procedure is using a full dynamic query?

Me: Explained in detail. Ex: SET FMTONLY, using a script task etc.

Interviewer: What are the various HA and DR features you worked on?

Me: Explained!

Interviewer: What is the most difficult issue you faced in working with Replication?

Me: Given a scenario and explained how we did RCA and resolved the issue.

Interviewer: What are the top reasons that cause failures in database mirroring?

Me: Explained the top reasons

Interviewer: Can you tell me one issue that you couldn't resolve?

Me: I have got assigned to a problem request to identify causes for SQL Server frequent unexpected restarts. I found there were memory dumps created and we unfortunately couldn't find a proper solution and raised a case with Microsoft. MS engineer analyzed the issue and suggested to apply a CU and increase memory.

Interviewer: You are assigned as a single point of contact for a Database Environment. Sunday its holiday and you didn't get a chance to look through notifications. When you come to office on Monday morning you could see that your production application is not working and when you checked it one of the drive is full and "Available Bytes is: 0." What is your immediate step?

Me: I'll quickly try to find out a decent sized file from that drive and I'll move it to other drive, in next minute I'll send a notification to the all concern teams and open an incident.

Interviewer: Good, then what's your next step?

Me: I'll try to quickly check the SQL instance to make sure all databases are online and then check error logs to find out the root cause.

Interviewer: Ok, you might have seen these disk full issues right? What are the top 3 reasons that might full the disk suddenly?

Me: Yes! From my experience, Auto growth enabled Log File size might be increased, A huge log/ differential backup generated due to a maintenance job or a huge Data feed, a SQL mini or full dump might be generated.

Interviewer: Ok XXXXX I am done from my side, any questions?

Me: Asked about the position and responsibilities.

Interviewer: He took 20 min to explain the roles, responsibilities and the business environment

Break time:

First Round Completed. After 15 min wait Staff member came to me and asked me to wait for the next round. I felt very relaxed and confident as I given answers to almost all of the questions. I was excited as I qualified in the first technical round, but somewhere in thoughts I was more confident as interviewer giving more flexibility and time to answer questions. At this moment I didn't have any clue how many interviews I need to attend ☺

Technical Interview - 2

After 20 more min I got a call from **Interviewer**, he came to lobby and called my name. I introduced him and he offered me a coffee. We both had a coffee and had to walk for 3 min to reach his cabin. Meantime we had a general conversation. I already had a long discussion in first round and this guy seems like a cool guy. I felt more confident and here is the discussion happened in second round:

Interviewer: Hay, just a moment

Me: No problem! (He started working on his laptop)

Interviewer: Can you tell me something about your experience and current role?

Me: Started giving details about my experience and current responsibilities

Interviewer: Hay, don't mind as I am not looking at you, it doesn't mean that I don't here you, please continue

Me: Have explained about my education background

Interviewer: Ok XXXXX, we'll start from a simple topic then we'll go through complex things

Interviewer: On which basis you will define a new full text index?

Me: Well I am not really sure on this (This is really unexpected, I really felt bad as missing the first question, is this a simple question?☹)

Interviewer: Hmm, what is the T-SQL predicates involved in full text searching?

Me: I am not sure as I didn't get a chance to work on full text indexing but I remember one predicate "Contains." (From this question I got to understand that he is trying to test my stress levels. I clearly said that I didn't work on full text indexes but he is still asking me questions on the same area)

Interviewer: Ok, there is a transaction which is updating a remote table using linked server. An explicit transaction is opened and the database instance is on Node-A. Now actual update statement is executed and a failover happened to Node-B before commit or rollback. What happens to the transaction?

Me: I tried to answer. I know how a transaction will be handled in case of a cluster node failover but not sure in this case as it's a distributed transaction. (He is typically trying to fail me☺)

Interviewer: Ok, you know any enterprise environment is having various environments right, like Development, Test, Stag, and Production. You have developed code in development environment and it needs to be moved to test. How the process happens?

Me: Explained about versioning tools and how we moved code between environments

Interviewer: Hmm, ok your project doesn't have a budget to use a versioning tool and the entire process has to be go manual. Can you design a process to move code between environments?

Me: Explained various options. Like having a separate instance and replicating code changes and versioning using manual code backup processes.

Interviewer: If we need to move objects between environments how do you priorities objects?

Me: Explained! Like first move user defined data types, linked servers, synonyms, sequences, tables, views, triggers, procedures, functions etc.

Interviewer: Do you know what composite index is?

Me: Explained! (Chapter 11)

Interviewer: Ok, while creating composite index on which basis we need to choose order of the columns?

Me: Explained with an example. (Chapter 11)

Interviewer: What is the difference between Index selectivity and index depth?

Me: Explained! These two are totally different terms. (Chapter 11)

Interviewer: Can you draw a table diagram when a partition created on that?

Me: Could not answer

Interviewer: What is the 9th page in first file of the primary file group?

Me: I can't get it (OMG!☹)

Interviewer: Ok, What will happen if this page is corrupted?

Me: I don't want to guess on the fly! (This guy is testing me for sure)

Interviewer: Ok leave it. We have configured Always on Failover Cluster and I have added a database in AlwaysOn availability group. As requirement comes in we have configured log shipping and replication for the same database. Now the database is participating in AlwaysOn availability group with 2 replicas and log shipping with a single secondary and acting as a publisher in Peer-to-Peer transactional replication with 4 subscribers. Now my question is a transaction updated 100 rows in our database, before the commit happen a failover initiated and the database failed over to the other node. Can you tell me the transaction impact on Log shipping secondary, secondary replica in AlwaysOn AG and all 4 subscribers?

Me: Hmm… the transaction should follow ACID properties and it shouldn't impact any secondary database or subscribers (My inner feelings Ok, I think I can go and have lunch at home today, next time I should prepare well when coming to MS interview)

Interviewer: How could you identify query which is causing blocking

Me: I explained how we capture query information from SQL handle

Interviewer: Ok, let's say when you find the blocking query is a stored procedure and the procedure is having 10000 lines of code, can we be able to get the exact query which is causing a block?

Me: I remember there is a way that we can do using statement_start_offset, statement_end_offset from a DMV DM_EXEC_REQUESTS.

Interviewer: Ok, if the blocking query is from a nested stored procedure or with in a cursor, can we still be able to get the exact query details?

Me: I am not sure on this.

Interviewer: No problem, leave it

Interviewer: We have a backup plan for a database as: Full backup – Saturday Night, Differential Backup Everyday Night, Transactional Backup on hourly basis. Now we lost the database at Wednesday at 9:15 AM. How to deal with the situation and recover data?

Me: Explained how we need to get the database back. Restore recent Saturday full backup and the latest (Tuesday night) differential backup and all transactional logs (Last Log backup must be taken at 9:00 AM Wednesday) followed by the differential backup and then apply if tail log backup is available.

Interviewer: Ok, when restoring Saturday night full backup we came to know that the full backup corrupted and not possible to restore. But we have all differential backups and log backups are available. Is it possible to recover data?

Me: Yes if all transaction logs are healthy.

Restore the previous week Saturday full backup (11 Days back)

Restore the last differential backup before the latest Full backup (5 Days back)

Restore all subsequent transaction log files till the last one.

Note: Sunday, Monday, Tuesday diff backups are not useful as the full backup is corrupted

Interviewer: You are assigned to a new client; they are setting up IT infrastructure for their new applications. You are supposed to design, build and take care of End-to-End delivery of database systems. They don't have a budget for buying a monitoring tool and asked to build a native notification tool using T-SQL programming or any other native programming. How do you handle this? Can you do that?

Me: Yes! I can, I already implemented native notifications using T-SQL and PowerShell scripts.

Interviewer: Great to hear, can you briefly explain how you implemented that?

Me: Sure! We have created a centralized dedicated SQL Server instance only for DBA activities and reporting purpose. Created centralized database and deployed PowerShell scripts to capture information from all SQL Server instances (140). It captures information about ERROLOG, Job Execution details, CPU, Memory, I/O and other performance counter details etc. Stored Procedures written for capturing this information and deployed in all servers, PowerShell scripts executes those procedures and fetch the details. Also we have designed SSRS reports to showcase the SQL Server current status.

Interviewer: That's pretty much enough, and what if that dedicated instance down?

Me: We had a log shipping setup for that dedicated instance

Interviewer: How are you comfortable with SQL coding?

Me: Yes! I am good in SQL coding

Interviewer: Can you write a query to split a comma separated string into a table rows

Me: I have written a query using CHARINDEX and SUBSTRING

Interviewer: Ok, now we need to implement the same logic for all incoming strings, can you explain how?

Me: I wrote a user defined function and using that function in main procedure

Interviewer: Can you tell me why you used a function here? What are the plus and minus in using functions?

Me: Explained about reducing code redundancy and may impact on performance

Interviewer: Ok, so there is a performance impact while dealing with large datasets if we use functions. Now write a query to do the same job without using a user defined function.

Me: Wrote a query by adding xml tags to the string and cross applying with nodes ().

Interviewer: Is there any other way?

Me: I am not getting.....

Interviewer: That's ok! Can you write a query for reverse scenario? Form a comma separated string from column values.

Me: I wrote a query...

Interviewer: Have you ever used query hints?

Me: Yes! I have

Interviewer: Can you explain what are all those and in which scenario you used?

Me: Explained Recompile, No Expand, Optimize for etc.

Interviewer: Ok, which is the best way, leaving optimization part to optimizer or controlling from developer end?

Me: Explained reasons for using query hints and finally justified that the optimizer is always right in a long run.

Interviewer: Ok, What are the other query hints you used?

Me: I know few more query hints but I didn't use them, explained other query hints

Interviewer: Any idea about statistics in SQL Server?

Me: Yes! Explained about the statistics

Interviewer: Ok there are two options in updating statistics right, which is the best option?

Me: It's not we can directly define the best option, it depends on the environment and data inserts/updates and explained how to choose the best option in both cases OLTP and OLAP

Interviewer: Ok, what is synchronous and asynchronous auto update statistics?

Me: Explained in detail.

Interviewer: How do you know if statistics are outdated?

Me: Given a query using STATS_DATE or from actual and estimated row counts or sp_spaceused may give wrong results.

Interviewer: How do we update statistics? In our production there is a huge traffic expected between 11 AM and 5 PM, is there any impact if we update statistics in between 11 and 5?

Me: Yes there might be chances that impact the procedure/query execution. It might speedup or slower the execution.

Interviewer: What do you know about ISOLATION levels?

Me: Explained about all available isolation levels

Interviewer: What is the default Isolation level?

Me: Read Committed

Interviewer: What is the problem with Read Committed isolation level?

Me: Non-repeatable Reads and Phantom Reads still exists in READ COMMITTED

Interviewer: Have you ever used "WITH NOLOCK" query hint?

Me: Yes! Explained about it

Interviewer: Ok, so do you mean that when specifies NO LOCK, there is no lock is being issued on that table/row/page?

Me: No! It still issues a lock but that lock is totally compatible with other low level locks (UPDATE, EXCLUSIVE).

Interviewer: Are you sure that is true? Can you give me an example?

Me: Yes I am sure let me give you an example. Let's say we have a table T with a million rows. Now I issued a command "SELECT * FROM T" and immediately in other window I executed a command "DROP TABLE T." DROP TABLE will wait till the first executed select statement is completed. So it is true that there is lock on that table which is not compatible with the schema lock.

Interviewer: What is the impact "DELETE FROM T WITH (NOLOCK)"?

Me: Database engine ignores NOLOCK hint when using in from clause with UPDATE and DELETE

Interviewer: What is Internal and external fragmentation?

Me: Explained in detail.

Interviewer: How do you identify internal and external fragmentation?

Me: Using INDEX PHYSICAL STATS and explained about AVG FRAGMENTATION %, AVG PAGE SPACE USED.

Interviewer: There is a simple relation called "Employee." Columns Emp_ID, Name, Age. Clustered index on Emp_ID and Non-Clustered index on Age. Now can you draw the Clustered and Non-Clustered index diagram? Fill the values for Leaf level and non-leaf nodes. Let's assume there are total 20 records and id's are sequential starting from 1001 to 1020 and Age Min Age 25, Max Age 48.

Me: Drawn a diagram by filling all employee ID's in clustered index also drawn non clustered index by filling all clustered index key values.

Interviewer: Has given 3 queries and asked me to guess what kind of index operation (SCAN/SEEK) in execution plan

Me: Given my answers based on the key columns used and kind of operation ("=," "LIKE")

Interviewer: What is a PAD INDEX option? Have you ever used this option anywhere?

Me: While specifying fill factor if we mention PAD INDEX same fill factor applies to NON-LEAF level nodes as well.

Interviewer: Can you write a query for the below scenario.

Previous_Emp_ID, Current_Row_Emp_ID, Next_Emp_ID

Me: Given the answer "Using LEAD and LAG"

Interviewer: How do you write query in SQL Server 2005?

Me: Written query using "ROW_NUMBER ()"

Interviewer: Write the same query in SQL Server 2000

Me: We can do this but have to use a temp table with Identity column to hold the required data and by self-joining the temp table we can get the required resultset.

Interviewer: Can you be able to write this without temp table?

Me: Am not getting ....

Interviewer: I am done from my side do you have any questions foe me?

Me: Actually nothing, I have got clarity on job roles and responsibilities.

Break Time:

Best thing I observed "Each **Interviewer** passes his/her feedback to the next level" based on that feedback you will be asked questions. But this is the longest interview I never attended. Mostly he tried to put me in trouble and tried to fail me to answer the question. I understand, in second round my stress levels were tested. Almost for each question he was very strong and cross checking and confirming back, I could hear "Are you sure?," "Can you re think?," "How do you confirm?" etc. This time I am not sure on 2nd interview resultL. I had snacks followed by a strong coffee and was waiting for the feedback.

One of the staff members came to me and told me that I need to go through one more discussion. I was very happy to hear and got a call from **Interviewer** after 45 min.

Technical Interview - 3

Interviewer: Hay XXXXX, How are you?

Me: I am totally fine......thanks!

Interviewer: How is the day today?

Me: Yah it's really interesting and I am so excited.

Interviewer: I am XXXX and working on BI deliverables, can you explain your current experience

Me: Explained!

Interviewer: Why did you choose database career path?

Me: Given the details how I got a chance to be in database career path.

Interviewer: Have you ever design a database?

Me: Yes! Explained the project details

Interviewer: Ok what are the phases in designing a new database?

Me: Explained in detail! Conceptual, Logical, Physical design.

Interviewer: Giving you a project requirement, can you be able to design a new database?

Me: Sure, will do that.

Interviewer: Take a look at these sheets, understand the requirement, choose a module, create data flow map, design OLTP tables and OLAP tables. Also design a backup plan, High availability and Disaster Recovery plan. All required details and SLA's are given in those sheets. I am giving you an hour time. Please feel free to ask me if you have any questions.

Me: Sure, we'll ask you if any questions. For me it took 1 and half hour to understand and to design tables for a simple module.

Interviewer: Can you explain the data flow for this module?

Me: Explained!

Interviewer: Can you pull these 5 reports from the designed tables?

Me: I wrote queries to fulfill all those report requirements. Luckily I could be able to pull all reports from the created schema.

Interviewer: Can you tell me the parameters to be considered in designing a new database?

Me: Explained various parameters needs to be considered category wise. For example Performance, Scalability, Security, Integrity etc. (1 or 2 examples for each category).

Interviewer: What is Autogrow option? How do you handle this?

Me: Explained about Autogrow option and explained 2 modes and their uses

Interviewer: You worked with versions from SQL Server 2000 to 2014 correct?

Me: Yes!

Interviewer: Can you tell me the features which are in 2000 and not in 2012?

Me: This is strange☺; you mean to say deprecated features which are in 2000 not in 2012?

Interviewer: Exactly ☺

Me: Well, I believe 90% things got changed from 2000 to 2012, anyways will give you answer "Enterprise Manager", "Query Analyzer," "DTS Packages," "System CATALOGS," "Backup Log with Truncate Only" etc.

Interviewer: Can you tell me top 5 T-SQL features that you most like which are in 2012 and not in 2000?

Me: Sequences, TRY/CATCH/THROW, OFFSET/FETCH, RANK/DENSE_RANK/NTILE, CTE, COLUMN STORE INDEX etc.

Interviewer: Have you ever worked on NO SQL database?

Me: No I didn't get a chance to work on No SQL

Interviewer: Any idea about Big data?

Me: Explained about Big data and how it is getting used in analytics. (I expected this question and got prepared). Talked on Document DB, Graph DB, Key based, Map Reduce etc.

Interviewer: Ok, will you work on No SQL database if you will be given a chance?

Me: Sure will do.

Interviewer: What is Microsoft Support to Big data in latest SQL Server?

Me: Explained details on ODBC drivers and plugin for HIVE and HADOOP (I prepared on this as well☺)

Interviewer: What is the maximum database size you used?

Me: I answered

Interviewer: What are the top parameters you suggest while designing a VLDB?

Me: Parallelism, Partitions, Dimensional/De-Normalizing, Effective Deletes, Statistics Manual Update

Interviewer: What is the big change in SQL Server 2014?

Me: There are many features and changes but I remember In-Memory OLTP introduced and Cardinality estimator redesigned.

Interviewer: That's great, how do you know that cardinality estimator redesigned? Did you observe any changes in query execution?

Me: ☺ Not exactly I just attended the Microsoft TechDays on 2014 introduction.

Interviewer: We have a simple table Employee with ID, Name, Age, Salary, DeptID, and Location. Can you take that marker and design the table storage? Table is having 5000 records.

Me: You mean how HEAP pages are allocated?

Interviewer: Yes

Me: Have designed a heap table pages (I really don't have any idea, randomly created boxes in square box)

Interviewer: Ok, now I have created a clustered index on ID column, can you draw the same table diagram now?

Me: Have designed a clustered index B-Tree by giving values based on the count 5000. (This time I am lucky I knew how CI allocates)

Interviewer: Ok, now I added a Non-clustered index on DeptID. Can you design Non-clustered index tree?

Me: Created the tree

Interviewer: Ok, this time I added a composite non-clustered index on (ID, DeptID). Can you draw how index looks like?

Me: Created the tree for composite index

Interviewer: Ok, this time I added a covering index with ID, DeptID in main clause and all other columns in INCLUDE clause. Can you draw how covering index looks like?

Me: Created the tree for Covering index (I am sure main clause columns values are used in all mid-level but include columns are placed only on leaf level)

Interviewer: Ok, this time I added a filtered index on column salary. Can you draw the index diagram?

Me: Created the tree for filtered index (But not sure if it's correct or not. I think I'll be in trouble if he continues asking questions on the same area)

Interviewer: Ok, this time I partitioned the table Employee based on DeptID. Can you draw the indexes diagram?

Me: Hmm....sorry I am not getting idea how Indexes are aligned (My guess was correct I caught finally with partitions)

Interviewer: No problem!

Interviewer: Can you tell me the critical issue you faced in your recent times?

Me: I explained that problem faced due to bad perimeter sniffing and explained how I resolved it.

Interviewer: Can you tell me top 10 best security practices for SQL Server?

Me: I explained as I do follow the enterprise security policies in our environment. Explained about SQL Injection prevention, dealing with sensitive data, encryption, physical security, server/ database configurations and Audit etc.

Interviewer: Fair enough, any questions?

Me: Yes I have one, in a very short span we can see SQL Server 2016 is in pipeline, may I know the major features in SQL Server 2016.

Interviewer: (Explained!) Any other questions?

Me: Nothing, but thanks.

Interviewer: Thanks for the patience, please be wait in lobby.

Break Time:

I sat down for 10 min, had a coffee, I was too tired. I had to wait for another 30 min and then one of the staff members told me that I can expect a call on next week. I drove to the home and had long bath☺. I knew I hadn't been perfect in answering all questions and but I just gone through 9 hours of interview which is a longest interview in my experience.

On Monday I was so curious to know about the result and was being waiting for the call. I was disappointment as I didn't get call till Tuesday EOD. Finally I have got a call on Wednesday by saying that there is another discussion scheduled for next Saturday.

Day -2

Technical Interview - 4

I reached MS campus and then took a local shuttle to reach the R&D building. I was so curious and wanted to know what kind of a discussion it was. HR told me that there might be another round of technical discussion followed by a behavioral discussion.

I have got a visitor badge and was being waiting in visitor lobby. **Interviewer** came to me and took me to his cabin.

Interviewer: Hi buddy how are you today?

Me: Hah, am very fine thanks, how are you?

Interviewer: Me pretty good man, can you introduce yourself?

Me: Explained (the same for the 4th time)

Interviewer: Ok what is your experience in SQL?

Me: Given detailed view on SQL Administration and Development experience

Interviewer: Can you take this marker. I'll give you few scenarios you just need to write a query. You can use any SQL language where you feel more comfortable.

Me: Sure (This is crazy I don't have experience other than T-SQL ☺ I took the marker and went to the board)

Interviewer: We have an employee table and columns are (EmpID, Name, Mgr_ID, and Designation). I'll give you input manager name "Thomos." Now I want you to write a query to list all employees and their managers who reports to the manager "Thomos" directly or indirectly.

Me: Have asked some questions like what is the MgrID for top level employees Ex: CEO and how do we need to display NULL values etc. I wrote a query using recursive CTE.

Interviewer: Write SELECT query syntax and place all clauses that you know

Me: Wrote syntax, included all possible clauses (Distinct, TOP, WHERE, GROUP BY, ORDER BY, Query Hints etc.)

Interviewer: I have a table called T. In that each record should be inserted twice. Now the requirement is write a query to remove rows which are more than twice?

Me: Have written a query using ROW_NUMBER in CTE.

Interviewer: How do you do this in SQL Server 2000?

Me: Given a query that can run in 2000 (everyone asking how do you do it 2000, I believe their intention is how can we handle the scenario when there is now shortcut)

Interviewer: Have you ever used covering index?

Me: Yes in lot of situations.

Interviewer: Ok, why covering index and when we need to use?

Me: Explained

Interviewer: Ok, then what is the difference between Covering Index, indexed view, composite index and filtered index?

Me: Explained in detail, how and when we need to use those with examples

Interviewer: What is top advantage in using the covering index?

Me: It's performance gain for covering index usage queries, mostly on analytics databases

Interviewer: What is the disadvantage in using covering index?

Me: Two reasons one is "Slow down INSERT/UPDATE/DELETE" and the other one is "Extra Space"

Interviewer: Ok, what is the main impact in adding more columns in covering index include list?

Me: It increases the Index Depth and then need to traverse the entire tree etc....

Interviewer: That's fair enough, what exactly the Index Depth is?

Me: Explained!

Interviewer: We have 30 distributed systems located across the globe. All are maintaining sales information. Each system follows its own schema. Now I am assigning you to build a centralized data warehouse. What is your approach? How do you design the process?

Me: Took 15 min and explained with a diagram. Created three tier architecture using "Source," "Stag," "Destination." I explained data flow between source and destination through staging. We also discussed on technical mapping, data flow, package design, Integrity, performance, business rules, data cleansing, data validations, final loading and reporting.

Interviewer: That's fair enough.

Interviewer: You are assigned to have a look at a slow performing stored procedure. How do you handle that?

Me: Explained in detail, execution plan, statistics etc.

Interviewer: Which is better Table Scan or Index Seek?

Me: Explained, it depends on data/page count. Sometimes Table Scan is better than index seek.

Interviewer: Can you give me a scenario where Table Scan is better than index seek?

Me: I have given an example where majority of rows needs to be retrieved and in that case of course index scan is better than index seek. When a table is having 1 million records and a query needs to retrieve 90% of records then one index scan can get the result set faster than 9 lakh index seek.

Interviewer: One of the SSRS reports is taking long time, what is your approach and what are all the options you look for?

Me: Explained step by step to tune a SSRS report. Discussed about local queries, data source, snapshot, cached report etc.

Interviewer: Data feeds are loading into a data warehouse on daily basis, requirement is once data load happens a report has to be generated and the report needs to be delivered to email for a specific list of recipients. What is your approach?

Me: We can use the data driven subscriptions by storing all required information in SQL Server database and it can help us in dynamic report configurations.

Interviewer: What is the most complex report you designed?

Me: Explained

Interviewer: I have two databases one is holding transactional tables and the other one is holding master relations. Now we need master table data with transactional aggregations in a single report. How do you handle this?

Me: We can use Lookup (He asked me in more detail and explained in detail)

Interviewer: Do you have idea on Inheritance concept? Can you give me an example?

Me: Have taken an entity and given example for inheritance

Interviewer: Can you write a code to showcase inheritance example? You can use DOTNET or Java

Me: Written an example

Interviewer: You are assigned to a premium customer and you need to setup infrastructure environment for new database instance. What are the best practices you follow?

Me: Explained the list of best practices to design a secure and optimized environment

Interviewer: Any idea about instant file initialization?

Me: Yes! I explained the zeroing process in detail.

Interviewer: What is the option "lock pages in memory"?

Me: Explained the option "Lock Pages in Memory"

Interviewer: Can you explain how memory allocation happens to SQL Server in Windows Server 2000 and 2012 R2?

Me: Explained how memory allocation happens for SQL Server and other processes. (I attended a performance tuning session there I learnt this).

Interviewer: What are the top performance counters we need to monitor for tuning database performance?

Me: Explained.

Interviewer: Using GUI or using Scripts which method you feel more comfortable for administrating and monitoring database environment?

Me: Well GUI is easier but I like SCRIPTs method as we have more flexibility for customization.

Interviewer: Can you explain how database snapshots works in SQL server?

Me: Explained in detail. How data captures when rows modified etc.

Interviewer: Have you ever used snapshots? What are the cases these are useful in?

Me: Explained the scenarios where we used snapshots. For example releasing scripts in prod VLDB etc.

Interviewer: What are the data encryption features available in SQL Server?

Me: Explained!

Interviewer: Can you explain what semantic model means is?

Me: Explained

Interviewer: What is SQL injection?

Me: Explained with examples

Interviewer: Your system is compromised and confirmed that there is SQL injection attack. What is your immediate action plan?

Me: Explained step by step. Remove access to Database, keep application in maintenance mode, data analysis, finding the effected location, reverse engineering, fixing the problem/restoring/ rollback, make DB online and allow application users.

Interviewer: That's fine. What are all possible reasons that cause TEMPDB full?

Me: Explained! Internal, Version Store, User defined objects, TEMPDB page latch contention and related trace flags.

Interviewer: You have written a stored procedure as business required. What are all the validations/ tests you do before releasing it to the Production?

Me: Explained about code reviews, performance, security, integrity, functionality, Unit, Load, and Stress etc.

Interviewer: That's fair enough. You have any questions?

Me: I am actually clear with the job roles and responsibilities; may I know on which area we are going to work? Mean I know usually in any Product organization there are various product engineering groups. I am curious to know which area we are going to work.

Interviewer: Well.... (He explained the detail).

Interviewer: It's nice talking to you, please be waiting outside you may need to go through one more discussion.

Break Time:

I went to visitor lobby. After 10 min got a call from staff member told me that I need to meet a Manager. I need to catch up a shuttle to reach the next building. I reached the venue and was waiting for the Manager. He came to me and took me to the cafeteria. We had a general discussion and he offered me lunch. We both had lunch it took 30 min. He looks very cool; I actually forgot that I was going to attend an interview☺. After other 10 min we reached his cabin. Actually I did a lot of home work to remain all successful, failure stories and experiences and prepared well as I have an idea about behavioral discussion. I am sure we cannot face these questions without proper preparations.

Final Interview – 5

Interviewer: Hi XXXX, I am XXXX, development manager, can you tell me about your background?

Me: Explained!

Interviewer: Reporting server is not responding and this is because of low memory issue. You have any idea about memory configuration for SSRS server?

Me: Explained about Safety Margin, Threshold, Working set Maximum, Working set Minimum

Interviewer: What is application pooling?

Me: Explained! Advantages, threshold and timeout issues

Interviewer: Any idea about design patterns?

Me: Explained! Creational, Structural, Behavioral and Dot net

Interviewer: What are the top 3 parameters that impact the performance of SQL Server?

Me: Explained! Server/Database configurations, Database Design, Index & Statistics Maintenance

Interviewer: If you are asked to design a new database what is your question to be asked?

Me: Answered! OLTP or OLAP?

Interviewer: You have got a request saying that one of the new applications is not able to connect to the SQL Server. Can you quickly list out the possible reasons?

Me: Answered! We need to check SQL Server error log that can quickly help us in understanding the correct problem. Reasons might be giving wrong (password, username, server/IP, instance name, port number) details in application configuration file, Remote connections may not be enabled at SQL Server, Port might be blocked, access may not be enabled, using the named instance name and browser service may not be running etc.

Interviewer: From your personal or professional life what are your best moments in your life?

Me: Answered!

Interviewer: Can you tell me a situation that you troubleshoot a performance problem?

Me: Explained!

Interviewer: Let's say you are working as a business report developer you have got an email from your manager saying that its urgent requirement. You got a call from AVP (Your big boss) and gave you a requirement and said that should be the priority. How do you handle the situation?

Me: Answered! Justified

Interviewer: You are working for a premium customer and planned for a final production deployment, you are the main resource and 70 % work depends on you. Suddenly you got a call and there is an emergency at your home. What is your priority and how do you handle the situation?

Me: Answered and justified.

Interviewer: How do you give time estimates?

Me: Explained! Taken an example and explained how I give time estimates.

Interviewer: What is your biggest mistake in your personal or professional life?

Me: (It's really tough) given a scenario where I failed.

Interviewer: Did you do any process improvement which saved money to your organization?

Me: Yes! I did. Explained the lean project I initiated and completed successfully.

Interviewer: For a programmer/developer what is most important, expertise in technology or domain/business?

Me: Answered! Justified

Interviewer: Can you tell me you initiated a solution something innovative?

Me: Answered!

Interviewer: Have you ever stuck in a situation where you missed the deadline?

Me: Yes it happened! Explained how I managed the situation.

Interviewer: Ok, your manager asked to design, develop and release a module in 10 days. But you are sure it can't be done in 10 days. How do you convince him?

Me: Answered! How I do convince.

Interviewer: From your experience what are the top 5 factors to be a successful person?

Me: Answered!

Interviewer: If you get a chance to rewind any particular moment in your life what it would be?

Me: Answered!

Interviewer: If I give you chance to choose one of the positions from Technology Lead, Lead Business Analyst, customer Engagement Lead, what is your choice? Remember we don't bother about your previous experience will train you on your chosen role.

Me: Answered as Technology Lead! And justified

Interviewer: Why you want to join Microsoft?

Me: Answered! Justified (I have been working on SQL Server from years and MS is the owner for the product SQL Server☺)

Interviewer: Since you said you have been using Windows and SQL Server and other products from Microsoft, what is the best in Microsoft?

Me: Operating System, yes it is the leader and driving the software world. As per the statistics 95% people start learning computers using Windows OS.

Interviewer: Just imagine if you are given a chance to develop a new product for Microsoft what you develop? Any plans around?

Me: Will build a new R&D team and design a mobile device that works based on artificial intelligence☺. So our new mobile comes with a virtual personal assistant that is fully automated and it can read emails for you, it can remain you certain things based on your daily routine, it can talk to you it can here you, it can search the internet and can get the latest news that you most interested in, you can create his/her shape and you can choose the voice etc.......

Interviewer: That's awesome. Do you have experience in mobile OS?

Me: No! I thought of learning it but it's totally a different stream ☺

Interviewer: It's nice talking to you, please wait outside, will call you in 10 min.

After 10 Min wait, a staff member came to me and told me that I may expect a call in 2 or 3 days.

4 Days later when I was in office I missed a call from recruiter☹. I got a message that she has an update for me. I called her back that when she gave me the good news that they are going to offer. Within next half an hour I received an email with the salary breakup and formal offer letter. I didn't expect that as we didn't have any discussion on salary. That was a super deal for which nobody can say "NO." I came out of the room I was like dancing ☺ finally 4 weeks of hard work, endless hours of practice it had all paid off. I called my parents and close friends and that's one of the best moments in my life.

Stored Procedure Code Review Checklist

In any enterprise environment developing a database system includes the database code review. Especially when you are aligned with a product based organization a DBA should take care of code reviews along with the maintenance. We have to document and follow the best practices in designing and developing database code. Most of the time while interacting with the customers we may need to answer the question "What you consider in reviewing the code?" Here I am going to showcase stored procedure code review checklist that we use for reviewing or unit testing a stored procedure.

Stored Procedure Development Life Cycle:

First let's see what are the steps followed in developing a stored procedure:

- Get the requirement - all required inputs and expected outcome
- Write the test cases to validate the business requirement
- Design and create the code/stored procedure
- Debug, Compile and Run the procedure
- Cross check all test cases passed
- Send it for code review
- Apply suggested changes if any from code review
- Deploy it to the intended environment
- Document the process

Why Best Practices/Code Review?

In enterprise environment we do follow a best practices guide for developing and reviewing database code. Now we'll see what are the advantages in following the best practices guide/ reviewing the code?

Dependency: It minimizes dependency as all database objects follow a specific standard anyone can easily understand and deal with the code easily.

Integration: Easily integrated with the existing environment

Optimization: We can see the best optimized and error free code

Stored Procedure Code Review Check List:

We have defined checklist in category wise. Below are the various categories in stored procedure code review check list.

- General Standards
- Scalability
- Security
- Transactions
- Performance
- Functionality
- Environment Based Settings

General Standards:

(Code Format, Naming Conventions, Datatype and Data Length, Syntax):

- Always follow a template in designing stored procedure so that it can easier developer job while designing and integrating. For example each stored procedure should be defined as various blocks such as "Comments Section," "Variable Declaration," "Actual Body," "Audit," "Exception Handling," "Temp_Obj_Removel" and define environment sections if any required.

- Check proper comments are used or not. Always describe procedure, inputs and expected output in comments section.
- Check naming conventions are used properly for procedure name, variables and other internal objects.
- Check all objects used inside the procedure are prefixed with the schema name and column names are referencing with table alias.
- Check all table columns used/mapped are using the correct datatypes and column length.
- Check if all required SET based options enabled are not.
- Check if there are any temporary objects (Temporary tables, cursors etc.) used, if yes make sure these objects closed/removed once their usage is done.
- Make sure Errors are handling properly.
- Define NULL acceptance in the procedure and code accordingly.
- Lining up parameter names, data types, and default values.
- Check spaces and line breaks are using properly.
- Check BEGIN/END are using properly.
- Check parentheses are using properly around AND/OR blocks.

Scalability:

- Use fully qualified names (Ex: Instead of PROC use PROCEDURE) for a better integration.
- Check if we are using any deprecated features.
- Check if any other/nested dependent objects used and make sure that all objects are available in DB and all functioning properly and add them into dependent list.
- Never use "SELECT *" instead use all required columns.
- If there are any triggers defined on tables used inside the procedure, make sure these triggers are working as expected.

Security:

- In case of any errors make sure that the complete error information is not throwing to the application instead use a centralized table to hold the error information and send a custom error message to the application.
- Apply encryption procedures while dealing with sensitive information (Ex: Credit Card numbers, passcodes etc.).
- If any dynamic SQL is used make sure it executes through only SP_EXECUTESQL only.
- Prefer views instead of tables wherever is possible.
- Document all permissions required to run the procedure.

Transactions:

- If any transactions are used, check it is following ACID properties as per the business requirement.

- Keep the transaction length as short as possible and do not select data within the transaction rather than select required data before starting the transaction and process it inside the transaction.
- Check commit and ROLLBACK is available happening as expected, cross check when using nested stored procedures.
- Avoid transactions that require user input to commit.

Performance:

- Cross check we are selecting/retrieving only required data throughout the procedure, always use Column names instead of "SELECT *."
- Check the column order in where clause, we should remember it impact the index usage, change the order if required.
- Avoid using functions/conversions while selecting and comparing, If result set is having 30 rows means that function is called >=30 times. let's say "WHERE <TAB.ColName> = MONTH (@DateParam)," we can fulfill this by creating a local variable and assigning this value to that and we can use that variable in where clause.
- Cross check if we can have a better/short way to get the same outcome with fewer joins.
- Always do filter data as much as we can and then apply required operations.
- Have a look on aggregations if any. Always do aggregations on a possible shortest dataset. Example we have a requirement "We want to know the top selling product details on each eStore." Now do not join Product_Orders, Product_Details and group by on e-store name by selecting max of revenue e-store wise. Instead of doing this first get the productID's with highest income e-Store wise and then map it with Product_Details.
- Check if there is any chance for bad parameter sniffing: Make sure that procedure parameters are assigning to local variables and referring these variables in queries instead of directly referring PROCEDURE parameters.
- Choose the best temporary object (Temp_Table, Table_Variable, CTE and Derived_Table) based on the requirement, here we should predict the near future.
- Try to use TRUNCATE instead of DELETE whenever is possible, remember we should know the difference and the impact.
- Check the response/execution time and make sure it is under the benchmark.
- Avoid cursors, use while loop instead.
- Check for the alternatives for costly operators such as NOT LIKE.
- Make sure that it returns only the required rows and columns.
- Analyse cost based execution plan to make sure No Bookmark/RID Lookup, No Table/ Index Scans taking more cost, No Sort – Check if we can use Order By, Check Estimated and Actual counts.
- Have a look at Optimizer Overrides - Review the code to determine if index hints or NOLOCK clauses are really necessary. These hints could be beneficial in the short

term, but these overrides might impact negatively when data changes happen or database migrated to new version.

Functionality:

- Prepare various test cases and make sure all test cases works fine. Example prepare test case to send all possible inputs to a PROCEDURE, define the expected output and compare with the actual output.
- Check Code is error free and parsing correctly and executing without any issue.
- Check output result set is coming properly, number of rows, number of columns, column names, data types etc.

Environment Based Settings

- Document all environments based settings and follow those instructions in designing the procedure.

  Ex 1: In a highly secure database environment, all procedures should call a nested Audit procedure which collects all session details and stored in an audit table.

  Ex 2: In an environment before performing and bulk operation we have to get the latest lookup values in lookup tables.

Summary:

- Always define your own standards and follow best practices in designing database code.
- Prepare an excel sheet with the required checklist and make sure that the SQL developer/DBA is filling the sheet before sending it to the code review.
- Initially it might take some extra time in development phase but it simplifies the code review process and leads to the best productivity.

Database Career Paths

We usually get in touch with the followers to discuss on various databases related issues. If we need to give rating to the questions that we answered, Top 1 will be "I would like to make/change my career into database systems and I am more confused on various database roles from job market. Can you explain/suggest the database career paths?" If you are interested in database systems and want to make your career in database path, first you should get clarity on "DATABASE ROLES." There are three basic paths available to make your career in database systems. Below are the 3 paths.

Database Designing & Development: Database Designers and Developers design and develop a database to hold and process data to support a front-end application which enable end users to do transactions online.

Database Administration: Database Administrators maintain the designed/developed systems to prevent the interruptions during the transactions and makes sure databases/database servers online 24X7.

Data Warehousing: Data Warehouse teams analyze the captured data and process it to find out the area where the business can be extended or improved.

First let's have a look on what are the various roles available in each path.

Database Environment Roles

Database Designing & Development:

- Database Architect
- Data Modeller
- Database Designer
- Database Developer/Engineer

Database Administration:

- Application/Development DBA
- Core DBA

Data Warehousing:

- Data Architect
- ETL Developer
- Database Analyst
- Report Developer
- Data Scientist
- + Roles under Database Design and Development may also applies to this category

Now you have some idea what are the roles available. Now we'll look into each role and its responsibilities. If you get a chance to choose, select the right path that suits your interest.

Database Designing and Development

Nature: They do architect, design and develop database systems that support On-Line Transaction (OLTP) Processing and On-Line Analytical Processing (OLAP). Most of the environments follow one of these frameworks "SDLC" or "AGILE."

Database Architect (Business + Structure + Data + Operations): Plan and execute the entire project and should have knowledge on all phases (Business + Technology). He/She should be able to answer all the questions related to database system.

> **Ex:** Analyzing client operations and customer requirements, mapping business requirements to technology, designing secure and optimized database systems.

Data Modeler (Business + Data + Structure): Work on mass/raw data and give a structure to that. To simply say that he/she will act as a bridge between business and IT. Means they understand the data and convert business requirements into conceptual, logical and physical models that suit the requirement.

> **Ex:** Separating data and operations, Identifying Entities and Relations etc.

Database Designer (Data + Structure): From the requirement analysis he/she should be able to design database by following best practices.

> **Ex:** Designing Databases, Tables, Data types, Capacity Planning etc.

Database Developer/Engineer (Operations): Based on the design developer/engineer develop database code to fulfill the actual business requirement.

> **Ex:** Creating Procedures, Functions, Views etc.

These People…

- Closely work with client/business team
- More chances to work at onsite
- More programming experience
- Can be expertise on a particular domain which is an added advantage
- Work is planned and mostly long term challenges
- Can see experts in SQL programming and business functionality
- Plays key role in building database systems

Database Administration

Nature: They do maintain database systems to make sure databases/database servers are up and online by 24*7. Mostly DBA works in ITIL environments.

Application DBA: Usually they work on Development, Test and Stag environments to support the database systems. Apart from database systems they should have knowledge on application configurations and business up to some extent.

> **Ex:** Troubleshooting App-DB connectivity issues, Deploying Scripts, Debugging Scripts etc.

Core DBA: Core DBA's are who responsible for PRODUCTION database servers/databases.

> **Ex:** Running Health Checks, High Availability, Troubleshooting issues, handles Service Requests, Problem Requests etc.

These People…

- Closely work with end customers/users
- Can be expertise in Technology Infrastructure field
- Mostly work from offshore
- Have to face unplanned outages
- Mostly have to face the daily challenges
- Most of DBA's work in shifts
- Usually do not have much knowledge on business functionality
- Would see more experts in server and database internals
- Plays key role in database infrastructure maintenance

Data Warehousing

Nature: Deigning and creating a centralized repository and process the past trends to predict the future trends.

ETL Developer: Design and develop an ETL (Extract Transfer Load) process to integrate data between various systems.

> **Ex:** Developing SSIS packages to integrate data from legacy systems to SQL Server 2014.

Database Analyst: Analyze the business requirements and confirms the project requirements. He/She analyze monitor data feeds and tune database systems when required.

Ex: Monitor test strategies to check they are matching with the requirements

Report Developer: Design, create business reports that helps management to take the right decisions.

Ex: Creating sales reports using SSRS

Data Scientist: The Data Scientist is responsible for designing and implementing processes and layouts for complex, large-scale data sets used for modeling, data mining, and research purposes.

These People:

- Closely work with business team and architects
- More chances to work at onsite
- More analysis experience and having knowledge on business functionality
- Can be expertise on a particular domain which is an added advantage
- Work is planned and mostly long term challenges
- Plays key role in decision making systems
- Mostly work with OLAP systems.
- Can see experts in data and business analysis
- Work with huge datasets

Resource Utilization

Remember these roles and responsibilities vary based on organization policies, management and environment. If below are the various phases in designing and developing a database.

- Requirement Gathering and Analysis
- Conceptual Design
- Logical Design
- Physical Design
- SQL Coding
- Testing
- Optimizing
- Version Maintenance
- Build
- Deploy
- Maintenance

Let's see how resources allocated in different environments:

Enterprise Environment:

- Database Architect
- Data Modeler
- Database Designer
- Database Developer
- Build Engineer
- Database tester
- DBA

Mid-level Environment

- Database Architect
- Database Developer
- DBA

Start-Up

- Database Engineer
- DBA

This is just an example how resource are utilized in various environments. It always depends on the business and budget.

How to become an Expert in your Career

Recently we conducted an interview for a SQL DBA with 6–8 years of experience for one of the critical project. We could hardly shortlisted 2 members out of 18. These 2 are experts at least in their stage. We can't say that remaining 16 people are not good, they can manage and deliver the task but still we need experts why?

Experienced people can manage their work and deliver the project on-time.

Experts tackle problems that increase their expertise, approach a task in a way that maximizes their opportunities for growth which can take business to the next level.

We had a discussion with various engineers, architects from different organizations and we have prepared a list of points which can help an experienced/fresher to become an expert.

Key points that make you an Expert in your chosen Path:

- **Know the Internals**
- **Expertise Your Profile**
- **Performance Tuning**
- **Accurate Estimations**
- **Never React Always Respond**
- **Keep your own best practices and Troubleshooting guide**
- **Training, Learning and Knowledge Sharing**

Know the Internals

We do work on various items in a typical working day. While working on an activity apply the formula WHW (What-How-Why). Most of the people knows "What" and "How" but ignore "Why" except **Experts**. One simple WHY can create multiple WHAT and HOW questions but if you question WHY then you will gain the more knowledge. Have a look at below examples.

Let's say you are a fresher and joined in an organization:

DBA:

Your lead asked you to create a database in SQL Server and keep .MDF on X drive and .LDF on Y drive.

WHAT are MDF and LDF? You co-worker can help you or you can know by surfing internet.

HOW to do this? Again internet can help you on this

Your work is actually done. If you wanted to become an expert ask the next question "WHY"?

"Expert Zone"

WHY should we keep MDF and LDF in different drives?

Ans: To improve the accessibility

HOW it improves accessibility?

Ans: Each drive is having a separate set of I/O busses. Since both files are in different drives, more busses will be available to complete the task.

WHAT is the problem if both are in same drive?

Ans: Task has to be completed using the limited I/O busses which delays the execution time.

WHAT else we can benefit if we can put these files on separate drives?

Ans: While choosing the drives we should consider the access requirement. For MDF its dynamic access required for LDF its sequential access so we can choose the dedicated drive which improves the I/O performance.

Developer:

Your lead asked to create a procedure. Use a temp table to hold some data and process it etc.

WHAT is a Temp Table?

How to create a Temp Table?

"Expert Zone"

WHY Temp Table? Why not a Table Variable or a CTE?

WHAT actually happens in database when we use Temp Table?

WHAT is the most optimized way of holding temporary data?

Ask "WHY" if you want to become an expert in your path and know the internals. Since timelines are really matters in IT we can't always spend some extra time. But remember you just have to know the answer for "WHY."

Expertise Your Profile

Your profile is the first piece of information that shows what you are. Let's say Person A and B is having 8 years of experience. If person "A" worked on Oracle for 8 years, Person "B" worked on SQL Server for 5 Years, on Oracle for 3 Years and Person "C" worked on SQL Server for 5 years, Oracle 2 years and also experienced in cloud computing using AWS. Can you guess who are having more chances to get good career opportunities and growth, it's absolutely person "C." Do not stick on a technology and never miss a chance to work on other (Similar) technology. Which mean you should be strong in at least one technology and should ready to learn new/other/similar technology.

Database Administration:

A SQL Server DBA Expert should have experience in:

- Database Server Installation and Upgrades
- Database Capacity Planning
- Day to Day Database Monitoring Maintenance
- Backup and Recovery
- High-Availability Solutions
- Disaster Recovery Solutions
- Performance Tuning (Server and Database Level)
- Troubleshooting and providing instant solutions
- Planning, Testing, Implementation and Maintenance of a SQL Server Instance
- Database Maintenance Automations
- ITIL Standards
- Securing Database servers
- Good Contacts with Technology Masters
- Recommended Certifications
- T-SQL
- PowerShell Script
- Native Plus Third party Monitoring Tools usage
- Using Version Tools – SVN, TFS
- DBA in other RDBMS (Oracle, My SQL, DB2 and one of NoSQL)
- Able to Work in a Team or Individual

A DBA should be expertise in one or two and should be experienced in remaining.

Design and Development: An Expert SQL Server Database Engineer should have experience in below:

- Requirement Gathering Analysis
- Designing a database

- Good Understand in Basics – Joins, Procedures, Functions, Triggers, Views, and Synonyms etc.
- Database Level Performance Tuning
- Execution Plan analysis
- Index Tuning
- T-SQL/PL/SQL
- Writing Secure and Optimized database code
- Integrity/Domain/Functional Testing for Database Code
- Using Version Tools – SVN, TFS
- Preventing/Handling SQL Injections
- Good Contacts with Technology Masters
- Recommended Certifications
- Knowledge on Front End Technology (.Net, Java etc.)
- Expertise in a Domain (Banking, Financial, Insurance, Healthcare, Media, Law etc.)
- At least work in two RDBMS (Oracle PL/SQL, SQL Server T-SQL)
- Should be experienced in Code Reviews
- Able to Work in a Team or Individual
- Familiar with SDLC/Agile

Performance Tuning

Performance tuning is the key aspect and which is actually tell about you whether you are an expert or just experienced. It's all about End-User satisfaction in using your application, they won't bother about the technology rather they just see how application is performing. It applies to all designing, development, maintenance, administration and warehousing. Also remember that any enterprise environment requires a specialist who can tune/optimize their database systems. Whenever designing or creating new database/database object experts should do proper analysis and ask as many questions as possible:

Database Administrator:

Your manager asked you to prepare a new SQL Instance and configure it. What are all the things you should consider to build an optimized and secure instance? Below

What is the business all about?

Ex: OLTP or OLAP

What is priority – Concurrency or Huge Data Processing?

Ex: DB to support online transactions or it for business reports

What is the Minimum and Maximum Memory required?

Ex: You should predict/determine the future usage based on the existing environment and the requirement

How many processers required?

Ex: You should predict/determine the future usage based on the existing environment and the requirement

What is the data growth expected?

Ex: Based on this we can allocate data and log files to drives also decide on Auto Grow option.

Determine MDF, LDF and TEMPDB file locations

Ex: Based on drives specifications keep MDF/LDF on separate drives. For TEMPDB keep these files separated from user database files.

What is the Index fill factor percentage to choose?

Ex: It depends on data modifications. For example when expecting more data modifications it can be 80 to 90 percent, if it is static/archive data it can be 100%.

What is the disk system required?

Ex: You should have command on RAID levels

What is the backup policy required?

Ex: It depends on Service Level Agreement (SLA) between organization and vendor.

What are the disaster recovery/High – Availability options required, if not now in future?

Ex: It again depends on the business and the down time accepted.

Can we have a shared instance on the same machine?

Ex: Decide can business allow us to have more than one instance on a same machine or not

Is that instance is under organization security policy?

Ex: Get clarity if any special permission required as per the business requirement and configure all security related parameters including Audit

What exactly basic maintenance required for the new instance?

Ex: Apart from basic maintenance any data feed jobs required etc.

What is the cost/time estimation?

Ex: A DBA should know about the database server licensing this as he/she has to suggest the team for a better available choice. Work and give the accurate Time estimation.

What are the best suited configuration options?

Instant File Initialization, Lock Pages in Memory, MAXDOP, Auto growth etc....

Did you get required Trace Flags?

Ans: What is the trace flags need to be enabled?

A DBA should know answers for all these questions to build an optimized and secure instance.

SQL Developer/Designer:

Now we'll see what a SQL Developer should know before starting a task. Let's assume that your manager asked you to create a table and create a stored procedure to insert data. You should be able to answer below questions:

Check if it can be normalized

Ex: Figure out the Key column and make sure all columns are fully dependent on key column. There are some areas where we need not bother about normalization. For example when a table is too small but the table is expected to participate in joins with the tables which are huge. In that case we'll get the performance gain if we do not normalize this small table. This is just an example we have to predict the table usage in your environment and design it accordingly.

Check any partitions required?

Ex: If that table is going to hold millions of rows and already other tables portioned check with your manager if it needs to be portioned.

Follow the correct naming conventions:

Ex: Always use the schema name with object name. If we do not use a schema name, DB engine first search the default schema for this object. Do not use reserved key words.

Use the correct data type for columns

Ex: Always choose the right data type for a column. We have to consider below while assigning a data type

Data Range – Minimum and Maximum expected values

Data Length – Fixed or Variable

Null value acceptance – Depends on business requirement

Domain value acceptance – Check your requirement document

Determine the null acceptability

Ex: Correctly define the NULL acceptability in a Table. We should predict the future when we are designing NULLABLE columns. Let's say we have designed a column with CHAR (10) NULL. Can you imagine if the table is having 25 Million Rows and in this column filled for 10 K rows only? Now let's see how the space is occupied for this column. Total space for this column (25 Million – 10 K) X 10 Bytes. In that situation we can consider creating other table with Primary Key from this table and this column. Now we can save the space. This is just an example to say that we need to predict/estimate the future while creating any single object in database.

Decide on table usage

Ex: Determine the security level; see if we need to create a view with limited columns

Choose the correct key column

Ex: Follow best practices in choosing key column, usually it should be a numeric.

Determine the index possibilities

Ex: Choose a correct index when it needs to be created.

Choose the right constraints

Ex: Always choose the correct constraint. On employee table there is constraint on Age (>22). This can be implemented using CHECK Constraint and TRIGGER as well. But CHECK is the right constraint here.

Are you following any template for writing procedures?

Ex: Define a master template based on your business requirement and follow the template across the database.

Any specific SET options we need to use?

Ex: Based on your environment enable all SET options. Ex: SET NOCOUNT ON

Any chances that your procedure execution will result into a Deadlock?

Ex: If yes, take the steps to prevent deadlocks.

How you are going to handle errors?

Ex: Are you using any centralized table to capture error information? If not start a framework that suits your environment.

How we are handling datasets inside procedure?

Ex: Choose the best available object based on the requirement and the size of data. Temp Table, Table Variable, CTE, Derived Table etc.

What is the acceptable maximum response time for stored procedure?

Ex: Have you defined maximum response time in your environment, if not determine it and tune all objects which are not under the defined time.

What is the default ISOLATION level as per the business requirement?

Ex: Decide what ISOLATION level your business required.

Are you closing/de-allocating all blocks, temp objects and transaction in procedure?

Ex: It's always a best practice that deleting/closing temp objects and loops.

These are the various questions for which you should know answers before starting the actual task.

Accurate Estimations

The most common question that you here from your reporting manager/Client is "How long will you take to get it done?" Here comes the time estimates, this is also a key area which tells about you whether you are an Expert or just an Experienced. Below are the points that you should consider before giving the time estimation for any task/project.

Do you have the Exact Requirement?

Ex: You should have clarity on what is exactly the expected output.

Do you have all required Inputs?

Ex: Once you know answer for the above point then list out all required inputs to finish your task that includes "GAP Analysis in requirement," "Resources required" etc. It always depends on the task and the environment.

Do you have priorities with you?

Ex: First break down your task into small chunks and then give the estimates for each task. It calculates the final cost estimation for the complete task. Once the task list is ready then prioritize the tasks and do finish the tasks with high priority first. It all depends on the criticality of the task and dependency.

Always Expect a Delay:

Ex: Make sure you are including some extra buffer time when giving estimates. Below points will give us why we should need buffer time:

- Expect a meeting or discussion
- If any unexpected issues comes in
- Resource and Infrastructure unavailability

Review the progress:

Ex: Review the task progress and give updates to the customer/task owner periodically. We can put some extra effort if you observe any differences.

Note: Accuracy in cost estimation comes from your experience. Do maintain a template for giving cost estimations thereof accuracy comes when giving estimations for the similar tasks.

Never React always Respond

One should think of three points when something wrong happens in your environment. One of my senior managers taught me how to habituate this. Here are three points we should never forget especially when we are working on critical environment:

- Humans do Mistakes – Think of a situation where you did a mistake
- We can't control the past
- What is the solution?

To be successful in your career this is the first point you should remember "Never React Always Respond." This is not easy as we said; there is a simple technique to habituate this: "Separate the Person from the Problem." Ok, now let's see some examples as below.

Ex: One of your team members accidentally deleted a Table from production instance and he didn't notice it until customer complaining that they are getting errors in their application side. How do you deal with this?

"Why did you run that command, I have told you lot many times……etc." will increase the problem density and situation becomes more complex.

Start thinking towards the solution:

"Is there any way that we can stop/rollback that command?"

"Is that happened during implementation of any specific request?"

"If Yes! Did you take any backup or snapshot before running the script?"

"Can someone be able to quickly get the table data into a temp table from the latest backup?"

"What kind of data, is that a static or transactional data?"

"If it is static/lookup can we get it from other similar environment?"

- Instead of reacting if you start asking questions towards the solution, people around you will start thinking in a positive way and they too work on the same goal.
- You can take the proper action once the solution provided and situation comes to normal. Ask your people to provide a complete report with a detailed RCA. And then you can take the proper action to prevent such kind of mistakes in future.

Keep your own best practices and Troubleshooting guide

Maintain your own document/guide, create a template in documenting problems. Whenever you come across with a problem note it down along with the possible solutions and the actual solution worked out for the current situation. You can save your time and energy if the same problem comes again.

Training, Learning and Knowledge Sharing

Irrespective of the role that you are working in you should go through some training on monthly/ Quarterly/Yearly basis. Learning and trainings should include below.

- Latest Technology (SQL Server 2014, Oracle 12c, Big Data Platform, Cloud Technologies)
- Process Oriented (ITIL, Lean & Six Sigma, Information Security, Agile, PMP etc.)
- Personality Development
- Communication
- Follow the Product Blog (For the latest updates on the product that you are working on)

Share your knowledge:

- Share your knowledge through various platforms available
- Document simply and share in your team
- Write a blog port
- Participate in technology forums
- Etc.

Finally: Identify your strength and choose a career path which most suits to you, you love it, you enjoy it, automatically dedication comes in, output is the best productivity, Expertise in your path, you grow, let your organization grow, best opportunities comes to you, reach your goal. Maintain a well-balanced life between Personal & Professional lives, have a lot's of beautiful moments, earn more, save more, serve something☺. Wishing you all the very best for your career.

www.ingramcontent.com/pod-product-compliance
Lightning Source LLC
Chambersburg PA
CBHW081454050326
40690CB00015B/2795
9781946390974